CONTROLLING CONTRABAND

Mentality, Economy, and Society in Eighteenth-Century Rio de Janeiro

ERNST PIJNING

Copyright © 2025 by Ernst Pijning

All rights reserved.

No portion of this book may be reproduced in any form without written permission from the publisher or author, except as permitted by U.S. copyright law.

Library of Congress Number: 2024926241

The cover illustration: "Mappa geral do rendimento das Reaes Casas de Fundação das 4 comarcas da Capitania das Minas geraes, Vila Rica, Sabará, Rio das Mortas e Serro Frio." 1753.

This picture was redrawn by Charlese Bell.

Original: Arquivo Histórico Ultramarino (Lisbon), Rio de Janeiro, papeis avulsos catalogados, Castro e Almeida, 16267.

Online: Projeto Resgate, National Library of Rio de Janeiro.

https://resgate.bn.gov.br/docreader/DocReader.aspx?bib=017-1_RJ&pagfis=34029

In memory of John Russell-Wood, George Winius, Eddy Stols, David Higgs and Paulo Cavalcante.

FORWARD BY KENNETH MAXWELL

One of the great strengths of Ernst Pijning's book is his very skillful and comprehensive integration and interrogation of the historiography of late colonial Brazil and his highly original reflections on why Brazil took a different path to independence from the rest of South America. Independent Brazil after all remained a monarchy and was led by the eldest son of Portugal's monarch and then his son for much of the 19th century. Brazil did not fragment like Spanish America.

Pijning explains why Brazil had become virtually independent in the decade before the Portuguese Court was forced to relocate to Brazil from Lisbon during the Napoleon invasion of the country in 1807. He delineates how Brazilian commerce and trade (and above all the contraband or "illegal" trade) allowed Brazil to escape from Lisbon's mercantilist straight-jacket. Brazil was in effect by 1800 no longer in practice following the economic strictures issued in Portugal and the most important vested interests in Brazil had effectively escaped from the economic decrees issued from Lisbon.

The focus here is on Rio de Janeiro and the South Atlantic and Pijning often takes to task other historians who have gone before him, usually politely, but no less devastatingly. This will not make him very popular in some academic circles. But it is a great strength of his book that he has so effectively integrated these historiographic themes and questions into his work. He provides a scintillating review of the arguments among Portuguese and Brazilian worthies at the time over economic policy and free trade and a review of the remarkable debates in Brazil and in Portugal over corruption and thievery and ethical dilemmas.

What Pijning has done in convincing detail, based on a remarkably wide range of archival sources, is to show how contraband and illegal trade, and official and unofficial commerce, both locally, regionally within South America, and within the Portuguese empire in São Tomé, in West and Southern Africa, and in Asia, intersected. And how this rich and complex chiaroscuro worked in practice. It is a fascinating journey into the past of imperial history. And it explains in part why Portugal's imperial endeavour was so flexible and lasted so long.

Above all he follows the lives and activities of individual traders, large and small, of governmental officials and military offices, of viceroys and magistrates, of bishops, priests and monks, of slave traders and market stall holders, and itinerant hawkers, all of them benefiting from and taking advantage of the loopholes in a system that was sometimes enforced by the authorities but was also often contravened. Examining a myriad of both official and unofficial cases, Pijning has followed a remarkable paper trail in multiple archives which he has exploited to great advantage.

This then is a study of the entrails of empire. We meet the Benedictines who though a hole in the wall of their convent in Rio de Janeiro conducted an illegal trade with the contrabandists of Rio's Prajanha beach. In fact isolated beaches out of the sight of the authorities (or with their connivance) were a favorite location for the illicit exchange of goods and commodities and slaves along the coast of Brazil. Here foreign vessels were also involved though if they arrived in the port of Rio de Janeiro, they could (and were) seized by the Portuguese authorities. Pijning provides fascinating details of several of these cases. We meet the individuals involved and their trials and tribulations. The mentality and social values and social status determined the degree to which individuals were allowed to engage in "illegal" activities.

The overlapping jurisdictions and responsibilities in Brazil facilitated these manoeuvres. As did the conflicting competences of the various oversight official bodes in Portugal. The foreign nations in Portugal had their own sovereign jurisdictions often granted in return for the promise of military assistance to Portugal in time of need. England and the Dutch obtained these privileges as a consequence of peace treaties. The first in the aftermath of Portuguese independence from Spain in 1640 and the latter as a consequence of reconciliation after the Dutch conquests of Portuguese colonies in the West and East Indies. Ties with England were strengthened by the commercial treaty negotiated by Methuen in 1703 and the Dutch two years later signed a similar treaty. There was a symbiotic relationship between trading privileges and contraband trade. The Portuguese regarded these privileges as providing loopholes for illegal trade.

Some of this "illegal" commence in Brazil was sanctioned, especially with the Spanish American port of Buenos Aires on the Rio de la Plata or though the Portuguese outpost of Colônia on the northern bank of the Rio de la Plata. Here was the source of the silver from Potosi in Upper Peru which the Portuguese and Brazilians desired for their trade with Africa and Asia. Tobacco and Cachaça (distilled spirit from sugar cane) from Bahia was exchanged on the off-shore Portuguese controlled island of São Tomé with Dutch, English, and French merchants to purchase slaves in West Africa. Some dozen of Bahia's leading merchants were involved in this profitable enterprise.

The rewards of this "illegal" commerce were very high. Throughout the 18th Century gold and gold dust flowed into Rio de Janeiro from Minas Gerias in one of the world's first great gold rushes. Gold dust in particular was often smuggled out of Rio de Janeiro on the Brazil fleets from Rio de Janeiro to Lisbon and then from Lisbon to England via the Falmouth packet boat. Diamonds from the far interior of Minas Gerais were also a glittering export from Brazil, easily concealed in the baggage of many sailors.

Pijning's archival research is astounding, and its originality and scope is astonishing, using Brazilian, French, Dutch, British, American, and Portuguese archives in six countries. Few historians have the enviable linguistic skills of Pijning, and he uses these skills to great advan-

FORWARD BY KENNETH MAXWELL

tage in this book. In this he is a worthy successor of Charles Boxer, the great British historian of the Portuguese and the Dutch empires. C.R. Boxer was also a mentor to the late Professor John Russell-Wood, who was Pijning's academic adviser.

Professor John Russell-Wood was a punctilious British scholar who taught in the history department at John's Hopkin's University in Baltimore for much of his academic career, where he encouraged a remarkable group of young PhD students over the years, perhaps uniquely so among scholars of the Portuguese imperial endeavour, and Ernst Pijning's was one of them. Pijning's careful archival work and the originally of his research and conclusions very much reflects Russell-Wood's influence, as it also reflects the influence of Professor George Winius of the University of Leiden in the Netherlands who was also an early Pijning mentor.

This is an astonishing work of history. It is accessible, detailed, engaging, and very well written. It provides a widow into the hidden realities and complexities of Atlantic history. It is a major contribution to our view of the 18th century world and its empires. Above all it is a revelation of the role of a fascinating cast of characters navigating their way through the complexities and challenges of everyday life in the 18th and early 19th centuries.

FOREWORD BY ADELTO GONÇALVES

I

After almost three decades of incomprehensible lack of interest on the part of Brazilian and Portuguese publishers in a text of exceptional importance for the History of Brazil and Portugal, American publisher Robbin Laird (*Second Line of Defense*) has decided to bring to light this doctoral thesis defended in 1997 at Johns Hopkins University in Baltimore, Maryland/USA, by Dutch historian Ernst Pijning (1963), who has been a full professor of History at Minot State University in North Dakota/USA since 1999.

This partially corrects this inadmissible gap, since it seems that a Portuguese version of this thesis is also due to be published soon by a Brazilian publisher.

The subject of Pijning's research is the contraband trade in colonial Brazil and its relations with Portugal and the Netherlands (Holland), especially in the period from 1690 to 1808. In his work, the researcher discusses not only the mechanics of smuggling and the actions of the participants in this illegal trade, but also the various factors that led to Portuguese, metropolitan and colonial measures to prevent this clandestine trade from spreading.

In other words, the historian analyzes how these measures represented a compromise between different interests, such as the role of the monarch, the integrity or malleability of royal authority, the application of this legislation and the types of penalties imposed on offenders. In this sense, he raises questions about what constituted legal or illegal actions, as well as broader questions about ethics and public morality in colonial Brazil.

II

For Pijning, smuggling was not seen by the Portuguese authorities as an ethical or moral contravention, but as part of Portugal's commercial interests. In this way, depending on the social scale of the possible offender, the practice was tolerated. Not to mention that the authorities who were supposed to combat smuggling often acted as intermediaries in this trade, which was illegal to begin with. And several viceroys returned to Portugal overly enriched, which always allowed suspicions to arise that they had profited greatly by contributing to smuggling running wild.

"But if smuggling was a ubiquitous and acceptable practice, how can we explain the fact that some people were arrested and persecuted?" asks the historian. And he himself replies: "It's because there were two types of smuggling: one condemned and the other permitted by the authorities." In other words: illegality depended on the social *status of* those who practiced it and the interests of the government that represented the Portuguese Crown.

Pijning points out that, in order to understand this dubious position, it is necessary to take into account the context in which Portugal lived, since the country was militarily and economically dependent on other nations in order to survive. Not to mention that neighboring Spain was threatening to occupy Portuguese territory and was only waiting for a valid pretext to extend its rule, as it had already done in the province of Galicia, whose language is practically a sister language of Portuguese.

Faced with the weakness of the Portuguese Crown, some internal groups had an inordinate influence over the economic and social policy put in place: for example, various branches of commerce, such as salt, fishing or whaling and coastal fishing, were monopolies. And those who held these monopolies were practically above any law.

FOREWORD BY ADELTO GONÇALVES

This was also the case with the illegal trade with Buenos Aires and the entire Río de la Plata, which was openly encouraged by the Portuguese authorities. Trade between Lisbon and Falmouth, in Jamaica, would also, in theory, be prohibited, but the Crown used to sign licenses so that it could take place.

Pijning notes that any estimate that can be made of the magnitude of this illegal trade will be highly speculative, since there are no official statistics in the Portuguese or Brazilian archives. In any case, the researcher points out that, among other documents, there is one in which Dom Pedro Miguel de Almeida Portugal e Vasconcelos (1688-1756), Count of Assumar, governor of the captaincy of São Paulo-Minas do Ouro from 1717 to 1721, estimates the illegal gold trade in 1733 at 166 arrobas from various ports in Portuguese America, such as Salvador, Rio de Janeiro, Recife, São Luís do Maranhão and Belém do Pará, to Lisbon, Angola, the Azores, Colônia do Sacramento, Mozambique, Madagascar and Guyana. The legal gold trade during this period would have reached 990 arrobas.

III

Pijning also recalls that, as Portugal depended on other European countries, such as England, France and Holland in particular, to maintain its independence from Spain, it had to make many concessions to these nations, to the point of functioning virtually as a British colony.

To this end, Lisbon only obliged foreign merchants to trade with Portuguese America through Portuguese intermediaries. "It should be noted that a significant proportion of products imported by Portugal from England were destined for Brazilian ports," he adds.

At one time, merchants from England and Holland had greater privileges both in Portugal and in the Atlantic possessions, which made it easier for them to engage in illegal activities through Portuguese merchants. In addition, they were judged by their own magistrates and according to the laws of their countries. They also had discounts on customs and freedom of belief.

According to Pijning, while King João V's (1689-1750) policy against illegal trade was characterized by passive resistance, his successors would adopt a more active stance against smuggling, especially after the actions of Minister Sebastião José Carvalho e Mello (1699-1782), the Marquis of Pombal, secretary of the kingdom of Dom José I (1714-1777), who sought to reduce the presence of the high nobility and clergy in state affairs and encourage the creation of a new class of aristocratic merchants. "Pombal advocated reforms in industry and agriculture, restructuring education as well as reorganizing the royal administration," he says.

According to Pijning, direct moral condemnation of smugglers was rare. "Portuguese legislation called illegal trade 'pernicious', not because it was immoral, but because the smuggler was stealing the king's wealth or defrauding the people of their property, while at the same time damaging the smooth running of honest trade," he observes. "

"But if smuggling didn't harm the royal treasury or complement normal commercial activities — as in trade with Buenos Aires — then it was tolerated and even encouraged. In other words, sometimes breaking the law was seen as something very positive," he concludes.

IV

Ernst Pijning, who specializes in the history of Latin America in the 18th century, received his undergraduate and master's degrees from the University of Leida in the Netherlands and his doctorate from Johns Hopkins University in Baltimore, Maryland. He is co-author of the book *La Guinée équatoriale aux archives nationales - XVIIIe-début XXesiècles* (Editions L'Harmattan, 2016), together with historians Valérie De Wulf, Jean-Marc Lefebvre, Gustau Nerin and Jacint Creus Boixaderas, which tells the story of the slave cycle in Equatorial Guinea, based on research into original documents from the National Archives in Paris. It is a study that allows the reader to discover how the histories of all parts of the world were intertwined, in particular the three continents that surround the Atlantic Ocean.

After completing his doctorate, he expanded his research into smuggling in the 18th century, also gathering information from French and English archives. He has published several articles and chapters in journals and collections in Brazil, Portugal, Canada, Colombia, France and the Netherlands. He has given several lectures at international symposia, especially at the University of São Paulo (USP), at universities in Goiás and at other university institutions in Brazil, Portugal and various Latin American and African countries.

(*) Adelto Gonçalves, journalist, Master in Spanish Language and Spanish and Hispano-American Literatures and PhD in Letters in the area of Portuguese Literature from the University of São Paulo (USP), is the author of *Gonzaga, um Poeta do Iluminismo* (Rio de Janeiro, Nova Fronteira, 1999), *Barcelona Brasileira* (Lisbon: Nova Arrancada, 1999) (São Paulo, Publisher Brasil, 2002), *Fernando Pessoa: a Voz de Deus* (Santos, Editora da Unisanta, 1997); *Bocage-o Perfil Perdido* (Lisbon, Caminho, 2003), (São Paulo, Imprensa Oficial do Estado de São Paulo - Imesp, 2021), *Tomás Antônio Gonzaga* (Imesp/Academia Brasileira de Letras, 2012), *Direito e Justiça em Terras d'El-Rei na São Paulo Colonial*(Imesp, 2015), *Os Vira-latas da Madrugada* (Rio de Janeiro, Livraria José Olympio Editora, 1981, Taubaté-SP, Editora LetraSelvagem, 2015), and *O Reino, a Colônia e o Poder: o governo Lorena na capitania de São Paulo - 1788-1797* (Imesp, 2019), among others. He wrote the preface to the book *Kenneth Maxwell on Global Trends* (*Second Line of Defense*, Arlington Virginia, 2024).

ACKNOWLEDGEMENT

Over the years my research has been financed by Minot State University, Prins Berhard Fonds, in the Netherlands, Fundação Luso Americana para o Desinvolvimento, and Fundação Calouste Gulbenkian, the John Carter Brown Library and the Johns Hopkins department of history. Two of this book's chapters have been published in earlier versions in the *Portuguese Studies Review*, and in *Arquipélago-História*.

I would like to thank the following people for their aid and help to make this possible: my colleagues at Minot State University, Bethany Andreasen and Joseph Jastrzembski for their many modifications of my English, Dan Ringrose and Lauren Young for their moral support, Raman Sachdev for his interpretation of the cover illustration, and Mark Singer for his everlasting patience and help with the images. Charlene Bell has been responsible for redrawing the cover illustration.

In Portugal I especially like to thank Albino, Carlos Alberto, Fernando, Jorge, Leão, Octavio, Pires, and Sintra, all former functionaries at the Arquivo Histórico Ultramarino for their comradery and support. I also like to thank Tiago C. P. dos Reis Miranda and Ângela Domingues for their support and friendship. In Brazil, I like to

ACKNOWLEDGEMENT

thank Fernanda Bicalho, Luciano Figueiredo, and Adelto Gonçalves com muito saudades. In the Netherlands I like to thank my family and friends, especially Theo Bolhuis for letting me visit many bookstores and for his hospitality and Frank Kanhai at the Nationaal Archief for his service.

CONTENTS

Introduction	xix
1. The Diplomacy of Contraband Trade: Between Passive Resistance and Proactive Reform.	1
2. Regulating Illegal Trade: Foreign Vessels in Brazilian Harbors	42
3. Monopolizing the Marketplace: Regulating Urban Space	84
4. The Politics of Punishment: Defining The Boundary Between Condoned and Proscribed Illegal Trade	104
5. Institutionalized Illegality: Colonel Administration and Contraband Trade	123
6. Discourse on Illegality	149
7. Conclusion	171
Postscript	176
Portugal and Brazil Confront the Contemporary World Series	181
Notes	185
Bibliography	233

INTRODUCTION

Smugglers' tales have vividly captured the human imagination. According to the *Oxford English Dictionary*, contrabandists in literature are depicted as outcasts of society in expressions such as "a large vagrant population of idlers, gypsies and contrabandists" and "scroundel, what do you want, contrabanding in these seas?"[1]

This book restores the contrabandist to his or her rightful spot in the eighteenth-century Lusophone world, that is, as entrepreneurs belonging to the establishment and having good connections with the governing elite.

Therefore, an analysis of contraband trade becomes a perfect tool to study colonial Brazilian society. Not only does the study of contraband trade provide an insight to any analysis of the functioning of mercantilism, the judicial system, as well as public and private ethics in the Luso-Brazilian world, it also has wider implications for our understanding of values and collective behavior in the early modern Atlantic.

Contraband was inherent in the early modern Atlantic economy and it equally permeated Luso-Brazilian society and its counterparts in Europe, Africa, and the Americas. What, then, was the significance of illegal trade? If contraband was so ingrained in society, how do we explain the fact that some people were indeed prosecuted and convicted? In order to answer this question, I distinguish between two types of contraband trade: first, contraband trade that was condoned by the authorities; and second, illegal trade that was the object of universal proscription.

Condoned illegal trade was a controlled commerce which was allowed to take place by the very persons whose official positions should have made them the very ones to combat it. In other words, it is more important to know who did it, rather than how much was smuggled. By analyzing why some people were prosecuted caught while others were not, it is possible to determine where the boundary between condoning and proscribing illegal trade lay.

Often it was the status of the people involved, rather than ethical concerns, which defined these boundaries. This point poses a further question: what determined the status, either collectively or individually, that helped to define these boundaries?

To determine this, I examine status as evident at three levels: The first level is the international, which discusses the negotiation on an interstate sphere to engage in illegal activities; the second are the metropolitan policies which were meant to influence the flow of illegal trade; finally, the third level is the regional interest in the colonies and the formation of alliances in order to pursue and regulate illegal trade.

Through the distinction between condoned and proscribed illegal trade, I clarify the different natures of illegality prevalent in the Atlantic and I analyze this topically through the different chapters.

The first chapter examines transnational aspects of illegal trade and how illegal trade was part and parcel of international exchange. British, Dutch, and French diplomats represented their nation's economic interests to the Portuguese courts. An important aspect of these policies was to benefit the British, Dutch, and French trade interests even if these policies were against Portuguese law. For instance, according to Portuguese law, gold from Brazil was not supposed to be exported to Britain and yet this practice was widespread. Indeed, both the Portuguese government and its British, Dutch, and French partners used trading privileges as a bargaining chip in the economic, military, and political theaters. In practice, diplomats and governments negotiated the ability to permit smuggling for their own nationals.

INTRODUCTION

Chapter two bridges the global and the local by examining the fate of foreign vessels sailing into Brazilian harbors. In theory, foreigners were prohibited to enter Brazilian ports. However, in practice, many British, Dutch, French and Spanish ships did call to Rio de Janeiro, claiming that they were in distress. For this purpose, Portuguese authorities set rigid rules, to which the captains and crews needed to follow if they wanted to avoid confiscation of any goods and their vessels.

In practice, local authorities used these rules to their advantage in order to regulate all legal and illegal commercial activities. Therefore, once foreigners disobeyed these rules and disallowed local authorities to act as intermediaries in commercial activities, they were subject to the full enforcement of the law. Once local authorities confiscated foreign vessels, the courts and government in Portugal itself then renegotiated their restoration according to the rules of international diplomacy as outlined in the first chapter.

Chapter three considers the urban space of Rio de Janeiro. The idea that markets are inherently free and that exchange of products is determined solely by price has been sufficiently refuted by historians. This chapter demonstrates that markets are inherently not free and monopolized. Officials, soldiers, merchants, and peddlers tried to control the harbor, beaches, markets, and streets of Rio de Janeiro. These groups' spatial control translated into market control, and hence a social stratification of the marketplace.

Chapter four details the fate of smugglers who were prosecuted by the colonial administration. This analysis of the legal system explains that being suspected of smuggling in itself was a punishment. Although very few suspects were actually convicted for a crime, they had to endure the ordeal of being imprisoned for the duration of the criminal investigation. The intentional delays of the judiciary system empowered both the crown and colonial administrators in their rulings over anyone who crossed the line between condoned and proscribed illegal trade.

Chapter five returns to the interaction between colonial and metropolitan rule. Through an examination of colonial administrators, the main intermediaries in commercial activities, it becomes clear that

INTRODUCTION

colonial rule is a dialogue between Portuguese and Brazilian administrators. This chapter examines changes over time in the colonial administration focusing on three key points: the ability of different colonial entities to control illegal trade; the manipulation of colonial administrators' jurisdictions by metropolitan measures; and the professionalization of colonial rule. Changing patterns in colonial administration determined the shifting balance between what illegal trade was condoned and what was proscribed throughout the eighteenth century.

The final chapter explains how contemporaries wrote about the phenomenon of illegal trade. In foreign travel accounts and officials' letters, illegal trade was condemned only when it was done by "the other." This double standard is still prevalent in today's historical perceptions of smuggling. Very few eighteenth-century authors attacked smuggling on moral grounds, and, when they did, it was generally in reaction to political crisis or natural disasters.

The conclusion clarifies the need to view Luso-Brazilian society as extremely flexible. Conducting illegal trade was only one aspect open to negotiation, as was the institution of slavery, the meaning of race, and the sacrament of marriage. Moreover, it is time to move beyond copying eighteenth century accounts on the immorality of illegal trade when it concerns people of other nationalities. Rather, a reflective look into every modern society will clarify that breaking the law is to what extent condoned and to what extent proscribed.

In a postscript, I would like to clarify one aspect of illegal trade that I did not fully address previously, namely the amount of illegal trade. This postscript considers estimations of the size of contraband trade, as well as how illegal trade was conducted. I am particularly concerned about the qualitative aspects of illegal trade, how much smuggling occurred with the consent of officials (condoned illegal trade), and how much went beyond the official trading networks (proscribed illegal trade), rather than the sheer quantity of illegal commercial activity. Moreover, I will analyze the changes over time between "proscribed" and "condoned" illegal trade.

Originally there were two appendixes to this work. The first appendix contains a list of all the cases of persons persecuted for illegal

INTRODUCTION

trade I encountered in the archives; the second appendix the salaries and donativos (tax paid to take possession of the office) for colonial administrators. Unfortunately, it was impossible to include these in this publication, however, I will be happy to provide them personally to any interested reader.

Just as it is hard to make estimations of contraband trade, so too, has the history of Brazilian smuggling frequently been a difficult topic for academics. The historiography on Brazilian smuggling is an exercise in self searching. Paulo Cavalcante is one of the very few historians who published a book on contraband trade in colonial Brazil.[2] Part of the disinterest was related to the supposed lack of documentation about this issue. While this lack of sources is relevant, the issue is broadened by the methodological debate of the importance of contraband trade. Their understanding of illegal trade has changed over time and these historians' views of colonial society in general, and smuggling in particular, is closely related to how Brazilians consider themselves.

Brazil is not the only country where illegal trade was equated to national identity. The case of the United States combining smuggling with national heroism provides a similar example. The idea that the Boston Tea Party was an act of liberation against British oppression is deeply ingrained in United States history. That smuggling was at the center of Bostonian merchants complaints was not contradictory to the ideal of "liberty."[3]

However, whenever smuggling deals with "the other," the story is quite different. When smuggling takes place in the Northern Mexican borderlands, United States historians view this as a form of weakness and a legitimation of Spain's loss of political control over this area.[4] Contraband trade then becomes more than breaking the law; indeed, how historians understand this phenomenon depends on their geopolitical ideas, as does their selection of sources for such a study. Historians are source-driven and understanding their sources of information explains their interpretations. There are five different methodological periods worth distinguishing.

The first are the writers of the colonial past who had few opportunities to write without censorship about illegal activities. The second group are the nineteenth-century historians who were engaged in positivist writing, which typically more informational than interpretative. These were historians writing for future generations where it was assumed that readers could interpret the sources for themselves. The third group of historians were of the pre-World War II generation. This group were more romantic inclined, as Brazilian history becomes more introverted and concerned with what it means to be a Brazilian. The fourth group are the post-World War II generation, when history became more structuralist and Marxist, mostly in opposition to the military regimes, interpreting Brazil's inhabitants as casualties of colonial exploitation. Finally, the fifth period of historical writers are of the post-modern era. This period is defined by historians attempting to reclaim Brazilian's autonomy in economic activities.

The first generations of Brazilian authors had enormous obstacles to face. Unlike Spanish America, Brazil did not possess a printing press or a university. All works about Brazil had to be printed in Portugal and they were therefore more oriented towards a metropolitan audience.

Moreover, publications had to be authorized by the censors, the representatives of the king and of the church. Any administrative or religious career needed to be formalized by entering a Portuguese university, since no institutions of higher education existed in Brazil before the arrival of the Portuguese court in Brazil in 1808. Given these measures, it will not come as a surprise that the earliest publications on colonial Brazil were Portuguese-centered. Brazil was part of the Portuguese empire and was not recognized as a separate entity.[5]

The earliest accounts of the colonies were therefore related to territories under Portuguese administration elsewhere, such as India. Practices in administration and commerce in India predated those in Brazil by more than a century, and it was logical that Portuguese merchants and readers connected Brazilian practices with those in India. Critique on Portuguese colonial administration came from the most distinguished echelons of society, and in Portuguese India this was Diogo do Couto.

Diogo do Couto was the official historian of Portuguese expansion overseas. He inherited the works of his predecessor, João de Barros, who started a list of the Portuguese heroic deeds in the *Décadas da*

Asia. As the keeper of the Goan archives and a former employee in Asia, Diogo do Couto had access to many official sources and he could draw on his own memories.

Based on these materials, do Couto's legacy folds into two major publications: the official story as laid down in *Da Asia* and the unofficial story as told in his *O Soldado Prático* (The Experienced Soldier). The latter was not published until 1790, but the manuscript circulated among his contemporaries.[6]

O Soldado Prático was a book by a frustrated historian. The book itself is not about illegal trade per se; rather, it explains the problematic governance of Portuguese India. When the book was written, Portuguese India was in decline, and Diogo do Couto pointed out the circumstances that led to Portuguese India's downfall and how to remedy this. Corruption, rather than smuggling was the main problem in Asia, but that corruption encompassed the failure to pay correct taxes at the customs.[7]

Diogo do Couto's dialog is similar to many accounts on the perversion of Portuguese administration over its colonies and his beliefs that bad administration led to the decadence of the empire was, what he considered, a divine punishment.[8]

Arte de Furtar (*The Art of Thieving*) elaborates on Diogo do Couto's problems in India. It deals with corruption in Portugal at the turn of the eighteenth century. Meant to be sarcastic, the author explains how corruption has reached every level of Portuguese society, from a yeoman to the king. Like in India, the author assumes that the greatest thieves are the persons supposed to prevent this crime, whether these are judges, noblemen, clergy, or officials of the customs.[9] The message from India and Portugal is clear: illegal trade should be considered at the same level as corruption and thieving, as both are deeply ingrained in Portuguese administration and society. However, can one assume the same about Portuguese America?

Whereas the treatises on Portuguese India and Portugal warned the readers of the deeply ingrained abuses and explained them as a manifestation of worldly and spiritual downfall, the first histories of Brazil remained more informative, giving reasons to attract colonists to the newly encountered world. Portuguese inhabitants of Brazil

INTRODUCTION

authored several first-hand accounts on the conversion of Amerindians, the fertility of the land, and chronicled the activities of the first settlers.

One of these books was written by Pero Magalhães de Gândavo, a friend of Luís de Camões, who elaborates on the history of the province of Santa Cruz (the name Cabral gave to Brazil).[10] Apart from relating the most recent history of Portuguese Brazil from the arrival of Cabral to the 1570s, the book also explains that the Province of Santa Cruz is a very fertile land, open to colonists who will encounter gold and gems in the interior. The book details the sites of most Portuguese settlements, elaborates on its economies, and outlines its relations with the local populations. In similar terms, Ambrósio Fernandes Brandão wrote optimistically in his late sixteenth-century account of Brazil. The New Christian sugar mill owner argued that, even though banished criminals were exiled to Brazil in the first decades, the lust for opportunity ennobled its settler population.[11] This book not only served as a propaganda tool to attract new Portuguese settlers, but it was also used as a guide for Dutch, English, French, or Spanish competitors.

Given the subsequent wars with the Dutch republic and France, one can imagine that not all these publications were welcomed by the Portuguese crown. Indeed, one of the most important treatises was immediately forbidden and all copies taken out of circulation.

The prime example of a forbidden book is Antonil's (assumed to be the pseudonym for João António Andreoni, S.J.) *Cultura e Opulência das Drogas do Brasil* published in 1711, and immediately taken out of circulation. The book details four major economic activities in the Portuguese colony: the cultivation of sugar, the growing of tobacco, gold mining, and cattle herding.[12]

The book minutely describes the methods of cultivation and mining, their finances, and the interior of Brazil including some maps. However, after several foreign invasions at the end of the War of Spanish Succession that led to the brief occupation of Rio de Janeiro by a French fleet in 1711, the Portuguese administration was quite reluctant to make such information public. Gold was found in Brazil during the 1690's and this made the colony even more attractive to

European competition, which the Portuguese king did not wish to encourage.

Antonil was the first to put the issue of illegal trade in print. This was especially in the case of tobacco cultivation and gold mining. He explained what will happen if farmers and miners refused to pay the full taxes on their products: according to Antonil, the king had a natural right to this taxation, and in the end transgressors would be caught, have their goods confiscated, and leave their families in poverty.[13] His work legitimized the Portuguese administration over Brazil and explained the consequences for those who did not obey the king's rules. Antonil's book is the best contemporary witness of Brazil's economy and it has been widely used by historians of colonial Brazil.

Historians have used two types of publications for their sources on the economy and society of eighteenth-century Brazil. The first are memoranda written to improve the Brazilian economy by Portuguese and Brazilian authors and the second are foreign travel accounts of visitors to Brazilian harbors. Both are similar, since the eighteenth century was influenced by the scientific academies where all captains and sailors learned the role of informant and most were willing to comment on the state of Brazilian development and how to make improvements.[14]

Scientific societies reached Brazil and Portugal during the eighteenth century. Local elites ran these organizations to promote the arts, letters, and the economy. Their members promoted themselves and their local community through the presentation of memoranda, musing on their illustrious past and promoting future development of the economy. Educated officials were highly represented in these organizations and they tried to improve their status by sending these memoranda to the Overseas Council, the secretary of state, and the Sovereign in Lisbon.

By the late eighteenth-century these memoranda became fashionable. Several were published in the annals of the Lisbon Academy of Sciences to which several university-educated Brazilians contributed.[15] As illegal trade was rife in that period, this topic was addressed in order to improve revenues, the local economies and Brazilian allegiance to Portugal.

INTRODUCTION

Most memoranda dealt with the utilization of natural resources for economic purposes. For instance, Balthazar da Silva Lisboa, a crown judge, wrote extensively about conservation and utilization of several types of wood.[16] His brother, José da Silva Lisboa, wrote extensively about the liberalization of the Brazilian economy and the elimination of crown monopolies.[17] The Bishop of Pernambuco, José Joaquim da Cunha de Azeredo Coutinho, was likewise engaged in the transformation of the regulatory system of the Brazilian economy in order to promote growth, which was not so surprising given the bishop's close ties with the Portuguese regime. The later Secretary of State, Dom Rodrigo de Souza Coutinho, did likewise.[18]

The works of these statesmen were signs of loyalty. Their primary goals were to improve the economic and political relationships between colony and mother country in a time when smuggling increased dramatically and signs of Brazilian resistance to Portuguese overlordship became more obvious.

Not all officials were as loyal as the four statesmen referenced above. However, literary works from Gregório de Matos and Tomás António Gonzaga were full of satire and fully blamed the incompetence of Portuguese administrators for the failure of the Brazilian economy. Both had to pay dearly for their comments: the first was exiled to Angola the other to Mozambique after conspiring to overthrow the government of the Mining districts.[19]

The works of Luso-Brazilian authors about their economy were highly influenced by foreign travelers and philosophers. One can hardly underestimate the international leverage of esteemed authors such as Captain James Cook, Abbé Raynal, and Adam Smith, whose work greatly influenced the Brazilian scientific community and whose opinions were echoed throughout the European intellectual word.

Unfortunately for the Brazilians, these esteemed scientists did not rate the Portuguese colony very highly. Indeed, most European travelers and intellectuals looked down upon Brazil, defining its population as "indolent" and any trade obstruction as illegitimate. Not only have these visitors been a source of information for future historians but they also set the debate for the issues for the next two centuries.

None of the distinguished British and French writers had good

INTRODUCTION

words for the governance, society, and economy of Brazil. Captain Cook, for instance, made some very negative descriptions of Rio de Janeiro after he was virtually sent away from the Brazilian capital by the Viceroy. Cook declared that the rule over Brazil was "very despotic," the population of Rio de Janeiro were too devotional since "they pray and sing their hymns with such vehemence, that in the night they were very distinctly heard on board the ship," that the women in Rio de Janeiro "make less difficulty of granting personal favours, than those of any other civilized country in the world," and that the greater part of the land is "wholly uncultivated, and little care and labour seem to have bestowed upon the rest."[20]

One of the most widely read books on colonial societies was that of Abbé Raynal. The first print of his *Philosophical and political history of the establishment and commerce of the Europeans in the Indies* was in 1770 and it remained a standard work for many the elites ever since. Not surprisingly, Raynal looked disdainfully upon the economy of colonial Brazil and the French philosopher paid particular attention to smuggling and the poor Portuguese administration. Raynal comments that Brazil was a rich colony, and that the Portuguese were the first to open up trade to Africa and the Orient.[21]

Unfortunately, Portugal had fallen into decadence for two main reasons. The first were the regulations of commerce through monopolies, increasingly so after the Lisbon earthquake of 1755 that decreased commerce and stimulated illegal trade. The second was through the dependency of the Portuguese economy on the British, which weakened Portugal's economy.

Not so surprisingly for a Frenchman, Raynal argued that the British administration had Portugal and its colonies in its grips, and the only way out of this situation was to open Brazilian trade to all foreign nations. Raynal never visited Brazil so he worked with travel accounts as his sources. This is obvious in his judgment on colonial Brazil, since many a foreigner expressed her/himself in similar terms. However, the political economy of Raynal's work is new, and it was soon to be mimicked by generations of Brazilian and European intellectuals.

The celebrated Scottish philosopher Adam Smith's thoughts on the Political economy of Portugal, Brazil, and their relations with Great

Britain were in line with Raynal's beliefs. Smith's *Inquiry into the Origins of the Wealth of Nations* was published only three years after Abbé Raynal's historical and philosophical history, at a time when the relations between Britain and Portugal came under scrutiny.

Adam Smith argued against the mercantilist principles of his time. He stated that Britain's close economic relationship with Portugal was negative for the former. Adam Smith reconsidered the advantages of the famous Methuen Treaty of 1703, in which Britain promised to import wine from Portugal at a lower price than Portugal's competitors, in exchange for Portugal importing British textiles at a lower price than its competitors.[22]

Contemporaries and historians have always considered this treaty as the basis for British economic power over Portugal, since Britain was able to import gold cheaply from Brazil as there was always a surplus on the Britain's side that needed to be paid off.

Smith, however, argued otherwise. He argued that the treaty was unnecessary, since Britain would have supplied textiles cheaper than its competition, and now it was forced to import Portuguese wine.[23] Moreover, since Britain had a trading surplus with almost all European countries, gold would flow in its direction either directly from Portugal or indirectly from other countries trading with Portugal.

Smith and Raynal both believed that Portugal's economy was badly organized by its monopolies, trade liberalization would be good for all (especially to Britain and France), and this would end the oppressive economic stronghold that Portugal had over Brazil. Brazilians have followed the two examples of Raynal and Smith. They used Raynal's concept of economic and governmental exploitation by Portugal over Brazil and they looked favorably on Smith's ideas on the opening of the Brazilian economy as a way to further progress and development.

Using the first generation of writers as a source, the second generation of positivist historians became sheer collectors of information. Historians of the colonial era depended on local sources, their own experiences, or travel accounts. They freely copied one another in an age where copying other authors was an honor rather than an offense. With the prohibition of a printing press in Brazil, the necessity to have all publications approved by both secular and religious institutions, news from Brazil remained scarce. This changed with the transfer of power from Lisbon to Rio de Janeiro in 1808 and the subsequent opening of Brazilian borders to foreigners. The secretive mind-set disappeared and foreign interest in the country opened.

With this new philosophy, foreign historians gained a renewed interest in Brazilian history, generated new sources of information, and had access to others. The early part of the nineteenth century saw an increase of foreign travelers who were not limited to coastal cities but who could visit the Brazilian interior by themselves. The French court painter Debret, the British visitor John Mawe, and the Swiss mining specialist Von Eschwege were among the many guests whose impressions of Brazil were printed, and whose books would be an important source for Brazil's economy and society for future generations of historians.[24]

The first comprehensive *History of Brazil* was written by the English poet Robert Southey and it was based on extensive research of official correspondence. Southey's book was inspired by "A collection of manuscripts not less extensive than curious, and which is not to be equaled in England. The collection was formed during a residence of more than thirty years in Portugal, by the friend and relation to which this work is inscribed."[25] Southey's friend and relation was Herbert Hill, reverend of the English nation in Lisbon, who remained Southey's sponsor through his life and who encouraged the poet in his project to write a comprehensive history of Brazil.[26]

Southey's work reflects the conclusions of the official correspondence. They also combined Raynal and Smith's ideas on the political economy of the Portuguese empire with those reflected in Portuguese administrators' reports. On the one hand, smuggling was a burden to the Portuguese treasury; on the other hand, extensive contraband networks reflected the Portuguese state's weakness to assert its authority over the Brazilian colony.

Southey's view on contraband trade became most clear in his analyses of gold smuggling. Mimicking an eighteenth-century document, Southey explained that smuggling gold dust was so profitable that it was hard to avoid. He stated that "the traders into whose hands it [gold dust] passed debased it so greatly, that if it found its way to the

Mint, there was usually a loss of ten or twelve per cent upon the assay, in addition to the twenty per cent deducted for duty."[27]

Furthermore, Southey became more philosophical and explained smuggling from a moral point of view. He wrote that "among those persons who are trained up to consider the acquisition of riches as the great object of their lives (and this is always the scope of vulgar education) there will be a large proportion in every country who care little concerning the manner by which this object might be obtained. Fraudulent practices in the common course of trade, are but too frequent in countries where the standard of morality is higher than Minas Geraes: but no practice could be so gainful as that of clandestinely exporting gold; and less scruple is always felt in defrauding governments and corporate bodies, than in cheating individuals."[28] Although Southey believed that illegal trade was caused by exceptionally low morality in the interior of Brazil, he also neatly pointed out that contraband trade was a more general phenomenon.

As foreigners investigated Brazil, so also did Brazilians look outside their country. Brazil's elite looked at France and the United States as an example for its future development. These more "advanced" countries paved the way for Brazilians for cultural and economic development. As admiration for "the West" increased, so did historians seek for sources in these countries.

During the nineteenth century, Brazilian gentlemen historians started the foundation of the discipline by copying documentation in foreign archives and by publishing them through national and local historical institutions such as the National Library and the Historical and Geographical Institutes.[29] Several historians were diplomats, such as Adolpho Varnhagen, and they visited French, British, Dutch, Portuguese, and Spanish archives in order to acquire crucial documentation about the new nation's past.[30]

Current historians profit from the nineteenth and early twentieth century positivist actions of reproduction of documentation where the reader could interpret the past.[31] The copied documents consisted mainly of diplomatic records as well as official correspondence sent by the viceroy and other to Lisbon. In Portugal, the originals could be found in the Overseas Archives, which housed the documentation of

INTRODUCTION

the Overseas Council (*Conselho Ultramarino*). The first substantial inventory of this documentation was made by Eduardo Castro e Almeida and subsequently published in the Annals of the National Library in Rio de Janeiro.[32]

Varnhagen and Almeida's work formed the foundation for historians on colonial Brazil up to the late twentieth century. Varnhagen's *História do Brasil* remains a treasure for Brazilianists. In the same tradition, others wrote copious Brazilian histories. Pedro Calmon is a wonderful example of this continuation from Southey and Varnhagen. His six volume work chronicles Brazil's past using the same type of documentation as Varnhagen, supplemented by sources acquired through his own tour of Portugal.[33]

Thus, Calmon's work became a well-researched work, reflecting the same interpretations viewing Brazilian history from the viewpoints of governors, rebellions, and occurrences described in the official correspondence and travel accounts. Calmon distinguishes himself from the nineteenth-century authors by using a more thematic approach. He classified contraband trade as part of general commerce. His observations anticipate the dependency historians, claiming that through the commercial Treaty of Methuen (1703), Portugal became the intermediary in the colonial commerce where Brazil delivered its goods (legally or illegally) to England.[34] According to Calmon, England profited greatly from Brazilian products, yet it brought only marginal advantages to Portugal and Brazil as the king invested his profits in palaces and it gave Brazilians the incentive to explore its interior.[35] Brazil's underdevelopment was thus explained by the relative backwardness of Portugal.

Underdevelopment by Portugal was followed up by resistance against the repressive regime, which was the main theme of the 'romantic" third generation of Brazilian historians. This could not be an acknowledgment of Portuguese superiority over Brazil, but rather how Brazilians were able to overcome Portuguese pressure through smuggling.

These stories could not come from official stories from the administrative correspondence but were a part of local oral histories and thus of the "real Brazil." Two examples of these romanticized stories are

INTRODUCTION

those of Xica da Silva and Dona Beija, who were legendary women who beat the system.[36] They demonstrated the cruelness of colonial exploitation, as well as the incompetence and corruption of officials and the local nomenclature, and the valiant struggle of the commoner to beat the system.

In the case of diamond mining, Feliciano dos Santos asserted that the contractor, João Fernandes Oliveira was all powerful and his will was obeyed by everyone in the mines. However, his slave turned lover Francisca (Xica) da Silva could manipulate the contractor into doing whatever she preferred. Only Pombal, the Secretary of State in Portugal, could overcome the contractor's power and the despot in Lisbon and he forced the all rich and powerful contractor to return in Lisbon.[37]

This interpretation of history with the emphasis on Brazilian strength and honor built a new national identity, where Brazilian resilience was represented through the mulatta and the underdog. The idea of contraband as form of resistance remains, even though the oral histories themselves have been proven to be factually incorrect.[38]

After World War II, the fourth generation of Brazilian historians began to use a more economic approach. Rather than explaining illegal trade though administrative failure, it was portrayed as a part of economic systems that were underdeveloped. For this approach, economic historians continued to use the diplomatic and official records, combining them with eighteenth century colonial thinkers such as Abbé Raynal and Adam Smith, while being influenced by Marxist thinking on cycles of economic development.[39]

The most influential historian was Caio Prado Jr., whose economic history explained that:

> "It is the so called "colonial pact" destined to reserve the national market of every country more and more for the products of its respective colonies, and the maritime commerce under its flag. This national exclusivism put Portugal and its colonies in a very bad position; without a navy ... and without a large national market, it restricted the exportation of its colonial goods."[40]

He argued that the absence of extensive manufacturing, no big market, and no shipping prevented economic development of Portugal and its colonies. The subsequent system of monopolies prevented industrialization of the Iberian country and its overseas possessions. Without a free market, economic development would become more difficult.[41] Caio Prado's ideas are close to the dependency theorists. His work was continued by historians throughout the military dictatorship. These academics investigated both quantitative and qualitative materials, and found renewed evidence to confirm Caio Prado's conclusions.

José Jobson de Andrade Arruda was a quantitative historian. He backed up his findings with balances of trade made in the late eighteenth and early nineteenth century. Considering this early statistical material, he discovered that Brazil even had a positive balance of trade with Portugal, which Arruda saw as clear evidence of the failure of the "old colonial system."[42]

Corcino Medeiros dos Santos used similar material, aided by early statistics found in Brazilian archives which described the flow of commerce in Rio de Janeiro and other main port cities.[43] His work was a supplement by Virgílio Noya Pinto and Michiel Morineau, who used materials from French consuls in Lisbon and French newspapers to estimate the value of the annual fleets as well as the gold production in Brazil.[44]

Although these historians were not the first to use statistical material, they was the first to analyze them in depth and Arruda even used the numbers to calculate an estimate of the amount of illegal trade in tobacco.[45] Unfortunately, almost all these historians took the eighteenth-century statistics on face value, as the Portuguese historian José Pedreira was able to point out.[46]

Caio Prado found his strongest disciple in Fernando Novais, who wrote the most read book on dependency and crisis of the colonial system in Brazil.[47] Novais made an in-depth analyses of the materials from Lisbon and especially the many reports on the decay of the Brazil trade and increase of illegal trade by Brazilian and Portuguese administrators. Using this material, Novais confirmed that the Portuguese colonial system had entered in a stage of crises at the end of the eighteenth century.

According to Novais, the phenomenon of illegal trade can not be seen without understanding the Old Colonial System, because "it is subservient to the total of the economic relations between the economies of the centers and the peripheries."[48] By principally using sources from the Portuguese administration, Novais and his disciples came to the conclusion that the Old Colonial System was powerful enough to undermine economic development in Brazil.[49] However, these ideas came increasingly under scrutiny as Brazilianists were starting to analyze agency beyond the administrative elites.

In Brazil, a fifth generation of social/cultural/economic historians started to integrate the sources and the conclusions of their colleagues interested in slavery and gender issues. Historians of slavery have long considered the idea that slaves had leverage in their unequal relationship with their owners.

However, the nature of this relationship had not been codified until these historians started to use testaments and documentation of religious organizations just like social historians.[50] Especially crucial was the publication of an inventory of all archives with documents related to slavery in commemoration of the centennial of its abolition in 1988.[51]

This opened up a wide array of new sources that could provide both more reliable answers to old questions which allowed Brazilian historians to reconsider the nature of their own economy beyond the dogma of colonial exploitation.[52]

One of the first to use notarial records to trace commercial transactions was João Fragoso.[53] He argued that the slave trade was fundamental in building capital in Brazil, thereby for the first time denying Portuguese hegemony of commercial activities. Increasingly, Brazilian historians started to view the Brazilian maritime economy from a Southern Atlantic perspective and let loose the idea that it was only run by major export products such as sugar, gold, and diamonds.[54]

At the same time, Portuguese historians started to assert the role of their country in Brazilian trade. Jorge Pedreira demonstrated that not only British products but also Portuguese textiles had a large market share in Brazil.⁵⁵ This new generation is now training home grown graduate students. Rather than moving to France, England, or the United States these students are using state universities in various parts of Brazil. Masters and doctoral students are now exploring local archives in their vicinity from Rio de Janeiro to Tocantins.⁵⁶

Unfortunately, too many theses have remained sheltered from a national audience, as local publications are not well distributed. Nevertheless, national and regional ANPUH (National Association of University Professors in History) meetings have been instrumental in bringing their works to a wider academic public and demonstrating the importance of other parts of Brazil beyond the colonial centers.

These new historiographic tendencies might easily give the impression that the metropolis asserted minimum influence over the colony. Historians need to reevaluate old and new evidence and explain the importance of colonial rules over Brazil. Rather than explaining all in terms of resistance and exploitation, it is better to think about accommodation and incorporation. The newest wave of historians is grasping with that situation, by rereading old sources, by studying uncovered foreign archives, and by studying previously uncovered areas.⁵⁷

CHAPTER 1

THE DIPLOMACY OF CONTRABAND TRADE: BETWEEN PASSIVE RESISTANCE AND PROACTIVE REFORM.

"Great Britain is, by long alliance & ancient engagements, by her political system, by her situation, and by her maritime force, the nation of all others, to which Portugal should give preference."

Dispatch Earl of Kinnock, British plenipotentiary to the Portuguese court, to the British Prime Minister William Pitt esq., October 11, 1760, National Archives in London [N.A.L.], [State Papers Portugal] SP 89, vol. 53, fl. 131v-132r.

Countries are human, implied the British diplomat, in the above statement. The idea of a "country as an actor" is echoed in diplomatic histories. L.M.E. Shaw, a British historian of Anglo-Portuguese relations during the early modern times, for instance, made the following claim about the 1654 treaty between the Portuguese and English governments. "Portugal delayed its ratification for two years and, after being forced to ratify it, endeavoured not to observe it for 156 years."[1]

The actors become the countries "Portugal" and "England" who behaved as if they were an individual, to whom the historian attributes characteristics such as "in England, commerce was considered to be of importance" or "Portugal was a Catholic country."[2] Diplomats like

Kinnock used attributed characteristics to demonstrate superiority of the inhabitants of their country of origin. British diplomats in Lisbon claimed the superiority of their fellow countrymen given the political, military, cultural, and economic characteristics of Great Britain. Kinnock's assumed superiority of Great Britain over Portugal as a nation therefore should result in exemptions from Portuguese national jurisdiction, which could lead to allowing British merchants to trespass the Portuguese government's laws and commercial regulations without impunity. This interest of British diplomats in encouraging merchants trading with Portugal increased starting in the 1690s, when gold was found in Brazil.

Gold was a highly valued commodity as the most coveted of the noble metals used in coins and the possession of gold established credit. Money meant military power as the loyalty of troops depended on the prompt payment of their wages. Moreover, the availability of ready cash smoothed commercial activities. The wealth of nations was counted in their gold and silver reserves.

Thus, management of the gold flow from Brazil through Portugal became an object of international competition. This rivalry involved mainly three European maritime powers: Great Britain, the Netherlands, and France. Governments from all three urgently needed gold supplies in order to stimulate commerce and to finance their recurrent wars against each other. All three administrations used trade as a strategic weapon. The Portuguese crown restrained the British, Dutch, and French governments' pretensions in order to keep as much Brazilian gold as possible within the Luso-Brazilian economy.

The Portuguese king forbade foreigners from exporting Brazilian gold from Portugal as well as trading directly with Brazilian ports. Still, what constituted violation of contraband laws by foreigners was negotiable. Depending on the status of the nation and of the person involved, there was a degree of latitude which allowed for some illegal trade. This chapter will discuss the foreigner's circumscribed activities involving contraband trade by demonstrating how foreign diplomats stimulated illegal gold trade. Then, I will show the tools with which the Portuguese king responded to these unlawful exports.

The ability of the Portuguese government to restrain an illegal trade in gold depended on Portugal's military and economic position in the international arena. This position was not very strong. From a military point of view, the Portuguese state had to seek allies both to preserve her independence from their Iberian neighbor and to keep equilibrium with other important European powers who otherwise might be tempted to invade her European and overseas territories. Economically, the Portuguese state was partly dependent on foreign nations to supply textiles and other products to its colonies and additional grain to feed its own population. Therefore, the Portuguese crown relied on foreign military and economic support in order to survive as a nation and preserve the integrity of her overseas empire.

Recognition of these harsh realities forced the Portuguese administration to be flexible regarding trading practices. One concession was partial allowance of contraband trade. In theory, such concessions took the form of granting privileges to foreign nationals or "nations," resident in Portugal, and of signing commercial treaties with national governments. Such treaties were concluded with the governments of England (1642, 1654, 1661, and 1703), the Netherlands (1661 and 1705), and France (1667). In practice, Portuguese officials raised obstacles to the implementation of concessions made by diplomats at the negotiating table and abrogated to themselves the authority as to whether to enforce mercantile laws.

These privileges and other measures taken by the Portuguese government are by no means a new topic for historians.[3] In fact, at least 14 historians have analyzed the diplomacy of trade from British, French, and Portuguese perspectives.[4] Notwithstanding of their differing national perspectives, all of the above historians wrote about the importation of Brazilian gold from Portugal by Great Britain and France and about Portuguese measures to curb this flow. As for sources, these authors consulted diplomatic correspondence and consequently paid considerable attention to the role of treaties and privileges. According to these authors, the concessions of such privileges made Portugal virtually a British colony.

This view is especially prominent in the works of Francis, Manchester, Shillington and Wallis Chapman, all of whom authored detailed diplomatic histories. These scholars do not point out, however, how such privileges stimulated and enhanced the ability of foreigners to engage in contraband, or in what ways the Portuguese government resisted such illegal commercial practices. Rather, they tend to regard Portugal as a colony or vassal state of Great Britain since the strategically vulnerable position of Portugal gave its government little option but to accede to the coercive terms of these treaties.

As British, Dutch, and French diplomats assumed the superiority of their respective countries above that of Portugal, they maintained the right of their countrymen to trespass commercial legislation of their host country. Negotiating commercial legislation and practice became the cornerstone of diplomatic interaction and this determined the leverage of the administrations in limiting or expanding illegal trade.

Therefore, in this chapter I analyze this political economic discourse during two distinct periods. The first period considers the Joanine reign (1706-1750), during which Brazil's gold production was the object of royal attention, and the second period considers the Pombaline and post Pombaline period (1750-1808), during which the Portuguese government was more pressed for financial means resulting in a more direct confrontation of foreign diplomats' pretensions.

In the first period, King John V was especially preoccupied with gaining administrative control over the mining district known as Minas Gerais.[5] The king concurrently issued policies to materialize the economy of Portugal itself. To counter the foreign impact on the Brazilian and Portuguese economies he took regulatory measures, which constituted a form of passive resistance against foreign merchants engaged in illegal trade. King John V did succeed in restraining foreign trade, but he provided little impetus to foster Portuguese commerce itself.

Ideas on ways to stimulate the Portuguese empire's economy did come from several statesmen such as Dom Luís da Cunha and Sebastião José Carvalho e Mello (later Marquis of Pombal).[6] But other voices, such as those of António Rodrigues da Costa and José da Cunha Brochado, influential members of the *Conselho Ultramarino* (Overseas Council) and the *Conselho da Fazenda* (Treasury Council), respectively, put forth policies with no goals other than to impose royal authority on Brazilian territories by the instruments of legislation and military fortification.[7]

Policies attributable to innovative and more sophisticated conceptions of the Portuguese and colonial economies, such as those of Dom Luís da Cunha and the Marquis of Pombal, were fully implemented only during the reign of King Joseph I (1750-1777), when persons espousing this line of thinking obtained absolute power.[8]

Foreign nations that supported the Portuguese crown were rewarded with trading privileges. Not surprisingly, many of the privileges that the Portuguese crown conceded to the English, Dutch, and French sovereigns had been made during the seventeenth century.

After 1640, when Portugal regained its independence from Spain, Portuguese policy was directed towards securing its territorial integrity from Spanish aspirations. Therefore, the Portuguese king sought alliances with the three most important seafaring countries in seventeenth century Europe: England, the Dutch Republic, and France. Portuguese diplomats initiated peace negotiations with all three countries and all three exacted a stiff price for lending their support to Portugal.

Concessions that the Portuguese government had to make to foreign nations included allowing them to have sovereign jurisdiction over their own residents in Portugal through a judge conservator granting them the right to have consuls in Brazil and agreeing to the residence of four families in the three most important port cities of Brazil, and conferring upon them the privilege of using their own vessels for trade to Portuguese America, albeit as part of Portuguese fleets. In return, those nations promised to provide military protection for Portugal.

Both the governments of the Dutch Republic and England obtained these privileges as a consequence of peace treaties, as these governments fully honored their pledges of support to Portugal. The first, immediately in the aftermath of Portuguese independence in 1640 and the second, only after bitter hostilities over Dutch conquests of Portuguese colonies in the East and West Indies had given way to an era of reconciliation.[9]

The French government remained more reluctant to support

Portugal, siding with Spain against Portugal after the signing of the Peace of the Pyrenees in 1659. Still, French diplomats were able to secure the same privileges as their English and Dutch counterparts with fewer long-term guarantees. Its peace treaty with Portugal in 1667 was valid for only ten years and the Portuguese authorities claimed that concessions were tolerated only as a favor once the treaty had expired.

In the beginning of the eighteenth century, the favored status of the English and Dutch merchants trading to Portugal was strengthened whereas the less desirable position of their French competitors further increased. Portugal joined the Anglo-Dutch coalition against the French and Spanish in the War of the Spanish Succession (1702-1713).

Ties with England were strengthened by a peace and a commercial treaty negotiated by Methuen in 1703. At the heart of this agreement was the exchange of English textiles for Portuguese wine. Each country promised to import the other's product at a lower tariff than its competitors. Two years later the Dutch government signed a similar commercial treaty which was never ratified by the Portuguese.[10]

French diplomats tried to obtain equal advantages but two attempts to conclude such a commercial treaty failed.[11] After the signing of the Peace of Utrecht in 1713, the French government tried to take advantage of tensions between the Portuguese and Spanish administrations, with the French king seeking more favorable concessions as a price for his role as an intermediary. In 1740, a similar situation occurred when tensions between the Portuguese and Spanish kings almost led to war. In both cases, French diplomatic efforts to gain commercial concessions met with failure.

There was also a relationship between trading privileges and contraband trade. Portuguese authorities saw in those privileges a loophole whereby foreign nationals could engage with impunity in illegal trade. This view was well-founded and foreign diplomats expressed identical opinions as will become clear from the following incidents with French diplomats.

In particular, French diplomatic reports fully document how France saw privileges in this light. For instance, in 1714 the French ambassador to Lisbon advocated the settlement of French consuls in Brazil as a means of helping direct illegal trade to that country.[12] The French consul to Lisbon, Mr. du Verger, held ideas similar to those of his superior. He also tried to gain the support of Portuguese governors in Brazil for French contraband trade. Du Verger's claims that governors in Brazil were less corrupt than their colleagues in Spanish America did not deter him from promoting proposals for illegal trade to Portuguese America. He recommended that great numbers of French vessels should anchor in the port of Salvador and, by their sheer numbers, would force the Portuguese to accept the reality of contraband trade.[13]

Furthermore, Du Verger was convinced that, if he could persuade one Brazilian governor to allow this contraband trade, then others would follow suit and condone such commerce. Thus, in a partly coded dispatch he suggested:

"When the fleets depart from here, and there are some changes of governors in some parts [of Brazil], we should solicit the new opportunities and by teaching them to hope that their intervention will be appropriately compensated, we will obtain their promise that they will permit such vessels to enter their ports as they will be advised of it in advance."[14]

Du Verger recommended that to have any success, this process should be handled discreetly.[15] This was wishful thinking. The cautious approach failed when Mr. Cangard, supposedly a diplomat appointed by the French king to become vice-consul in Rio de Janeiro, arrived in Lisbon in 1714. The French ambassador reported, with embarrassment, that Mr. Cangard talked openly about his plans to open direct trade with Brazil and that he had already made his personal arrangements with local merchants for this commerce.[16]

As a consequence, the ambassador remarked:

"It is not easy to destroy the impressions which the Portuguese already entertain that they are forewarned that the French are established in the [Portuguese] conquests in order to let the whole nation engage in direct commerce with them."[17]

It must also have been extremely painful to both French and Portuguese diplomats when, in 1728, the French Captain Le Gentil de la Barbinais published his journal in Amsterdam. This journal openly related how he had traded with the authorities in Salvador 14 years earlier.[18]

Therefore, it was hardly surprising that Portuguese authorities began to curtail foreign privileges in an effort to restrict any kind of concessions that might unwittingly promote illegal trade. To this end, the Portuguese government took three measures: expulsion of foreigners from Brazil; refusal to allow foreign vessels to enter Brazilian ports even if they were incorporated in the annual fleets from Portugal; and, finally, expulsion of those consuls and merchant families who had taken up residence in Brazil as the result of the peace treaties. It is beneficial to consider such measures and their ramifications at greater length.

During and shortly after the War of the Spanish Succession, Portuguese authorities began to curb privileges that permitted active participation by foreign subjects in Brazilian trade. Henceforth, Portuguese America would be closed to foreign influences and all trade to Brazil would occur only through the intermediary of Portuguese merchants. Thus, the appearance of foreigners in the Brazilian gold mines was looked on suspiciously by the Portuguese crown.[19] As early as 1702, the Brazilian governor general, Dom Rodrigo da Costa, warned about the negative consequences of their presence.[20]

More serious was the French and Spanish presence on Ilha Grande, an island off the Brazilian coast just opposite the port of Paratí and South of Rio de Janeiro, which was also the terminal of the road to the mining regions. Acquisition of leadership positions in the community by such foreigners, and intermarriage with the local population, made the Overseas Council uneasy and the councilors pleaded for their immediate expulsion.[21] The councilors' opinion was not unfounded: at least one Frenchman, Ambroise Jauffret, wrote a long memorandum on the mines in Brazil to the French king after his stay in São Paulo.[22]

In what was to be a comprehensive package of measures against foreigners, the first act was an order for the expulsion of certain individuals.[23] First to be expelled from Brazil were the French Capuchins.[24]

The Portuguese government decreed that no new friars should be sent to Brazil, even though the secretary of state had commended their services to the French consul. The French diplomat remarked that:

> "One treats this case as an affair of state. The foundation for all decisions now being taken is apprehension that foreigners should not know too much about what is happening in Brazil."[25]

A year later, six out of the nine Capuchins had already arrived in Lisbon from Brazil while their fellow priests, deep in the interior, were to be sent over immediately.[26] A royal letter of 1713 ordered that any foreigner who was not a merchant and who did not have a Portuguese spouse and children should be expelled from Brazil.[27]

This order remained in force throughout the eighteenth century but there were exceptions. For example, when foreigners had skills that were needed in Brazil they were allowed to stay. However, if they subsequently became public nuisances then they were ordered to leave. Such was the case of two foreign doctors who both wanted to stay in Rio de Janeiro. One of them, the German John Adolph Scharan, petitioned in 1730 for dispensation from this ruling. The outcome of the case was not recorded.[28]

The other, Jose Strukz, a Flemish doctor from Bruges, who arrived on the Dutch vessel *Vredenburg* in 1789, successfully treated several people. Since there were only four doctors for the whole population of Rio de Janeiro, viceroy Luís de Vasconsellos e Sousa pleaded to the secretary of state for the physician's continued presence in Brazil.[29]

Others were less fortunate. Pedro Folgman, a naturalized Dutchman, was very helpful to his fellow countrymen in Rio de Janeiro when the Brazilian authorities confiscated their vessel *Don Carlos* in 1725. The governor, Luís Vahia Monteiro, did not appreciate this help and ordered his expulsion.[30]

The expulsion of all foreigners from Brazil was virtually impossible.

Indeed, there were foreigners in Brazil of whom the authorities had no knowledge. For instance, in 1776 the Scotsman Charles Campbell wrote to the English plenipotentiary in Lisbon, Robert Walpole. Campbell had lived for about 50 years in the region of Sabará, formerly one of the richest gold mining districts of Brazil. At the age of 72, Campbell wanted to sell his lands in Minas Gerais and return to his native country. Only through the personal intercession of the Earl of Weymouth, the English secretary of state, was he able to achieve this goal.[31]

The crown took further restrictive measures in 1710. For the first time, it ruled that vessels sailing with the three Brazil-bound fleets (Salvador, Rio de Janeiro, and Recife) must be of Portuguese origin.[32] The British consuls in Lisbon and Porto protested, fearing that if they gave in to these measures, inevitably Portuguese authorities would feel no inhibition about abolishing other privileges.[33] These protests fell on deaf ears.

At the same time, another set of measures was promulgated. These ordered the expulsion of English and Dutch merchant families and consuls who had settled in Brazilian ports. The British community in Lisbon complained that they could no longer travel freely to Brazil and that effectively this measure precluded the settlement of new families in the three main port cities of Portuguese America.[34]

Dom Luís da Cunha, the Portuguese ambassador to Great Britain, asked the British king to renounce the privilege of settling four families in the main ports of Brazil. This would make French competition more difficult. Da Cunha pointed out that according to the terms of treaties with France, French nationals had been granted the same privileges as their British colleagues. If the British forwent these privileges British merchants would be in a competitive advantage over French merchants, Da Cunha stated, since British merchants had established enough contacts already in order to successfully engage in commerce, they did not need the four families. Da Cunha argued that curtailment of privileges granted to French nationals would eliminate them as potential trading rivals, especially since the French government was planning to use those families and consuls for the purpose of engaging in illegal trade.[35]

The British merchant community in Lisbon did not agree with Dom Luís da Cunha's argument, because they did not fear competition from French traders and saw in Da Cunha's specious claims an attempt to curb their own participation in commerce.[36] The Portuguese government resorted to drastic measures, which was reflected in draconic actions of governors and viceroys. The British trader Ralph Gulston arrived in Lisbon from Rio de Janeiro with the fleet of 1716. A merchant who had resided for about seven years in Rio de Janeiro, he had built up a successful business. Suddenly, the governor executed orders from Lisbon to expel him using charges that he had committed criminal offenses.[37] Similar problems arose in Salvador. The viceroy, Count de Angeja, arbitrarily tried to expel three British families, who were only successful in postponing their expulsion for a year.[38]

Remonstrances by the British plenipotentiary in Lisbon to the Portuguese secretary of state, Diogo de Mendonça Corte Real, had no effect. The Portuguese secretary replied that, because of his trading with French merchants, Ralph Gulston had been a *persona non grata* in Rio de Janeiro for years and that the king had long wanted to recall him. Corte Real claimed that this measure would not be an obstacle to British families continuing to live in Brazil.[39] The only result of the English diplomatic protest was that Ralph Gulston was allowed to return to Rio de Janeiro for one year in order to liquidate his commercial interests.[40]

The expulsion of British merchants continued. The next fleet from Brazil brought the news that all British merchants in Salvador had been required to show licenses from the Portuguese king authorizing their continued residence.[41] The British consul general openly expressed his fears that all three British families would be expelled, thereby rendering any privileges null and void. He received the reassuring answer from the Portuguese secretary of state that all but one merchant could stay with the justification that the two year term had expired. The secretary went on to say that the terms of treaties would be fully upheld.[42]

Although the Portuguese crown was only partly successful in expelling British traders from Brazil, the British community became very uncomfortable. Indeed, all foreign merchants intending to settle in Portuguese America faced considerable obstacles. In February of 1723 a British merchant tried to take up residence in Salvador and, although he promptly obtained a license to settle in the Brazilian capital, a full two years elapsed before he obtained all the necessary permits to travel to Brazil.[43]

The Portuguese government also claimed that the quota of families had already been filled. British envoys protested that all British persons in Brazil had been counted in this quota, including sailors who had jumped ship and settled in Brazil, taking Luso-Brazilian wives.[44] British diplomats continued to bring bring up the issue of establishing merchants in Brazilian ports throughout the eighteenth century, but they never fully realized their goal.

Dutch traders and diplomats experienced similar problems. In 1711, the king refused to give permission for two Dutchmen to settle in Brazil.[45] In 1729, the governor of Pernambuco expelled the Dutch merchant and consul, Pieter de Graaf, and his companion, Nicolaas Couse. They were sent to prison, with their release conditional on signing a document stating that they would not return to Brazil.[46]

Dutch diplomats strongly opposed these new Portuguese measures and threatened to withdraw their promise of military support for Portugal. When, in 1712, news of Duguay Trouin's conquest of Rio de Janeiro arrived to Portugal, the king summoned Dutch and British diplomats to ask them for military support. The Dutch resident sent home a secret dispatch that suggested making such military support conditional on Portuguese adoption of a more benign policy on matters of commerce.

> "On this occasion it seems important to me to suggest to the States General, that this would be the appropriate time to demand satisfaction from the Count of Tarouca concerning the bad treatment of the Dutch here, especially in regards the price of salt, and the commerce in grain, and refusal to allow the Dutch to settle in Brazil, although this prerogative is established by treaties."[47]

In other words, the Dutch government linked military support to commercial concessions, a connection that English diplomats would vigorously stress at a later stage.[48]

Whereas British and Dutch envoys negotiated for the continued presence in Brazil of merchant families and consuls, French diplomats had to start from zero if they were to have some French representation in Portuguese America. In this, they achieved a measure of success. French envoys succeeded into acquiescing to their demands by threatening to renegotiate the terms of the Treaty of Utrecht (1713) if their privileges were not fully restored. The Portuguese diplomatic position vis-à-vis the French was fundamentally untenable. So intense was the pressure on the Portuguese government that the English plenipotentiary repeatedly remarked on what he viewed as excessive French influence in Portugal. He even thought that Portugal had concluded a secret commercial treaty with France which would permit French nationals to trade directly to Brazil.[49]

Although these rumors were without merit, French diplomats did negotiate for a vice consul in Salvador, something both their British and Dutch colleagues had failed to accomplish. This was no mean achievement. France had a consul in Salvador before the War of the Spanish Succession and had attempted to reclaim this right after both countries were once more at peace. Despite hesitancy and recalcitrance on the Portuguese side, French diplomats were persistent and nominated a Mr. de Pantigny, who presented his credentials to the Portuguese king. After two months, he was "excusado," or flatly refused.[50]

The French ambassador's immediate reaction was to inform his superiors in Paris that the problem was bureaucratic, namely, that the *Desembargo do Paço* (Supreme Court of Justice) had favored the nomination but, in the *Conselho Ultramarino* (Overseas Council), the *procurador da coroa* (royal prosecutor) had opposed it.[51]

Nevertheless, a few days later, Diogo Mendonça Corte Real, the Portuguese secretary of state, coolly explained to the French ambassador that the English and Dutch were not allowed to have a consul in Salvador and that a vice consul would suffice. The secretary remarked that if His Excellency, the French Ambassador, were to let the matter drop then the secretary of state would review the issue of the establishment of French merchant houses in Salvador. The ambassador was left in little doubt that the outcome would be positive.[52]

Although Portuguese authorities finally relented, two years passed before a French vice consul was allowed to go to Salvador. The new Vice Consul was not Monsieur Pantigny, who had left for Gibraltar on secret business matters, but a Monsieur Du Vienne, a wealthy and trusted French trader in Lisbon who had enough capital to provide French vessels calling at Salvador with the necessary credit.[53]

As might be expected, French merchants were not to enjoy this exclusive privilege for long. The Portuguese king withdrew the privileges once the problems with the signing of the Utrecht peace treaty had been resolved. A mere three years later, Du Vienne reported that the viceroy wanted to expel him. The following year this became effective. The viceroy claimed that Du Vienne's patent as vice consul had been granted for three years and that the Portuguese king could no longer tolerate a French consular presence in Brazil.[54]

French consular problems with Portuguese authorities were not confined to Brazil but also to the more accessible Atlantic islands. The Atlantic islands were frequently used for provisioning by vessels bound to or from Brazil and served as an excellent opportunity for both legal and illegal commercial transactions. Similar difficulties arose in the Azores, where local authorities acted autocratically. The French consul in Fayal found out how precarious his position was when he protested a new tax imposed by the Municipal Council. He was told that he could accept the new tax or appeal to Lisbon to reverse the ruling but, that until a decision was reached in Lisbon and communicated to the Azores, he would remain in prison.

Whereas merchants from the more loyal Great Britain and the Netherlands could count on full fledged support of the consuls on the Portuguese islands, their French competitors had to overcome several commercial obstacles.[55] After the expulsion of priests and diplomats from Brazil, the third measure that the Portuguese government used against foreign influence consisted of restrictions placed on the jurisdiction of judge conservators in Portugal itself. Portuguese officials maintained that the jurisdiction of these judges, one for each national group, represented a serious threat to their authority. Foreigners could not be arrested or brought to trial without the approval of their own judge conservator whose country of origin or nation paid his salary. The Portuguese administration had acquiesced to this arrangement with great resistance. However, this was far from the end of the matter. In 1742, the Portuguese king determined that economic disputes between Portuguese and British merchants would be judged by the Municipal Council in Lisbon rather than the judge conservators. There were many protests against this measure, especially by British and Dutch diplomats, but all were in vain.[56]

The Portuguese strategy of eliminating foreigners from Brazil trade had been a success, at least temporarily. Portuguese authority was reasserted and the position of Portuguese merchants in Brazil trade strengthened. Foreigners were allowed to stay in Brazil only on Portuguese terms or their position became untenable. Direct foreign participation in the fleet system had diminished and foreign merchants were obliged to trade with Brazil using Portuguese colleagues as intermediaries. After minimizing direct trade to Brazil, the Portuguese government was now in a position to move toward gaining more control over the flow of Brazilian gold entering and leaving Portugal itself.

Portugal, Great Britain, and many other countries had longtime passed laws forbidding gold exports.[57] Sovereigns looked unfavorably upon the export of noble metals but, in the absence of paper money, these metals were essential to the maintenance of a monetary system. Noble metals were also the preferred medium for paying soldiers. During the many wars of the seventeenth and eighteenth centuries, the outcome of such hostilities was as much determined by the availability of gold and silver reserves to the respective warring factions as by their tactical skills in the field. Brazilian gold became very attractive to both foreigners and nationals. Regulation of the flow of gold bullion was hotly contested and highly controversial.

Throughout the first half of the eighteenth century, Britain had an overwhelmingly positive balance of trade towards Portugal (Graph 1.1). A significant proportion of products imported into Portugal from Britain had Brazil as their final destination. In particular, cheap English textiles were attractive to both free and slave populations of Portuguese

America. In order to pay for these commodities, much of the gold exported from Brazil passed through Portugal to Britain. While technically forbidden, this export was condoned in order to obtain goods from Britain and other European countries. The Portuguese prime minister, the Marquis of Pombal, openly admitted this.[58]

Therefore, the question was not whether illegal traders should be prosecuted but how exports of gold from Portugal could be streamlined and regulated.[59] An opinion issued by a councilor of the *Conselho da Fazenda* (Council of the Treasury) held that the export of gold by foreigners should be allowed but not to such a degree that Portuguese merchants would be starved for capital or that there would be insufficient money in circulation.[60]

Illegal shipments of gold from Portugal to Great Britain generally were transported by packet boats and military vessels. Because these vessels enjoyed diplomatic immunity, they could not be searched by customs or other harbor authorities.[61] A clear distinction should be drawn between different kinds of illegal exports of gold: the export of gold dust, which had not been taxed by the Portuguese and Brazilian authorities, and the export of coins minted from gold, on which the fifth due to the crown had been paid. Even though authorities frowned on the latter practice, the former was clearly more detrimental to the king's treasury.

There were many reports about the illegal transportation of gold dust. The French consul in Lisbon, De Montagnac, observed after the arrival of the fleet from Rio de Janeiro in 1725:

> "That an English warship left the harbor, which twelve days earlier had entered and anchored in the middle of this fleet. We are convinced that a considerable quantity of gold was transferred to this vessel and loaded without having been duly registered."[62]

The fact that such activities were carried out quite openly and blatantly was an embarrassment to the Portuguese. In fact, transshipment of Brazilian gold in Lisbon was conducted on the waterfront, directly under the nose of King John V who, from his open palace windows, had a good view of the frequent disputes between British sailors and Portuguese authorities.[63]

In all cases, British diplomats protested the imprisonment of their countrymen and the confiscation of their holdings in gold. In virtually all cases, these persons were freed and their gold restored to them. In the case of one British merchant whose gold coins were seized by Portuguese custom officers in 1734, the British plenipoteniary, Lord Tyrawly, was reluctant to intervene.[64] The British minister claimed that the British merchant had been so imprudent about his smuggling activities that his arrest and the confiscation of his goods had been his own fault.[65]

In His Excellency's opinion, indiscretion and blatant defiance of Portuguese authority were clear reasons for confiscation and arrests. The confiscation of gold from important persons threatened the condoned export of gold and was so fundamental to the Anglo-Luso alliance that it gave rise to some "tests cases." One example was the case of the banker Mr. Wingfield in 1726; Wingfield's arrest by the Portuguese authorities after his house in Lisbon was searched and gold found, much in dust form, provoked outcries of indignation from the British government. Only after the British government threatened to send warships to enforce his release was the case resolved amicably. One outcome was the Portuguese suggestion that henceforth these exports should be allowed but that a small duty would be levied on exports of gold and silver.[66]

Tolerance for the illegal export of gold, provided that it was licensed, became a reality in the 1740s when the *juiz da saca de moeda* (judge of money exports) signed documents to this effect.[67] Still, payment of even these taxes was avoided by some merchants who lived on brokerage fees derived from the differential rates charged to export gold not only by the Lisbon authorities but also by merchant ships, packet boats, and military vessels.[68]

British merchants were not alone in exporting gold from Portugal. Often there were Dutch man-of-war vessels in the harbor of Lisbon awaiting the arrival of gold transports from Brazil.[69] French consuls tried to interest their government in sending military vessels but their proposals were ignored, though Portuguese officials did arrest some French merchants.[70]

Export of gold to Great Britain, while forbidden by law, was in practice condoned by the Portuguese. The officially illegal status of this trade permitted Portuguese authorities to correct some of the abuses and to partially diminish the gold flow, especially of untaxed dust gold. But in general, there was little that the Portuguese authorities could do beyond setting some examples.

Another way of regulating commerce was the creation of trading companies. The Portuguese government made some attempts in this direction during the Joanine period. Still, state interests were limited, and it proved difficult to attract capital, either foreign or national, to invest in these projects. One such example was the Corisco Company, organized in 1724 by a few foreign merchants of whom the most important was the French captain Jean Dansaint.[71] The purpose of the company was to erect a fortress near the Mina Coast on the island of Corisco and to use it to deliver slaves to Brazil. The project provoked much foreign opposition: the British consul talked one of his compatriots out of it and French diplomats treated Dansaint as an enemy of the state.[72] But it was the Dutch West India Company (W.I.C.) that destroyed the fortress the Portuguese company had erected on Corisco after Dansaint had captured several of its vessels.[73] Moreover, the W.I.C., had argued that the peace treaty of 1661 gave them a monopoly on the slave trade, and did not tolerate any Portuguese competition on the Mina Coast.[74] Therefore, the Corisco Company survived for only three years.

Although the short-lived Corisco Company ended in a failure, it did start off a debate about the necessity of such companies.[75] A major problem of such trading organizations was that they needed substantial start-up capital, which had to come from foreign and national investors. This support was difficult to obtain since financiers lacked confidence in such projects. Only when the state actively began to participate in these trading companies did they enjoy any degree of success.[76] However, among Portuguese ministers of state and advisers, there was no unanimity of opinion on this issue, and only during the

Pombaline administration did such projects obtain full governmental support.

The Joanine anti-contraband trade policy may be summarized as follows: consistency in restraining the participation of foreign nations in the gold trade; favoring those countries that offered protection against Spain; using one country against another; passive resistance to restrain foreign influence in Brazil as much as possible without modifying the basic organization of the Luso-Brazilian economies.

Portuguese administration, both in the metropolis and in Brazil, significantly evolved in the period from 1700 to 1750. By the end of the 1730s, the governor of the Southern Brazilian provinces, Gomes Freire de Andrade, imposed a workable form of administration on Brazil's mining districts. As a consequence, larger quantities of gold flowed to Portugal. At first there was no need to restrict foreign nations' share in this gold stream as such restrictions could only lead to the alienation of nations on whom the Portuguese government depended for military protection. Official thinking at the time was that it was preferable to impose a degree of acceptable regulation over this trade rather than to use brute force in an attempt to stop all illegal commerce. By the early 1750s, with the royal treasury facing financial exigency, the promotion of policies calculated to generate revenues for the royal fisc became a matter of national priority. Thus, there came into existence new policies which, it was hoped, would actively promote Portuguese industry. These new policies coexisted with older policies, policies that had been effective in limiting the degree to which foreign nations and their nationals could have an impact on the Luso-Brazilian economy.

During King John V's administration, policies to prevent illegal trade were mostly confined to legal measures to confine North European traders to Portugal and the Atlantic islands. During the successive administrations of King Joseph I (1750-1777), Queen Mary (1777-1793), and Prince Regent John VI (1793-1822), the administration took a more active stance. During their reigns, their goals encompassed nothing less than the total reform of the Luso-Brazilian economy and society.

The individual most identified with these new proactive policies was Sebastião José Carvalho e Mello, better known as the Marquis of

Pombal. Pombal, as prime minister (*secretário do reino*) to King Joseph I, transformed Portuguese society in more than one aspect. With the increase of the assertion of the state over society, Pombal and his successors conducted fund raising efforts which required an overhaul of the social order in Portuguese society.

Pombal sought to diminish the role of the high nobility and the clergy and to stimulate a new class of merchant-aristocrats. He stood for industrial and agricultural reforms, restructuring education, and reorganizing the royal administration. During Pombal's later years, state control diminished but the basic idea of state intervention to foster economic wealth remained.

The new policies that emerged after King John V's death reflected a modification in the mind-set of the Portuguese ruling class towards the ideas of the "estrangeirados" (politicians who had been abroad) of the 1730s. Introducing a new education curriculum entailed reducing the role of the clergy as it was seen as keeping the population mired in "superstitious beliefs." With the Portuguese people encouraged to assume the responsibility as stewards of the national economy, those who showed an entrepreneurial flair were in great demand while those lacking such talents were removed from decision-making positions. The Royal Exchequer would have to streamline its collection and disbursement processes by professionalizing its administrative personnel. This was a period rife with the formulation of new policies and a readiness to implement reform.

Policies of active reform could not be enacted without encountering some degree of resistance. King Joseph I and his prime minister Pombal relentlessly pursued persons who resisted their reform program and bestowed patronage on persons who were in their camp. Pombal took draconic measures such as the expulsion of the Jesuits, bringing the Tavoras to trial, and the mass imprisonment of political opponents. Pombal's patronage rewarded his supporters with participation in controlled monopolies on commerce, economic development, and public offices.[77]

Confronted with these two facets of Pombal's administration, a restructuring of Portuguese society and a brutal suppression of its opponents, most historians have chosen sides, with one camp stressing the positive effects of Pombal's measures on Portuguese society and the other highlighting the negative effects of his repressive measures.[78] The two historians who have dominated this discussion are Jorge Borges de Macedo and Kenneth R. Maxwell. Jorge Borges de Macedo has argued that Pombal's reform program represented a continuation of, rather than a break with, earlier Portuguese economic policies. He concedes that some changes did occur but asserts that these were consequences of the prevailing economic situation.[79] Kenneth R. Maxwell, on the contrary, demonstrates the innovative quality of Pombal's economic and institutional reforms which resulted in increased state control over the Portuguese economy.[80] Moreover, he reconciles Pombal's reforms with his despotic repression by admitting the paradoxical existence of both aspects in his policies.[81]

Pombal's policy is coherent: despotic government was necessary in order to bring about long-lasting reforms. Reform had to be imposed from above since there was no incentive for it to come from below. In contrast to earlier periods of transformation, during and after king Joseph I's 27-year reign, reforms became institutionalized. Following Joseph's death, policies of protectionism, demonopolization, and stimulation of local interests replaced older ideas. Testimonies to the institutionalized discussions of these policies included numerous economic reports, experimentation with new types of production in agriculture and manufacturing, attraction of foreign specialists, and the foundation of scientific and literary academies.[82]

Pombal's policies also included a more active stance against illegal trade by foreign nationals. His reintroduction of sumptuary laws, protectionism, and the formation of monopolistic trading companies forced a restructuring of the parameters of illegal trade. On the one hand, Pombal's policies allowed the condoning of contraband trade, which was reserved for those who supported the new ideas. On the other hand, the new economic policies lifted the boundaries between proscribed and condoned illegal trade to a higher level. The main driving forces behind these new avenues of the political-economic mind set was embedded in a multi-national context.

In the 1750s, the bulk of illegal trade still consisted of the export of noble metals to Britain. The Portuguese government tussled with the problem of how to stop Brazilian gold from flowing to Great Britain. Policies of passive resistance, such as raising barriers to foreign settlement in Brazil, were only partially successful. The huge trade deficit ruled out measures aimed at Great Britain and Northern Europe. Confronted by this insolvable problem, the Portuguese government opted for a program of revitalization of the Portuguese manufacturing sector.

Textiles were the most important product that foreigners provided to Brazil. In order to stimulate Portuguese manufacture of textiles, the Portuguese government, just before the end of the reign of King John V, turned to an old and proven method: the introduction of pragmatic or sumptuary laws. In the last decades of the seventeenth century, the Count of Ericeira, then prime minister, had also used these laws to revitalize Portuguese industry.[83] Although a sumptuary law was meant to ban luxury goods, in practice it restricted the import of certain types of textiles into Portugal and its colonies.

The government had already introduced the first pragmatic law in 1749, the last year of King John V's reign. This law hit French merchants hard since the prohibition targeted textiles produced in that country. French nationals were forced to withdraw products from the Portuguese market products that they had already previously sold to local retailers and export them back to France. In the beginning the law was strictly enforced. People who infringed clauses of this law were arrested on the streets of Lisbon.[84] Soon after King Joseph I came to power, the sumptuary laws were strengthened. These new measures excluded not only French merchandise from the Portuguese market but also some Portuguese manufactures.[85] Pombal's policies, besides aiming at the revitalization of the Portuguese economy, were also designed to provide exclusive access to the internal market to those foreigners and nationals who supported his policies.

How effective were these measures? In the French case, the results seem to have been rather meager. The numbers in Graph 1.1. below indicate that, at least on the short run, French commerce did not suffer as much as their own diplomats claimed. The French consul in Lisbon based his ideas on taxes levied on cargoes of French vessels that arrived in Portugal which gave a different view from the balances of trade drawn up in France. The French historian Labourdette explains this disparity by suggesting that many French goods entered as contraband: the goods supposedly originated from another country and many French captains refused to pay the consular duties.[86]

Sumptuary laws, however, were not altogether effective in eliminating French textiles from Portuguese markets. There was extensive contraband trade: one expedient resorted to by

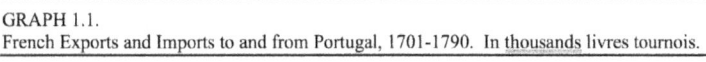

GRAPH 1.1.
French Exports and Imports to and from Portugal, 1701-1790. In thousands livres tournois.

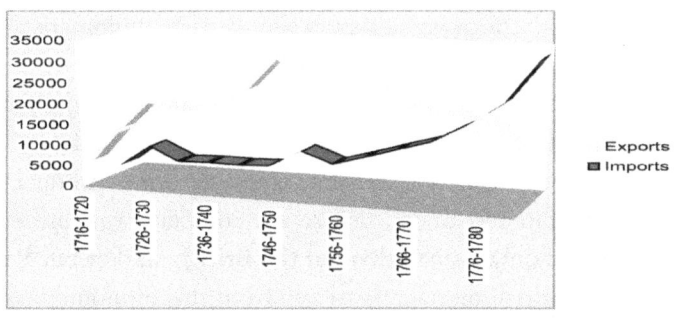

Source: Jean-François Labourdette, La Nation Française à Lisbonne de 1669 à 1790 entre Colbertisme et Liberalisme (Paris: Fondation Gulbenkian, 1988) 638-640.

French merchants claimed was the claim that the textiles they imported were of Dutch manufacture. For a time, the Lisbon customs condoned this deception, even though officials knew that the textiles were of French origin. In 1786, however, the Portuguese enforced the law against the imports of French textiles and French diplomats complained once more.[87] This sterner stance by the Portuguese was attributable to the fact that Portuguese manufacturers had, by then, started to produce the same kinds of textiles.[88] Sumptuary laws served not only to exclude unfriendly nations from the market but also to promote Portugal's own industry. Entrepreneurs investing in manufacturing obtained state support by monopolistic legislation aimed at protecting the Portuguese market.[89]

Therefore, the Portuguese government's policy came to focus on the establishment of a national manufacturing sector. The first casualties of these new policies were those nations that had the least favorable relations with Portugal. This did not mean that British and Dutch manufactures could be imported with impunity but that they suffered from increased taxation and partial exclusion from the market. The former reflected an increase in commodity-specific taxes as well as from modifications to the *pauta* or customs list.[90] The latter was due to the result of the establishment of Portuguese monopolistic trading companies for particular markets, notably the *Companhia do Alto Douro* in Portugal and the two companies of Pará and Maranhão and of Pernambuco and Paraíba for trade to Brazil.[91] These trading companies led to many controversies between British diplomats and the Marquis of Pombal.

The *Companhia do Alto Douro* was a good example of the monopolization of the market by both foreign and national merchants.[92] Port wine from specific districts became the sole wine product to be exported to Britain and Brazil. Before the company was formed, port wine had enjoyed only a small share of the British market but Pombal's policies forced British merchants to buy from this monopoly company wines from a demarcated region.[93] Pombal thereby favored important wine growers and merchants who were loyal to his cause and bankrupted his opponents by excluding them from the market. This system favored big landowners and reduced the number of small wine growers.[94] His goal was not to drive British merchants out of their roles as intermediaries for their own market but to force these foreign merchants to play according to the company's rules.[95] This monopoly was undermined by illegal mixing of Port wines with wines from regions out of the demarcated zone. Although this practice occurred on a large scale, the law did enable Portuguese authorities to put foreign wine exporters in a vulnerable position by occasionally imposing punishment.[96]

British merchants and diplomats were not pleased with Pombal's trading companies. In 1760, the Count of Kinnock, British ambassador to Portugal, wrote a long memorial protesting the new Brazilian companies as a threat to British commerce. In the very first paragraph Kinnock stated the essence of his complaint:

CONTROLLING CONTRABAND

"The erection of the trading Companies, from hence [Portugal] to the Brazil must necessarily produce the most destructive consequences to the British commerce, not only diminishing the export of our manufactures, but also by lessening the import of the coin of Portugal into Great Britain."[97]

In fact, such monopoly companies did not have any say over commercial practices in the major captaincies (provinces) of Brazil. The Count of Kinnock noted with apprehension that he had been informed that preparations were afoot for the creation of a company for Bahia and he expressed his concern that other companies might be instituted for Rio de Janeiro and Minas Gerais.[98]

At the same time, there was a reduction in policies of passive resistance. Between 1767 and 1786, there was almost no prosecution of illegal exporters of noble metals from Portugal. True, British diplomats continued to complain about the behavior of the Portuguese government, especially concerning the monopoly companies and the problems British merchants encountered trying to settle in Brazil. This gave rise to some eccentric diplomatic exchanges.

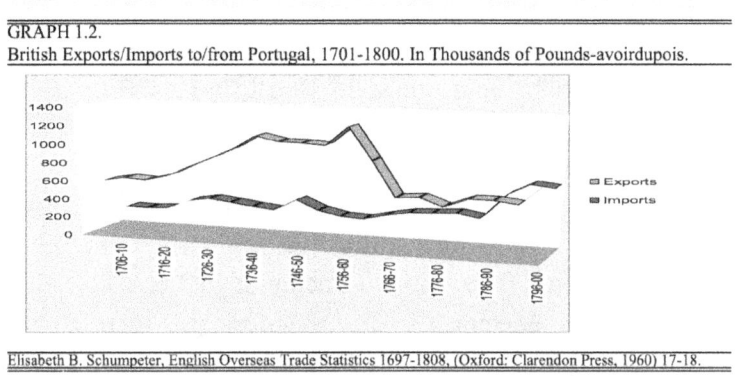

GRAPH 1.2.
British Exports/Imports to/from Portugal, 1701-1800. In Thousands of Pounds-avoirdupois.

Elisabeth B. Schumpeter, English Overseas Trade Statistics 1697-1808, (Oxford: Clarendon Press, 1960) 17-18.

The nature of British complaints can be better explained by examining the balances of trade. These showed a decrease during the 1760s in the hitherto preeminent position of Britain. The decline of British commerce was related to the diminishing value of British exports to

Portugal (Seen above in Graph 1.2). However, Portuguese exports to Britain remained fairly stable, with a small temporary decrease attributable to the Lisbon earthquake of 1755.

Several explanations have been advanced for the decline of British trade to Portugal. The British secretary of state, Lord Rockford, formulated five reasons: diminished gold mining, problems with the Spanish in the La Plata region which diminished silver exports, heavy investment in construction materials from countries other than Britain after the Lisbon earthquake disaster of 1755, the establishment of the new Royal Treasury which impeded reinvestment, and the burning of the Lisbon Customs House.[99]

Robert Walpole had, at an earlier stage, attributed the British losses largely to bad investments by English merchants, many of whom had entrusted their merchandise to *commisários volantes* (itinerant peddlers) who embarked on the ships of fleets bound for Brazil. British merchants, like their correspondents in Brazil, hoped to gain exorbitant profits by the use of those peddlers. Unfortunately, such hopes were often dashed because often merchandise was never paid for, and the consignors faced heavy debts.[100]

Walpole's assertion is interesting and may have contributed to some short-term decline of British trade. However, on the long-term, historians have attributed the diminishing of British trade to the decreasing amounts of gold mined in Brazil.[101] Less Brazilian gold meant a reduced capacity to make up for the trade deficit between England and Portugal. Therefore, commerce between the two countries would tend naturally to decline. Considering Graph 1.3, which portrays amounts of gold mined in Brazil as estimated by the Brazilian historian Virgílio Noya Pinto and the amount of gold transported from Brazil to Lisbon as assembled by Michel Morineau, there is coincidence between the period of decline of gold mining and the decline of British trade. However, the decline of gold imports into Portugal was not as drastic as the differences in the decline between British imports and exports to Portugal. This suggests that other factors existed.

CONTROLLING CONTRABAND

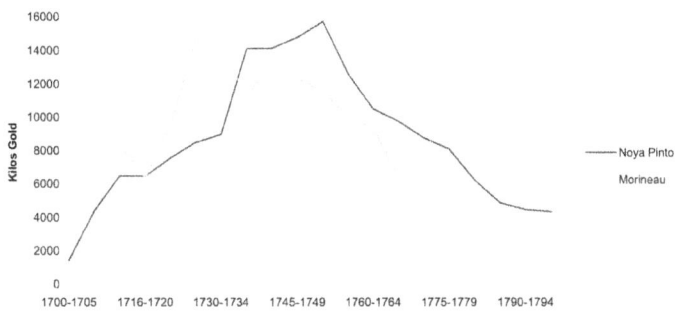

GRAPH 1.3.
Estimates of Gold production in Minas Gerais, Goiás and Mato Grosso 1700-1799 (N.P.) and of gold transports from Brazil to Lisbon 1711-1769 (M.). Quinquennial avarages in kilos.

Sources: Virgílio Noya Pinto, Ouro Brasileiro e o Comércio Anglo-Português (2.ed.; São Paulo; Companhia Editora National, 1979) 114; Michel Morineau, Incroyables Gazettes et Fabuleux Métaux. Les Retours des Trésors Americains d'après les Gazettes Hollandeses (XVIe-XVIIIe siècles) (London: Cambridge University Press; Paris: Maison des Sciences de l'Homme, 1985) 136-139.

The British historian, H.E.S. Fisher, gave a good overview of the possible reasons.[102] These were the decline of gold mining and silver exports from La Plata which coincided with a decline in sugar prices and a decline in the grain trade from Great Britain. Jorge Borges de Macedo even spoke about a period of crises in the Portuguese economy which was overcome by the end of the next decade.[103] The positive balance of trade in Portugal's favor in the 1790s is attributable to the increase in the cotton trade and rising sugar prices on the international market in the wake of the Haitian revolution.

The relative differences between French exports to and imports from Portugal tended to exceed slightly the figures for British trade (Graph 1.1). This discrepancy can be explained by the fact that French merchants had access to fewer Portuguese products with which to equalize their balance of trade. The French figures underline these findings about British trade: the balance changed at the same time. But, in contrast to the British numbers, there was already a marked growth of Portuguese exports to France in the 1760s. The French historian Labourdette attributed this growth to the increased cotton trade from Brazil and to the rise in Portuguese imports of French grain.[104] During the 1780s, French traders clearly began to lose ground

27

on the Portuguese market. Previously exports had remained fairly stable, now they began to decline sharply. The French political situation and problems in its colonies were the most likely reasons for this decline.

GRAPH 1.4. Revenues from the tenth of the customs (*dizima da alfândega*) of Rio de Janeiro, 1711-1805. In Contos de Reis (million reis).

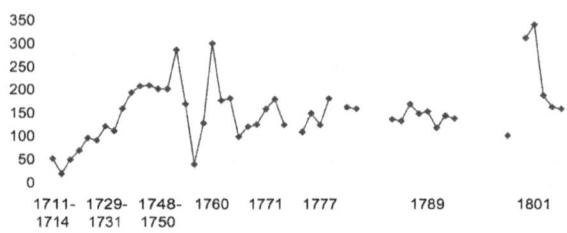

Sources: Arquivo Tribunal das Contas (Lisbon), Erário Régio, Fundo Geral, cód.4057; AHU, Rio de Janeiro, p.a., caixa 53, doc.9; caixa 60, doc.44; caixa 69, doc.68; A.N.R.J., Col.caixa 495, pac 1 and 2; BNRJ, ms.I-12,1,9 and 14; RIHGB 254 (1962) 266-274.

Revenues from the custom taxes in Rio de Janeiro reflected this decline of the gold trade. Still, one of the most important taxes, the tenth, stabilized at about 150:000$000 reis (Graph 1.4). This demonstrated that commercial activities had diversified and had become less dependent on the trade with Britain or even with Portugal. Increasing commerce with Britain did have an impact as the revenues from the tenths started to rise again when British trade increased. It should be noted that this was also a period of increasing price levels so that rising revenue from the tenths are inflated.

British diplomats refused to accept a decrease of their share in the Portugal trade. About 1774, the Portuguese government, experiencing serious problems with the Spanish in the river Plate area, sought British assistance.[105] These Portuguese requests were not always appreciated in London. In October of 1774, the English plenipotentiary to Lisbon, Robert Walpole, had an audience with the Portuguese secretary of state, the Marquis of Pombal. Walpole argued that British support for Portugal against Spain was conditional on Portuguese willingness to recognize redress to English grievances. Pombal became angry:

> "The Marquis de Pombal upon this, was very much agitated & disturbed, and said, than this was not the time to set up such trifles in contradiction to the great Business in question, which was no less that the loss of defence of the Dominions of Portugal."[106]

Whereupon Walpole answered in similar terms as his Dutch colleague had done during the War of the Spanish Succession:

> "That His Majesty as he is a zealous friend and ally to the King of Portugal, is no less the Protector of his subjects and of their trade; and has a right to require that justice be done them, and that their Grievances be redressed; and that as upon the present occasion, the Court of Portugal must be fully persuaded of the services & good offices of the King, His Majesty expects with great reason a suitable return from the Court of Portugal."

The Portuguese government did not easily yield to such pressure, especially after Colônia do Sacramento, an important smuggling post for the English in Spanish America, changed from Portuguese to Spanish rule.

After the forced resignation of Pombal in 1777, Portuguese politics continued to stress innovations. Reforms continued in the formation of the Academy of Sciences which promoted technological changes in agriculture and manufacturing in order to increase revenues and to improve exportation of Portuguese and Brazilian products on the international market. The Portuguese government stimulated product diversification, improved quality improvement of goods, and assisted foreign workers and industrialists in order to promote manufacturing and administrative reforms. These measures extended not only to the Portuguese mainland but extended to all overseas territories. The post-Pombal administration abandoned the notion that the central government should, or could, regulate everything. His successors further eroded the mercantile system by abolishing monopolistic trading companies and by giving greater freedom to local initiatives without changing Portugal's privileged position on the Brazilian market.

British diplomats and merchants continued to proclaim their grievances to the Portuguese crown and, by the 1780s, the queen was forced to respond to these diplomats. Therefore, the crown could no longer continue to confine its response to active reform alone. Under the regimes of Queen Mary I and her son Prince Regent Dom John (later King John VI), Portuguese anti-contraband policies came to present more of a balance between economic improvements and diplomacy.

The last decades of the eighteenth century saw the apogee of the production of memorials, a genre of politico-economic expression that promoted change in the economic system in order to preserve and improve the economy of the Portuguese empire. The Portuguese government encouraged the publication and dissemination of these memorials, especially by the Academy of Sciences. These publications, whose authors included contemporary luminaries, such as Dom Rodrigo de Souza Coutinho, José da Silva Lisboa, José Joaquim Azeredo Coutinho, and Domingos Vandelli. These memorials had specific economic objectives: their suggestions for modifying methods of agriculture, mining, and manufacturing, both in Portugal and Brazil often became crown policy.[107] One author of such memorials was Joaquim de Amorim Castro, a crown judge (*juiz de fora*) and tobacco inspector in Cachoeira, Bahia. He addressed the need to improve methods of tobacco cultivation, to exert regulatory controls, and to improve revenue collection in the backlands of Salvador.[108] Some of his ideas were adopted and he was promoted to high court judge in Rio de Janeiro for his services. Many reform policies met with a favorable response and were put into practice. Nevertheless, the Portuguese government found yet another means to curb foreign aspirations to increase illegal trade. This was by means of negotiating commercial treaties.

Negotiations of commercial treaties had occurred with British and French diplomats during the eighteenth century but in fact only two such treaties had been signed: the Methuen Treaty of 1703 with the king of England and the Treaty of 1705 with the Estates General of the Netherlands.[109] To English and French diplomats, such treaties were instruments whereby they could regain earlier privileges. But Portuguese officials saw the negotiations, essential prerequisites that might or might not culminate in the signing of such treaties, as instruments to frustrate any such intentions.

French diplomats were in a rather difficult position. In the Treaty of Utrecht (1713), they included a clause that a separate commercial treaty with the Portuguese crown would be negotiated. Their privileged status was conditional on this commercial treaty, at least in the official Portuguese interpretation. There was a powerful incentive for Portuguese officials not to conclude any such treaty but to instead use these negotiations as a tool to threaten French diplomats' aspirations. Therefore, Portuguese authorities claimed that French privileges depended not on any treaty but on the goodwill of the respective governments.

The negotiation of a commercial treaty became a real headache for French envoys. After the breakdown of the first diplomatic efforts, just after the Utrecht Peace Treaty of 1713, new negotiations had to wait for more than two decades. From 1737 to 1743, French representatives tried to negotiate a commercial treaty with Portugal.[110] The stakes were high and did not involve Brazil. The French crown's objectives were that the French and Portuguese territories in the East Indies would unite under the administration of the French East India Company, that madeira wine could be bought on the same terms as British merchants enjoyed for usage overseas, and that French textiles would be allowed into Portugal. In return, the Portuguese diplomat's objective was the introduction of Brazilian tobacco into France. The treaty was never realized as French authorities refused to accept the exchange of Portuguese tobacco and Portuguese officials realized that such a treaty might excessively anger the British government. The French economy did not have much to offer their Portuguese counterparts, especially since many of their export products were the same making the two nations competitors rather than potential allies.[111]

Commercial negotiations were long and tedious as both French and British diplomats wanted concessions that Portuguese authorities found unacceptable. Instead of opposing their partners outright, Portuguese officials adopted the tactic of delaying the process endlessly until French and British negotiators finally understood that it would never be concluded. Although the Portuguese government sometimes gave way on minor points, often they found an excuse to take everything back. For instance, in 1783 negotiations were reopened with French officials but they ended in just over a year. French authorities, despite their eagerness to conclude a commercial treaty with Portugal, made a *faux pas* in a dispute about Cabinda (Angola) which provided Portuguese authorities with an excuse to end discussions.[112]

British diplomats did not fare much better. Already at the end of the 1730s, the Royal African Company, which had hoped to import gold and letters of exchange failed in its negotiations to obtain an *asiento* (a contract to deliver slaves).[113] Contraband trade was not an unexpected result of these types of contracts, as the *asiento* to Spanish America served as a cover for a substantial illegal trade.

The Portuguese authorities were masters of the art of negotiation. Martinho de Mello e Castro and his successor Luís Pinto de Souza, Portuguese secretaries of state between 1786 and 1795, were superb negotiators who managed to keep British diplomats talking for almost a decade without needing to compromise on any Portuguese positions. However, the results of these tactics were not always what Portuguese statesmen expected.[114] British authorities started to make threats before negotiations got under way. Previous British representations had failed in matters such as the admission of Irish textiles into Portugal on the same basis as English, the power of the judge conservator, the establishment of English merchants and consuls in Brazil, and especially on the high taxes imposed on English textiles. Reacting to this failure, the English consul, John Hort, wrote an aggressive and voluminous memorial to Martinho de Mello e Castro. The memorial, dated October 1, 1784, stated that one result of Portuguese policies of imposing high taxes and prohibiting British imports was that every year 12 ships had left Britain for Brazil to engage in direct trade. He added that if the secretary of state doubted this, he should consult the English gazettes brought by the packet boats to Lisbon. The consul warned that a well-known and highly respected Brazilian merchant was launching plans to start a trading association to operate this illegal trade.[115]

Hort's reaction marked a turning point in British trading policies towards Portugal and Brazil. One of the main British officials' goals of these treaty negotiations was that there should be no extra taxation of British goods entering Brazil via Portugal. In order to achieve this objective, British officials threatened to conclude a commercial treaty with France.[116] Portuguese diplomats tried to call the British diplomats' bluff but had misgauged the British position. The result was an Anglo-French commercial treaty. The British crown and Parliament openly defied the Methuen Treaty by lowering tariffs on French wine while taxes on Portuguese wine remained the same.

There is some evidence that suggest that a British policy of stimulating direct illegal trade to Brazil developed in the last decade of the eighteenth century. In a suggestive questionnaire sent to the British consul in Lisbon, the Board of Trade asked for the amount of British textiles carried to Brazil and the volume of illegal trade between Portugal and Britain. It also inquired whether Portugal could do without Britain for its supply of textiles for the Brazilian market.[117]

John Hort's memorial hit a sensitive spot for Portuguese officials. It did not alter Portuguese diplomatic policies towards Great Britain but instead provoked a strong reaction towards Brazil. De Pina Manique, the superintendent charged with curbing contraband, wrote a long review of Hort's memorial. Pina Manique claimed that contraband trade was the main cause of the diminishing trade between Portugal and Brazil.[118] Two months later, Martinho de Mello e Castro sent a dispatch to the viceroy in Rio de Janeiro, Luís de Vasconsellos e Souza, with Hort's memorial and Diogo de Pina Manique's review. Instead of lowering tariffs on British manufactures or liberalizing the trade to Brazil, the Portuguese authorities reacted by deciding to compel Brazilian dependence on Portugal by legislative means. They did this by prohibiting all manufacture in Brazil in the hope of stimulating Portuguese industry.[119] Portuguese textile exports to Brazil did indeed increase in the last two decades of the eighteenth century, auguring well for a successful result.[120]

Economic and political relationships between Portugal, Brazil, and the rest of Europe changed drastically at the end of the eighteenth century. The Brazilian historian, Fernando Novais has argued that the old colonial relationships between Portugal and Brazil entered into a stage of crisis after the death of King Joseph I and the resignation of Pombal in 1777.[121] Novais pointed out that economically, Portugal was becoming unnecessary to Brazil and that this new reality found political expression in the form of several revolts. The Portuguese historian, Valentim Alexandre, however, stated that the political crisis was solely related to the imminence of a French invasion of Portugal since 1794. He also asserts that there was no crisis in the economic relationship between Portugal and Brazil nor in political terms given the absence of any coherent movement towards independence in Brazil.[122]

Was there a crisis in Brazil at the end of the eighteenth and beginning of the nineteenth century and, if so, what were the reasons? Both Novais and Alexandre have invoked balances of trade as part of their economic argument. Novais and José Jobson Arruda de Andrade demonstrated that the balances of trade had turned around in the period from 1794 to 1807.[123] Formerly, the balance between Portugal and Britain was in favor of the latter, and between Portugal and Brazil, in favor of the former. But these 13 years witnessed considerable change: the balance of trade between Portugal and Britain reversed to favor Portugal and that between Portugal and Brazil changed to Brazil's advantage. What generated these shifts? According to Novais and Andrade, increased prices for Brazilian products were combined with greater diversity in products and markets. On the other hand, Portugal was increasingly unable to meet the demand of the Brazilian market, especially as a result of the far cheaper goods that foreigners introduced in Brazil through illegal direct trade. As a result, the colonial system came under pressure and Brazilians started to revolt against it.

The two Portuguese historians, Valentim Alexandre and Jorge Miguel Pedreira, contest the assertions of their two Brazilian colleagues.[124] Through a more profound study of the balances of trade, Alexandre and Pedreira corrected the finding that the balance of trade between Portugal and Brazil changed completely in favor of the latter (Graph 1.6). Besides pointing out that consignments of money had been included in this balance, their analysis also revealed miscalculation of re-exports of foreign textiles which was attributable to the fact that items had been placed in the wrong rubrics in the original balances. Furthermore, Pedreira demonstrates that textile manufactures in Portugal did not enter into a period of crisis. On the contrary, Portuguese textile manufacturers increased their exports to Brazil until the French invasion of 1807 and continued to produce for the Brazilian market afterwards.[125] Both Portuguese historians concluded that there was no crisis in the relationship between Portugal and Brazil and that direct illegal trade between Britain and Brazil was insignificant.

There may be some truth to both schools of thought. There is overwhelming evidence of an expanding illegal trade in the years before the transfer of the royal court to Rio de Janeiro. One indicator was the number of foreign vessels that entered the port of the Brazilian capital on the pretext of distress (Table 1.5). In the 1790s, these numbers averaged somewhat less than twenty-five per year. This number doubled after 1800.

TABLE 1.5. Number of foreign vessels entering the Port of Rio de Janeiro between 1791 and 1807.

1791: 9	1794: 19	1797: 24	1800: 70	1803: 54	1806: 59
1792: 34	1795: 26	1798: 27	1801: 64	1804: 32	1807: 47
1793: 29	1796: 16	1799: 39	1802: 51	1805: 38	

Sources: ANRJ, Col., caixas 492 and 493, cód. 156 and 157; AHU, Rio de Janeiro, p.a., caixas 148-243, passim.

Although feigned emergency entries into ports were a common strategy for engaging in illegal trade all over Spanish America, it is not always certain that the crews engaged in contraband activity. Three considerations must be taken into account. First, many British ships were whalers on their way to or from the South Seas. According to the British consul's report in 1784, notices of British ships bound for Brazil were openly published in British newspapers. Lloyd's List indeed mentioned those vessels, but many ships with the destination "Brazil" was often returning from other destinations. Examples are the "South Seas" or the "Falklands" with carried whale oil.[126] Therefore it was by no means clear that these vessels would have unloaded all their cargo in Brazilian ports for the purpose of illegal commerce. Rather, it seems likely that they fished off the Brazilian coast, although such legitimate activity does not preclude their possible engagement in contraband trade.[127] Secondly, many vessels came and went to Buenos Aires and Montevideo. Although this trade was officially illegal, it was condoned and even promoted by the Portuguese crown.[128] Thirdly, Spanish vessels often sailed for Rio de Janeiro and Salvador in order to join convoys to Europe, in accordance with the terms of an agreement negotiated between the Portuguese and the Spanish governments.[129]

Notwithstanding these cautionary notes, one can not but consider the significant circumstantial evidence stemming from official correspondence between Lisbon and Rio de Janeiro, inquiries, and travel accounts.[130] There are many examples that point in the direction of an increasing illegal trade. The commanding officer of the Portuguese fleet, the Briton Donald Campbell, wrote lengthy reports about the huge amount of contraband trade and the impossibility of solving this problem since the coastline was too long to be controlled.[131] The viceroy, the Count of Arcos, opined that contraband trade had become so common that it could not be seen as a crime.[132] The procurator of the Municipal Council claimed that rarely did a day pass without foreign vessels unloading contraband in the harbor of Rio de Janeiro.[133] *The Pilgrim*, an American vessel, was confiscated because its passport gave its destination Rio de Janeiro.[134]

Donald Campbell found correspondence on board an abandoned English vessel, *The Duke of Clarence*, with instructions to buy tobacco in Brazil and sail for the Mina Coast.[135] Further testimonies can be found outside Portuguese sources, such as the travel account of the British captain Thomas Lindley and in the few extant papers of merchants, such as the correspondence of Ives and Brown in Providence, Rhode Island.[136]

Having established that there was indeed an increase in illegal trade during the last years before the transfer of the royal court to Brazil, the balance of trade still demands an explanation. Valentim Alexandre demonstrated that, between 1796 and 1807, the balance of trade between Portugal and Brazil was less negative for Portugal than Brazilian historians have asserted. In some years (1797, 1798, 1799 and 1802) it was even heavily positive for Portugal.[137]

GRAPH 1.6. Portuguese Exports and Imports to and from Brazil, 1796 to 1807. Currency exports excluded. In 1:000$000 reis.

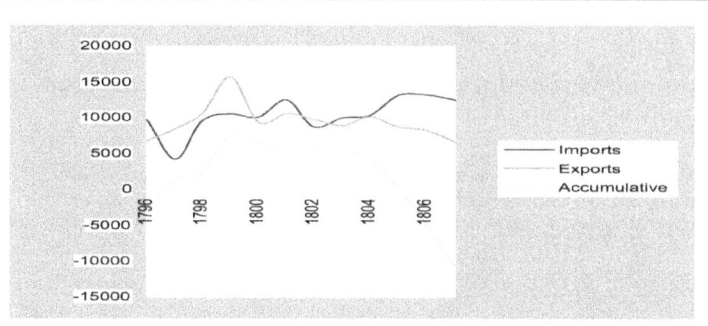

Source: Valentim Alexandre, Os Sentidos do Império. Questão Nacional e Questão Colonial na Crise do Antigo Regime Português (Porto: Edições Afrontamento, 1993) 64, quadro VI.

Alexandre and Pedreira are walking on thin ice when they claim that the balances of trade were an indication of contraband trade. Whereas Novais argued that a positive balance of trade for Brazil was indicative of a significant amount of illegal trade, the Portuguese historians asserted that Brazil's accumulative positive balance of trade between 1796 and 1805 (Graph 1.6) must necessarily indicate that there was no significant increase in contraband trade.[138]

There are several objections to the claim that the size of illegal commerce can be deduced from the balances of trade. Any contraband trade was a surplus over and above legal trade. Therefore, an increase in Brazilian demand and unexpected profits could have resulted in more demand for Portuguese textiles. Yet, this assertion does not exclude the possibility there was also greater demand for legally and illegally imported foreign textiles.

There are indications that the flexibility in the balance of trade numbers as a function of the growth of Brazilian demand. In the years between 1797 and 1801, sugar prices on the international markets rose substantially (Graph 1.7.) Therefore, Portuguese merchants who were engaged in overseas trade must have enjoyed substantial profits trading colonial goods to European markets. Payment for those goods to their Brazilian correspondents took some time, which may explain the temporary positive balance of trade for Portugal. Demand could also have risen as profits from the inter-American market grew, especially since the slave trade to Rio de la Plata opened new and profitable opportunities. Moreover, Luso-Brazilian merchants earned profits transporting Spanish American goods to Europe and vice-versa.

Graph 1.7. Prices of Brazilian Sugar on the Amsterdam market, 1789-1807. In Cruzados by Amsterdam Pounds (weight). Highest price mentioned.

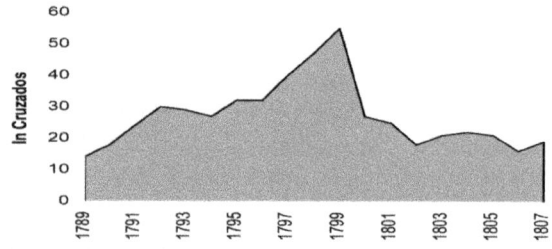

Source: N.W. Posthumus, Inquiry into the History of Prices in Holland (Leiden: E.J.Brill, 1946) 1:124, 610-616.

Pedreira demonstrates that Portuguese textile production increased after the 1770s and continued to enjoy a significant share of the market after Brazilian independence. Portuguese textiles could compete successfully on the Brazilian market. But Pedreira also recognizes a decline in the five years preceding the official opening of the Brazilian market in 1808.[139] The period of decrease in exports of Portuguese textiles to Brazil coincided with a substantial increase in the numbers of foreign vessels in Brazilian ports.

In my opinion, the growth in illegal trade is best explained not by resorting to quantitative data but by considering changing circumstances. In the last decade of the eighteenth century, the Portuguese government lost its power to regulate illegal trade. The most acute crisis facing the government arose not in Brazil but in Portugal itself, which became very vulnerable to invasion after the French Revolution and the campaign of Rousillion. As Alexandre points out, the Portuguese government played a rational diplomatic game in order to preserve the country from disaster.[140] For the first time, the British were not able to assist Portugal against the threat of French and Spanish invasion by land. Had France become an ally of Portugal, the French would have been unable to help Portugal against any British aggression toward its colonies.

With the Portuguese king fearing a French invasion of the mother country, Portuguese diplomatic overtures and economic policies towards their French colleagues changed. Both French and British merchants yearned for Brazilian gold. Since the Portuguese government wanted neutrality, French officials demanded that the Portuguese administration disallow commercial advantages that British merchants had enjoyed. The French government demanded their Methuen Treaty, as Brazilian gold would enable France to pay for her wars in Europe.[141] Therefore, the French directory flatly refused to ratify the treaty concluded with the Portuguese administration in 1797 and opted for a policy of conquest of Portugal:

> "The interest of France demands that its government not leave any stone unturned to indemnify the French people for the sacrifices it has made, the rich stores that increase in Portugal will furnish a sum of almost one hundred and twenty million livres from the rich mines of Brazil and the sum of ten million, which stems from diamonds mined there, in addition to goods from their colonies in Asia and Africa and especially their eighteen ships of the line and more than twenty frigates lying in their harbors. Those are the compensations the republic must demand from our enemies this and to the greatest detriment of England which hitherto has enjoyed a virtual monopoly on such benefits."[142]

The Portuguese king also feared a British invasion of his colonies and not without reason. British forces did invade Madeira under the pretext of protecting the island against the French navy. British troops occupied Buenos Aires in 1806, increasing Portuguese officials' suspicions of a takeover.[143] The increase in British contraband trade to Brazil was no secret to the Portuguese government but Portuguese authorities did not have the political power to combat illegal trade actively. Since French merchants were allowed access to the Portuguese market, the direct trade of British merchants to Brazil would have to be condoned.

Alexandre is correct in asserting that there was no economic gain for the French government by invading Portugal.[144] But the invasion itself was not the result of a strategic miscalculation, not family politics, indeed, its specific goal was to secure for France the possession of the Portuguese colonies and above all of Brazil. According to British diplomats, French policies were to achieve the capture of both Portugal and of the Portuguese prince regent, thus guaranteeing the French revolutionary government's possession of Brazil.[145] Therefore, the Portuguese prince regent had to walk a tight rope between the preservation of Portugal and that of its colonies. The transfer of the court to Brazil became the trump card of the Portuguese crown.[146]

British diplomats also wanted the king to transfer the Portuguese court to Brazil. In this way, Portugal would not be further subject to the blackmail of French diplomats and Brazil would remain out of reach of the French armies.[147] Caught between two fires, the Portuguese prince regent bought both off. On the one hand, he was obliged to pay reparations to the French government so that it would not invade Portugal; on the other, he had to pay the price for condoning illegal trade in order to keep the British navy from invading the Portuguese colonies.[148] The policy of the French ambassador to Lisbon was to gain the confidence of the Portuguese prince regent so that he would choose not to sail for Brazil. This policy failed as France armies did invade Portugal and the court did withdraw to Brazil. The prince regent was forced to conclude a new commercial treaty with Great Britain that legalized the contraband trade that had been carried on for the last decade.

Illegal commerce was a psychological weapon in the relationships between the Portuguese government and that of the most important European seafaring powers. Further, contraband trade was an issue in negotiations over trade privileges, foreigners' ability to settle in Portuguese colonies, and their direct participation in the Brazil trade. The struggle over privileges and commercial concessions was part of a vigorous debate over how far contraband trade should be condoned. Friendly nations that gave military support, or nations on whom

Portugal depended for her national security, could obtain concessions that allowed them to participate in the Brazilian gold trade. The Portuguese administration's policies were directed towards restricting foreign participation in the Brazil trade as far as possible, thereby minimizing the illegal re-exportation of Brazilian gold from Portugal. To this end, the crown adopted various strategies over the course of the eighteenth century. In the first half of the eighteenth century, Portuguese authorities used passive resistance in the form of legal prosecution, curtailment of privileges, and tax increases to achieve their goals. In the second half, Pombal introduced a policy of proactive reform. Promotion of export diversity and incentives to improve agricultural and industrial productivity in Portugal were prominent up to the last decades of the eighteenth century.

The Portuguese government was able to establish authority over the flow of bullion in the beginning of the eighteenth century and maintained this control for many decades. But after the 1790s, there was an increase in direct contraband trade between European countries and Brazil: the Portuguese government had to condone illegal trade to Brazil as its military position weakened. The transfer of the court from Portugal to Brazil embodied the choice that the Portuguese prince regent was so reluctant to make between the preservation of the mother country and continued possession of Portugal's overseas colonies.

CHAPTER 2
REGULATING ILLEGAL TRADE: FOREIGN VESSELS IN BRAZILIAN HARBORS

> "If the same duties at the custom-houses in Brazil were not paid for goods which were imported in British as in Portuguese vessels, the consequences would be, that every English merchant must resort to smuggling, or be obliged to give up all idea of competition with the Portuguese."
>
> Henry Koster, *Travels in Brazil in the years 1809 to 1815* (Philadelphia: M. Carey & Son, 1817) 2:268.

Henry Koster was a British settler who came to Pernambuco after the opening of the Brazilian ports for trade with friendly nations. He vehemently defended the commercial treaty that was just concluded with Great Britain, in terms that reminded him of the pre-1808 situation. British vessels had to anchor in Brazilian ports for spurious reasons and they could trade goods only illegally. Whereas Koster focused on British merchants as protagonists, Dauril Alden also pointed out the crucial role of royal administrators, stating that "the captains of unchartered foreign vessels frequently sought admission to Brazilian ports on a variety of grounds, including storm-caused structural damage to hulls, masts, sails, and rigging, making their vessels unseaworthy; outbreak of disease, particularly scurvy, among passengers and crewmen; shortages of fresh water and provisions; even loss of bearings. It was up to the senior administrative officer in each port to determine whether the captain was speaking the truth or was merely advancing pretexts in order to violate Portuguese laws against direct foreign trade with the colony."[1]

In the previous chapter, I discussed how Portuguese administrators attempted to use diplomacy to streamline foreign commerce to Brazil. In this chapter, I take this to the local level and analyze how Brazilian administrators influenced international trade through control of foreign vessels calling at their ports. How local administrators treated those foreign ships was an indicator of the degree in the enforcement of regulations concerning illegal commerce.

By law, all commerce with the colonies had to pass through a Portuguese entrepôt where goods were transshipped to Portuguese bottoms, which were the only vessels permitted to trade with Brazil. There was no justification for a foreign ship to anchor in a Brazilian harbor, other than one in distress, or conducting illegal trade. Brazilian port officers considered suspect the entrance of any foreign ship and had at their disposal a wide range of measures designed specifically to prevent any landfall by a foreign vessel. Yet local officials used such legislation, which was meant to combat illegal commerce, for the regulation of contraband trade. Captains and crews of foreign vessels had to comply with coercive acts by local authorities if their contraband trading was to be condoned by these same officials.

The degree of local control over illegal trade changed over the course of the eighteenth century, with three distinct periods. The first of these, from the discovery of gold in the 1690s to the end of the 1720s, was characterized by policies aimed at asserting crown authority over unruly mining communities in Minas Gerais and establishing control over the production and taxation of gold. During this period, Portugal was particularly vulnerable to intrusions by foreigners who, in the absence of adequate coast guard patrols and fortifications, had virtual *carte blanche* to engage in contraband trade. During the half century, from the 1730s to the 1770s local authorities were able to establish and maintain their authority over foreign ships that called at

Brazilian ports as long as they arrived in small numbers. In this period, most illegal trade was concluded by Portuguese or Brazilian vessels sailing to Portugal and to Africa. After the 1770s, Brazilian authorities gradually lost their authority over contraband trade. The growing number of foreign ships calling at Brazilian ports as a result of the South Sea whaling fishery, the opening of La Plata trade, and a more intensive coastal trade all made official regulation increasingly difficult.

This chapter analyzes how colonial authorities used metropolitan rulings to regulate illegal trade by foreign vessels. Central to my analysis are case studies demonstrating the way in which Brazilian officials received foreign ships. Authorities condoned illegal trade, but only in so far as foreign vessels adhered to an unwritten code concerning regulation. Cases of confiscation demonstrate what constituted the demarcation line between officially condoned contraband and punishable illegal trade. Because Portuguese authorities legalized the illegal trade to Spanish America, they will be dealt with separately in the second part of this chapter.

In the two centuries after Cabral's 1500 landfall in Brazil, foreign and Portuguese vessels shared the trade. In the sixteenth century, the Portuguese had competed with French interlopers for the supply of commerce in Brazilwood. During the seventeenth century both Dutch and English ships were incorporated into the annual Brazil fleets. Only at the end of the seventeenth century, when the discovery of gold became common knowledge, did the Portuguese king enforce the rules that excluded foreign vessels to sail outside the fleet system to Brazil.[2]

During the first three decades of the eighteenth century, the political and military situation in Brazil remained unstable. The Portuguese administration sided with their English and Dutch counterparts against the French and the Spanish monarchs during the War of the Spanish Succession. This made Brazil vulnerable to French and Spanish corsairs and invasions and led to the successful ransacking of Rio de Janeiro in 1711. Southern harbors, such as Paratí, Santos, and Angra dos Reis, remained defenseless against foreign pirates. Moreover, even their supposed ally, the Dutch West India Company, attacked Brazilian slave vessels on the West African coast. There were also internal problems which seriously impeded effective regulation of the production, taxation, and flow of gold until the end of the 1730s, when stability was imposed upon Minas Gerais.[3]

It was during this unruly era that local policies towards foreign vessels took on a definitive form. The centralization of local administration, the end of civil strife in Minas Gerais, and the re-routing of the gold trails made it possible to regulate illegal commerce possible. During Gomes Freire de Andrade's government of the southern Brazilian provinces (1733-1762), Luso-Brazilian administrators finally consolidated their authority over contraband trade.

TABLE 2.1. Foreign Vessels Confiscated in Brazilian Ports, 1700-1807. Excluding Spanish ships.

Year	Nationality	Name	Restored.
1. 1715	French	La Reine de Nantes	Restored.
2. 1716	French	Le Succès	Restored.
3. 1718	French	La Subtile	Unclear.
4. 1718	British	Saint Joseph	Restored.
5. 1720	French	L'Aspirant	Unclear.
6. 1721	French	La Françoise	Unclear.
7. 1721	French	S. Jean Baptiste	Restored.
8. 1725	French	Le Comte de Toulouse	Restored.
9. 1725	Dutch	Don Carlos	Not Restored
10. 1770	British	Argyle	Restored.
11. 1773	British America	Leviathan	Not Restored
12. 1780	British	Hind	Restored.
13. 1793	French/Spanish	Buen Viaje	Restored
14. 1797	British	Mary of Bristol	Not Restored
15. 1800	British	Packet	Not Restored
16. 1801	British	Duke of Clarence	Not Restored
17. 1801	U.S.A.	Pilgrim	Not Restored
18. 1802	U.S.A.	Samuel	Not Restored
19. 1802	French	Diligent	Restored.
20. 1803	British	Saint Peter	Not Restored

Sources: see text.

The law of February 8, 1711, ruled that Brazilians could not have commercial ties with foreigners, and the law of October 5, 1715 clearly specified regulations concerning the handling of foreign vessels entering Brazilian harbors.[4] These laws delegated absolute authority and jurisdiction over foreign vessels to port officials. All ships were to be inspected once they came within cannon ball range of fortresses. The most severe sanction was confiscation, which was applied when the governor or viceroy judged that the vessel had no good reason to enter the port. Such a decision had to be confirmed by the High Court, which resided in Salvador. Only after 1751 did a second Brazilian

High Court function in Rio de Janeiro. If a foreign vessel did not have enough money to pay the fines, the captain was permitted to pay in kind. His cargo was sold to the royal treasury and sent to Portugal, while the captain had to pay double duties. Several cases of confiscation and the protracted process leading to final resolutions eroded any vestiges of resistance to these laws.

The laws of 1711 and 1715 buttressed the legal authority and jurisdiction of local officials over foreign vessels.[5] These laws were executed selectively, namely only in cases of flagrant disobedience and disrespect for local authorities. It was significant that so many confiscations took place within a single decade from 1725 to 1735. During this time the governor of Rio de Janeiro and the viceroy in Salvador applied the law of confiscation to seven French vessels: (*La Reine de Nantes* [1715], *Le Succès* [1716], *La Subtile* [1718], *L'Aspirant* [1720], *La Françoise* [1721], *Saint Jean Baptiste* [1721], and *Le Comte de Toulouse* [1725]), one English boat, *Saint Joseph* (1718), and the Dutch ship *Don Carlos* (1725) (table 2.1).[6] These cases, in which such drastic measures were taken, merit more detailed analysis as they demonstrate how local officials enforced their authority over foreign visitors in order to regulate illegal commerce.

To begin with, we might ask why so many French vessels were confiscated. As demonstrated in the previous chapter, French diplomats were not subtle when it came to policies in support of their nationals' direct trade to Brazil, a fact that did not escape the attention of Portuguese authorities.[7] English diplomats even feared that local officials in Brazil were acting on behalf of French captains. British representatives protested to the Portuguese king about French contraband trade to Brazil, and inquired whether there existed a commercial treaty between Portugal and France that legitimized such trade.[8] Their suspicions were further aroused by the preamble to the 1715 law against foreign ships entering Brazilian harbors, which referred only to breaches of the law committed by captains of British vessels. The British envoy to Lisbon explained that: "A suspicious mind might think they did either permit, or connive at the French Trade, and would fling the Odium of strangers trading thither directly, only on the British Nation."[9]

Confiscation of vessels occurred when foreigners refused to accommodate themselves to local procedures and denied the local officials their role as intermediaries in illegal commerce. The governor of Rio de Janeiro and the viceroy in Salvador confiscated the *Reine de Nantes* because they did not approve of a maneuver designed to circumvent the law. In 1715, Jean Dansaint sailed his vessel *La Reine de Nantes* into the harbor of Rio de Janeiro with a cargo of slaves from the Mina Coast. In order to dispose of his 450 slaves in Brazil, Jean Dansaint had sold his vessel and its cargo to the crown judge (*ouvidor*) of the island of Príncipe in the Bight of Benin, making the vessel officially Portuguese. For this reason, Dainsant was legally able to sell its slaves in a Brazilian port.[10] The governor of Rio de Janeiro judged this to be a contrived transaction, and therefore confiscated the vessel.[11]

Such uncompromising enforcement of the policy towards foreign ships trading outside of the official realm also occurred in 1725. The viceroy in Salvador confiscated another French vessel, *Le Comte de Toulon*, in identical circumstances.[12] Had the governor of Rio de Janeiro and the viceroy in Salvador approved the sale of these vessels in Africa to a Portuguese official, they would have been condoning illegal trade conducted in an area beyond their jurisdiction. Yet by refusing to recognize the legality of the new ownership, the governor and viceroy preserved their authority over the regulation of contraband trade.

Brazilian officials took other French vessels by force in small harbors along the coast south of Rio de Janeiro. Brazilian authorities had at their disposal a wide range of measures designed to prevent, at best, or to forcefully discourage, at worst, any landfall by a foreign vessel. Local officials invoked such measures not to combat, but to regulate illegal trade. Such was the case of the captain and crew of *La Subtile*, who sold textiles for gold in Rio de Janeiro with merchants who had contacts with Minas Gerais.[13] The French privateer was ultimately captured and a boarding party sailed it to Santos where local authorities condemned the ship.[14] The French captain, Mr. Geslain, told a different story claiming to be a slaver in need of provisions on his way from São Tomé to La Plata, but local officials had refused to allow him to enter a harbor in Ilha Grande.[15] After nine members of the crew had absconded with a sloop, Geslain sailed for Santos, where the local governor confiscated the vessel. In this case, the French vessel traded along the coast without using the local authorities as intermediaries. The perils of such a lack of cooperation became readily apparent. The governor of Rio de Janeiro labeled the ship a "pirate" and made it subject to confiscation.

Brazilian authorities captured three other French vessels along the Southern Brazilian coast, all of them trading outside the jurisdiction of the Carioca officials. *St. Jean Baptiste* was confiscated for illegal slave trading on Ilha Grande.[16] *L'Aspirant* was also caught with a cargo of slaves off Ilha Grande and brought to Santos for confiscation.[17] *La Françoise* was a small vessel constructed in Santa Catarina for the French captain George Bourdain, who sailed it along the Brazilian coast to the island of São Sebastião and Ilha dos Porcos, where it was captured by Portuguese authorities.[18] These examples demonstrate that all French vessels trading on the coast south of the Bay of Guanabara might possibly be confiscated, and they almost certainly would be if they had skipped the harbor of Rio de Janeiro.

The one Dutch vessel, *Don Carlos*, confiscated in Brazilian waters was also done so over a matter of jurisdiction.[19] First anchored off Ilha Grande, where it was reported to have traded with the local population, the ship then sailed to Rio de Janeiro. There it stayed for three months, while the captain waited for seasonal winds (monsoons) to carry it to the Pacific. But the governor of Rio de Janeiro grew impatient, especially after the Dutch captain refused the offer of the governor's services for repair and provisioning of the vessel, and ordered the *Don Carlos* to leave without returning to Brazilian territories. The Dutch captain defied this gubernatorial order and did return to Ilha Grande rather than continue his voyages and risk the rough weather rounding Cape Horn. The governor sent the coast guard which brought the ship back to Rio de Janeiro, where the governor confiscated the *Don Carlos*.

Without exception in all these cases of confiscation, the authority of a local governor was at stake. Trade was conducted outside the Bay of Guanabara in the myriad of safe havens far from the watchful eyes of crown officials. By trading outside the major ports, captains placed themselves, their cargoes, and their vessels under suspicion. *Ipso facto*, crown officials assumed that such vessels were engaged in illegal trade and confiscated them, since this illegal commerce was unconditionally proscribed as it afforded no opportunity for mediation by an official.

That foreign vessels could trade with impunity was amply demonstrated by Le Gentil de la Barbinais, commander of an anonymous French vessel that sailed into the harbor of Salvador at the end of 1717.[20] His ship, which was one of three, was damaged and needed repairs. The vessel was richly loaded with merchandise from Peru and China. Upon entering Salvador, the owner of the ship disembarked to have an audience with the viceroy, the Marquis of Angeja.

The viceroy explained the measures that would be taken against the vessel and warned that it might be confiscated if the captain failed to make a strong case to justify entering the harbor. He stressed that many French vessels had visited Salvador, and that prior experience with these vessels had let him to mistrust the crews. This thinly veiled warning did not restrain the French, although the conversation with the viceroy made an impression on them. They presented the visiting inspectors with gifts to gain their goodwill. The inspectors reluctantly accepted the gifts but had other matters on their minds. They were interested in determining who should be permitted to have access to the French vessel for the purpose of trade, as becomes clear from the continuation of le Gentil de la Barbinais' account.

The officials reported to the viceroy that indeed the vessel urgently needed repairs. More importantly, they advised that the ship should be left in a dock for repairs, and the cargo stored in a warehouse. The French disagreed and the ship was repaired in the harbor. This permitted illegal trade to be conducted in the harbor itself, where the visiting inspectors had less authority. Military guards in sloops surrounding the ship were less hostile to the crew. They offered the crew their good services, with the result that every night local merchants came to trade with the ship.

Le Gentil de la Barbinais' trading scheme did not contribute to the goodwill of the three inspectors: the chief inspector of the treasury (*provedor da fazenda*); the customs inspector (*provedor da alfândega*); and a high court judge (*desembargador*). On the contrary, they became obstructive, delaying the process of repairing the ship and even threatening to confiscate the vessel. The viceroy abstained as much as possible from these intrigues but was sympathetic to the well-being of the French merchants. He knew that the intention of the three inspectors was not to scrupulously implement the execution of the king's orders, but rather to obtain their share of the trade cake. Their revenge for not receiving it was to come shortly afterwards.

It took seven months to repair the French vessel. Upon leaving the capital of Brazil, Le Gentil de la Barbinais discovered water was still leaking into the ship. On his return to Salvador some friendly officials informed the captain that:

> "Prisons ... are filled with unfortunate Merchants who have traded with the French, and whose goods were confiscated for having transgressed the Kings Orders. ... They added that the three Inspectors [Judges] of the Treasury, avaricious and corrupt persons, would do all in their power to persecute him. ... The Frenchman answered that as the Inspectors [Judges] of the Treasury were avaricious people, it should not be difficult to win them over to his side, by promising them a good deal."[21]

As a result of a scheme implemented by Le Gentil de la Barbinais, the French did win the support of the local authorities. Decision on the fate of the vessel was taken by a board consisting of the viceroy, whose vote counted double, the three inspectors, and and an additional two high officials. The opposing inspectors were forced into a minority opinion because the two high officials and the viceroy were more positively inclined towards the French. Consequently, the carpenters responsible for the shoddy repairs were imprisoned, the inspectors obtained more gifts from the French, and the vessel was soon on its return voyage to France.

The court in Lisbon heard appeals against confiscations and did, in some cases, restore vessels to their owners. Such restitution depended on another set of variables: the exigencies of the Portuguese king's diplomatic relations with France and the Dutch Republic, respectively. As a result, French and Dutch petitions for the restitution of vessels were judged differently. The Portuguese king tried to stay on friendly terms with the French, so as not to get involved in the continental wars, as well as the Spanish, who were the natural allies of the French. Given these political considerations, the Portuguese had no alternative but to condone both French and English illegal trade. French vessels were, in general, restored to their owners.

Still, illegal trade could not be seen to go completely unpunished, and therefore the Portuguese bureaucracy punitively delayed the process of restitution for several years or even decades. Furthermore, the Portuguese were not willing to countenance full restitution of confiscated vessels. For instance, the owners of the vessel *St. Jean Baptiste*, confiscated in 1721, received only a part of the value of the vessel and its cargo in 1725. A complete financial settlement had to wait until 1734.[22] The affair of *Le Succès*, confiscated in Salvador in 1717, promised to be speedily resolved in view of the fact that within 12 months the Portuguese king ordered its return. Such hopes were unfulfilled. Two decades later the French consul was still pleading for a final settlement.[23] In the case of *Le Comte de Toulouse*, the Overseas Council even admitted that the delay was intentional, arguing that since similar cases involving Portuguese ships were pending before French courts, the case should be prolonged even though John V had ordered the vessel's return.[24] And, indeed, while the ship had been confiscated in 1725, five years later French authorities were still pleading for redress.[25] Concerning the English vessel, the *Saint Joseph*, confiscated in Salvador, the only information was that it was restored to the owner as a royal favor.[26]

In the case of *La Reine de Nantes*, the Portuguese king turned the confiscation to his own advantage. The sale of the ship to the judge of São Tomé raised a fine point of law, and Portuguese courts dealt with the case for more than a decade.[27] The Portuguese government offered a settlement to the captain, Jean Dansaint, which was conditional on his entering the royal service as the main director of the Corisco Company, a short-lived trading company that defied the Dutch West India Company on the Mina coast. With the profits, Dansaint was to recoup the money the Portuguese government took from him in the confiscation of his vessel. Although this plan failed, the French captain did stay in Portuguese service, and the king even bestowed upon him the Order of Christ.[28]

Dutch diplomats' attempts to gain restoration of the vessel *Don Carlos* met with failure.[29] At the time, the Portuguese and Dutch governments were engaged in diplomatic tussles over jurisdiction on the Mina Coast. The Dutch West India Company claimed that, as a result of the 1661 peace treaty, Portuguese vessels had to trade with their fortress at Whydah. As the Brazilian slavers refused to comply with this demand, the Dutch West India Company started to capture Brazilian vessels, and the Portuguese government undertook harsh reprisals.[30] The *Don Carlos* was confiscated in Rio de Janeiro even though Dutch representatives pleaded that the *Don Carlos* was not a West India Company vessel. The Portuguese king was only prepared to restore the vessel if a solution could be found to the Mina Coast issue.[31] The owners suffered such a financial loss that in 1782, 57 years after the confiscation of the *Don Carlos*, they were still pleading for restitution.[32]

During the first 30 years of the eighteenth century, Portuguese and Brazilian officials established their authority over illegal trade. Whenever contraband trade was beyond their jurisdiction and control, they confiscated vessels. The fact that a relatively high number of ships were confiscated was indicative of the officials' determination to regulate this illegal commerce. The period from the 1730s to the 1770s was marked by stability. The control that Luso-Brazilian officials had gained over trade remained unchallenged over these four decades. Significantly, Brazilian officials did not confiscate any foreign vessels during this period (Table 2.1). The absence of confiscations did not mean that captains and crews of foreign ships were not engaged in illegal trade. If illegal trade did take place, it was condoned because now local officials were able to regulate these activities.

Although illegal trade was of major concern to both Portuguese and Brazilian administrators, they also took military and strategic factors into consideration. Luso-Brazilian officials took safety measures to diminish foreign presence in Brazilian harbors. Published travel accounts routinely contained full descriptions of a port's fortifications, which aroused suspicion in the minds of Portuguese and Brazilian officials as to a visitor's real intentions.[33] Such reports influenced the conduct of the local governor or viceroy towards incoming

CONTROLLING CONTRABAND

foreign ships. This was especially so in the 1730s to the 1770s, which was a period of war and territorial contestation in the colonies. However, I would argue that local circumstances, and especially the conduct of foreign captains, such as their recognition of the Brazilian officials' authority over the harbor, deeply influenced the way officials received foreign vessels.

The exceptionally long and capable governorship of Gomes Freire de Andrade rule over Rio de Janeiro and the southern captaincies (1733-1762) changed the balance of power. Under his leadership royal authority was definitively established in the mining areas and southern Brazil. Recognizing officially what had long since been apparent, namely that Rio de Janeiro was the most important city of Brazil, the king made it the *de facto* capital of Brazil and the seat of the viceroy in 1763. Southern ports were fortified against foreign vessels, and routes from Minas Gerais to the coast were diverted to the city of Rio de Janeiro. Foreign vessels that called at ports of southern Brazil were obliged to sail to Rio de Janeiro. Foreign captains had to obey local authorities. Those captains who chose to be recalcitrant would be subjected to a degree of harassment and lack of understanding that made their stay in Brazilian ports less comfortable. That a system of *quid pro quo* prevailed, with compliance bringing cooperation, was illustrated by the case of the French vessel *Arc-en-Ciel*.

Upon the *Arc-en-Ciel*'s arrival at the bar of the Bay of Guanabara in 1748, the captain sent a sloop to inform the governor of Rio de Janeiro of its presence, and to seek advice as to the number of cannon salvos required by protocol on passing the fortress of Santa Cruz.[34] By this gesture, the captain paid due respect to the person and authority of the governor and recognized his jurisdiction over the ship while within territorial waters. The *Arc-en-Ciel* was a French warship, sent and manned at the expense of the French king and bound for the East Indies, during the War of the Austrian Succession (1740-1748), in which Portugal remained neutral. Gomes Freire de Andrade reacted positively to the arrival of the *Arc-en Ciel* because the Portuguese king, being an ally and friend of the French king, had given express orders to offer every assistance to French vessels that entered into his territory.[35] The captain was given his own country house, where Gomes Freire de

Andrade paid him several visits and helped the captain solve his credit problems. The captain was also allowed to buy provisions freely in the market of Rio de Janeiro, without the usual intermediaries. Further, the governor assigned a hospital in town for treatment of the scurvy ridden crew. Moreover, the captain and crew were free to circulate wherever they liked, and Gomes Freire de Andrade even accepted an invitation to dinner on board the *Arc-en-Ciel*.

In the case of the *Arc-en-Ciel*, the deferential behavior of captain and crew and the status of the vessel led to the most favored treatment possible. Captain and crew could freely stay in town, the French vessel was not guarded, and provisions could be delivered to the vessel by any person the captain requested. This latitude meant that no Brazilian official would verify that all payments had been made for deliveries of provisions or whether any member of the crew had sold French textiles to the citizenry. Credit could not be obtained from the royal treasury but, with the governor's assistance, monetary support was secured from local merchants. The captain and crew of the *Arc-en-Ciel* played by the rules and their compliance rewarded with cooperation on the part of Brazilian officialdom.

Conversely, the circumstances surrounding the visit of the British vessel *Endeavour* under the command of captain James Cook illustrated that failure to comply could bring its just results. In 1768, on an expedition to chart the transit of Venus, Cook went into the Bay of Guanabara in order to obtain provisions, to do research on the indigenous flora and fauna, and perform astrological observations.[36] James Cook, conscious of his "Higher Mission to the Profit of Mankind," assumed that he would have the full cooperation of any officials that he might meet on his voyage of circumnavigation. He was soon to learn that such lofty goals would not absolve him from following regulations required of any captain of a foreign vessel putting into a Brazilian port.[37] The viceroy, the Count de Azambuja, was determined to teach the young British navy lieutenant a lesson in protocol and instill in him respect for the appropriate procedures to be observed to by any residing vessel.

When he arrived in the harbor of Rio de Janeiro, James Cook was unfamiliar with the protocol on arrival in a Brazilian port, and sent his

CONTROLLING CONTRABAND

first officer to the viceroy. The first lieutenant asked for a pilot and indicated the place where he would like to anchor. He had orders from James Cook to reveal as little as possible about the purpose of the journey. The lieutenant was promptly arrested, sloops with soldiers surrounded *Endeavour*, the vessel was boarded, and Brazilian authorities interrogated the crew. The viceroy noted that these measures were in full compliance with His Majesty's Orders and port regulations, as detailed in his dispatch of November 17, 1768, to Captain Cook:

> "I am not surprised at the Novelty that Lieutenant James Cook finds in the treatment that his Ship had in this Port; being in all its points which he takes Notice of, in Conformity not only with the Orders of His Most faithful Majesty my Master, but also to the Ancient Custom of the same Port ... And this is the reason why before any thing else the Solemn Ceremony was made I practised with your Officers, in asking them if you would subject yourself to the Customs & Orders that are in this Port, because only under this Subjection & the information that is taken in the Visit which is made that you put into this Port with real necessity, it is that you are admitted. Wherefore, if you think it hard Submitting to what in your Memorial you Express, it is in your power to leave the Port ... Ships have always Subjected themselves in these Ports to all cautions that are taken to this End, which is never more necessary to be put in Practice than when the same Ships oppose them; because they become more suspicious."[38]

In the following weeks, James Cook protested in vain against all these "cautions" and suffered humiliation on several occasions. The Count de Azambuja did not honor his request to be relieved of the guard, whom the viceroy had ordered to escort him while he was on shore and Cook was required to buy provisions through the intermediary of a factor appointed by the viceroy. No other crew member was permitted to go ashore, nor were two of his scientists, Sir Joseph Banks and Dr. Solander, who had planned to measure the transit of Venus over the sun. According to Cook, the viceroy was incapable of grasping the meaning of this project, and somehow thought that what Cook had in mind was that the North Star would pass over the South Pole.

Indeed, the viceroy reported to the secretary of state that Cook's unyielding requests for permission to make observations of the "star" [sic] Venus and examine the Brazilian flora and fauna made captain and crew very suspect in his view.[39]

Mistakenly thinking he could dominate the viceroy by his behavior, Cook demanded permission for Sir Joseph Banks and Dr. Solander to go on shore, the removal of his guard, and freedom to trade. He was surprised when the Count de Azambuja held fast and denied all such demands. Not merely contemptuous of an Englishman who did not behave in a manner deemed appropriate and respectful, the viceroy accused James Cook of being a smuggler and claimed that illegal trade was the reason for his calling at Rio de Janeiro. Cook did his best to clear his name of such an allegation. Azambuja treated the English gentleman with caution because "Notwithstanding all care I [the viceroy] am informed that always your People have Smugled [sic] some goods."[40] That the viceroy's suspicions were fully merited was confirmed by Sir Joseph Bank's journal entry of November 26, 1768:

> "I myself went ashore this morning before day break and stayed till dark night; while I was ashore I met several of the inhabitants who were very civil to me, taking me to their houses where I bought from them stock for the ship tolerably cheap."[41]

James Cook went so far as to suggest that the viceroy should have kept a closer rein on his own personnel, as "This would have prevented such of them as even under His Excellency's roof [i.e. in the Palace of the Viceroy] from tempting such of my People as were ashore ... [to carry on] Contraband trade."[42] Cook also observed that some Spanish ships from Buenos Aires had arrived and received far more favorable treatment. He sent his report and supporting documentation to the Admiralty, hoping that the Portuguese and English Courts would rule against the unfriendly reception of English vessels. In fact, he should have been grateful that his ship was not confiscated. The merchants who did trade with Cook, one of them a naturalized Englishman, were arrested and endured many difficulties before being released.[43]

In fierce contrast to the elegant behavior of the French admiral of the *Arc-en-Ciel*, the recalcitrance of James Cook stood out. The former was rewarded by being granted free movement of his sick mariners and total liberty to purchase all the goods that he wanted from any source. The French were free to go wherever they liked and had no credit problems. Had the French conducted illegal trade, officials were more likely to have turned a blind eye. Captain Cook's behavior, on the other hand, earned him the fate of being constantly under guard and having to buy all provisions through a single intermediary.

Regulation of commerce was critical. That failure to control trade would have led to anarchy can be best demonstrated by the case of a French squadron of six vessels, under the command of the Count d'Aché, that entered Rio de Janeiro in 1757.[44] The squadron was on its way to the East Indies to combat the English at the beginning of the Seven Year's War, and a stop in a Brazilian harbor for provisions was deemed inevitable. Aware that such a landfall might cause problems, the French authorities gave instructions to the Count d'Aché to cooperate fully with Brazilian authorities.[45] His Most Christian Majesty judged that Ilha Grande was the best place to anchor, since provisions were abundant in that area.[46] The Brazilian authorities had advised all foreign vessels that visited Southern Brazil to go to Rio de Janeiro. When the governor of Rio de Janeiro received notice of the squadron's arrival at Ilha Grande, he requested the French squadron to put into his harbor.[47]

The arrival of so many French ships and troops created such panic among the Carioca population that even foreign diplomats in Lisbon reported on the event.[48] Gomes Freire de Andrade was in Minas Gerais and the acting governor could not handle the situation. The populace was openly hostile to French soldiers and an inhabitant of French origin was accused of engaging in illegal trade.[49] It was only with the return of Gomes Freire de Andrade, that order was reestablished.[50] After the departure of the French squadron, the governor arrested some Brazilians for engaging in illegal trade with the French troops.[51] In Portugal, there was also a fiercely negative reaction to the arrival of this and other French squadrons off Ilha Grande. The Portuguese secretary of state, Sebastião José de Carvalho e Mello (the later Marquis de Pombal), called the French military "intolerably arrogant, abusing the laws of hospitality."[52]

In the period from 1730 to 1770, local officials were able to regulate foreign vessels that entered Brazilian ports. The sources are remarkably silent about contraband trade by foreigners. Whenever documentation mentions illegal trade in this period, it involved Portuguese vessels in the Bay of Guanabara or occurred elsewhere, such as at the Colônia do Sacramento on Río de la Plata.

This situation began to change in the 1770s. Whalers from Britain and North America appeared in the South Seas; other vessels were attracted by the opening of commerce with Spanish America. As a consequence, the number of foreign ships off the Brazilian coast began to increase, creating new problems. Matters came to a head during the last decade of the eighteenth and the beginning of the nineteenth century. So great were the numbers of foreign vessels putting into Brazilian ports that Brazilian officials were no longer capable of controlling commerce (Table 2.4).

An indication that contraband trade had become less regulated was the resurgence in confiscation of foreign vessels. The viceroys Marquis of Lavradio and Luís de Vasconcellos e Souza confiscated two British ships, the *Argyle* (1770) and the *Hind* (1780), and one American vessel, the *Leviathan* (1773). Their cases are instructive, as they underline the fact that by this time defiance of regulation, rather than proven involvement in illegal trade, was a sufficient cause for confiscation. Therefore, some vessels were confiscated in the port of Rio de Janeiro proper.

Both the *Argyle* and the *Hind* were vessels in the service of the British East India Company. The *Argyle* had sailed from the African coast to Rio de Janeiro, where it had made a rendezvous with another British ship.[53] Since foreign vessels could enter Brazilian ports only for emergency reasons, this entry was sufficient legal cause to confiscate the vessel. The viceroy, Marquis do Lavradio, was especially upset by the behavior of the *Argyle's* captain, who had forced his way into the Bay of Guanabara, despite the viceroy's reluctance to let him enter. During his presence in the harbor, the captain of the *Argyle* remained recalcitrant. Thus, when it became clear that the *Argyle* had indeed arranged a rendezvous with another British vessel within the harbor, the viceroy had sufficient grounds for confiscating the vessel.

The confiscation of the *Hind* had the same judicial basis.[54] The *Hind* arrived from St. Helena, claiming that the vessel needed provisions and repair. The pretext for the *Hind*'s arrival was that the governor of St. Helena needed materials. The Brazilian viceroy stated unequivocally that it was not up to a British governor to decide whether a British ship could enter a Brazilian harbor. The viceroy confiscated the ship because, under Portuguese law, it was illegal for a vessel to enter a Brazilian harbor unless in distress.[55] In both cases, the authority of the viceroys over the port was at stake. And, for the first time in decades, the viceroys gave no quarter to anyone who contested his authority. Yet in contrast to previous confiscations, this took place in the port of Rio de Janeiro itself, rather than in the smaller ports. Thus, the boundaries between what had been condoned and proscribed illegal trade had narrowed in the 1770s.

As legislation was more strictly enforced in the 1770s, so too, did the restitution of the two English vessels go more smoothly than that of the confiscations of French vessels in the 1720s. The restitution of the *Argyle* was more protracted, because the infringement of Portuguese law was more blatant. Only after three years of petitioning did the British consul, Robert Walpole, receive official notice that the *Argyle* would be restored to its owners.[56] Even then, the Portuguese authorities delayed the sailing of the *Argyle* from Rio de Janeiro to Lisbon for another year.[57] In this case, only a royal pardon helped to restore the vessel after legal condemnation. Therefore, any claim for damages was made moot.[58]

One year after its confiscation, the viceroy returned the *Hind* to the representative of the British East India Company as an "act of grace." This restitution set a record for promptness: the total process from confiscation to restitution had taken only 15 months.[59] As with the case of the *Argyle*, all claims for compensation by the English East India Company were declared invalid.[60]

Both cases of confiscation were provoked by violators of procedures: the captains had acted inappropriately and defied the viceroy's authority. In 1773, there was one other confiscation, that of a Rhode

Island whaler, but this one was grounded in pragmatism combined with national interest.[61] Upon the arrival of the American vessel, the *Leviathan*, the viceroy, the Marquis do Lavradio, noticed that the crew were specialists in fishing for spermaceti whales, a technique with which the Brazilian whale contractor was totally unfamiliar. For this reason, the viceroy decided to confiscate the Rhode Island whaling ship on the somewhat spurious grounds of suspicious behavior. Captain and crew were afforded the choice of being jailed or offering their services to the Brazilian whaling contractor in order to teach his personnel how to catch spermaceti whales.[62] After a few voyages, the American captain refused to cooperate further, and he perished in prison. Two of his crew members survived incarceration and reached the Portuguese capital in 1779, three years after British diplomats had learned of their fate.[63]

In the period between 1790 and the arrival of the Portuguese court in Brazil in 1808, Brazilian administrators confiscated at least five British, two American, and two French vessels (table 2.1). The British vessels were the *Mary of Bristol* (1797), the *Packet* (1800), the *Duke of Clarence* (1801), and the *Saint Peter* (1803); the American, the *Pilgrim* (1801) and the *Samuel* (1802); and the French were the *Buen Viaje* (1793) and the *Diligent* (1802). This relatively high number of confiscations indicates that officials were less able to regulate illegal trade.

British and American whalers played a pioneering role in the opening of South Atlantic commerce. Their vessels began to appear regularly in the South Atlantic in general and off the Brazilian coast in particular during the 1780s. Drawn by the information they had about the potential for commercial activities, they intruded on the local trading patterns even when these were unrelated to whaling activities.

The genesis of this illegal trade can be traced back to the period of the American Revolution, when British whalers were manned with American crews that had emigrated from New England, especially from Nantucket. The British government encouraged those American fishermen to settle in Milford Haven in South Wales.[64] These sailors often behaved secretively. For instance, when the British Privy Council on Trade questioned Mr. Enderby, one of the most prominent owners of whaling vessels, about whether a spermaceti whale had ever been captured by his crew, the answer was that: "Mr. Enderby never heard that it was - if it is the sailors do not let us know, but sell it privately."[65] Whaling crews frequently engaged in smuggling and the owners of the whalers often defended their actions. Such was the case when the *Emilia* returned in 1790 from the South Seas with foreign alcoholic beverages on board.[66] Concerned British customs officials confiscated the liquor. However, the Privy Council on Trade ruled favorably on Enderby's plea to restore the beverages and stock them in a warehouse until the sailors could make proper use of them during the ship's next voyage.

TABLE 2.2. British vessels owned by the Enderbys calling at Rio de Janeiro and Santa Catarina (S.C.), 1788-1807.

Enderby, (Anderby) Charles & Co, London; November 1802, *William*; January 1799, *Kent*.
Enderby, Father and Son, London; February 1793, *Rattler*.
Enderby, Samuel, London; February 1792, *Speedy*; June 1803, *Brittania*; February 1799, *William*; July 1797, *London*; April 1797, *Carolina*; February 1794, *Speedy*; November 1793, *Atlantic*; November 1793, *William*; August 1793, *Emilia*; March 1792, *Brittania*.
Enderby, Samuel and Charles, London; November 1796, *Greenwich* (S.C).
Enderby, Samuel and Son, London; January 1793, *William*; December 1792, *Hero*; August 1792, *Greenwich*; June 1792, *Emilia*; March 1792, *Atlantic*; October 1791, *Hero*; October 1791, *Kent*; August 1790, *Emilia*; October 1789, *Emilia*; December 1788, *Emilia*.
Enderbys, London; August 1804, *Rebecca*.

Sources: "Autos de Exame," A.N.R.J., Colonial, caixas 492 and 493, códices 156 and 157, A.H.U., Rio de Janeiro, p.a.n.c., caixas 141-241.

Illegal trade by South Sea whalers was of concern to the Privy Council on Trade, which in a 1791 meeting suggested a penalty if illegal commerce in the harbors of the South Seas continued.[67]

The owners of South Sea whalers explained that this only worked if all stopped trading illegally in those ports:

"They did not think it would operate as any detriment to the said Trade or Fishery, if the owners, masters, mates, and other officers of the ships employed therein, were to be bound in a bond not to be concerned in any illicit trade contrary to law or treaty."[68]

However, there is no evidence that the owners could have had any such influence over their crews. On the contrary, as Table 2.2 demonstrates, quite a few whaling ships did enter Brazilian ports, even though they sailed with enough provisions for 20 months.[69] The ship owners justified calling at South American ports by claiming that crews suffered from scurvy.[70] Although their need for fresh provisions was plausible, Brazilian authorities became suspicious about the quantity of whalers and other adventurers that entered their ports.

Whenever British ships defied the authority of the local officials, they incurred the threat of confiscation. In 1795, the Brazilian viceroy, Count de Rezende, complained that British captains always had spurious pretexts for entering Brazilian ports:

> "The debates ... are immense, and always indecorous and offensive to the immunity of the King's Orders, to the character of the Minister, and to the respect that a Viceroy's signature deserves."[71]

Such was the case with the *Saint Peter* in 1803.[72] Carrying a load of timber, the ship entered the harbor of Rio de Janeiro, claiming that it leaked, the steering wheel was malfunctioning, and that they needed provisions.[73] The Brazilian officials who examined the vessel did not believe the English captain, since the ship had visited three other Brazilian ports, namely Paraíba, Pernambuco, and Salvador, before arriving to Rio de Janeiro. This convinced the Brazilian examiners that the *Saint Peter* was a smuggler's ship. Moreover, all the reasons given for their arrival in Rio de Janeiro proved untrue. The *Saint Peter* had left Salvador only eight days before, rendering the captain's claim of need for provisions unlikely and the steering wheel showed no malfunctions. To verify whether the vessel really did leak, the authorities demanded that the vessel be unloaded. When the captain and crew complied as slowly as possible, so that the vessel would not be empty before dark, the Brazilian examiners became impatient and started to unload the ship themselves although they still did not complete the unloading before dark. As soon as the officials left, the guards noticed the English crew below deck with torches. By the following dawn, the *Saint Peter* did indeed leak. The officials argued that the leak had been created under cover of darkness. The viceroy's response to such furtive behavior by the captain and crew and their lack of respect for his authority was to confiscate the vessel.

The Lisbon authorities stood firm on these confiscations. Although the British plenipotentiary in Lisbon did his best to obtain the return of the *Saint Peter*, his efforts were in vain and even aggravated the matter.[74] On a later occasion, when the subject of such reclamations of confiscated British vessels was broached, the Portuguese secretary of state remarked to a British diplomat that:

> "But, I never can believe that the British Government will degrade itself by exposing the cause, not of injured subjects, but of detected smugglers. His Royal Highness knows too well what is due to his own rights to give up to the enemies of his manufactures, the very weapon with which they carry on their warfare against them."[75]

The judicial procedures were very arbitrary. Depending on the goodwill of local authorities, confiscation could be avoided, as illustrated by the case of the *Ann Joseph*, which arrived in Rio de Janeiro from St. Helena and Capetown in 1802 on the pretext that the main mast was broken. In order to hide the fact that it was not, the crew had put ropes and cables all along the mast and resisted officials' close examination.[76] The viceroy thereupon confiscated the vessel. Then, the captain changed his mind, claiming that there was another reason for his arrival, namely, he did not have enough water. Re-inspection of the *Ann Joseph* bore this out and, remarkably enough, the ship was released, but the captain was forced to leave within 48 hours and, according to the viceroy, without conducting any contraband trade.[77]

When a foreign vessel put into one of the many minor ports along the Brazilian coastline, local authorities were more than eager to receive some part of the cake. Trading outside of the big port cities of Rio de Janeiro, Salvador, and Pernambuco was a blatant attempt to circumvent the highest authorities, who did not hesitate if they could find any pretext for confiscation. In 1797, the *Mary of Bristol*, a sailing vessel equipped for hunting seals, sailed into the harbors of São Sebastião (captaincy of São Paulo), twice to Rio de Janeiro, and once more into Salvador under various pretenses.[78] The ship was finally confiscated in Ceará, where the captain and some members of the crew put ashore in a sloop. Although no illegal trade was proven, the ship was sailed to Recife, where local officials confiscated it. Still, the suspicious behavior of the captain of the *Mary of Bristol* was an excuse for these decisive actions by the Brazilian authorities.[79]

In most cases, it was difficult to prove that illegal trade had taken place but there were exceptions. One of these was the privateer, the *Duke of Clarence*, which the coast guard encountered near Cabo Frio without captain and mate.[80] On board, the Portuguese authorities found documentation of commerce in tobacco, gold, and slaves. The *Duke of Clarence* had sailed to Santos, where it had loaded a cargo of slaves and tobacco. However, near Cabo Frio, the British captain and mate had a fatal encounter with a Spanish vessel sailing under a Portuguese flag. The Spanish captain, pretending to be Portuguese, invited the British captain and mate over for dinner on board his vessel. When the Britons came on board the Spanish ship, they were instantly killed and the crew of the *Duke of Clarence* fled immediately to shore. The Brazilian authorities caught some of the crew, and their fate was to perish in a Brazilian prison.[81]

Another case was that of Thomas Lindley, captain of the *Packet*, who eventually published an account of his experiences as a contrabandist along the Brazilian coast.[82] In 1800, the English adventurer and his wife were sailing off the Brazilian coast in their own vessel. Lindley urgently needed repairs and provisions, which he found in the harbor of Porto Seguro in the captaincy of Bahia. He was welcomed by the local judge (*ouvidor*) who suggested a lucrative sale of brazilwood. Lindley eagerly consented but talk of these commercial activities ran quickly through town.

Unfortunately, the judge had some enemies who profited from this intelligence to oust their adversary. Lindley was advised to leave, even though repairs were not completed. The *Packet* returned to sailing along the Bahian coast and found another safe harbor at the mouth of the river Carcarelos. By now the governor of Bahia had been informed about Lindley's activities, and the governor dispatched the coast guard to intercept the British vessel. The troops arrested Lindley, his wife, and the crew of the *Packet* and brought them to Salvador. The crew was soon released, but the captain and his wife were not. After a year, Lindley and his wife managed to escape to Lisbon, and they sailed from there to Great Britain from there.

Even though Lindley's guilt was obvious, he did try to reclaim his vessel and cargo.[83] Lindley's argument was that: he had assumed that the trade of brazilwood to be legal trade since the local crown judge himself had suggested it. The British plenipotentiary did petition the Portuguese secretary of state to this effect.[84] As the diplomat himself expected, the result was not positive.[85] In contrast to other cases, anti-authoritarian behavior by the captain was not the reason for this confiscation. Lindley was the victim of his own naivety. He could not have known that he was dealing with the wrong officials.

During the decade preceding the opening of Brazilian ports to international trade (1808), the situation deteriorated. In 1799, a Portuguese captain remarked that the British market was filled with gold dust and diamonds from Brazil.[86] A year later, the Portuguese representative in Sweden received a startling request from the royal court. A Swedish East India vessel had anchored in Rio de Janeiro and engaged in contraband trade. So lucrative was this commerce that the company's officers suggested to the Portuguese Court that permission be granted for all its ships to enter the harbor of Rio de Janeiro and engage in such trade.[87]

The Portuguese court was both offended and shocked by such a suggestion. Confronted with the large number of foreign vessels sailing along the Brazilian coast and claiming their right to enter Brazilian harbors under diverse pretenses, Donald Campbell, a British commander in Portuguese service, exclaimed:

> "Every nation has the right to defend its revenues by laws that it judges appropriate to impose. I cannot imagine for one moment that Portugal is likely to cede its rights in favor of the English, or any other nation. Still, we are not here discussing nations but contrabandists, who in all parts are subject to the force of the law of the land wherever they are without ever giving the just motives for causing offense to their own nation."[88]

Whereas the British had become experienced smugglers, the newly independent American republic still had much to learn. Thinking that trading with Brazil was normal, United States custom officers issued passports listing Brazilian destinations. Two ships, the *Pilgrim* and the *Samuel*, were victims of this negligence. The Pilgrim, sailing out of Rhode Island, entered the port of Rio de Janeiro in February of 1802. The captain, Samuel Staples, argued that the ship urgently needed repairs and the inspectors were skeptical. When they read the passport, signed by Thomas Jefferson, that bluntly stated the destination of the ship as Rio de Janeiro, confiscation was unavoidable.[89] In 1802, the *Samuel*, also carrying a passport mentioning Rio de Janeiro as its destination, sailed from Boston to Montevideo with a stop in Rio de Janeiro. Running into problems off the coast of northeast Brazil, the ship entered the small harbor of Porto de Touros in Rio Grande do Norte. The local officer arrested the American captain and crew immediately and sent them to Recife, where the American captain died in prison.[90] There was no redress for confiscation of either the *Pilgrim* or the *Samuel*. The captain of the *Pilgrim* was eventually set free, since the authorities could not but believe his ignorance. In the case of the *Samuel*, all appeals failed since its rich cargo of textiles convinced Lisbon authorities that smuggling had been the objective of captain and crew.[91]

There were also some confiscations involving French nationals by Portuguese authorities, though few occurred in Brazil and most of the French faced the better end. In 1793, two Frenchmen and one Frenchwoman sailed to Brazil with the Spanish ship the *Buen Viaje*, which was confiscated in Paratí for illegal trade. All three French nationals, Mr. Bonnafous, Mr. Sauvaget, and Mme d'Entremeusse, received redress for their specific cases in the beginning of the nineteenth century.[92] The *Diligent*, a French vessel confiscated in Recife, was also restored to its captain.[93] British diplomats complained about the favored treatment of the French.[94] The explanation lay not in Brazil but in Lisbon, where the prince regent took advantage of every opportunity to forge good relations with representatives of the French government and looked favorably on private citizens of that country.

The study of the confiscation of foreign vessels is central to understanding illegal trade. Paradoxically, contraband trade could be condoned only when regulated by Brazilian administrators. Once officials were no longer in the position to regulate this illegal commerce, foreign captains crossed the line between having their actions condoned or proscribed. In the latter case, confiscation was inevitable. The absence of confiscations in a given period signified that contraband trade was regulated. However, for other periods it is essential to understand why vessels were confiscated to understand the degree of authority that officials had over this contraband trade.

In the first three decades of the eighteenth century, when Brazilian officials had not yet established their authority, confiscations occurred regularly. This pattern changed in the next four decades, when illegal trade took other forms, namely within the Portuguese fleet system itself. After the 1770s, more foreign vessels were engaged in illegal trade on the Brazilian coast. Ships confiscated in the 1770s and 1780s were taken because they did not comply with the stipulations of Portuguese law and the captain defied the authority of local officials. Defiance of authority continued to be a strong reason for confiscation in the 1790s and 1800s, but, during this period, in contrast to the 1770s and 1780s, the authorities lost control over illegal trade. Only in the 1790s and 1800s, when smugglers did not need officials as intermediaries of illegal trade, was royal authority seriously defied.

In the last decade of the eighteenth century and the first of the nineteenth century, Portuguese authorities became reluctant to restore confiscated British and American vessels. Contraband trade had gotten out of hand and, if the Portuguese authorities were ever to reassert their authority, they had no alternative but to adhere unswervingly to a strict policy of enforcing the law. Such was the opinion of the secretary of state, the Viscount da Anadia, writing to a colleague:

"The contraband trade in which foreign ships engage in Brazilian harbors is so manifest and scandalous, and the cunning with which they in the majority of cases circumvent the laws under pretext of emergency entries into harbors, demands that on those few occasions that it is proved beyond doubt ... legal action must be taken against the infractors to the full extent of the penalties prescribed in these laws."[95]

French vessels were excluded from such stringent enforcement because the Portuguese government wanted to please the French and keep them from invading their country. The French were permitted to defy Portuguese authority, just as the English had in earlier decades.

Spanish and Spanish-American trade was not unlike the French, since they had an exceptional position. This was because Spain was a threat to both Portugal and Portuguese colonies, and because Spanish America offered lucrative opportunities to Luso-Brazilian merchants and to the Portuguese crown.

The relationship between Portuguese and Spanish-America during the eighteenth century deserves special mention. Spanish vessels from the Río de la Plata area were excluded from the Portuguese prohibition on direct trade by foreigners with Brazil. The Portuguese government considered trade between Portuguese and Spanish America "less illegal" for two reasons. The first and most important was the delivery of silver. Silver, not unlike gold, was a noble metal, essential to the minting of coins and for commerce with the East Indies. Secondly, Portuguese authorities saw their commercial activities in the Río de la Plata area as a means of territorial expansion. There was a parallel policy for the Amazon region, in recognition of the fact that this waterway was the means of access for Portuguese manufactures to the market in Quito.[96]

The Spanish government was uneasy with the Portuguese lust for expansion, and it was not until 1777 that the nations established good relations with the Treaty of Santo Ildefonso, the signing of which was conditional on resolution of the problem of Colônia do Sacramento. Sacramento was founded in 1680 on the north bank of the estuary of Río de la Plata for the purpose of asserting Portuguese territorial claims to the north bank and sharing in the profits from the silver mines of Potosí. Thus, Colônia do Sacramento became a smuggler's paradise, used by Portuguese and other foreigners to participate in commerce with the viceroyalty of Peru.[97] Spanish troops captured and blockaded Colônia several times, stopping Portuguese illegal trade.[98]

Yet, under British and Portuguese pressure, the Spanish authorities were subsequently forced to restore the territory at the peace negotiations.

The Treaty of Madrid, celebrated in 1750, altered this situation. The Portuguese statesman Alexandre de Gusmão, realizing that Colônia do Sacramento was less important to the Portuguese king than had been previously believed, was able to exact large concessions from the Spanish government for its return.[99] Unfortunately, the main treaty could not be fulfilled, because a prerequisite, namely the dissolution of the seven Indian/Jesuit villages in the Cisplatine region, proved impossible and the treaty was nullified. War over the Platine region ended in a complete Spanish military victory in 1775 with the Colônia do Sacramento falling to the Spanish crown. Working from a newly acquired position of strength, the Spanish administration cultivated neighborly relations with their Portuguese neighbors by joining in condoning "illegal" trade between Spanish and Portuguese America.[100]

The Portuguese government's policy of showing more tolerance towards illegal trade by Spanish ships than by vessels of other nations was not new. Welcoming the silver carried by Spanish vessels, Portuguese authorities did not object to their presence. Especially during war, Spanish merchants and officials profited from Portuguese neutrality by transporting goods and persons under a the Portuguese flag.[101] The Portuguese state had the good fortune not to participate in the War of Austrian Succession (1740-1748) and the War of American Independence (1778-1783), and remained neutral during the first two years of the War of Spanish Succession (1701-1714), for five years during the Seven Years War (1756-1763), and as long as possible during the wars following the French Revolution (1792-1814).

Therefore, the 1777 treaty of Santo Ildefonso or treaty of Defensive Alliance (*Aliança Defensiva*) contained a novel provision, namely that "contraband" trade was to be officially encouraged by both Portuguese and Spanish authorities. Illegal trade that had hitherto been conducted directly, but clandestinely, in La Plata now became visible.[102] In 1782, the Portuguese and Spanish governments established an official arrangement: Spanish vessels incorporated into Portuguese fleets and transportation of Spanish goods in Portuguese vessels was permitted.[103] These measures allowing Spanish ships to enter Brazilian harbors and Portuguese vessels to anchor in Spanish American ports actively stimulated illegal coastal trade between the colonies of both countries in South America. As Robert Walpole, the British plenipotentiary in Lisbon, remarked, these actions were "against the general system of jealousy and exclusion that has constantly prevailed."[104]

The Portuguese administration's objective was limited to gaining access to silver originating in Potosí, for which La Plata was a major exit route.[105] Spanish American merchants wanted to trade slaves from the Portuguese African colonies in exchange for local commodities such as hides, meat, *herba maté* (herbal tea), and tobacco. Since the Portuguese authorities were reluctant to permit Spanish participation in the slave trade and wanted to obtain silver in return for their products, there was a discrepancy between the respective expectations and aspirations of the two nations. With regards to the Spanish American point of view, the situation was quite different. Intercolonial trade was important for the Río de la Plata area. The general opinion was that African slaves were essential to the economic development of Alto Peru. For this reason, many foreign vessels, especially British and French, transported slaves to Río de la Plata in the eighteenth century. Serious interruptions to this slave trade occurred during the frequent European wars. Throughout these periods, Spanish and French vessels could not safely enter the ports of Buenos Aires, Montevideo, or Maldonado. At such times, the trade ceased or shifted to Portuguese colonies.

As long as Colônia do Sacramento remained under Portuguese rule, the slave trade could utilize this free port. But Spanish authorities were unwilling to accept the implication that the slave trade could be re-routed and thereby removed from the control of Spanish authorities in Buenos Aires. After the 1777 treaty of Santo Ildefonso, the slave trade was diverted from Río de la Plata to southern Brazilian ports.

One complication was that authorities in Portugal declared the slave trade from Brazil to Río de la Plata illegal. Moreover, Brazilian authorities were ordered to accept only silver and hides from Spanish vessels, and limited those Brazilian products that the Spanish Americans could receive in return. If these regulations had been executed in full, commerce between Spanish and Portuguese America would have stagnated. In practice, Brazilian officials retained some authority because they could threaten to confiscate Spanish-American vessels if their captains did not acquiesce to the officials' wishes.

The practical workings of "illegal commerce" between Río de la Plata and Brazil is aptly demonstrated by the case of the *San Juan y San José*, one of the first Spanish ships to enter the port of Rio de Janeiro after the treaty of Santo Ildefonso.[106] In 1780, the Spanish viceroy in Buenos Aires permitted this ship to sail for Rio de Janeiro in order to exchange a cargo of salt, flour, and silver for Brazilian tobacco.[107] Officially, this voyage contravened the terms of the Portuguese law of 1715, which forbade the entrance of any foreign vessel unless it was in urgent need of assistance. Yet the Brazilian authorities admitted the *San Juan y San José* in order to maintain "good harmony" between the crowns of Spain and Portugal.[108]

The Brazilian viceroy, Luís de Vasconcellos e Souza, consequently started to negotiate with the captain of the Spanish vessel. He forbade the Spanish captain to sell any product other than silver in exchange for tobacco and threatened him with confiscation if he did not obey. The Brazilian viceroy was successful in bringing about the sale of all available tobacco and thereby extracting as much silver as possible. He sold about 1365 arrobas of tobacco to the Spanish ship. When this was not enough, he traded slaves and various commodities for the rest of the silver.[109] A law in 1751 forbade trade in slaves to foreign territories but Luís de Vasconcellos e Souza broadly interpreted this legislation, claiming that exceptional circumstances justified his actions, namely:

> "That one can put an end to that frequent transgression of the above-mentioned law, which as far as I can remember was published for the sole reason of satisfying foreigners who made complaints about the large amount of contraband through the introduction of these slaves." [By Colônia do Sacramento].[110]

The Brazilian viceroy thus interpreted the legislation to his own advantage, but it did not follow that others could take the same liberties with the law.

The *San Juan y San José* did not leave Brazilian waters as soon as these commercial transactions were completed. After official negotiations with the viceroy, the captain of the *San Juan y San José* traded on the beach of Nossa Senhora da Glória, just outside the urban boundaries of the city of Rio de Janeiro, and on the Enseada das Palmas, on Ilha Grande.[111]

Whereas the Brazilian viceroy rationalized his own transgressions of the law, infringements by others were not condoned. Reports about illegal trade by this Spanish vessel led to several official inquiries. In Rio de Janeiro, two merchants were found guilty of trading with the *San Juan y San José*: with the full knowledge of the military guards on board they had traded meal for gunpowder.[112] As a result, a second lieutenant and a corporal on duty at the time were arrested and sentenced to death by the War Council in Rio de Janeiro.[113] The viceroy protested and refused to carry out this severe verdict, whereupon the king commuted the sentence to banishment to Angola for ten years. The guards were to be employed in Angola in the same military positions they had held in Rio de Janeiro.[114]

On Ilha Grande, judicial inquiries led to confiscation of the Portuguese vessel *Bom Jezus de Iguagipe*. Several witnesses declared that the ship had sailed from Salvador for the specific purpose of conducting illegal trade with the *San Juan y San José*.[115] On an unguarded beach, out of view of all officials, the crews had traded sugar, tobacco, and slaves for Spanish flour.

Some other Spanish ships were to follow the example of the *San Juan y San José*, and the viceroy in Buenos Aires invited Brazilian vessels to sail to Río de la Plata where they would be well received under the pretense of emergency situations.[116] Luís de Vasconcellos e Souza did not complain about the illegality of this trade. Rather, he was concerned about "*o espírito de má fé, que lhes-hé inherente*" (the spirit of bad faith, that is inherent to them), by which he was referring to the Spanish authorities' ability to set all the terms for this illegal commerce.[117] The Brazilian viceroy related the following incident. Two Spanish vessels called at the harbor of Rio de Janeiro and announced that the viceroy in Buenos Aires was eager to receive any Brazilian vessel that entered Río de la Plata. The Spanish captains freighted some Brazilian ships for this purpose. The Spanish authorities in Montevideo cordially welcomed a Portuguese vessel, until they received news of a richly laden Spanish fleet bound for the same port. Then the officials admitted only the goods that Spanish merchants had paid for from these Brazilian ships and wasted no time in returning the vessel with the Brazilian merchants' goods.

Still, La Plata trade involved cooperation between Spanish and Portuguese merchants, and even joint ownership of vessels. Especially in times of war, ships flew the flag that was the safest. For instance, a Spanish merchant in Cadiz, the Count of Reparas, sent six vessels flying the Portuguese flag from Lisbon to Montevideo via Rio de Janeiro in the name of the Portuguese merchant Fernando José Ferreira.[118] In 1781, the captain of the *Rio Grande*, José Joaquim de Freitas Lisboa, came upon the *Nossa Senhora da Conceição*. This vessel was sailing under a Spanish flag off Rio Grande de São Pedro, but the captain raised British colors on his approach. The ship proved to be a British privateer, eager for information about commerce between Portuguese and Spanish ships.[119]

During the War of American Independence (1778-1783), the Portuguese and Spanish governments made arrangements to their mutual benefit.[120] Spanish goods and persons would now be transported via Rio de Janeiro in order to guarantee their safety from capture. One problem remained: who was going to set the terms for this trade? Luís de Vasconcellos e Souza remained reluctant to let Spanish goods be carried in Portuguese vessels to Lisbon. He claimed that the Spanish were just taking advantage of the Portuguese vessels' substantially lower freight costs.[121] The Brazilian viceroy also stated that merchants from Spanish America entered Rio de Janeiro under false pretenses to trade in slaves.[122]

Luís de Vasconcellos e Souza resented the way the Spanish merchants conducted this trade, since Spanish authorities denied Brazilian merchants their fair profits. Reports about this commerce diminished as soon as peace was concluded in 1783 but were revived during the wars of the French Revolution.

TABLE 2.3. Spanish Slave Vessels sailing from Río de la Plata to Brazil, 1793-1806.

1793	1794	1795	1796	1797
2	2	0	2	2
1798	1799	1800	1801	1802
7	15	9	1	9
1803	1804	1805	1806	
7	16	9	3	

Source: Elena F. Scheuss de Studer, La Trata de Negros en el Río de la Plata, (2 ed.; Buenos Aires: Universidad de Buenos Aires, 1958), appendix, cuadro xv.

After the French Revolution, Portuguese and Spanish authorities were even more eager to engage in coastal trade between Brazil and Río de la Plata. The coastal captains frequently infringed the Portuguese ruling that they could not engage in the slave trade and should carry only silver to exchange. A petition by merchants of Rio Grande de São Pedro in 1800 claimed that seventy ships were engaged in illegal trade between Río de la Plata and Rio de Janeiro to the detriment of their own commerce.[123] These merchants alleged that products from Spanish America were the same as those from the southern part of Brazil and that they could not compete with such low prices. Three years later, an official from Rio Grande de São Pedro wrote an alarmist report that this contraband slave trade in exchange for agricultural products elevated the price of slaves, diminished the number of workers in the fields, and competed with Brazilian goods. In order to convince the Lisbon authorities of the case's gravity, he added a list of 16 ships that had sailed to Buenos Aires and Montevideo.[124]

The attentive British commander of the Portuguese fleet, Donald Campbell, devoted part of his long memorandum to the thriving Río de la Plata trade.[125] Campbell recognized the importance of the silver that Portuguese merchants received from this commerce, and its crucial role in the India trade. Textiles, especially from India, were as essential to the slave trade from Angola as was Bahian tobacco to the slave trade to the Mina coast.[126] However, Campbell claimed that the loss of slaves to Spanish America was harmful to the Brazilian economy. The Portuguese secretary of state was less impressed with the

CONTROLLING CONTRABAND

Campbell's report, and suggested that his main focus should be to combat contraband by captains of English vessels.[127]

TABLE 2.4. Number of Spanish Vessels and Foreign Ships entering Rio de Janeiro, 1792-1807.

1792	1793	1794	1795	1796	
5 (34)	0 (29)	3 (19)	6 (26)	2 (16)	
1797	1798	1799	1800	1801	1802
2 (24)	14 (27)	25 (39)	30 (70)	4 (64)	9 (51)
1803	1804	1805	1806	1807	
10 (54)	8 (32)	6 (38)	1 (59)	1 (47)	

Spanish vessels are the first mentioned numbers; the total number of foreign ships are between brackets.
Sources: A.N.R.J., Colonial, caixas 492 and 493, códices 156 and 157; A.H.U., Rio de Janeiro, p.a.n.c., caixas 151-243, passim.

It is difficult to estimate the number of vessels engaged in the commerce between Brazil and Río de la Plata. One problem is the incompleteness of customs records for Portuguese and Spanish America. Even where reliable records were kept, trading beyond the official routes remained unregistered. The intensity of such commerce is indicated by the following reconstruction based on Brazilian sources, namely the *autos de exame* of all foreign vessels that entered the port of Rio de Janeiro (Table 2.4). These records were probably complete, but do not include Spanish vessels that went to small Brazilian ports along the coast. Spanish vessels arriving to await incorporation into convoys to Lisbon were also mostly exempt from this examination. These figures (Tables 2.3-2.5) represent the minimum numbers of vessels engaged in the trade. Data for the years of 1803 and 1804 are the most complete. If we add Corcino Medeiros dos Santos' numbers (Table 2.5) to those of Elena F. Scheuss de Studer (Table 2.3), the total number of Portuguese and Spanish vessels that sailed between Río de la Plata and Brazilian ports for 1803 and 1804 are 31 and 60, respectively.

Yet, even if this trade formed but a small part of the total commerce in Rio de Janeiro, its impact remained important. That Carioca authorities had lost their control over this trade was highly significant, as will become clear from the study of some cases of capture of contrabandists in Southern Brazil. The case of the *Nossa Senhora da Conceição e Santa Rita* demonstrates well how commercial networks in the southern ports of Brazil were intertwined. In 1794, the vessel left Santa Catarina for Montevideo with a cargo of slaves and after the cargo was sold, set sail for Salvador. But, buffeted by contrary winds, the ship had to return to the island of Santa Catarina. There, the inspector of the treasury (*provedor da fazenda*) was tipped off about these illegal actions and alerted the interim governor of the island. After correspondence with the Spanish viceroy, the Count de Rezende demanded the transportation of the crew and ship to the Brazilian capital. The crew of the *Santa Rita* was immediately imprisoned, and the ship taken into custody in Rio de Janeiro. The ensuing judicial inquiry into the actions of the mate, captain, crew, and owners of the *Santa Rita* was one of the most extensive investigations of its time.[128]

TABLE 2.5. Luso-Brazilian Vessels entering Montevideo, 1803-1806.

1803	1804	1805	1806
9	12	30	22

Luso-Brazilian Vessels entering Buenos Aires, 1803-1804.

1803	1804
15	22

Source: Corcino Medeiros dos Santos, O Rio de Janeiro e a Conjuntura Atlântica, 201, 202.

The arrest of the ship, captain, and owners had been in error, but was a *fait accompli*. The owner of the *Santa Rita* was João Marcos Vieira, the highly respected director of the whaling company in Rio de Janeiro. When the confiscation took place in Santa Catarina, Jacinto Jorge dos Anjos wrote him a letter expressing his feelings about the incident:

> "There are no words adequate to express my feelings and there is no person on this island [Santa Catarina] who does not feel likewise, seeing the insult heaped on the patron of this community and his clientele."[129]

But Jacinto Jorge dos Anjos explained that they could do nothing about the situation. The *provedor da fazenda* himself had made the denunciation to the interim governor. Though highly touched by what had occurred, the appointed governor was too ill to act on Vieira's behalf. Still, the same letter writer was full of hope for justice since:

> "A favorable outcome to this controversial action depends on our beloved and most Honorable Viceroy, who possesses piety and compassion that shine through in all his actions and make his illustrious government so memorable. He will not fail to exercise them on behalf of Your Excellency in such critical circumstances."[130]

Even though Vieira was a favorite of the viceroy, justice prevailed.[131] A high court judge in Rio de Janeiro conducted a thorough interrogation, in which all the crew of the *Santa Rita* confessed that they had been in Montevideo and had sold slaves. The judge needed evidence to determine the matter of guilt. In regard to the ownership of the slaves, eight crew members, including the slaves, testified that the mate, the second mate, and six of the sailors had sold slaves and goods.[132] The zealous investigators had found João Marcos Vieira's correspondence, attesting that most of the slaves came from João Marcos Vieira and the merchants he was dealing with. Along with the testimony of several witnesses, the confiscated correspondence proved that Vieira was a busy merchant with an extensive commercial network, including merchants from Santa Catarina, a priest, a merchant from Porto Alegre, a lieutenant in Rio de Janeiro, a merchant in Rio Grande de São Francisco, and both the former governor and *provedor da fazenda* of Santa Catarina.[133] There was evidence that Vieira had been trading since 1787 with Spanish merchants and had contacts in Montevideo.[134]

The whaling contractor did not confess to his crime. Vieira claimed to be stunned by the fact that the *Santa Rita* sailed not to Salvador but to Montevideo, which was certainly not his order.[135] He pleaded ignorance as to the identity of his correspondents and reinterpreted their letters. For instance, an entrepreneurial friar, António de Santa Anna Palha, bluntly related the difficult time he had with a small vessel full of contraband goods. Failing to make headway against contrary winds, he beached his vessel and had to sleep on the beach in order to guard the cargo so that it would not be stolen.[136] João Marcos Vieira told the interrogators that "this friar, being something of a gallant, used the term contraband to refer to women."[137] The outcome of the case is not fully known, but Vieira's goods were confiscated on royal order and the six seamen were imprisoned.[138] However, by 1797 Vieira had regained his old position, even though his case was still proceeding in Lisbon.[139]

This case study illustrates how the trade to La Plata had become incorporated into the coastal trade in southern Brazil. Spanish merchants in Montevideo and Buenos Aires were equal partners with merchants in Porto Alegre, Santa Catarina, and Rio de Janeiro. Moreover, military officers and senior civil servants were involved in this illegal trade. Even the governor of Santa Catarina and the viceroy in Rio de Janeiro participated, and Vieira expected, and probably obtained, protection from the king's personal representative. Vieira's case became too public to be ignored and a full legal prosecution was inevitable. Yet, as in many other cases, after the legal process in Lisbon had finished, he returned to his old place in the sun.[140]

Reports about local involvement in illegal trade to Río de la Plata became more and more frequent. Several cases in the year 1796 suggest the extent of this trade. In one case, there circulated the denunciation that the captain of Ubatuba, a city south of Ilha Grande, was a main contractor in the slave trade to La Plata and had a Carioca merchant as his commercial contact.[141] In another case, a captain of a Spanish vessel in the harbor of Rio de Janeiro wanted to buy slaves. His request was denied by the authorities, who assumed that the vessel would take on slaves once it was out of sight of the harbor. Further, sending the coastguard would not help, since smugglers knew when the coastguard would go on patrol.[142] On yet another occasion, the inspector of the treasury had his doubts about an inhabitant of the Valongo, the slave market area in Rio de Janeiro. Though he claimed to be bound for Angola, the inspector had heard that his real destination was Montevideo.[143] Finally, on Ilha dos Porcos, the coastguard arrested three Brazilians, who had been on board a Spanish vessel loaded with slaves that came from Rio de Janeiro.[144]

The officials fought with no avail against this commerce. If the trade could not take place in the port of Rio de Janeiro, then captains sought other venues such as the southern harbors, Salvador, or even just outside the bar of Rio de Janeiro. Measures such as a prohibition on fishermen sailing by night and registration of all slaves arriving in Rio de Janeiro did not diminish the number of reports of such illegal activity.[145] This contraband trade went on, with or without the approval of local officials. In some cases, the Portuguese authorities still showed their teeth. Around 1800, a Spanish vessel, the *Miercoles*, was a victim of sporadic official efforts. This Spanish vessel was on its way with slaves from Salvador to Montevideo when it encountered the coastguard vessel *Voador* on patrol off Cabo Frio. This time, the officials on board the *Voador* were alert and confiscated the Spanish ship.[146] The *Miercoles* was held by the coastguard at Cabo Frio and then brought to Rio de Janeiro. The Spanish owner, Pedro Dubal, called this an infraction of the terms of the treaties and a threat to harmonious relations between Portugal and Spain.

Of course, there ensued protests by the Spanish ambassador in Lisbon.[147] The stance adopted by the owner of the vessel was instructive, pointing out exactly what was illegal, but condoned.[148] He claimed that this trade was essential to Spain, since it supplied their American colonies with the labor needed to promote agriculture and industry. This was the very reason given by the Portuguese government in prohibiting a slave trade to Spanish America. At issue was the fact that, should the Spanish claim be upheld, then Brazilian officials would lose their authority to regulate illegal trade. The confiscation of vessels was one way in which local functionaries could assert their authority. Dubal also stated that his vessel was commanded by a Portuguese captain and was therefore Portuguese. This claim only made his case worse, since the employment of Portuguese persons in Spanish service could lead to their loss of nationality. This kind of practice was considered an act of treason. Pedro Dubal pleaded ignorance of the law forbidding the transport of slaves from Brazil to Spanish America.[149] The secretary of state could not believe this ignorance given the circumstances of the case: namely that the slaves had been embarked clandestinely under cover of darkness and off the bar of Salvador.[150] Pedro Dubal was correct in his views that this commerce was illegal, but condoned. There were good reasons for him to question the grounds for the confiscation of his vessel, since such trade was common practice. However, the Portuguese authorities did not alter their opinion and, in 1805, the Spanish ambassador was still petitioning for a more favorable outcome.[151]

If this case was meant to set an example, then it failed. At least three other Spanish vessels were confiscated after the *Miercoles*: the *Belisario*, *Espada de Hierro*, and *Monte Toro*.[152] This illegal trade became even more blatant. There were numerous petitions from Spanish captains who wanted to trade in Spanish American goods, and memoranda that indicated the extent of contraband on this route.[153] Petitions took on an increasingly defiant tone. One such was by a Carioca merchant who asked the prince regent to permit him to engage in trade with Río de la Plata, especially since the merchant had a running account with a Spanish merchant.[154] On another occasion, the Spanish ambassador in Lisbon, acting on behalf of a Spanish merchant, requested permission to negotiate the exchange of 2000 slaves from Brazil for 2000 mules from Río de la Plata.[155] Contraband trade ceased to be considered illegal. The last viceroy in Rio de Janeiro, the Count of Arcos, made this clear in a letter to the Prince Regent a few months before the transfer of the Portuguese court to Brazil:

> "The crime of contraband trade is so prevalent as to have lost the taint of criminality because of the frequency and familiarity with which it is engaged by the inhabitants of Rio de Janeiro, and it has rapidly gained acceptance as an innocent and legal enterprise."[156]

By this time, local authorities had lost all ability to regulate illegal trade. On each side of the Atlantic, there were distinctive positions as to what should be considered illegal trade. Utility was the main standard for Portuguese authorities. If contraband trade was beneficial to the mother country, then it should be condoned even though it was prohibited by law. The trade with Río de la Plata was beneficial since it brought in silver and appeased the Spanish, who entertained political aspirations in Europe. Local authorities in Brazil reacted differently. The illegality of contraband trade was useful, since this allowed officials to regulate illegal commerce. Once illegal trade became legalized by authorities in Portugal, a local bureaucrat's position as intermediary became endangered. Portuguese rulings that outlawed the distinction between condoned and proscribed illegal trade undermined the authority of Carioca administrators. The acceptance by the local merchant community of illegal trade as a form of free trade challenged not only the legitimacy of the bureaucrats as commercial intermediaries, but also the very pattern of a monopolistic economy.

The Bay of Guanabara with Rio de Janeiro in 1767. **Cartas topographicas da capitania do Rio de Janeiro** mandadas tirar pelo Illmo. e Exmo. Sr. Conde da Cunha Capitam general e Vice-Rey do Estado do Brazil, 1767. National Library of Rio de Janeiro. http://objdigital.bn.br/objdigital2/acervo_digital/div_cartografia/cart512339/cart512339.pdf

Barracks on the waterfront of Rio de Janeiro in 1775. *Part of Map: Planta da cidade de S. Sebastião do Rio de Janeiro. National Library of Rio de Janeiro. http:// objdigital.bn.br/objdigital2/acervo_digital/div_cartografia/cart325890/cart325890.jpg*

Benedictine Cloister on Rio de Janeiro's waterfront in 1775. (Number 27) *Part of Map: Planta da cidade de S. Sebastião do Rio de Janeiro. National Library of Rio de Janeiro. http://objdigital.bn.br/objdigital2/acervo_digital/div_cartografia/ cart325890/cart325890.jpg*

The whole waterfront of Rio de Janeiro (1775) *Part of Map: Planta da cidade de S. Sebastião do Rio de Janeiro. National Library of Rio de Janeiro. http://objdigital.bn. br/objdigital2/acervo_digital/div_cartografia/cart325890/cart325890.jpg*

CONTROLLING CONTRABAND

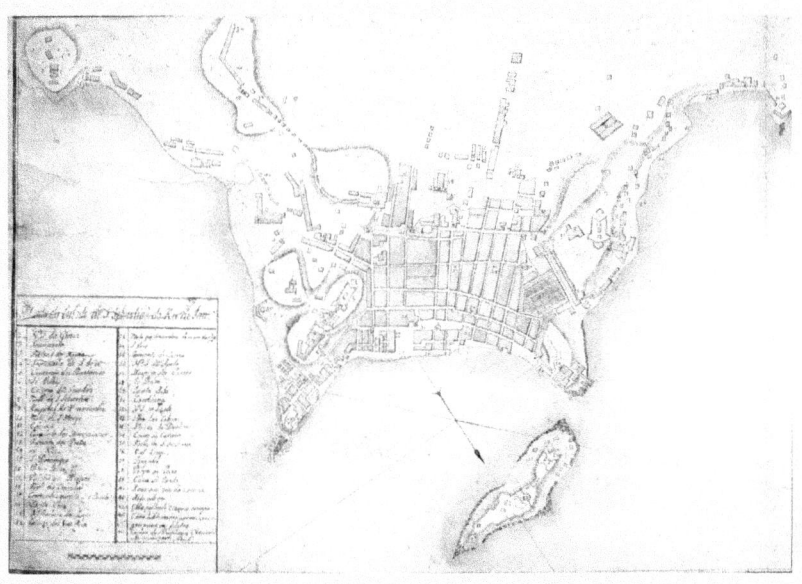

Streetmap of Rio de Janeiro (1775) Part of Map: Planta da cidade de S. Sebastião do Rio de Janeiro. http://objdigital.bn.br/objdigital2/acervo_digital/div_cartografia/cart325890/cart325890.jpg

CHAPTER 3

MONOPOLIZING THE MARKETPLACE: REGULATING URBAN SPACE

"These different kinds of monopolies are enormously profitable, but it must be confessed at a very considerable cost on the personal liberty of the subject, in the true interest of commerce and interior trade, and of course in the real and ultimate good of the public ... it is this imprudent way, that this indolent and thoughtless government supplies its treasury, at the expense of public good."

John Turnbull, *A Voyage Round the World, in the Years 1800, 1801, 1802, 1803 and 1804,* (2nd ed.; London: printed for C. Chapple, 1813).

Monopolies and contraband were common features of Portuguese colonial trade. John Turnbull, an Englishman who visited Rio de Janeiro during his voyage of circumnavigation, expressed the views of many observers of the Luso-Brazilian scene when he condemned the thoughtlessness of a government that enhanced its own coffers through monopolies that were detrimental to the public good. Such commentators held that the prevalence of contraband was a problem for any government and one indicator of the attenuated authority of the monarch.

It was difficult for those visitors to conceive that such a monopolistic society could be dynamic. On the one hand, monopolies and trade legislation were designed to regulate the local economy, which assured the inhabitants of an economic basis according to their social status. On the other hand, smugglers diminished the financial burden on the consumers of products through illegal commerce. Monopolies and contraband trade were not merely common features but a central part of colonial economy and society. The legal economy monopolies did lead to an increase in the price of goods. Contraband trade could provide a corrective to high cost of products. Luccock and other foreigners were intrigued by the absence of a free marketplace in colonial Rio de Janeiro. With every inhabitant occupying a discrete place in society, the potential for individual mobility and initiative in the economy was highly restricted. The exceptions to this rule were those persons who, aided by a governmental system that farmed out certain public services and sections of the economy to individuals, abrogated governmental responsibility, which led to foreign charges of Portuguese indolence. Tax farmers and administrators of monopolies enjoyed royal authority in the exercise of their functions, and used this authority to regulate both the legal market and the illegal trade that followed its legal counterpart. Regulation of all commerce took the form of licenses and taxes, which were not only a means of collecting revenue, but also mechanisms for controlling space, prices, and the persons employed in selling a particular product, thereby controlling the flow of supplies to the urban area of Rio de Janeiro.[1] Officials also regulated the market by wielding their jurisdiction at will to punish those who transgressed the laws. In licensing and taxing certain products, the contractor and administrator had enormous latitude to favor certain persons arbitrarily at the expense of others, guaranteeing his own role as an intermediary of both legal and illegal trade.

Space, price, and personnel were three essential ingredients of a market monopoly. The capacity to restrict points of sale was central to the authorities' regulation of that part of the market over which they had jurisdiction. Commodity prices could be set and modified by both royal decrees and local needs. The exclusion of lower status persons, such as peddlers and vendors, led to a rigid stratification of both the legal and the illegal market.

Price levels for primary commodities such as manioc (cassave) and beef remained remarkably stable in big cities such as Rio de Janeiro and Salvador throughout the colonial period.[2] Although there were some problems with food supplies to Salvador during the early eighteenth century, which led to occasional price hikes, these food problems were less frequent after the 1720s.[3] In his excellent study of prices for manioc and other foodstuffs, Dauril Alden did not mention any marked increases in prices between 1736 and 1769, while only in 1721 did manioc prices skyrocket.[4] In contrast to Salvador, the provisioning of food to Rio de Janeiro was never a problem since the greater accessibility of food from the immediate and further hinterland. In the captaincy of Rio de Janeiro, farms specialized less in the cultivation of cash crops like tobacco and sugar than in the *Recôncavo* of Salvador.[5] Harold B. Johnson has demonstrated that prices remained stable for most of the second part of the eighteenth century. Only in the 1790s and 1800s, did prices of primary foodstuffs increase as a result of local policies and the Napoleonic wars.[6]

The marketplace has not received the treatment it deserves in the historiography of colonial Brazil. Many historians and economists have perceived the natural state of the market as free and unrestricted; when issues such as monopolies and petty trade are raised, they are usually treated in terms of context of exploitation and criminality.[7] There are few studies of local economies in the colonial era. Luiz Mott, chronologically documenting local fairs and small commerce in colonial Brazil, demonstrated that the diversification of the local economy was a necessary precondition for the existence of fairs.[8] There are several books focusing on a single population group and its economic functions. Mary Karasch wrote extensively about slaves in the urban context of Rio de Janeiro, demonstrating their diverse commercial activities in the peddling trade.[9] Luciano Figueiredo concentrated on females in colonial Minas Gerais, where he showed how local governments regulated the internal market and demonstrated that women constituted the largest single group of small vendors.[10] A.J.R. Russell-Wood's comprehensive study of colonial Rio de Janeiro and Salvador as port cities linked commercial and professional activities in an urban setting.[11] However, a historiography combining the role of space, ethnicity, and commerce, such as that offered by historians of the Andean regions, is nonexistent for colonial Brazil.[12] In this chapter, I stress the administrators' use of monopolies and illegal trade to regulate economy and society in eighteenth century Rio de Janeiro.

Monopolization of space, price, and human resources by public and private administrators could arise merely by virtue of their jurisdiction. Conflicts occurred between officials over the nature and extent of the jurisdiction and over who should regulate particular sectors of the legal and illegal economies. Control of space was the key to regulation of commerce. As can be seen on the enclosed map of Rio de Janeiro, most public spaces in Rio de Janeiro were the beaches and the water. On the waterfront, both small and large vessels were loaded and unloaded. The shore areas were focal points for small trade: fishermen delivered their catches and small vessels unloaded vegetables and other foodstuffs. Larger ocean-going vessels unloaded their cargoes of imported goods, either directly or onto lighters, depending on the tide. Beaches were also used served for unloading contraband. Each type of vessel had its specific mooring area in the harbor. Foreign ships had to anchor in front of the Ilha das Cobras, under the cannons of the fortress; Luso-Brazilian vessels from Europe or Africa had to anchor near the custom house; and ships from Brazilian ports had designated places along the waterfront, for instance, at the Praynha.

Negotiation over space started as soon as entering vessels crossed the bar of Guanabara. All ships had to pass a narrow entrance which was guarded by the fortresses of Santa Cruz and São João da Barra, which defended access to the bay. The fortress at Praia Vermelha faced a nearby beach close to the Sugarloaf (*Pão de Açucar*), where small vessels could unload their cargos without entering the bay of Guanabara. The purpose of these fortresses was to defend the city and to monitor access to the Bay. They also enabled the military to regulate commercial activities. Therefore, if illegal trade was to be conducted out of sight of the military, it had to take place on the more distant beaches of Tijuca, Copacabana, Guaratiba, and Sepatiba.[13]

Regulation of access by sea to the Bay of Guanabara translated into commercial advantages for colonial authorities. Whenever the military's control became excessive, protests arose and settlements were negotiated. One such group of plaintiffs was the fishermen of Rio de Janeiro, who since 1728 had to pay a tax to the contract farmer of the tenth.[14] In order to enforce this tax and license system, the contractors, complaining that fishermen were trading illegally outside the bar, sought the cooperation of the captains of the two fortresses at the entrance of the bay of Guanabara. The governor, Luís Vahia Monteiro, was responsive to the contractors' complaints and ordered officers of the fortresses to stop and inspect all vessels entering the bay.[15]

The military turned this order to their advantage and used, or abused, the right to inspect vessels in order to abrogate to themselves the regulation of the sale of fish in the city of Rio de Janeiro. This opportunity did not go unchallenged and complaints soon arose from fishermen that their vessels were stopped at the bar and on the waterfront. They alleged that after soldiers stopped fishing boats at the fortresses, soldiers bought the fish at low prices and then traded the fish on the beaches illegally, i.e. without paying taxes.[16] Luís Vahia Monteiro's order that the military should desist from this practice was ineffective, as was to become apparent from the continuing barrage of complaints to his successor.[17] Later, new powers were conferred upon the military to patrol the harbor in order to stop fishermen from selling their catches without paying taxes.[18] The role of the military as regulators and sellers remained an issue, as Governor Gomes Freire de Andrade pointed out that "there are many soldiers who sell fresh fish," as they "do not have any other profession to sustain them."[19] Decades after these incidents, similar orders were given, and the complaints continued.[20]

The custom officers in Rio de Janeiro also had a regulatory role over the coastal trade. All coasters needed to carry an on-board manifest listing the contents of their cargo. This rule was trespassed, even though the absence of such an official paper made shippers vulnerable to severe punishments when challenged by customs officers.[21] In small coastal towns where no customs existed, local military governors used this legislation to demand satisfaction from the shippers. In two instances, the captain of Guaratiba requisitioned a large part of the salt cargoes that Carioca vessels carried along the coast.[22] Legislation to buttress the powers of custom officers was promulgated throughout the eighteenth century. Until 1732, all vessels had to call at the custom house, even if their cargo consisted of non-taxable goods.[23] Because of endemic non-compliance, this measure effectively allowed the customs to have guards on all beaches around the city who taxed vessels on arrival.[24] Regulations over seaborne commercial activities were challenged, and officials had to find workable compromises. The Municipal Council, the governor, customs and treasury officials, and contract tax farmers all competed for regulatory authority over some sector of the fish trade. Overlapping jurisdictions with no clearly defined lines of demarcation resulted in rivalries and tensions. This potential problem was solved by allowing every official to have his share of the pie, as illustrated by procedures for the visits of foreign vessels. The ships were searched and inspected by a mixed commission of representatives drawn from all the governmental departments, each with a distinct role. This commission consisted of a crown-appointed judge, an interpreter, a surgeon, two high ranking military officers, and two delegates from the harbor authorities. The governor or viceroy made the final decision on a vessel's fate and the vessel was guarded by soldiers in rowboats, who were appointed by customs officials. Two groups were exempt from the jurisdiction of such a commission: members of the clergy and military personnel from Portugal. The exemption of these groups from search by local authorities inevitably led to disputes.

The clergy was immune from search by any secular authority. As a result, customs officers were allowed neither to levy fees, nor to search any vessel chartered or owned by a religious order.[25] The Benedictines were involved in illegal dealings capitalizing on the strategic position of their monastery, which was in the heart of downtown Rio de Janeiro. Through a hole in the wall, the Benedictines had illegal access to Praynha, a lively marketplace on the waterfront. Several reports denounced the illegal traffic that took place through this hole, but secular authorities had no jurisdiction to prosecute any trespassers.[26] The problems became more complicated in 1727, when the Benedictines demanded ownership of the Ilha das Cobras, a small strategically placed island some 100 yards in front of the town center. Had they succeeded, they would have been in a commanding position to regulate all trade. But aware of the checkered reputation of the order,

Governor Luís Vahia Monteiro reacted by expelling the Benedictines to a location 80 miles outside of the city. The Overseas Council in Lisbon did not approve of this draconian measure, but the Ilha das Cobras remained definitively in secular hands.[27]

The Portuguese military was also exempt from legal prosecution in the harbor of Rio de Janeiro. In the case of fleets from Portugal, such jurisdiction remained ill-defined and the object of contention. In some instances, the Portuguese fleet commander claimed full authority over his troops and vessels while in the harbor and city of Rio de Janeiro.[28] Such disputed authority could even result in the contractor being threatened with death if he tried to levy dues on soldiers.[29] Complaints arose over several issues, such as customs officers' inspections of vessels and the free movement of soldiers in the city of Rio de Janeiro.[30] Such clashes between the governor of Rio de Janeiro and the commander of the fleet reveal the consequences of this annual defiance of the governor's authority within the harbor of Rio de Janeiro. In 1795, the viceroy, the Count de Rezende, complained that the commander of the fleet, Manoel da Cunha Sottomayor, even surpassed the English captains entering his port in arrogance and incivility. Foreigners at least recognized the jurisdiction of the viceroy over the harbor, but the admiral of the fleet refused to even salute the fortress on the Ilha das Cobras.[31] In his rebuttal, Sottomayor denounced the *"violencias, ultrajes e despotismo"* (violence, insults and despotism) committed by the viceroy by ordering the arrest of soldiers walking on the streets after 10:00 p.m. The outraged Sottomayor also alleged that the viceroy had taken advantage of the admiral's illness to name a replacement and had ordered that no shipyard should repair his vessels.[32] Personalities did not always clash so fiercely. Sottomayor's successor, Donald Campbell, was one of the few persons who had no problems with the count of Rezende's conduct.

Various measures were taken to prevent illegal trading with the fleet by military, customs, or treasury personnel. Even before the vessels entered the harbor of Rio de Janeiro, they were welcomed by a coast guard vessel dispatched by the commander of the fortress at the entrance of the bay, both to guarantee safe passage into the bay and to prevent trading at the bar.[33] Entering the Bay of Guanabara, all ships were visited and watched over by guards of both customs and treasury.[34] These guards were to prevent individuals from embarking and disembarking before all goods were unloaded.[35] At the custom house, merchandise were carefully inventoried, their value assessed, and dues levied. Then, the goods were sealed according to the custom's list (*pauta*) and distributed to their owners. The vessels remained under armed surveillance until they left the bay of Guanabara.[36]

Whereas the Brazilian military-controlled access to Rio de Janeiro by sea and by land, civil officials regulated legal and illegal commerce inside the municipal boundaries of Rio de Janeiro. Still, attempts to completely exclude military participation in, and regulation of, the market within Rio de Janeiro proved impossible.[37] Soldiers not only traded, but also fished in the harbor, and they sold their hauls in order to supplement their meager wages which were often in arrears. In 1733, the Municipal Council, in an abortive attempt to bar military personnel from trading, catching, and selling fish, petitioned Lisbon for legislation that would prohibit soldiers from trading in fish.[38] But Gomes Freire de Andrade, as the incoming governor of Rio de Janeiro, objected to such a move. He reminded Lisbon officials that soldiers' pay was low, often in arrears, and sometimes not paid at all. The argument was valid for officers as well as for their troops.[39] Gomes Freire de Andrade argued successfully that the soldiers should at least be allowed to sell the fish they caught as would any other person, regardless of status or social condition.

Guard posts, custom posts, and private barracks on the waterfront enabled private persons and individual officials to conduct and regulate legal and illegal trade. By the end of the eighteenth century, a high court judge saw the problem as follows:

> "They leave no space open on the beach, and even the streets leading from the city are blocked with huts and stalls. Many are locked, taking up not only all the waterfront but also the adjacent sea. They have doors opening onto the beach, private landing stages, and other means for introducing contraband and for hiding contrabandists."[40]

The Municipal Council and the governor/viceroy competed for

control over the sale of commodities within the municipal boundaries of Rio de Janeiro. One way this jurisdictional confrontation came to a light was over buildings on the waterfront.[41] As early as 1647, the governor argued against all construction on beaches near the city on the grounds that they obstructed the effective defense of the city, and he proposed that all existing houses on the beaches be destroyed.[42] The Municipal Council of Rio de Janeiro vigorously opposed the removal of these houses, claiming lack of space within the urban boundaries of the city.[43] Orders for demolition were ineffective, and construction continued.[44] At issue were not only lofty ideals of public safety, but also contested jurisdiction over the regulation of commerce and vested interests which the presence of such structures encouraged.[45] Both governors and municipal councils argued in favor of building that would further their own interests or those of their friends. Luís Vahia Monteiro authorized a friend to construct a warehouse on the beach of Valongo.[46] The secretary of the Municipal Council, Julião Rangel, had his own coterie that wanted to construct facility to mend nets and prepare fish for market.[47] If different administrative organs could not agree with one another over the division of jurisdiction, at least they enjoyed a measure of success in obstructing their rivals from building on the highly contested beach. Such was the case with a slaughterhouse, whose construction on the beach was proposed on two occasions but each time withdrawn as the Municipal Council protested building in a public area.[48] Despite such challenges, private buildings on the beach proliferated.[49]

Wrangling over territorial jurisdiction provided a loophole for both legal and illegal commerce. As long as there was disagreement as to who had the authority to regulate the marketplace, illegal trade and free commerce could take place with impunity. Some attempts to monopolize the prime areas of commerce occurred. Although Rio de Janeiro lacked a central square comparable to any city in Spanish America, there were specifically designated markets for fish, meat and slaves, and storehouses for salt and grain. These spaces were owned either by private persons or by the government.[50] Efforts by shippers to unload cargos other than on the designated beaches met with obstacles.[51] Whenever it looked as if one vested interest was gaining the upper hand, the others protested. The viceroy's successful attempt at market monopolization and hoarding at the end of the eighteenth century was an example of the consequence of such monopolistic practices.

If the Count de Rezende was unpopular with the population of Rio de Janeiro, this was partly attributable to his attempts to monopolize the market.[52] On the pretext of enhancing the city's defenses, the viceroy decided to authorize construction of a warehouse on the beach for the salt contractor and for the storage of sugar.[53] According to the officers of the Municipal Council, such a construction would effectively end all free access to the beaches. Through its spokesman, Balthazar da Silva Lisboa, the Council vehemently protested and acted to prevent this construction.[54] The count persisted, claiming jurisdiction over all the beaches.[55] When the municipal councilors personally inspected the construction site and dismissed the workers, the viceroy reacted by sending a military patrol to the area and giving instructions to arrest anybody, even if they were members of the Municipal Council, if they obstructed execution of his orders.[56] After winning this monopoly over space, he was successful in obtaining another monopoly, this time over price controls.

Control over space was linked to the struggle for control over prices. Immediately after the viceroy and his clientele monopolized control over the supply, marketing, and distribution of salt and flour, prices of these commodities began to rise.[57] The crown judge and procurator of the Municipal Council did not tarry in reporting these developments to the prince regent. Balthazar da Silva Lisboa launched a new judicial inquiry into the high prices of *farinha* (flour).[58] He demonstrated that the chief inspectors of the customs and of the royal treasury artificially inflated the price of flour in Rio de Janeiro by forcing all ship captains to sell their cargoes at excessively low prices, and then offering the same commodities for sale at the storehouse at extremely high prices. Once they had gained control over the beach area, and consequently over both the legal and illegal markets, there were no obstacles to prevent the viceroy, administrators of the royal treasury, and customs officials from monopolizing all commercial activities. As a result, prices of basic foodstuffs rose sky-high, and civil unrest was in the air.

The most extreme market monopolization occurred through the creation of mandatory points of sale, which enabled administrators to regulate both the legal and illegal markets completely. In the beginning of the nineteenth century, an anonymous author gave a detailed description of the creation and consequences of one such mandatory point of sale in Salvador.[59] Like Rio de Janeiro, Salvador was a major port, and its urban conglomeration was dependent on the supply of provisions by sea from nearly towns and villages.[60] Salvador had more problems with its food supply than did Rio de Janeiro because its immediate hinterland produced cash crops such as sugar and tobacco, and farmers avoided growing manioc as much as possible.[61] That monopolization of a distribution point had even worse repercussions in Salvador than in Rio de Janeiro becomes apparent from an anonymous memorial describing a case that occurred in the old Brazilian capital. As was often the case, the proposal to build a permanent storehouse for the sale of flour was seemingly motivated by the very best of intentions. Hitherto the practice had been for captains of small vessels to sell flour offshore to intermediate vendors, who then resold the flour for at a higher price to vendors in the city.[62]

In 1785, the governor of Bahia made the widely acclaimed decision to create, for the good of the whole population, a public storehouse where all flour would be unloaded, stored, and made ready for sale at a moderate price. He levied a tax on flour of 20 reis an *alqueire* (72 pounds) to cover the costs of the building and administration of the storehouse, and for a contribution to the administrative costs of the local hospital.[63] The enthusiasm for such noble goals soon dissipated as it became apparent that the governor would have the exclusive right to nominate the administrators of the warehouse without having to seek royal approval. Consequently, the appointees were the governor's cronies, and they quickly abused their new position. Exclusive control over the nomination process led to immediate financial gains for the governor. By securing monopolistic control over both the market and the regulators of the commerce, the governor had guaranteed for himself a highly lucrative source of income. The administrators used and abused their position to enforce the 20 reis levy on the captains of flour-carrying vessels. Moreover, the captains were obliged to have a license from officials in the port towns of the hinterland (recôncavo), allowing them to transport flour to the city of Salvador. The price of flour was fixed at 640 reis an *alqueire*. Having bought the flour cheaply, the administrators resold this staple of nutrition to the populations of the city of Salvador and the captaincy of Pernambuco at the highest possible price, which in some cases attained 1$600 reis an *alqueire*.[64]

Nevertheless, even such exorbitant profits were not enough to pay for the costs of the local hospital and the administration of the warehouse, which were dependent on the 20-reis tax. Moreover, the captaincy of Pernambuco experienced two periods of hunger, provoked by inadequate supplies from Salvador. Monopolization had led to a decrease in the amount of flour transported to Salvador from the *recôncavo*, and the official profits from the warehouse declined. As a result of the oppressive monopolies, flour shippers avoided the port of Salvador, and, instead, sold their cargoes in other places. In 1795, the public warehouse remained empty for long periods. The new governor, Dom Fernando José de Portugal, deregulated the price of flour in order to attract new supplies. This had immediate repercussions. After a short while there was an upsurge in flour-carrying vessels arriving in Salvador, and the now free market price of flour went down to 480 reis an *alqueire*.[65]

That the officials regulated not only legal but also illegal trade became evident when, in 1796, Dom Fernando José de Portugal named a new administrator for the public warehouse. The new administrator revealed the abuses of his predecessor, such as the sale of licenses that allowed captains to sell their flour outside the harbor. He also discovered that the weights were inaccurate. The results of such revelations were short-lived, and scarcely made a dent in solving deep-rooted problems. The anonymous author of the description pointed out that a levy remained on flour vessels that sailed directly from Bahian ports to Pernambuco, without calling at Salvador.[66] When, in 1806, the new governor, the Count de Ponte, extended the jurisdiction of the public warehouse administration to raise more taxes, matters took a turn for the worse. In their attempts to increase their effectiveness in the collection of dues, tax collectors became so zealous that many captains had to pay taxes on more flour than they actually carried. Captains were not even consulted when the weight of the cargo was assessed. Flour on vessels bound for Lisbon was also taxed. From 1806, not only were captains liable for payment of 20 reis an *alqueire* in taxes, but so too were the flour buyers. Moreover, the officials of the public warehouse used their position to oblige the captains to hire the slaves of the officials to unload vessels. The price of flour and other essential foodstuffs rose again, leaving the population discontented.[67]

As the anonymous author observed, the root of the problem did not lie in the fact that the population had to pay the tax of 20 reis an *alqueire* on flour and other primary foods. Rather, it was the manner in which the taxes were collected, and especially the way the merchant-administrators used these taxes to establish a monopoly on the sale of these essential products. He noted the cynicism of such officials who abused the public trust on the spurious grounds that their actions were in the public interest. This abuse of power seriously undermined royal authority, the anonymous author stressed. Writing in 1807, he observed that these events in Brazil predated the French Revolution by a mere four years.[68]

The administrators of the public warehouse in Salvador used their authority to monopolize the market and to regulate both legal and illegal trade. This was not an isolated case. In the same city, municipal councilors used the threat of heavy penalties to coerce vendors to sell meat only in the municipal butchery.[69] The greater the degree of jurisdiction exercised by an individual or group of individuals, the greater the potential to regulate a particular sector of the market. This strict monopoly over both price controls and the use of public space led to an all-pervasive regulation of legal and illegal markets, resulting in artificial raised prices.

The same pattern of market monopolization occurred with another essential product: salt.[70] Salt was delivered to Brazil from Portugal. Its sale in Rio de Janeiro was farmed out by contract at a fixed sale price. Just as had happened with flour in the storehouse in Salvador, the actual sale price for salt was often much higher than the legally set sale price.[71] The contractor managed to get around this fixed price by selling salt outside the urban boundaries of Rio de Janeiro, because there he was not bound by price controls. The contract farmer colluded with local officials with the result that hardly any opposition was voiced to these abuses. The salt contract was abolished only when it began to infringe negatively on royal revenues derived from taxes. Salt was a necessary commodity during the pre-refrigeration age. It was essential for the preservation of meat, and it was also an important element in the curing of hides. High salt prices were the main reason that Brazilian hides could not compete with hides from Spanish America.[72] As long as municipal councils continued to control salt sales, they continued to play a key role in determining who could sell this product.[73] The fixed price protection afforded by the salt contract was valid only in the cities of Rio de Janeiro, Salvador, Recife, and Santos. Elsewhere salt contractors could charge whatever they liked.[74] In small harbor towns, the populace was even less protected from market monopolization than in big cities. In the coastal city of Paratí, south of Rio de Janeiro at the end of the old gold route, salt prices could reach as high as 4$000 reis an *alqueire*.[75] Since salt was often in short supply, high prices seemed unavoidable.[76] Moreover, in the struggle for power between competing interests in small townships, some councilors were no match for the influence wielded by the commander and officers of the garrison.[77] In towns such as Angra dos Reis and Cabo Frio, both important but small coastal cities, it was the commander of the garrison, and not the elected town councilors or the appointed officials, who held power and regulated all commerce.[78]

We have seen that control of space resulted in increased prices. A large army of vendors with access to basic foodstuffs profited from these monopolies to sell these essential products for a good price. These vendors were essential, since their capacity to distribute goods at low prices to households made life tolerable in expensive cities.

Goods for the city's inhabitants were made available at the marketplace in Rio de Janeiro by a broad spectrum of vendors, ranging from highly positioned merchants to street peddlers. At the upper end were merchants who regulated the supply of foodstuffs in the city by controlling supply networks that were both regional and extra-regional, and who could dictate the distribution of such foodstuffs in the city. Shopkeepers were dependent on the goodwill of such merchants for their goods, but themselves also exercised considerable control over whether to make these available for sale and at what prices.

Although the sales practices of merchants and shopkeepers were subject to regulatory control, they were in a better position to benefit from the benign neglect of regulating authorities, who could condone illegal practices and contravention of price controls. Peddlers and street vendors enjoyed no such official favor and were more likely to be prosecuted for illegal sales or for selling below the regulated prices. Still they did not abstain from illegal practices to obtain their goods cheaply and sell them below monopoly prices. Both groups were essential to the colonial economy. Merchants and shopkeepers regulated the sale of quality goods which they mostly obtained through the official trade. Peddlers and vendors made life more affordable by selling less goods of lesser quality or illegal goods for lower prices in the otherwise expensive cities.

Once goods were unloaded on the beaches, they were sold either to peddlers or to the middlemen and shopkeepers in the city. In the urban context, specific areas were assigned for many activities that could not be conducted elsewhere. Local administrative entities, such as the Municipal Council, the military, and the governor/viceroy used their jurisdiction over specific areas as an instrument to regulate the marketplace. John Hunter, an observant English visitor in late eighteenth-century Rio de Janeiro, remarked that commercial activities were concentrated in one street.[79] As in many European towns, designated areas of Rio de Janeiro were reserved for specific occupations, and street names reflected the services available: textiles were traded in the Rua da Quitanda and the Rua da Quitanda dos Pretos; fishmongers lived in the Rua dos Pescadores, and goldsmiths were concentrated in the Rua dos Ourives. As A.J. R. Russell-Wood remarked "every Port could count a Street of the Coopers, Street of the Shoemakers or Street of the Tinsmiths."[80] In Lisbon there was the Rua das Contrabandistas, which still exists to this day. If professionals did not have offices, at least they congregated at specific locations. John Luccock, an English resident in Rio de Janeiro for ten years (1808-1818), observed that all the local lawyers met at the corner of the Rua de Ouvidor and Rua da Quitanda.[81] Jean-Baptiste Debret, a Frenchman who served the Brazilian emperor in the first decades of the nineteenth century, mentioned that all merchants met at the corner of the palace square where all the vessels arrived.[82] Oftentimes there were specific trading places designated for specific goods. The slave market was at the Valongo, the fish market at the Praia do Peixe, and there was one central butchery for the sale of all meat. Still, in contrast to Spanish America, there was no central square where all goods were traded. Authorities controlling these multiple vending spaces were able to regulate this commerce, thereby setting prices and determining who was allowed to trade.

Peddlers were important to petty trade, both legal and illegal. Mary Karasch has demonstrated that in nineteenth-century Rio de Janeiro and Salvador peddlers were generally slaves and freed persons of both sexes. They supplied households in the city of Rio de Janeiro with cheap food and textiles, from whose sales both owners and slaves profited.[83] In Salvador, Afro-Brazilian women specialized in selling contraband textiles bought from foreign vessels.[84] Slaves and persons of lower status were intermediaries between consumers and vendors as neither group questioned the provenance of the commodities they bought and sold in trades that were mutually beneficial.

The poor, freedmen, and slaves peddled goods through the streets of Rio de Janeiro. Their goods and contraband were obtained at low prices, sometimes from small land holdings (*chacaras*) in the environs of the city, other times by buying goods directly on the waterfront.[85] Their goods were cheaper as they were procured directly from suppliers, at times without the payment of the requisite taxes.[86] Such practices could pose a threat to public health, as when female slaves sold low quality or even rotten meat that had been discarded from the slaughterhouse and washed in polluted water.[87]

The position of these petty vendors remained precarious since such activities were identified with free and enslaved colored females and with poverty.[88] Engaging in illegal trade could be even more precarious for the lower strata of colonial society than for slaves. If caught, free persons were especially vulnerable. Unlike slave vendors, some of whose owners were influential or colluded with local authorities and could gain acquittal of their slaves if they were arrested making illegal sales, free persons had no such protectors. The *Santa Casa da Misericórdia* helped poor prisoners in the city jails, but their resources remained limited.[89] In Salvador, the *provedor* of the Santa Casa complained that meeting bail for imprisoned slaves was too much of a financial drain, and that the brotherhood's philanthropy would stop if they were recidivists.[90] Poor vendors were also the first to suffer from all kinds of regulations enforced by the municipal and governmental guards who kept order in public spaces in Rio de Janeiro. In one case, slaves were punished because they were walking on the streets at night when the fleet was in the harbor.[91] In another case, guards were installed to keep order and avoid any skirmishes at points of sale for fish, flour, and salt.[92] As the words "*negros e mulatos*" were often equated with thieves and murderers, this population was disproportionately subjected to harsh treatment and harassment as regulatory mechanisms were applied to them with particular severity.[93]

The Municipal Council attempted to regulate commerce by issuing licenses. In 1776, the Council made a special effort, but with predictably limited results. It ruled that vendors (*quitandeiras*) could sell their goods only in front of the Municipal Council chambers and only after buying such licenses. This measure was executed despite vehement protests. *Quitandeiras* who did not purchase licenses were removed and their goods confiscated as contraband.[94] The *quitandeiras* demanded restitution of their goods. So numerous were the non-paying vendors and such was the demand for their products that the Municipal Council had to yield to pressure and reverse its decision.[95]

There was general resistance to monopolies and commercial regulations by the authorities, still, merchants, shopkeepers, and vendors invoked these regulations in order to gain advantage over their adversaries. When there was a proposition to prohibit the sale of *aguardente* (sugarcane brandy) in taverns outside the city even the chief inspector of the treasury reacted adversely, noting that:

> "This product by nature resists monopoly control ... moreover this

liquor is the approved remedy for any wound or injury in Brazil, and it would be totally inappropriate to prohibit its use outside the city."[96]

Merchants used bureaucratic regulations to exclude vendors from outside the city.[97] In an 1815 petition, these groups protested the toleration shown toward vendors of contraband who did not live in Rio de Janeiro in accordance with the law. The local merchants claimed to be "true" citizens of the city. They made the accusation that outside vendors (*mascates*) were seamen who came into the city and infringed on their market share. Therefore, the merchants demanded that these mascates were to be removed through the enforcement of old laws, so that the local merchants will regain their control of the marketplace.

The exclusion of outside sellers from infiltrating local commerce goes back to early legislation on itinerant traders (*comissários volantes*). There has been much mystery surrounding the existence of these peddlers, who were outlawed by Pombaline legislation on the grounds that they dealt in contraband.[98] Whether these traders were of great importance or not remains unresolved. The British plenipotentiary in Lisbon claimed that British commerce had declined considerably because of the trust that British merchants placed in these itinerant traders for their commerce with Brazil.[99] That the phobia towards itinerant traders might be based on legal propaganda by Pombal, and not on the actual situation, can be seen in the scarcity of references to *comissários volantes* in fiscal or regulatory documentation.[100]

Officially sanctioned artisans and merchants could be liable to prosecution, especially if their involvement in illegal trade was too obvious. The greatest blow to one such group of artisans was the expulsion of the goldsmiths. In 1766, the viceroy, the Count da Cunha, reported that much gold was illegally exported to Rio de la Plata as "this prejudicial street is frequented by thieves and vagabonds in the guise of goldsmiths."[101] The next year an unexpected royal order was issued prohibiting all but ten goldsmiths from practicing their profession regardless of their financial position in the city of Rio de Janeiro. Even though the viceroy pleaded that there were many honest persons in this profession, the order was executed to the letter.[102] Bachelors and apprentices were forcibly recruited into the military, and elderly goldsmiths left the city for their families in the countryside.

The salesmen and women in Rio de Janeiro, regardless of their financial means or social status, supplemented their income by selling illegally obtained goods. The strategy of both groups was to obtain a stronghold in one sector of the market by colluding with officials. Their role as intermediaries in commerce had positive and negative effects. They could break monopolies exercised by officials by obtaining goods cheaply without the administrators' interventions as intermediaries - but the vendors could also establish monopolies themselves. When the clamor of protests reached such a pitch as to become a public issue and require intervention by king, viceroy, or governor, it was a sure indication that one group had secured a strangle hold on a lucrative segment of the market and thereby provoked the resentment of competitors and rivals.[103]

The impression of foreigners notwithstanding, the marketplace in colonial Rio de Janeiro had great flexibility. The strength of the Brazilian economy lay precisely in the fact that it was not a free economy. In order to secure a place in both the legal and illegal markets, participants had to gain the support of administrators. The making and breaking of monopolies was well integrated into this economic and social system, and the regulation of the marketplace by officials guaranteed continuity of both royal authority and royal revenues. Such a protected social system maintained the status of all participants in the economy, although it should be emphasized that permeability and social mobility were possible. Persons who attained a higher status automatically acquired more rights in the legal and illegal economies, especially if they could link themselves to, or become members of, the local bureaucracy. Charges of contraband trade were leveled against persons who were of an inferior social status. Newcomers to the market, such as emigrants from Portugal, started in Brazil in such risky ventures as the slave trade. This could be highly profitable in the short term.[104] If successful, they quickly advanced socially and could engage in more secure enterprises. Their "Old World" connections were in high demand, but only if they were able to incorporate themselves to the local networks and proved themselves to be prosperous in business where they able to advance in the Carioca merchant community.

Competition did not occur in the physical marketplace, nor over who could produce the cheapest product, as was the free market ideal. The whole process was played out on another level, because only after a person had attained higher status though local networking could that person obtain a preferential market share. John Luccock, a British merchant who settled in Rio de Janeiro in 1808, thought that Carioca merchants were indolent, since they wasted their time talking to each other on the streets instead of selling products.[105] The extent of his misconception can now easily be revealed. Brazilian merchants did not waste their time selling products as cheaply as possible, because the essence of market competition lay not in the cheapness of their products, but in who could establish the best connections.

CHAPTER 4
THE POLITICS OF PUNISHMENT: DEFINING THE BOUNDARY BETWEEN CONDONED AND PROSCRIBED ILLEGAL TRADE

"His Sovereign Majesty is above all laws, as he protects his oppressed vassals against the personal moods of the executors of the law, who infringe and abuse them by virtue of this very legislation."[1]

A Brazilian merchant to the Prince Regent in 1805.

Distinctions between illegal trade activities that were condoned and those that were proscribed will become clear by analyzing the judicial system. As already noted, Luso-Brazilian officials condoned illegal trade as long as it remained within legal and extra-legal boundaries. This depended on both legislation and local customs. In this chapter, I will examine case studies of persons condemned for illegal trade to establish where these boundaries lay and how they changed over time. Of particular importance is the role of the sovereign, whose laws were applied to local circumstances by his officials. Yet, as the merchant above asserted, his supreme power meant that he still had the prerogative to bend the law to serve justice.

Administrators were intermediaries in illegal commerce by virtue of the fact that their jurisdiction to combat contraband trade also empowered them to regulate these illegal practices. The Portuguese king codified this jurisdiction in laws. Crossing the boundary between condoned and proscribed illegal trade could occur in three ways: direct trade without an intermediary; trade that awoke an unacceptable degree of attention; and trading beyond one's social status. For each of these infractions of the unwritten code, there was a corresponding form of prosecution. More than anything, the practices of the Luso-Brazilian legal system explain how the issue of illegal trade was dealt with by colonial administrators. The punitive value of legal systems was mostly in the tiresome qualities of its procedures because simply to level an accusation to someone in itself constituted a form of punishment. The Luso-Brazilian judicial system had a distinctive characteristic: while prosecution was required to prove guilt, a suspect was never fully acquitted even if the evidence against her or him did not meet the requisite burden of proof. The slightest shred of evidence against the accused was deemed enough to deny to her or him full acquittal and thus recognition of innocence. In such cases, the only recourse was appeal to Portuguese institutions or the king. However, even a royal pardon was not considered sufficient to clear the subject entirely. In fact, if a prisoner was pardoned by the sovereign, that prisoner could obtain release from jail and restitution of her/his confiscated goods only through difficult and time consuming bureaucratic procedures.

There was good reason to painstakingly avoid any action that might provide grounds and even a pretext for an accusation of illegal trading. The extreme hardship posed by arrest was itself a deterrent to potential transgressors. A single complaint (*queixa*) brought by a third person was enough to make any individual suspect. There was thus considerable pressure to act according to social convention. However, far from preventing illegal commerce, this pressure served to restrict engagement in contraband trade to individuals who, by virtue of their social status were considered eligible to participate in this illegal system. This interpretation of legislation and the functioning of the law differs somewhat from most current works by legal historians on Portugal and its colonies because many have focused on institutions rather than on cases. Literature on Portuguese law has increased dramatically in the last two decades. One major impetus was the seminal work of António Hespanha, who wrote for the first time, a comprehensive study of the development of legal institutions in Portugal.[2] His main argument was that in the seventeenth century, Portuguese institutions were fractured between different institutions and population groups (military, clergy, foreign nations, and other privileged groups.) Rather than taking a centralized and royal rule as their point of departure, it is the sharing of governance that was more convenient. In the case of legal institutions, regular judges (*juizes ordinários*) were common, and only after enough economic development might they be replaced by literate and trained *juizes de fora* (outsider judges). Similarly, historians, such as Lauren Benton, have elaborated on this issue in the Portuguese empire. Benton also argued for the shared jurisdiction as a commonality in the Portuguese empire, but rather than studying solely the privileged groups, she argues that Luso-Brazilian (and other European) authorities created or imagined runaway slave communities as judicial unities, which colonial governments could negotiate and even conclude treaties with.[3] Both Hespanha and Benton remain rather concentrated on institutions or on organizational contexts. However, the advantages of these scattered jurisdictions can be found in legal practices and the cooperation/antagonism of the different administrations. A problem in this is complete sources, as Arno and Maria José Wehling realized in their study of the High Court (*Relação*) of Rio de Janeiro. Even though they found an impressive amount of the High Court's legal decisions, complete processes and their outcomes were less readily available.[4] With the notable exceptions of António Manuel Hespanha's two articles on the role of pardons and the enforcement of the death penalty, Timothy Coates' book on exile, and Patricia Aufderheide's dissertation on deviance, historians have paid surprisingly little attention to the practice of law in Portugal and its overseas possessions.[5] Indeed, historians have concentrated on case studies related to the Inquisition and civil law, which was of only minimal relevance to illegal trade. Both civil and Inquisitorial procedures were different, even though a few cases were tried both by secular and religious institutions.[6]

Even though historians have not specifically focused on law enforcement, most publications mentioned the tediously long procedures. For example, according to Patricia Aufderheide, "Appealing to the Relação was slow and expensive."[7] This was seconded by Stuart Schwartz, who mentioned that the Bahian High Court's "workload seems extraordinary heavy."[8] Historians of colonial Brazil have paid scant attention to the enforcement of the law. Stuart Schwartz's book on the High Court in Salvador is largely a prosopographic analysis of the judges.[9] Silvia Hunold Lara, Patricia Aufderheide, and Leila Mezan Algranti use criminal cases in their studies of violence as related to slavery and social stratification in colonial Brazil.[10] A.J.R. Russell-Wood treats to the role of the *Santa Casa da Misericórdia* in assisting the prisoners.[11] Discussing legal prosecution in Rio de la Plata, Zacharias Moutoukias demonstrates that individuals could buy pardons in Spain for illegal trade even before committing the crime and stresses the importance of this purchased tolerance for the commerce of Buenos Aires.[12]

In this chapter, I will analyze three major cases of prosecution of illegal trade in Rio de Janeiro during the eighteenth century, focusing on the manner in which royal policies towards illegal trade and the machinery of prosecution evolved. In all three cases, changes occurred as a consequence of new royal policies. The first of these cases, the prosecution of merchants by Luís Vahia Monteiro, governor of Rio de Janeiro (1725-1733), was essential to the establishment of royal authority over the gold flow out of Brazil. This case corresponds with a peak in the number of prosecutions for illegal trade in Rio de Janeiro (Graph 4.1.) In the second case, focus will be on protests by merchants in Rio de Janeiro against the implementation of sumptuary laws in 1753, whereby a new royal policy altered the boundaries between what was condoned and what was proscribed, resulting in an organized local boycott of these new policies. The 1740s and 1750s were a period of compromise saw a low incidence of legal prosecutions in illegal trade (Graph 4.1.) Finally, the third case deals with the prosecution of goldsmiths between 1763 and 1767 as part of an attempt to put an end to organized illegal trade within the Portuguese fleet system. During this period, there was a short-term increase in the number of prosecutions for illegal trade. These three cases will cast light on the hidden boundaries that separated contraband trade that was tacitly condoned by Brazilian officials from what they refused to condone.

Next, the chapter will examine the judicial practices of punishing illegal trade and policy making which reveal a duality in the enforcement of the law, between *de facto* arrests and *de jure* judicial procedures. This duality served as an instrument for arbitration between local interests and royal authority. Local interests were served when suspects were arrested and were waiting for official prosecution. Royal authority was established by formal prosecution and the king's intervention in the event of granting a pardon. Changes in policies and in perceptions of what constituted illegal trade occurred in reaction either to highly publicized contraband cases or to new taxation policies that changed the boundaries between what was condoned and proscribed.

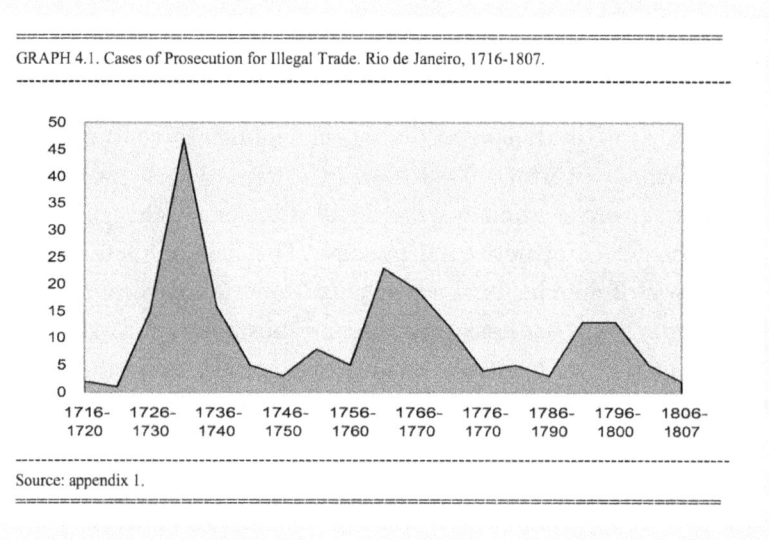

GRAPH 4.1. Cases of Prosecution for Illegal Trade. Rio de Janeiro, 1716-1807.

Source: appendix 1.

There are some distinct periods during which governors or viceroys tried arbitrarily to extend their authority, often resulting in mass arrests and in local protests. More than a few contrabandists ran afoul of local authorities when they failed to appreciate the shifting boundaries between condoned and proscribed behavior (Graph 4.1.) One case of mass arrests and protests occurred during the governorship of Luís

Vahia Monteiro (1725-1733).[13] This governor, a last minute royal appointee from the northern Portuguese province of Trás-os-Montes, became one of Rio de Janeiro's most disliked rulers.[14] During his governorship, he alienated many factions of society, including clergymen, high-ranking civil servants, and members of the Municipal Council.[15] The focal point of the governor's actions was combating illegal trade through unorthodox methods. During this period the district of Minas Gerais remained unruly. Monteiro's fellow governors of São Paulo and Minas Gerais had experienced great difficulty in pacifying the inhabitants, who at times even engaged in a minor civil war. Under these conditions, royal authority could hardly be enforced, much less the effective collection of the fifth (*quinto*) on gold. Monteiro directed his struggle to prevent illegal trade on two fronts: first, he tried to stop the export of powder gold; second, he combated the counterfeiting of gold bars. The first brought him into conflict with admirals of the Portuguese fleets, in whose vessels powder gold was illegally shipped; the latter incensed local merchants. An examination of arrests arising from these initiatives, subsequent investigations by the governor, and the Lisbon reaction sheds light on methods of establishing local and royal authority in colonial Rio de Janeiro.

In the 1730s, officials taxed all gold in mints situated in the provinces of Minas Gerais, São Paulo, and Goiás. These mints issued coins or bars bearing the royal mark and provided the owner of the gold with a certificate that tax had been paid (*guia*.) All bars were numbered and registered in an account book at the mint in the Brazilian interior. In Rio de Janeiro, merchants had to register their bars again at the local mint before loading them on the fleet for transport to Portugal. With merchants in Rio de Janeiro opposing the measures used by the governor to combat contraband trade in gold, the collection of the royal *quinto* on gold remained a constant challenge.[16] The governor of Rio de Janeiro introduced the draconian policy of confiscating all illegally minted gold and arresting all persons suspected of having engaged in this contraband trade. Monteiro implemented his new policy on a large scale. This was especially relevant after the discovery of an illegal mint in Minas Gerais in 1731.[17]

After the arrest of several persons suspected of selling illegally minted gold, Monteiro took two steps. First, he personally arrested all suspects who could not prove that their gold bars were legally minted. Second, he opened commercial letters and arrested the receivers if the contents did not please him. Even though the Lisbon authorities vehemently opposed the governor's controversial methods, they did praise him for arresting the suspects, whom they considered guilty even without evidence. During Monteiro's administration, there was an increase in the number of gold smugglers who were arrested (Graph 4.1.) His efforts were far-reaching but the crime was difficult to prove. One striking example of how difficult this was happened in 1725. Seeing a vessel bound for Pernambuco anchored at a spot where gold was loaded on a regular basis, the suspicious governor searched the vessel for three days but found no gold.[18] Without conceding defeat, the governor gave the captain the opportunity to give up voluntarily any gold on board in exchange for immunity from punishment, although the captain would have to pay the royal fifth. The captain refused but the governor received a tip telling him where the gold was hidden. Monteiro's efforts were finally rewarded when he found two small gold bars weighing 22 *marcos* (about 260 grams) embedded in timber.

The governor kept up an impressive record of capturing gold smugglers, even prior to the big catch of the illegal minters in Minas Gerais in 1730, which drew international attention.[19] The judge (*ouvidor*) of Minas Gerais arrested a large and well-connected gang of minters *in flagrante delicto*. Their presses were confiscated and they were arrested and sent to Lisbon.[20] Not only were these counterfeiters arrested, but so too were all persons in possession of fraudulently minted bars. These arrests seriously upset the merchant community of Rio de Janeiro. After a royal order in early 1730 prohibited the possession of powder gold outside the mining districts, the governor issued an ultimatum that failure to deliver all powder gold to the mint within two months would have drastic results.[21] When this deadline passed, Monteiro opened a judicial inquiry (*devassa*) on the smuggling of gold out of the harbor of Rio de Janeiro. He nominated the notary public of Paratí to conduct this inquiry because he did not trust any official from Rio de Janeiro.[22] The members of the investigating commission pronounced five merchants guilty of engaging in illegal trade.²³ The merchants were found either to have gold powder in their possession or to have left unregistered bars of gold at the mint in Rio de Janeiro, whose description did not match those registered in the mint of Minas Gerais.²⁴ Since the marks on the bars resembled those of the illegal mint, the governor of Rio de Janeiro imprisoned the suspects.²⁵ The arrests would have been on a larger scale if the governor of São Paulo had also sent the books from his mint, but he refused to cooperate.²⁶

Although they recognized the necessity of gaining control over the taxation of gold, Lisbon authorities viewed Monteiro's actions with suspicion. He had acted unilaterally without the cooperation of local officials, and immediately after the arrest of the merchants, a complaint (*queixa*) appeared stating that the suspects were arrested without knowing what the charges were.²⁷ Moreover, the Overseas Council (*Conselho Ultramarino*) did not accept the governor's contention that the mere fact that the marks were not registered in the Minas Gerais mint was enough to prove them counterfeit.²⁸

One of the imprisoned merchants was João Francisco Muzzi, whose personal reactions towards his imprisonment are known because his commercial correspondence to the Lisbon merchant Francisco Pinheiro has been published.²⁹ Muzzi's case was especially instructive, as it demonstrated the tensions between the need for due process on the one hand, and, on the other hand, the authorities' interest in properly taxing gold and punishing contrabandists.³⁰

The governor personally arrested the Italian merchant during an audience at his palace.³¹ After an interrogation on false gold marks and his connections with Minas Gerais, Monteiro imprisoned Muzzi and confiscated his goods. Soon after his arrest, Muzzi complained that the governor had intercepted his letters and that he had not been formally accused. He hoped that his Lisbon correspondent, Francisco Pinheiro, could help him by alerting Alexandre Metello de Souza Menezes, a member of the Overseas Council, who had visited Rio de Janeiro as an ambassador on his way to China. Having been born in Italy, Muzzi feared above all that he would be expelled from Brazil, as had been the case with Pedro Folgman, a Dutch settler forced to leave after a Dutch ship was confiscated.³² Muzzi's complaints were well received in

Lisbon. What drew the closest attention was the interception of his letters. The municipal councilors of Rio de Janeiro wrote to Lisbon to complain of the governor's despotic behavior.[33] The king and the Overseas Council decreed that opening of letters was prejudicial to the normal course of commerce and should be stopped immediately.[34] Even though Monteiro was reprimanded for his behavior, the prisoner's situation did not improve as a result.[35]

In addition to personal difficulties, the economic consequences of Muzzi's imprisonment soon were felt. His commercial papers were confiscated and the only possessions he was allowed to keep were his clothes.[36] Muzzi was losing his credit rapidly and his Lisbon partner became very preoccupied with the outstanding debts of his correspondent.[37] The financial repercussions of Muzzi's arrest became starkly apparent when Pinheiro's goods, which the governor had confiscated from Muzzi, were sold at very low prices the following year, in large part attributable to the deterioration in the warehouses.[38] The personal consequences of Muzzi's imprisonment were even more dramatic. Although magistrates never found him guilty and had every reason to hope that his case would soon be solved, his punishment was severe. The judge (*ouvidor*) pronounced Muzzi not guilty, but this did not mean that Muzzi was a free man.[39] The judicial process was prolonged by the king's order that all trials concerning gold be transferred to the High Court in Salvador.[40] This protraction in the process became even more devastating when members of the Overseas Council delayed Muzzi's request for temporary release (*fiança*) by requesting additional information from Brazil.[41] It took another two years for the High Court in Salvador to hand down an opinion.[42] Even though this ruling confirmed the ruling in Rio de Janeiro, Muzzi was still not released. A further order from the Overseas Council, requiring all cases concerning contraband gold judged in Salvador to be reconsidered by them, prolonged Muzzi's imprisonment for yet another year while the colonial High Court sent all documentation to Lisbon.[43] The next year's fleet brought no decision from Lisbon. Only through the personal intervention of a high court judge in Salvador, did Muzzi finally obtain his release from jail five years and nine months after his original arrest.[44]

Other cases demonstrated how officials used the ordeal of the judicial process as punishment. An arrest was as good as a verdict and the suspect's only hope of release lay in personal connections.[45] Some well-connected suspects could, for instance, be freed on bail with a special license in order to prove their innocence.[46] Others were less fortunate, and did not survive the circumstances of their imprisonment.[47] Even if a sentence was handed down the condemned had to wait a long time in prison before the actual enactment of the verdict.[48] Poor people could easily perish in prison.[49] In 1779, a soldier wrote to Lisbon that he had been imprisoned for 27 years, although he had been condemned only to a four-year exile to Santa Catarina and a fine of 200$000 reis.[50] Since this soldier lacked the financial means to protest against his circumstances, he was unable to obtain his freedom. Others were acquitted of charges against them but could not pay the clerks who supplied documents essential to end their captivity.[51]

The 1730s were important years for restoring royal authority over the taxation of gold. Unpopular governors such as Monteiro did the dirty work in punishing contrabandists who transgressed the newly established boundaries between condoned and proscribed illegal trade. Royal and administrative authority was confirmed since only a royal pardon could release prisoners after they had already undergone their punishment. Newly formed boundaries formed challenges to the sovereign's authority which was re-established by the moderating authority of the king and the royal prerogative power to pardon. Local protests were certain to arise whenever Lisbon authorities created new commercial regulations. These rulings modified the boundaries of condoned illegal trade and therefore raised new challenges to authority. Reassertion of royal authority over the taxation of gold brought with it numerous arrests, as royal authority was initially contested, but ultimately re-established in the 1730s.[52] Twenty years later, a new area of contention accompanied the implementation of new Portuguese policies following the introduction of sumptuary laws but officials and merchants were able to find common ground between commercial and state interest. As Graph 4.1. demonstrates, relatively few persons were arrested in the 1750s for illegal trade. These new policies sparkled with far reaching implications. When, in 1753, the sumptuary law of 1749 was implemented in Rio de Janeiro, local merchants staged such vocal and organized protests that they were reported all over Europe.[53] Foreign diplomats were interested in this issue because these laws also affected their nationals who had settled as merchants in the towns of Lisbon and Porto.[54]

These new measures shifted the boundaries between condoned and proscribed illegal trade. Royal instructions now declared some formerly legal goods to be contraband while they also demanded more elaborate searches of goods shipped from Lisbon to Rio de Janeiro. Such measures did diminish illegal trading activity. This zealous vigilance was too much for the merchants of Rio de Janeiro and they threatened to boycott all official commerce.

In 1753, the admiral of the fleet sailing to Rio de Janeiro handed over instructions to the governor that all goods from the fleet should be scrutinized by customs to ensure and that they were legal, and they had been dispatched in accordance with the new regulations.[55] A seal from the Lisbon customs indicated that each item had been individually inspected. If this seal was lacking, the goods were confiscated by officials of Rio de Janeiro and burned in a public place. Furthermore, the merchants to whom they had been dispatched were required to pay a penalty of three times the value of these goods.[56] In compliance, custom officers confiscated goods on the 1753 fleet to a total value of almost two million reis.[57] The merchants reacted to these measures immediately and vigorously by rallying together to protest vehemently as a corporate body, as they had done in previous crises.[58] The merchants protested the fact that some hitherto legal commerce had become illegal and that these measures had been implemented without warning. Formerly, they were not able to get away dispatching goods that were not taxed in Lisbon, and now, without prior notice, they had to adhere to a stricter policy.[59] But the governor, José António Freire de Andrade, returning from Serro do Frio specifically to deal with this crisis, held firm to the hard line, insisting on full compliance with all measures.[60]

The merchants reacted against these measures by refusing to buy any such commodities from the fleet, to pay the freights charges, and refusing to dispatch any goods in return.[61] No money arrived from

Minas Gerais and, consequently, the fleet's crew could not be paid. Now, there was not much of a cargo for the return voyage to Lisbon. Indeed, it looked as if there would be no fleet to Portugal that year.[62] The stalemate continued for several months, since neither governor nor merchants were inclined to give in to the other side's pressure. Arguing that these measures were new and unexpected measures seriously increased the amount of time it took for newly arrived consignments to clear customs. The merchants demonstrated that the absence of commercial activities had grave consequences for the economy and administration of both Brazil and Portugal. With some truth, they observed that without their input there would be no monies for the royal fisc, the colony, or the metropolis, and drove home to the king and governor how indispensable their contribution to the economy and society of Rio de Janeiro was.[63]

Only after much deliberation did the government finally relent. Petitioning the governor to no avail, the merchants were referred to the chief of the customs, who in turn referred them to a high court judge responsible for commercial affairs.[64] The judge ruled against the merchants and the governor accepted their decision. As a last recourse, the governor consulted all judges of the recently created High Court. Their opinions were divided: four agreed to the governor's hard line while four others opted for negotiation.[65] Since the deadlock had to be broken, the governor finally gave way by not penalizing the merchants for non-sealed goods, but this exemption applied only to cargo carried on the 1753 fleet.[66] This resolution was subject to approval by the Lisbon authorities, which came one year later.[67] Finally the fleet did sail to Lisbon, and in the following years merchants and officials complied with the new rules. But this was not the end of the affair. Learning from this experience, the Carioca merchants institutionalized the spirit of cooperation by formally incorporating themselves. Copying the examples of Lisbon, Porto, and Salvador, they created a merchant society, the *Mesa do Bem Comum*, whose statutes they sent to Portugal for approval in 1754.[68] The aim of the *Mesa do Bem Comum* was to enable the merchants to respond collectively against all unfavorable new governmental policies.[69] Although the organization's statutes proclaimed a strong religious and spiritual dimension, the objectives of its members were primarily secular. For instance, the *Mesa do Bem Comum* proposed to nominate the merchants who would be appointed to the Board of Inspection (*Casa da Inspeção*), a new institution created to control the quality of sugar and tobacco. The *Mesa* also opposed certain measures of the sumptuary laws.[70] It is not clear whether the statutes were ever approved. The chancellor of the high court voiced a negative opinion of them, especially the clause whereby the merchants sought to impose a customs tax in order to finance their own institution.[71] In any case, the *Mesa* never had a formal existence, even though a mass was celebrated and the sermon printed in its behalf.[72] The authorities never recognized the brotherhood and it did not survive longer than 1757, when Sebastião de Carvalho e Mello abolished the already existing *mesas do Bem Comum* of Lisbon, Porto, and Salvador.[73]

Nevertheless, the merchants of Rio de Janeiro had shown that they could organize collectively if their interests were at stake. The authorities were more than willing to compromise, since the merchants' goodwill was essential to the economy and administration of empire. In this case, the authorities had jeopardized this goodwill by establishing the boundary between proscribed and condoned illegal trade at an unacceptable level. The reaction of the merchants was predictable, but all parties finally complied with the new legislation. Under the governorship of Gomes Freire de Andrade (1733-1762), commerce and administration found a working compromise and relatively few persons were arrested for illegal activities (Graph 4.1.). Still, the new Pombaline legislation triggered another type of illegal trade: organized crime through the existing fleet system. After Gomes Freire's administration, new measures were deemed necessary to curb this type of illegal trade. One such measure, aimed at targeting nefarious activities by goldsmiths in Rio de Janeiro, did not inspire the same opposition as had the sumptuary laws because the illegality of gold contraband was less disputed there was general consensus that it should be proscribed. In the 1760s through the 1780s, illegal trade increasingly took the form of organized crime. Whenever it became too public, there was correspondingly greater likelihood of detection. Rampant contraband trading came to the public attention and gained notoriety. Furthermore, problems arose when merchants' financial wealth exceeded what betitled their social status as a consequence of their involvement in illegal activities.

There were several instances of exposure of such illegal trading companies. In 1735, Governor Gomes Freire de Andrade reported on a company trading with São Tomé that the viceroy in Salvador had exposed.[74] The company consisted of merchants in Brazil and members of the higher clergy and the administration in Africa, in the Colônia de Sacramento, and in Minas Gerais, São Paulo, Rio de Janeiro, Salvador, and Recife. The hub for the company's activities was in São Tomé, where Brazilian gold was traded for slaves with Dutch, English, and French merchants in Ajuda, Cacheu, Gambia, and Melim.[75] The size and extent of this company was formidable. Gomes Freire de Andrade estimated that the confiscations totaled one million cruzados and that it would take decades to settle all the accounts.[76] Had this company continued, he wrote to his colleague in Pernambuco, its members would have become powerful ("*poderoso*") in a few years. The implication was that they would become increasingly difficult to prosecute.[77] Such was already the case, since the company involved the eight most important merchants in Salvador.[78] Had the viceroy not pardoned these merchants, commerce in Brazil's capital would have been seriously disrupted.[79] In the 1760s, 1770s, and 1780s several cases of organized illegal trade came to light.[80] The study of one such instance, that of the goldsmith and diamond cutter Francisco Xavier Telles, demonstrates the devastation which unwanted publicity could wreak on such extensive trading networks, the thorough nature of the prosecution, and the use of pardons to re-establish royal authority.

Instructions to the first viceroy in the new Brazilian capital of Rio de Janeiro included an order to arrest five individuals suspected of illegal trade in gold and diamonds, and whose guilt had been established after extensive investigations in Lisbon.[81] These were: Francisco Xavier Telles, a goldsmith; António Rodrigues, his partner; Manoel de Almeida, a traveling merchant to Minas Gerais; and two other merchants resident in Minas Gerais.[82] When the Lisbon authorities inspected the *Xancarona*, a vessel just returned to Lisbon from Rio de

Janeiro, they encountered a substantial amount of undeclared gold and diamonds.[83] The Portuguese officials arrested the Lisbon merchant Carlos Manoel de Aguiar and found an extensive correspondence on this illegal trade at his house.[84] As soon as the royal order was received in Rio de Janeiro, the Brazilian authorities immediately arrested the five suspects and confiscated their goods. Proven guilty beyond any doubt by their commercial correspondence and administrative papers, the suspects had no alternative other than to confess despite their fear of harsh punishment. Francisco Xavier Telles, for instance, said at his first interrogation that he had few things to confess, but exclaimed that "if he deserved to go to Angola or to the gallows, they should send him."[85] Guilt was obvious and proven even before these hearings. The high court judge and inspector of gold, João Tavares de Abreu, made a rigorous examination of all the evidence. Not only did these suspects confess but accomplices and others implicated in this elaborate web of illegal trade also found guilty.[86]

How this network had come into being was revealed through the interrogations of Francisco Xavier Telles and his companions, António Rodrigues and António Attunes Ferreira.[87] In Rio de Janeiro, Telles had bought gold dust and diamonds from itinerant peddlers who walked the roads connecting Minas Gerais to Serro do Frio and Rio de Janeiro. These peddlers (*mascates*) also came to his workplace to sell their contraband.[88] The gold buyers thus implicated by Telles were Lisbon merchants who sold the prohibited goods to a British merchant with a Portuguese name, Manoel Dias Santos.[89]

These illegal goods were shipped with the consent of highly placed persons. Telles brought his gold and diamonds to three different captains of the fleet. He also entrusted them to two passengers, a clergyman and a military colonel.[90] The most powerful persons on board were in a position to guarantee the safe transportation of the contraband. In Portugal, the gold dust was handled over to the captain of the British packet.[91] Since Telles and his accomplices admitted to their crimes, they all faced a rigorous prosecution in Lisbon.[92] Despite his obvious guilt, given his confession and implicating correspondence, the king pardoned Telles in 1767.[93] Although the king prohibited him from returning to Rio de Janeiro, Telles' punishment was obviously lenient.

Telles' case was followed by the arrests of two more contraband groups. The principal suspects, Pedro Telma Lima and Francisco de Souza Braga, were both goldsmiths in Rio de Janeiro.[94] As in Telles' case, suspects appealed to be acquitted after legal procedures in Portugal.[95] This raises several puzzling questions about the functioning of the Luso-Brazilian judiciary.

In practice, only a few persons were prosecuted and condemned to the full extent of the law. My research has found evidence of 201 cases of persons prosecuted for illegal trade in Rio de Janeiro. The final outcome of the trials is known only in 67 cases. In only a third of these cases were the suspects condemned. Of these 67 men and women, 14 were pardoned and 28 were released despite sentences against them. Of the 25 remaining cases, 10 persons were sentenced to banishment and one was executed.[96] Further of the 10 people sentenced to banishment, one fled, another died in prison, and the other was forgotten in prison. In the other 14 cases, suspects suffered pecuniary loss in the form of confiscations and fines.[97] These numbers confirmed the findings of the Portuguese historian, António M. Hespanha.[98] In a sample of 294 crime cases which came before the High Court (*Relação*) in Lisbon between 1694 and 1696, Hespanha found that almost half of the suspects were acquitted. He also noted that capital punishment was rare in Portugal: during the seventeenth and eighteenth centuries only 467 persons were executed.[99] Actual condemnation was not the primary form of punishment, instead there was a tendency to draw out the judicial proceedings to make the suspects suffer. After hearing that a false minter had been imprisoned for 19 years, a member of the Overseas Council remarked that the policy of lingering imprisonment was as effective as the execution of the laws.[100] Seen in this light, it is not surprising that the outcome is known for only 67 out of the 201 cases. The judicial system intentionally moved slowly to delay the passing of a final sentence and imposition of punishment. A suspect could consider himself lucky to be informed of the charges against him and to have his sentence executed promptly. Full implementation of the law usually ended in imprisonment and, in many cases, restored confiscated goods, and more importantly, it ended the uncertainty of a prisoner's future.

The Portuguese judicial system operated on two levels. On the one hand, suspected complicity in a crime resulted in arrest, which usually meant confinement and confiscation of goods. For all practical purposes, to be suspect was tantamount to being found guilty. On the other hand, the actual judicial procedure required clear evidence of guilt, and the suspect was well protected. Even if sufficient evidence proving guilt was available, a suspect could be acquitted on the grounds of unjust judicial procedures or pardoned by the king. But, rather than adhering to the letter of the law and prescribed judicial procedures, Portuguese officials responded with a bureaucratic strategy that essentially relied on obstruction of justice - interminable inquiries, misplaced evidence, inefficiency, and delay. The functioning of the system, rather than the judges themselves, thus became the instruments for punishing transgression of the law. Therefore, these findings confirm Michel Foucault's findings that prisons were already an important means of punishment before the fall of the *Ancien Régime*, but it had not yet been codified as such.[101] Even though *de jure* imprisonment as a form of punishment to obtain moral reforms was not widespread in Europe and its colonies, *de facto* the Portuguese juridical system did work in this way.

After such procedures, structural measures were introduced to diminish the likelihood of illegal trade. Shortly after Telles was sent to Lisbon, the viceroy received orders to reduce the number of goldsmiths working in the Rua dos Ourives from 450 to 12.[102] Such flagrant cases of proven illegal trade forced Lisbon authorities to redefine the boundaries of condoned and proscribed illegal trade. In the 1770s and 1780s, the number of cases of prosecution for illegal trade showed a downward trend. Did this mean that there was less illegal trade?

The search for an explanation must be accompanied by a word of caution on these numbers: they include only those cases in which the names of the prosecuted felons were evident. It is possible that fewer persons were identified by name than were found guilty. Even though the number of cases leading to prosecution decreased in the sample, contemporary reports indicated an increase in illegal trade, especially the 1790s. Thus, it seems likely that the boundaries of illegal trade became blurred. Further, it appears that authorities were increasingly involved in illegal trade. Contraband trade evolved from organized to institutionalized crime. This shift explained the outcry voiced by the merchant cited at the beginning of this chapter.[103] He wanted royal protection from the law and its administrators since, in his view, his important role in Brazilian society and the attendant contributions to the royal treasury should have exempted him from legal prosecution by crown appointed judges. The merchant's protest also reflected the double standard of criminal punishment in colonial Brazil. The local judiciary could in effect punish any person who crossed the boundaries between condoned and proscribed illegal trade by prolonging protracted pre-judgment periods in prison. However, suspects could advance through the judicial hierarchy, shortening their process and even obtaining freedom. There was some negotiability, since the poorer a suspect was and the fewer connections he or she had, the less likely it was that he or she would receive a favorable treatment. If a suspect was very poor, the chances were high that he or she could perish in prison.

The king alone had the power and authority to weigh the degree to which illegal traders could be prosecuted without harming Luso-Brazilian trade, on which the royal exchequer depended for revenues. New policies were enacted after the discovery of an illegal mint in the 1730s, the introduction of a new sumptuary law in Brazil in 1753, and the arrest of goldsmiths in the 1760s. In the first two cases, these changes led to fierce protests in Rio de Janeiro and resulting accommodation by the authorities. By demonstrating flexibility in the application of laws concerning illegal trade, and by pardoning trespassers, the king established his authority as an arbiter above the law and protector of his vassals against the very judicial system that he had created. The boundaries between condoned and proscribed illegal trade shifted over time as did the degree and effectiveness of control over illegal trade. Cases that were pursued by the judiciary demonstrated not all illegal trade, but only illegal trade that was prosecuted. Prosecutions spiked in the 1730s and the 1760s with the implementation of new royal policies that shifted the boundaries of what was proscribed. The few instances of prosecution in the 1740s and 1750s indicate that Luso-Brazilian authorities and merchants had reached a compromise over what illegal trade was condoned and what was proscribed. In contrast, the fewer instances of prosecution for illegal trade, combined with more reports about contraband since the 1780s, seem to indicate that officials were losing control over these activities and that were condoning more illegal activities.

CHAPTER 5

INSTITUTIONALIZED ILLEGALITY: COLONEL ADMINISTRATION AND CONTRABAND TRADE

Brazilian officialdom's involvement in contraband trade has been described in script and scripture. The venality of the bureaucrat was infamous and widespread as the administration played the part of intermediary in illegal commerce. The officials whose responsibility it was to combat illegal trade were among its most prominent participants. Their power derived precisely from the jurisdiction they exercised over the fight against illegal activities. The Portuguese sovereign was by no means an inactive bystander. On the contrary, those in charge tried to assert authority by regulating these illegal practices through the manipulation of administrators' jurisdictions, incomes, and appointments.

The organization of Luso-Brazilian administration changed during the eighteenth century. In order to achieve both optimal tax income and full recognition of his authority, the crown pursued a double policy of increasing bureaucratic professionalization and decreasing the administrators' local ties. Both objectives were attained by appointing university-trained administrators to the highest bureaucratic positions, reducing the number of offices that were sold or farmed out, and prohibiting administrators from participating in the local society of their place of posting. Local reactions to these policies impeded their complete implementation. Therefore, the sovereign sought to maintain his supreme authority by keeping a fine balance between local economic interests and metropolitan financial needs. The sovereign used the prosecution of illegal trade as a pretext for controlling colonial administration. The crown's structural policies of professionalizing and displacing Carioca administrators were implemented locally on an *ad hoc* basis. The sovereign purposely delayed sensitive reforms until flagrant cases of illegal trade had come to light. These changes occurred especially after disputes among administrators from different branches of the bureaucracy, frequently followed by arrests of officials in those cases related to contraband trade.

A combination of institutional developments and local interests determined the regulation of illegal trade. On the one hand, letters or nomination defined an official's degree of jurisdiction over informal trade. On the other hand, personal relations and local networks determined the status accorded to an official by local leaders and thereby the degree of acceptance of his involvement in illegal activities. The crown showed considerable flexibility in allowing officials to regulate illegal trade. Yet, it tried to minimize the officials' role in these activities through a policy of conflict stimulation and centralized problem-solving, followed by measures intended to rationalize and displace the bureaucracy. This capacity for reform waned during stressful situations that strained the royal treasury, such as the threat of French, Spanish, Dutch and British invasions of Portugal. It was precisely at such times that colonial administrators had more bargaining power to advance their own interests. In the 1760s, this policy changed when the king granted more power to the High Court and the viceroy to streamline the administration. These changes also diminished the number of native-born office holders. The ouster of locally-born administrators led to imbalances in the regulation of illegal trade and provoked widespread defiance by colonists *vis-à-vis* the authority of the crown's appointees.

The focus of this chapter is on royal and local authorities' control over the Carioca bureaucracy. A survey of the branches of administration, their jurisdictions and their conflicts will set the stage for an analysis of how these bureaucracies developed and the degree to which they were vulnerable to local and royal pressures. I shall than examine the nature of the relationship between the administrators' income, the sale of offices and the role of officials in illegal trade. Finally, I will explain how administrators in Rio de Janeiro eventually lost their power to regulate illegal trade. Many authors have documented the widespread venality of Brazilian officials. Contemporaries described this phenomenon amply in sermons, satire, travel accounts, and official correspondence.[1] In some cases this information led to well-publicized arrests of administrators; in others, such issues were resolved locally as officials disputed over their jurisdictions. The area over which an official had jurisdiction was crucial because it set the parameters for authority over what would be the official's slice of commercial activities in Rio de Janeiro. As Clarence Haring has demonstrated for Spanish America, administrators' jurisdictions were often purposely vague and overlapping.[2] This makes it difficult, but not impossible, to make some generalizations concerning the administration's functioning and to discern the specific tasks and duties designed to its functionaries.

The units of importance for commercial administration can be divided into five parts: customs, treasury, judiciary, governor, and the Municipal Council. In theory, each of these entities of government was assigned discrete roles and tasks. Although these basic tasks entities remained invariable during the eighteenth century, the hierarchical structure in which the administrative units were arranged was modified significantly. The basic tasks of the different administrative branches can be summarized as follows. The customs (*alfândega*) taxed products entering and leaving the harbor of Rio de Janeiro by ships. The treasury (*fazenda real*) received revenues due to the crown, made disbursements in the royal name and farmed out tax monopolies. The viceroy or governor (*governador, vicerei*), as the senior crown representative and the person in the colony in who was vested royal authority, strove to ensure that the royal will was implemented, that disputes were resolved and that there was no disruption to public order. The magistracy (*ouvidor, juiz de fora, desembargadores da relação*) dealt with persons transgression of the law. Finally, the Municipal Council (*Câmara Municipal*) exercised authority in the urban context in the regulation of commerce and ensuring the well-being of the inhabitants.

At face value, the jurisdiction of each entity appears discrete, but in practice there was overlap, especially in prosecution of illegal trade. The governor, judge of the customs (*juiz ouvidor da alfândega*), chief treasurer (*provedor da fazenda*), municipal inspector (*meirinho da cidade*) and private contractor each had the jurisdiction to arrest transgressors of commercial laws. Major cases were handled by the crown-appointed judge (*ouvidor geral do crime*). With the exception of those cases involving persons exempt from the jurisdiction of the civilian magistracy, such as men of the cloth and members of the military others enjoyed the privilege of being tried by special courts. Although each official's degree of jurisdiction was clearly stated in his letter of appointment, such jurisdiction was often not recognized *in loco*. As the boundaries of their jurisdiction blurred or became ill-defined, their authority *de facto* depended on the degree to which other officials encroached upon their jurisdiction or permitted them a free reign. The most powerful administrator was the chief inspector of the treasury. Not answerable for his decisions, even to the governor, he exercised absolute authority. Judicial investigations and arrest of a chief inspector of the treasury could be carried out only with royal approval.[3] Equal freedom was given to the members of the city council. Citizens of Rio de Janeiro enjoyed the same privileges as citizens of the city of Porto.[4] All municipal councilmen, their children and grandchildren were citizens and enjoyed privileges, including immunity from arrest and exemption from military service.

Judicial investigations placed curbs on the actions of governors and crown-appointed judges, whose conduct was subject to a *residência*, a judicial inquiry, to scrutinize their conduct in office.[5] Such *residências* were critical because their outcome determined whether or not an administrator would receive recognition in the form of *mercês* (royal graces) on return in Portugal, or would fall out of favor and be refused future royal favors. Promotion was contingent on a positive *residência*.[6] At some periods the *residência* became virtually obsolete.[7] On other occasions an *ouvidor* could be arrested as a result of a negative *residência*. Given the high stakes, it was not unknown for the subject of such an investigation to try to influence the outcome, or for the investigating officer to act maliciously towards an official and destroy his hopes of further advancement.[8] In any case, the *residência* remained a powerful weapon in preventing local officials from disregarding practices and putting crown officials on notice that they were liable to sanctions if they disregarded local practices and criteria as to what constituted appropriate behavior. Complaints were powerful instruments used by residents to make public their views on an administrator's performance in office. Any individual could address a complaint (*queixa*) to the king, his secretary, the Overseas Council, the governor or any senior magistrate and claim that, if Lisbon authorities received too many *queixas*, an administrator was not behaving according to the norms, which, in turn, would earned said administrator a bad reputation. His conduct could become subject to investigation if his colleagues confirmed these complaints and that the administrator could be suspended from office and sent to Lisbon. Such checks exerted coercive effect forcing administrators to cooperate in order becoming target of such complaints; they also provoked conflicts by encouraging administrators to denounce uncooperative colleagues. If members of any single group became too powerful, grumbling and complaining (*mumurações*) by the population would prevent them from obtaining too much influence. Officials were thus forced to cooperate with each other, since various administrative entities all had a say in the management of affairs, they needed to agree on the implementation of policies. For instance, if a governor proved obstructive, a gentle reminder might take the form of delays in the payment of his salary from taxes levied by the Municipal Council or the customs. This mutual cooperation was a symbiosis of all interests. When jurisdictions were contested in cases of conflict usually focused on illegal trade the crown remained the final arbiter, and his role as moderator strengthened the sovereign's power to curb these practices.

Throughout the eighteenth century there was a trend towards modernization and professionalization of the administration. Rio de Janeiro in 1800 differed from the Rio of 1690. The city had risen from a regional capital to the unofficial center of empire. The population grew steadily, between 1760 and 1803, it increased from about 30,000 to about 45,000 inhabitants.[9] While in the 1690s Rio de Janeiro could still be administrated by locals lacking any specific training, by 1800 the administration had become more complex, demanding a professional approach and guidance. Senior posts in the administration were occupied by university-trained jurists, who checked on their subordinates. This fact did not mean that locals were excluded from the colonial administration: on the contrary, it included a substantial number of Brazilian-born graduates from the University of Coimbra, and policies forbidding such officials from maintaining local ties became more flexible.

Lisbon authorities recognized the fundamental role of the administration in the regulation of illegal trade. Royal measures to restrain contraband trade were usually combined with administrative reforms. Balancing local and metropolitan interests, the administrative organization was a flexible system of regulation. Jurisdictions of the different administrative branches over commerce were subject to significant change. In the course of the eighteenth century, fundamental reforms shifted the balance from a locally-based administration to one where upholding metropolitan interests predominate. The administration, however, was always able to adapt itself to these new regulations and reassert local interests. An analysis of four important reforms of the administrative system will illustrate this point, namely a royal decree of 1721 that reversed an earlier ruling permitting governors to engage in trade; reform of the Municipal Council in 1733; installation of the High Court in 1752; and appropriation of high administrative functions by the High Court between the 1760s and 1780s. This analysis will reveal the impact of such reforms on the regulation of legal and illegal trade and the ways in which local interests reacted against these reforms.

The issue of allowing governors to engage in commercial activities was subject to debate. In practice, many a governor did participate in trade, but though officially prohibited by law from doing so.[10] An exception was the period between 1709 and 1721, during which trading by governors was legal and authorized by the king.[11] At the heart of the issue was the availability of tax money to pay the governor's salary and the potential for abuse attendant on such trade.

The Municipal Council had been the first to petition in favor of allowing governors to trade in 1692.[12] The councilmen's concern was not to expose the king's senior representative to temptation, but the question of how to pay his salary. Until 1730, the Municipal Council was responsible for municipal taxation and collection of the customs dues, the governor's salary derived from these funds. Unable to levy enough taxes for this purpose, the council hoped that the Lisbon government would allow the governor and senior officials to trade on their own account. This was the background to the Municipal Council's petition of 1692 against a measure forbidding governors to engage in commercial activities.[13] The councilors denied that trade by the governor would adversely effect general commerce and argued that the population was grumbling against the introduction of a new tax on olive oil to pay the governor's salary.

The Municipal Council's took a pragmatic point of view, maintaining that royal prohibition would be ineffectual. Even if a governor did not trade on his own account, the councilors claimed, he would favor rich merchants and leave himself open to conflict of interest and corruption. Moreover, the fact that a governor engaged in trade would be of little consequence to the general commerce. The council did argue that governors should be restricted in certain trading practices: for instance, they should not be allowed to trade with foreigners, nor to collude with influential merchants to monopolize trade.[14] The Overseas Council supported the petition presented by the Municipal Council, asserting that the governors could trade regardless of whether this was permitted or not and sympathized with the view that the imposition of additional taxes to pay for his salary would place an intolerable burden on the local economy.[15]

The Overseas Council acted on this position in 1709 when it authorized trade by governors and senior officials to trade, despite the chances that liberalization would lead to venality.[16] This decision did not pass unchallenged. Two learned men speaking respectively against and in favor of the policy authorizing governors to engage in commerce.[17] Against the notion was Francisco Barreto, a Benedictine friar and member of the Lisbon based Academy of History, and the archbishop of Braga, Ruy de Moura Telles. Barreto argued that commerce in general was evil, and especially for governors, who would be likely to abuse their position. The friar reminded the king of Friar António Vieira's sermon on the venality of officialdom. In that sermon, it was argued that senior administrators should stay pure because they represented the king's virtues. The archbishop was more worldly in his reflections. His arguments reflected the stance of the Municipal Council: governors would not necessarily abuse their position if they traded, but rather would contribute positively to commerce. Telles asserted that measures taken to prohibit trade by governors and senior crown appointees were a waste of money. The alternative, placing a financial burden on the population, was unacceptable and still would not deter a governor from engaging in commerce. The archbishop wrote that circumstances could prevent laws from being implemented to the letter, and this was one case where it was preferable to adapt legislation to reality. In his view, this was preferable to tempting senior officials to flout the law or imposing taxes against the objection of the Brazilian population.

In 1721, the king revoked the measure permitting governors and senior officials to trade.[18] He had realized that trading by senior officials was detrimental to good governance, the governor's relation with the population and the king's coffers. Regardless of the renewed prohibition, contemporaries claimed that governors continued to trade.[19] There was substantial evidence to sustain these allegations.[20] The private correspondence of Governor General Ayres de Saldanha e Albuquerque (1719-1725) and that of Viceroy Dom Fernando José de Portugal (1801-1804) reveal their commercial activities.[21] The governor of Angola in the 1760s, Francisco Innocencio de Souza Coutinho, possessed gold mines in Minas Gerais.[22] Two governors of Minas Gerais, the Count of Assumar (1717-1721) and Dom Lourenço de Almeida (1721-1732) had amassed legendary riches during their terms of office.[23] The latter was even refused the customary audience with the king upon his return to Portugal.[24] Accusations against some viceroys were defamatory and groundless. Luís de Vasconcellos e Souza (1789-1793), for instance, was accused by an anonymous author who wrote to the British consul in the following unflattering terms:

"D. Luis Vasconcellos a man of weak intellect, destitute of honour capable of taking a bribe from a beggar, as well as from the most opulent; a man who during his Vice Royship of Rio de Janeiro received through the channel of his own servants even the meanest bribe for doing common justice, that he might enrich himself, whose injustice became so glaring that on his return he was denied admittance to the Royal Presence as a punishment."[25]

The inventory of Souza's estate after his death lent credence to one of these charges, but the others were without foundation. The former viceroy seemed quite affluent. Luís de Vasconcellos e Souza, Count of Figueiró, left his heirs a sum of one hundred million reis, a considerable amount worth more than ten times his annual income during his tenure as a viceroy.[26] Illiterate he was not, he left a library of more than 700 books, including works of Abbé Raynal, Montesquieu and Montaigne. Nor was Souza out of favor with the queen. After his return, the former viceroy kissed the hands of the Prince Regent, who was pleased to nominate him to preside over both the Treasury Council, the Supreme Court, and over the Royal Treasury.[27] Upon receiving the news of his safe arrival in Lisbon, the Municipal Council of Rio de Janeiro organized lavish festivities and even erected a statue of their former viceroy.[28] Precedence for such public recognition had been set by his predecessor, the Marquis of Lavradio, who was also honored with a statue after his death became known in the Brazilian capital.[29] In contrast, Vasconcellos' successor, the Count de Rezende (1794-1802), did leave a legacy of nepotism and improper commercial activities.[30] That Lisbon authorities condoned the viceroy's participation in commerce was evident from the fact that the secretary of state allowed the Count of Rezende to leave his vessel in Lisbon before inspectors could board to search for contraband gold.[31]

Few governors were prosecuted for their behavior. Exceptions were governors of Benguella (Angola), of Santa Catarina and of Colônia do Sacramento, who were sent in chains to Lisbon.[32] Only one governor of Rio de Janeiro was ever arrested, Francisco de Castro e Moraes was condemned for his behavior during the French invasion of Duguay-Trouin in 1711. As his goods were being confiscated, the Overseas

Council remarked that they should amount to an impressive sum. The governor had been engaged in a lucrative trade to Minas Gerais, but at a time when it was still legal.[33] Some 20 years after the confiscation, Moraes' wife was still petitioning in vain for the restoration of his property or for compensation.[34] Military defeat was evidently a worse crime than contraband commerce.

Low salaries provided an incentive for governors to engage in trade. One of the most vocal complainers about his salary was the Marquis do Lavradio (viceroy 1769-1779). Pointing out that he was an exception among governors because he had not traded privately, Lavradio declared that:

> "I am glad that I have not yet been thought of at home as a thief, tyrant or as being voluntarily in Brazil, which are the honorable titles to which we poor governors of America are exposed; I believe that the fact that they have not yet remembered to call me these despicable names is attributable to the services that I render to this government."[35]

In his private letters, Lavradio mentioned that he had incurred heavy debts for his services to the crown, and claimed that his salary as governor of Bahia, and later as viceroy, was even insufficient to cover all his expenses.[36] Like his predecessor, the Count da Azumbuja, Lavradio had to borrow money locally at high interest.[37] Yet, as Nuno Monteiro has demonstrated, many members of the high nobility in Portugal remained poor and deeply in debt. A posting as viceroy or governor overseas did not change their financial circumstances.[38] The most they could expect was to cover all the expenses they incurred in Brazil. On his return to Portugal, a governor or viceroy could look forward to recognition for his good services to the crown, in the form of either subsidies or titles, provided, of course, he was not refused an audience with the king as in the case of Dom Lourenço de Almeida.[39] The king's lukewarm reaction to this venality was no surprise. Trading was not generally seen as a nefarious activity. Rumor had it that even the king's son, the Crown Prince Dom José, was involved in illegal commercial ventures to Veracruz in New Spain.[40] Since the Municipal

Council was responsible for levying the taxes to pay the governor's salary, the councillors were in a powerful position. A governor who acted against their wishes could count on problems with tax farming, which provided the revenues for his salary. The Municipal Council in Rio de Janeiro comprised of five councillors, a procurator and a secretary. Not much is known about the way the councilors were elected, but it is safe to assume that, as in Salvador and other places throughout the empire, they were chosen at random by a child in a kind of lottery for a non-renewable period of three years.[41] The two permanent positions were those of procurator and secretary, who enjoyed exceptional power. The crown-appointed *juiz de fora* was the procurator and president of the council, represented metropolitan interests and acted as a curb on local excesses. The secretary was a local resident who owned his office by purchase or inheritance and remained in office for life.

The Municipal Council defended the interests of the colonial elites. Fernanda Bicalho has demonstrated how these local elites redefined themselves as a nobility who had won their position by cultivating and defending the colony at their own expense.[42] They petitioned for subsidies to let their sons study in Coimbra, and took steps to ensure that administrative positions would remain in their hands.[43] The pool of potential councilors was a closed community, many of whom lived outside the city boundaries.[44] They were protective as to who could or could not be elected to the senate, and protested immediately when "outsiders" such as New Christians (i.e. merchants) tried to enter their ranks.[45] In practice, only 'good men' *(homens bons)*, i.e. children and grandchildren of former councilmen could be elected to the senate. This exclusiveness led to disagreements with the merchants of Rio de Janeiro, who argued that Portuguese-born people should also be eligible.[46] The Municipal Council reported to the king whenever they agreed or disagreed with the policies of the judiciary, governors and clergy.[47] Conflicts among the different agencies of the government were endemic and were easily provoked by the constant infringement of one another's jurisdictions. In cases where the governor threatened the Municipal Council too aggressively, the councilors invoked the privileges exempting them from arrest.[48]

The dependency of governors and magistrates on the Municipal

Council for their salaries was a source of great friction. Should one or the other exhibit recalcitrance in reaching a *modus operandi* with the councilors, the Council retaliated by withholding their salaries. Both governors and *ouvidores* did complain about their incomes, which the Municipal Council used as a bargaining chip.[49] For their part, governors tried to interfere in the electoral process in order to gain the upper hand in this antagonistic relationship.[50]

The governor and the Municipal Council clashed intensely and repeatedly under Luís Vahia Monteiro (1725-1733).[51] Each side made severe allegations to the king about the other's improper behavior and transgression of the law. The governor accused the secretary of the Municipal Council of participating in, and upholding, illegal trade and thereby robbing the king's treasury.[52] The Municipal Council accused the governor of being despotic and oppressing the inhabitants of Rio de Janeiro, especially by his policies of suppressing illegal trade.[53] One major result, totally unanticipated by the councilors, was that the king finally overcame his hesitations and applauded the governor's measure ordering that the contracts for the customhouse be farmed out by the royal treasury.[54] This move was a severe blow to the power of the local administration, but essential to the coherence and consistency of tax farming not only in Rio de Janeiro, but in all major Brazilian ports.

The Municipal Council never recovered from this setback to its jurisdiction. Petitions to the king dwindled in number after Luís Vahia Monteiro's death, and mostly dealt with routine matters such as confirmation of privileges of its members, especially exemption from military service.[55] The Municipal Council became an institution confined to the sphere of local affairs, and the councilors became the objects of contempt for members of the royal administration.[56] Nevertheless, the king, the secretary of state and the Overseas Council continued to consult the Municipal Council in local affairs. Their voice was most strongly felt in the 1790s, with the strong personality of the controversial *juiz de fora* Balthazar da Silva Lisboa, did the Council regain some of its clout in governmental policies.[57] The same shift in power occurred in the small ports of the captaincy. The councilors of Paratí, Angra dos Reis and Cabo Frio did not enjoy the same protection from arrest as their colleagues in Rio de Janeiro. After many reports of illegal trade in gold with foreign vessels, the governor of Rio de Janeiro decided to 'defend' these small ports. A military detachment literally took over these ports, imprisoning the councilors and imposing the will of the governor on their population.[58] A repercussion of these drastic measures was that alternative gold-smuggling routes were taken over by the military personnel who were sent from Rio de Janeiro.

The Municipal Council in Rio de Janeiro yielded most of its jurisdiction to the royal treasury. One of the most important positions in the colonial administration, the office of *provedor da fazenda real* (chief inspector of the royal treasury) was sold and inherited in both Salvador and Rio de Janeiro.[59] In both cities, this position stayed in the same family for three generations in Salvador and for two in Rio de Janeiro. The local roots of the *provedor* made the office highly contested by the king and Portuguese born administrators. Like the members of the Municipal Council of Rio de Janeiro, the *provedor* enjoyed judicial immunity, but in practice this did not prevent him from being accused of abuse of office and being arrested.

The first person to exercise the office of chief inspector of the royal treasury in eighteenth century Rio de Janeiro was Luís Lopes Pegado, who served in this office since the 1690s.[60] Already in 1705 he was accused of abuse of office by the *juiz de fora* and imprisoned.[61] After putting this behind him, Luís Lopes Pegado left for Salvador where he bought the identical office, which remained in the family for three generations.[62]

In 1709, the king decided to put the office of *provedor* in Rio de Janeiro on sale again.[63] Apparently this was a controversial move because the king found it necessary to defend the policy by arguing that he was in dire financial need and that he should therefore be allowed to sell an office of such great use to the public. The same issue came up again in 1714. The office was sold by auction, but when Francisco de Amaral Gurgel offered forty thousand cruzados for the position, a new controversy erupted. The Overseas Council held that Gurgel was unacceptable for such an office, because he was a suspect in the murder of the previous *provedor* and was already too powerful.[64] The king opted to accept the lucrative offer and appointed Gurgel to the office. His tenure was short, Gurgel had to renounce his office when he was arrested on the murder charges.[65] This was a classic example of the royal will thwarted by the collective outrage of colonists and local magistrates. After Gurgel's resignation, Bertholomeu Cordovil Sequeira took over the office, which was to remain in his family for two generations, though not without problems. Already, within two years of his taking office, Bertholomeu left for Lisbon to defend himself against allegations that he had traded with an English vessel.[66] Although Bertholomeu was soon exonerated, he did have to give up his position for two years.[67] When Bertholomeu petitioned for compensation, which he estimated at 20, 000 cruzados, the Overseas Council ruled that a sentence of "not guilty" did not mean that he was innocent, and only granted him only a part of the official salary and not the emoluments. The council concluded that only a minor part of the total income which that position might reasonably have been expected to yield was sufficient.[68]

The offices of *provedor* could be bequeathed to a son, so when Bertholomeu fell ill after serving for 30 years, his rightful successor was his son Francisco de Cordovil Sequeira e Mello who petitioned to replace is father. Francisco promised to serve "with that same love, zeal and disinterest."[69] Gomes Freire de Andrade, governor of Minas Gerais and Rio de Janeiro, had very different views on the abilities of the *provedor*'s son. He had left instructions for the interim governor in Rio de Janeiro, Mathias Coelho e Souza, to let the secretary of the treasury, and not Francisco, succeed to the position.[70] This move caught Francisco by surprise, and he wrote a vehement protest to the king asserting that he was the legitimate heir to the office. The governor eventually did approve, but Francisco had to pay one third of his income as a *donativo*, a payment made to rent an office.[71] Francisco finally gained royal approval to inherit the office, but Gomes Freire continued to have reservations about the *provedor*'s performance.[72]

Francisco de Cordovil Sequeira e Mello was to face many investigations into his conduct. In 1748, the governor arrested him, along with the *juiz de fora*, over a jurisdictional dispute.[73] Arrested again in 1761 for a crime against a captain from Angola, he was sentenced to a three-year banishment in Rio Grande do Sul. The accusation was that the *provedor*, his wife, and his slaves had beaten up the captain in their own house.[74] After a three-year suspension the *provedor* was restored to office. He never had left for the south, because further investigations showed that the original testimonies in the original had not been made under oath.[75] The last and most serious blow to Francisco de Cordovil de Sequeira e Mello came in 1769, six years after Rio de Janeiro had become the capital of Brazil. The viceroy suspended him from office over alleged irregularities in the ledgers of the treasury.[76] Francisco had fallen victim to the legacy of Pombaline reforming zeal for greater professionalization in government: the royal treasury was being reformed, a new council of the treasury was created, and the viceroy sought any opportunity to oust him.[77] Similar incidents occurred in Recife and Salvador, leading to the replacement of such contractors by career civil servants.[78]

The king abolished *de jure* the office of *provedor da fazenda* in 1769, officially delegating this position to the treasurer of the king's coffer but unofficially, delegating the *provedor*'s functions to a high court judge.[79] Francisco was not a witness to such charges because by then he was incarcerated in a Lisbon jail where he was to spend for the rest of his life.[80] Significantly, he was not found guilty of any crime.[81] His son, Felipe de Cordovil e Sequeira e Mello, demanded compensation.[82] As a graduate from the University of Coimbra, Felipe asked for appointment to replace the high court judge in Rio de Janeiro, the *desembargador e provedor da fazenda real*, who had taken over his father's functions.[83] The son's request was denied, but the queen arranged a financial settlement in compensation, and Felipe did buy the office of secretary of the Municipal Council. There, he joined forces with the *juiz de fora*, Balthazar da Silva Lisboa, and became part of the vocal opposition against the viceroy.[84]

Forced resignations as an effect of professionalization were not limited to the royal treasury. The post of *juiz ouvidor da alfândega* (judge of the customs) was also affected. Placed on sale in the first decade of the eighteenth century, after being separated from the office of *provedor da fazenda*.[85] The post stayed in the hands of the same family until 1786, when the incumbent was suspended, and a high court judge took over his position.[86] The professionalization of the administration since the 1760s increased the power of high court judges at the expense of officials who had inherited their administrative positions. As a consequence, the administration came into the hands of individuals trained at the University of Coimbra and those mostly born in Portugal who were less likely to serve local interests. But, as the following study of the high court judges will demonstrate, local society did adapt to the new situation by incorporating these judges into local society. Before the installation of the High Court, all matters concerning crimes in Rio de Janeiro were handled by a *juiz de fora* and an *ouvidor geral*, both appointed by the king for a period of at least three years. The jurisdictions of these two functionaries overlapped, and the nature of their jurisdictions and functions stemmed from the different institutions to which they were appointed. Whereas the *juiz de fora* was associated with the Municipal Council dealt with local affairs, the office of *ouvidor geral*, as a separate branch of the crown administration with affairs that had an impact on governance of the state.[87] The *juiz de fora* would judge cases within the city or falling in the sphere of the Municipal Council, such as the customs contracts, the *ouvidor geral* took charge of civil and criminal cases of general interest to the whole captaincy of Rio de Janeiro. In 1752, the office of *ouvidor geral* became incorporated into the High Court, and the *juiz de fora* remained independent as the Municipal Council's president.[88]

The creation of the High Court in Rio de Janeiro was a milestone in the judicial and fiscal administration of southern Brazil. Its installation in 1752 was combined with the founding of the *Mesa da Inspecção*, the Inspection Board, and the application of new sumptuary laws. The Inspection Board, under the presidency of a "superintendent of gold," took over some of the responsibilities for quality control from the customs, as regarded sugar and tobacco.[89] The high court judges (*desembargadores*) were effectively second only to the governor or viceroy at the apex of colonial administration.[90] The king's prosecutor and the judge of the king's treasury (*juiz dos feitos da coroa e fazenda*) heard all cases appealed from the *provedor da fazenda*.[91] But the *provedor da fazenda* continued with the task of recording denunciations of contraband and passing them on to the *ouvidor do crime*, who had also become a high court judge.[92] Upon the "abolition" of the office of *provedor da fazenda*, another high court judge served this function. This shift of responsibilities from a proprietor office to a crown appointed high court judge coincided with the founding of the general treasury (*erário régio*) in Rio de Janeiro, whereby the *provedor da fazenda* assumed responsibility for the treasuries of Angola and Portuguese India.[93] High court judges as well as the *ouvidores* and the *juizes de fora,* received their training at Coimbra. In contrast to Spanish America, no university existed in Brazil or in any other Portuguese colony. As students, future high ranking officials of state discussed policies for empire, and although the Brazilians in Coimbra still formed an independent clique, a strong *esprit de corps* that developed in this arena was to be reflected in the expression of a Luso-Brazilian consciousness.[94] Not only high court judges but many of the senior administrators also received their education in Coimbra.[95]

This takeover by officials trained in civil law might suggest that administration had fewer local ties. That, however, would not be an accurate picture. Stuart Schwartz has elaborated quite extensively on the effects of the "Brazilianization" of the Salvadoran High Court.[96] Since the 1730s, all royally appointed judges had not been allowed to marry locally, unless they had royal consent.[97] Just after the installation of the High Court, one of the judges asked for such permission, which was denied.[98] Even though the bishop of Rio de Janeiro, the chancellor of the High Court and the governor of Rio de Janeiro pleaded in his favor, the king was very slow to yield.[99] The Secretary of State, Sebastião de Carvalho e Mello, later Marquis of Pombal, strongly objected to such marriages by crown judges, arguing that judges would lose their objectivity and would be prone to abuse of office and conflict of interests.[100] By the 1790s, this restrictive policy changed dramatically. So automatic and unquestioned was the granting of such permissions, that high court judges and *juizes de fora* did not even bother to give the names of their prospective brides when petitioning for such licenses.[101] Therefore, the delocalization and centralization of the administration that had taken place in the 1750s gradually achieve a balance between colonial and metropolitan forces. Arno and Maria José Wheeling's book on the Carioca High Court demonstrate similarities with these findings concerning the Carioca High Court.[102] Out of the 87 high court judges, they found 67 references to the judges' place of birth. Sixteen of the 65 were born in Brazil. Of those sixteen, five were born in Rio de Janeiro. Over time the number of Brazilian judges increased. The only Brazilian judge on the High Court from 1752 to the late 1760s was the first chancellor. Only two other Brazilian born judges were installed during the reign of Pombal (ended in 1777), and since then a steady stream of about three Brazilian-born high court judges per decade followed. The seven judges born in Rio de Janeiro were evenly spread over the decades, yet the Wehlings did not find any reference to a Carioca born judge in de early nineteenth-century. Yet throughout the period between 1752 and 1808, Brazilian born judges always remained a minority. Another mechanism to ensure the balance of royal and local authority was the nomination process for public office. The combination of sale of offices and low incomes for administrators was traditionally put forward as an explanation for the venality of the bureaucracy. In fact, in comparison to Spanish America, few offices in the Portuguese administration were either sold or farmed out, and even these limited practices declined. An analysis of the sale of offices and of officials' incomes provides an interesting perspective on the importance of the individual branches of public administration in colonial Rio de Janeiro.

An individual could accede to public office in three different ways: he could buy and own his office; he could lease an office in return for a financial donation (*donativo*); or they could be directly appointed to his office in return for past services to the crown. The number of office holders slowly diminished. Offices that had earlier been sold were leased as they became vacant.[103] Leasing could occur in two ways. Either a person could send a petition to the king asking for his recognition of military or administrative services given to the crown by himself or by his family or he could make a bid for a specific office. Judges, governors and viceroys were royal appointees. Until the 1770s, however, the senior positions of the treasury, the customs and the mint were bought and owned by Brazilian-born administrators.

The amount of money for the *donativos* could vary considerably. The reason was that some persons obtained their offices not only through payment, but also in recognition of their services. For example the administrator of the textiles in the customs paid *donativos* ranging between 30$000 and 650$000 reis to lease his office. One explanation for this discrepancy might be that there was a considerable difference in the administrators' tasks from one year to another. The secretary of the quartermaster (N.°34, *escrivão da almoxarife*) donated 17$500 and 84$000 reis a year to lease his office in 1744. Perhaps there were two secretaries, or the king received another offer after he had already accepted the first. The latter assumption would also apply in the case of the secretary of the balance of the customs (N.°38, *escrivão da balança da alfândega*) whose office was leased for the sums of 106$667 and 124$000 reis in the same year. Despite these problems with data, some general tendencies are discernible. There was a relationship between the sensitivity of the office and the *donativo*. The *donativo* was relatively high for offices that conferred individual regulatory authority over contraband trade. For instance, the inspector and the secretary of the register in Parahibuna (N.°XXVIII and N.°XXX) on the gold route to Minas Gerais paid a *donativo* amounting to 70 % of anticipated receipts, whereas the normal rate was one third.[104] Offices in Angra dos Reis and Paratí (N.°I-VII, XXXI-XLVII), towns situated close to the old gold route to Minas Gerais, sometimes yielded more in *donativo* than their estimated income, whereas the same offices in the less strategically situated towns of Cabo Frio and Macacú (N.°VIII-XV, XVI-XXVII) would find few bidders even at one third of the expected income.

With the sale of offices, the king unintentionally taxed venality. Since the yields on offices that were more sensitive were higher than officially stipulated salaries, the donor expected additional income derived from illegal activities. Not surprisingly, local administrators at times protested against the renting or sale of these offices.[105] Even though the king claimed that "it was never my royal intention that incapable persons should serve in these offices," the practice persisted, and the taint of unaccountability and of unreliability continued to be associated with such functions.[106] The practice of selling and leasing offices disappeared slowly, even as suggestions were made that all offices in Rio de Janeiro should be farmed out.[107] Before 1786, there were 18 offices in the possession of private persons, while 26 were nominated after paying the *donativo* and 122 were appointed. But by

1786, only five offices had changed from being owned or farmed out to being nominated.[108] The filling of offices by ownership, nomination and farming of offices subject to constant fluctuations. For many positions, I found only a single *donativo* payment. In yet other cases, a senior administrator or the treasury council nominated the office holders (Table 5.2).

Another indication of the importance of offices was their income. Data for incomes were based on sometimes contradictory evaluations by high officials such as the governor, crown judges, the royal treasurer, or the municipal councilors. The crown officials' level of income was not guaranteed, as only a part of it derived from salaries. Another part was contributed by emoluments during festivities, and a third by fees levied for certain services. Invariably, errors and inconsistencies in assessments were frequent, as is apparent from the assessment of income for the guard of the ships (N.°113, *guarda mor dos navios*), respectively assessed at 40$000 reis in 1694, 400$000 reis in 1734, and 42$000 reis in 1743. There was most probably a mistake in the 1734 assessment by the crown judge, perhaps because of a clerk's writing error. The higher the income the state derived from the office, the higher the official's personal income would be. This pattern becomes clear from analysis of data for the secretaries or scribes, whose incomes differed drastically depending under whom they served. In 1786, salaries in the 100$000 reis range went to the secretaries of the *alcaide* or bailiff, *almoxarife* or master of the storehouse (N.°34), and *meirinho da cidade* or municipal officer (N.°66) who handled local affairs not relating to illegal trade. Occupying the middle range were positions such as the secretaries of the treasury (N.°53) and of the orphan's trust (N.°76), who received 550$000 reis and 300$000 reis respectively. Most of the secretaries of customs officers had high incomes, 1:600$000 reis for the secretary of the customs (N.°33, in 1803), 600$000 reis for the secretary in charge of supervising the unloading of cargoes at the customs (N.°50), 1:200$000 reis for the secretary charged with the opening of the crates (N.°70), 1:000$000 reis for the *escrivão da mesa grande* (secretary of the big table) (N.°71). The exception was the secretary in charge of the weights used in the custom house (N.°38), who received only about 290$000 reis. The secretaries in the customs were strategically placed with respect to illegal trade. The taxation of incoming products was dependent on their judgment. Other secretaries in powerful, and thus lucrative, positions were the secretary of the court of appeal (N.°36), secretary of the judge for inheritances of absent people (N.°59), secretary of the *ouvidor* for criminal cases, secretary of the *ouvidor* in the captaincy (N.°78 & 79), and the secretary of the viceroy (N.°179) all of whom directly served high court judges and the viceroy.

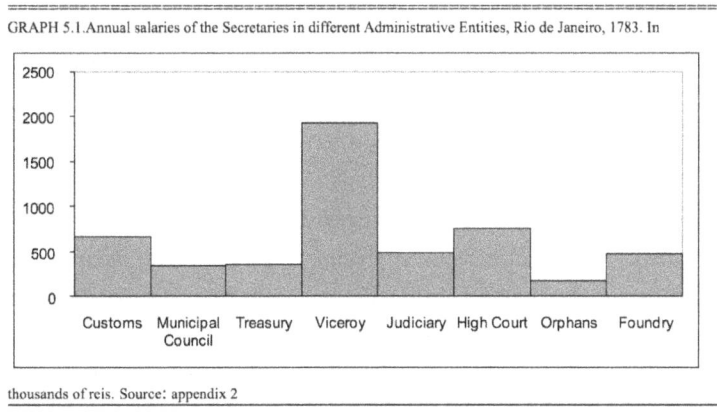

GRAPH 5.1. Annual salaries of the Secretaries in different Administrative Entities, Rio de Janeiro, 1783. In thousands of reis. Source: appendix 2

Secretaries' salaries are broken down by administrative branch (Graph 5.1). Obviously, the secretary of the viceroy earned the highest income in 1783. The high income of secretaries of high court judges underlined their importance. That secretaries in the customs were ranked third in terms of income should not be too surprising, given the sensitivity of their offices as regards illegal trade. At the lower end were secretaries of the treasury, of the Municipal Council, and especially of the orphans' trust, which reflecting their more circumscribed and less profitable areas of jurisdiction Royal efforts to modernize the administration met with strong local opposition. The best illustration of how centralized administration clashed with local interests was the state of arrears in the custom house since the late 1780s. The custom house was a sensitive administrative organ, since it was where most illegal trade took place. As the place where goods were assessed for taxation, customs was also the place where merchants could receive tax breaks. There was an elaborate and complex relationship between officials and merchants. If administrators needed to borrow money for their *donativo*, they turned to merchants. Family ties and shared interests also brought merchants and their regulators close together as Moutoukias demonstrated in the case in colonial Buenos Aires.[109] This situation did change in Rio de Janeiro towards the end of the colonial period. Indeed, the customs became an arena of constant bickering, dismissal of officials, discoveries of frauds and winking at illegal trade. This situation was attributable to the monopolization of power by the viceroy and important high court judges. The local elites defied this monopolization and, by 1806, illegal trade had become such an openly accepted part of colonial society that intervention by administrators would have been fruitless. The judge of the customs, José António Ribeiro Freire, described the situation to the viceroy as the follows:

> "The lack of execution of the aforementioned law, had as a result that the officials were not zealous in levying taxes. The officials are called names when they confiscate goods, not only by contrabandists and their partners, but also by the common people, who threaten their life at every moment of the day. Therefore. these administrators are evasive in their work, and close their eyes to contraband, with the most terrible consequences."[110]

Thus, just two years before the opening of the ports, the situation had worsened so much that not only the prince regent's, but also the administrator's authority was defied. Not only was condoned illegal trade accepted as normal, but measures taken to restrict illegal trade that had not been previously condoned now began to prove ineffective.

Both the organization of the customs and the economic situation in Rio de Janeiro contributed to this breakdown of authority. The custom office was reorganized after the old judge of the customs was laid off in 1786. A Coimbra-educated high court judge, António José Cabral de Almeida, took over the role of the local judge and set out to modernize the administration. If this reform had been carried through to completion, taxation on goods would have become stricter, leading inevitably to adverse reactions on the part of the merchants who were used to tax breaks.

TABLE 5.2. Nomination of Custom House Administrators: 1786 and earlier.

Office	Nominated in 1786:	Before 1786:
Administrador	Royal Treasury in Lisbon	Owner
Conferente da Porte	Treasury Council	No record
Escrivão da Balança	Treasury Council	*Donativo*
Escrivão da Descarga	Treasury Council	*Donativo*
Escrivão da Abertura	Possession by Customs Judge	Owner
Escrivão Mesa Grande	Treasury Council	Owner
Feitor da Abertura	Treasury Council	*Donativo*
Feitor da Balança	Treasury Council	No record
Fiel do Thezoureiro	Treasurer Customs	No record
Guarda Ajd. do Fiel	Treasury Council	No record
Guarda Mor	Owner	Owner
Guarda do Ponte	Treasury Council	No record
Guarda da Marinha	Treasury Council	No record
Guarda da Porta	Treasury Council	No record
Juiz da Balança	Customs Judge, Viceroy	*Donativo*
Juiz da Alfândega	High Court Judge serving	Owner
Porteiro	Treasury Council	Owner
Selador	Owner	Owner
Thezoureiro	Viceroy, Municipal Council	Municipal Council

Source: see appendix 2.

The suspension of the old judge of the customs, António Martins Britto, brought about a drastic change of administration and personnel in the customs. Both his immediate successors, António José Cabral de Almeida and José António Ribeiro Veiga, found that Britto's ledgers were in great disorder and rife with omissions.[111] The old judge protested against this inquiry, arguing that personal frictions and internal disturbances provoking viceregal intervention were the true grounds for his suspension.[112] Almeida did reorganize the personnel of the customs. He dismissed the *escrivão da mesa grande* (secretary of the big table), the *fiel da mesa da abertura* (steward of the table for opening packages) and the *porteiro da alfândega* (doorman of the customs) on suspicion of fraud. They were replaced by Almeida's confidants.[113] His successor, Veiga, suspended yet another two officials, the *escrivao da mesa da abertura* (secretary for opening goods), and *escrivão da descarga da alfândega* (secretary for unloading cargoes at the customs), after uncovering their fraudulent behavior.[114]

Another dimension of the actions of high court judges is that most officials of the customs were nominated either by the Council of the Treasury, which was dominated by high court judges, or by the viceroy. The Council of the Treasury consisted of the chancellor, the *provedor da fazenda*, the chancellor of the High Court, the king's procurator (*procurador da coroa e fazenda*) i.e. José António Ribeiro Veiga, and two lower officials.[115] Thus Veiga's and Almeida's moves asserted the High Court's authority over the nomination process of customs officials.

Dom Rodrigo de Souza Coutinho, Secretary of State in Portugal, took some steps against these policies, pleading for a reduced role of the High Court in financial affairs and for the Court's independence from the viceroy.[116] The high court judge's strategy was frustrated with the 1800 nomination of a new administrator of customs by the royal treasury in Lisbon nominated the administrator, Luís de Noronha Sorrizão, the only person in the customs directly appointed from Lisbon. This exceptional appointment led to immediate conflicts with the judge of the customs in Rio de Janeiro. After an exchange of words, the new administrator, Sorrizão, started complaining about abuses in the customs.[117] The main problem concerned jurisdiction, especially since the administrator claimed the authority to nominate other custom officials. The judge of the customs responded with the by now hallowed tradition: he opened a judicial inquiry into the administrator's behavior and found him guilty of neglecting to tax goods belonging to the merchant João Pedro Meyer.[118] Despite receiving powerful support from the viceroy (the Count de Rezende), the chancellor of the High Court and the *juiz de fora*, Veiga eventually had to yield because of Sorrizão's good connections at court.[119] The secretary of state naturally sent a letter of reprimand to the high court judge. Under the next viceroy, Dom Fernando José de Portugal, the judge appealed the case to Lisbon. The secretary of state asserted that Veiga's intrusion into the area of jurisdiction of the administrator was at the root of all the problems.[120] Both the judge and the administrator of the customs survived the judicial quarrels, but the judge started losing his grip on his own personnel.

Fraud was the *Leitmotif* of customs officials; this behavior did not change with the arrival of new personnel. There were some major problems in combating illegal trade that could not be solved merely by better bookkeeping methods. The High Court's increased control over nominations of minor functionaries furthered their susceptibility to bribes and at the same time royal legislation started to impede the lower officials from their profits if they prosecuted smugglers.[121]

A major source income for officials consisted of confiscations through denunciations, but misdirected legislation undid part of this fraud-prevention mechanism. The 1755 Statutes of the *Junta do Comércio* (Council of Commerce) stated that all confiscated contraband should be burned publicly.[122] This provision caused problems, since the officials traditionally received one third of the confiscated goods. Therefore, the judge of the customs suggested selling these goods to one of the captains of the many foreign vessels anchored in the harbor of Rio de Janeiro at the time of confiscation.[123] Still, the viceroy urged the judge of the customs to burn some illegal goods, and officials of the customs complained continually that they received no compensation for their discoveries of contraband.[124] Without the financial incentive to reward them, officials were unlikely to combat illegal trade nor was legislation against their venality of any effect. In July 1807, just a few months before Brazilian ports were officially opened to foreign vessels, the judge of the customs nailed a viceregal decree to the doors of the custom house.[125] It was a futile reminder that any cooperation between customs officials and contrabandists was strictly forbidden. By then, both crown and officials had already lost all authority over the prosecution of illegal trade.

The administration in Rio de Janeiro was caught between local and royal interests. Local interests were served by the entry of administrators into Carioca society: the more officials there were of Brazilian descent, married into Brazilian society, or with investments in the local economy, the more attention would be paid to local interests.

Royal authority was buttressed by the king's power to regulate officials' income and jurisdictions. As the only person who could settle problems of jurisdiction, the king determined who could regulate what part of the illegal economy. The king had long-term policies to improve his grip on the expanding economy, nevertheless he took local interests into account. The king depended on his subjects' willingness to pay taxes in exchange for his royal protection.

The ideal economy benefitted from a symbiotic interdependence between administrators and merchants. The administrators needed merchants in order to advance money for their *donativos* or bribes, while the merchants needed the administrators to earn tax breaks. This system ebbed away by the end of the eighteenth and beginning of the nineteenth century as Coimbra-trained high court judges who took over crucial parts of the administration breached the trust that Carioca society had placed in its commercial regulators. This massive change combined with the increasing presence of foreign vessels due to the Napoleonic wars, eliminated the gap between condoned and proscribed illegal trade. As a consequence, colonial officials in Brazil had lost their control over the regulation of illegal trade by 1808.

CHAPTER 6

DISCOURSE ON ILLEGALITY

Eighteenth-century laws, administrative correspondence, economic treatises, sermons, and satirical poems are filled with references to contraband trade, giving the impression that illegal trade was not merely a widespread phenomenon in Brazil, but an integral part of colonial economy and society. We have seen that officials condoned some illegal trade activities, whereas they took legal action against others. This dual policy presents a major legal issue: what were the circumstances under which an illegal act could be condoned? The analysis of discourse on illegal trade in this chapter pinpoints ways in which contemporaries tried to reconcile this legal issue with colonial mores.

An individual's or a nation's ability to conduct contraband trade with impunity was an expression of their higher social status or prestige. As the Brazilian historian Laura de Mello e Souza has argued for Minas Gerais, members of the lower class were "declassified" (*desclassificados*), outsiders of colonial society.[1] This meant that officials were more prone to prosecute poor and statusless persons for illegal acts, whereas those of a more elevated social status could be powerful (*poderso*) and thus above the law. The same social hierarchy is valid for the transatlantic world. British, French, and Dutch merchants claimed to be of higher social status on the grounds that Portugal and Brazil were dependent on their country for their political and military survival. In discourse about illegal commerce with foreign nationals, these nationals' ability to engage in contraband trade was a measure of their relative strength and higher status.[2]

The late eighteenth century, a period of rampant illegal trade, coincided with a revision of Brazil's role in the Portuguese empire. In this period the principle of primacy took precedence over that of utility. Portuguese economists argued that what was good for the mother country served the common well-being of both colony and mother country. Their visions reflected the influence of French physiocrats, who argued that agriculture was more important than manufacturing and that the market could be protected. Brazilian economists, however, were influenced by British free traders who held that manufacturing was more important and that there should be no restrictions on the market. This controversy gave rise to debates between the Portuguese and the Brazilian intelligentsia about what was most advantageous (*útil*) to Portugal and Brazil.[3] Portuguese authorities approached the issue by proposing the primacy of the mother country over the colony.

Illegal commercial activities were not inherently immoral, but condemned for their lack of utility. The results of illegal commerce were what determined whether this practice was despicable: if illegal commerce had positive effects, for instance the acquisition of silver from Spanish America, then contraband trade became indeed a good and advantageous act. The immorality of illegal trade depended not only on the results, but also on the actors' status. Contemporary discourse stigmatized some persons engaging in illegal commerce as "poor and destitute" (*pobre e miserável*) when their commercial activities were not advantageous to the general economy. This double standard in the application of the law meant that illegal activities could be condoned depending on the social status of the participant.

Morality became an issue only on special occasions, namely instances of national disaster and decline. An important theme in early modern Portuguese literature, and the notion of decline was seized upon particularly in times of military, political, economic and natural crises: the Battle of Alcazar Quibir (1578); the subsequent incorporation into the Spanish empire (1580-1640); the loss of the Portuguese Asian empire; the war with the Netherlands (1625-1661); the fall of sugar prices (1680s-1690s); the Lisbon earthquake of 1755; and the wars that threatened Portugal after the French revolution (1794-1807). Contemporaries sought, and found, divine retribution in such crises and their collective punishment for their immoral behavior.[4]

The most influential work on the relationship between mother country and colony, or the "old colonial system," was written by the Paulista historian Fernando Novais.[5] Novais revived an expression already used by colonial bureaucrats in the first years of the nineteenth century.[6] Arguing along the lines of dependency theory, Novais asserted that Brazil's economy was subordinated to that of Portugal and that Brazil's economic development was restricted as a result.[7] However, newer historiography, most notably from João Fragoso and Larissa Brown, has argued that the Brazilian economy can not simply seen as subordinate to Portuguese interests.[8] As I will demonstrate from my analysis of the discourse of illegality, Brazil and Portugal were on an equal footing in relation to each other. Even if Brazilian merchants ostensibly agreed that all European commerce with Brazil should be mediated by Portugal, they would in fact accept this condition when it worked in their favor. For the part of the eighteenth century, Portuguese discourse on political economy served to legitimize Portugal's position in the empire. By the end of the eighteenth century as commerce became based on a "primacy" principle, Brazilians challenged the "utility" principle that all European commerce should be conducted through Portugal. At the same time contraband trade spun out of the control of the local officials.

Contemporary definitions of contraband emphasized the identity of the perpetrators and the nature of the consequences rather than the act itself. These definitions legitimized the "utility" principle. Portuguese legislation described illegal commerce as "*descaminhos da fazenda real*," i.e. putting royal money in wrong hands, or embezzlement from the royal treasury.[9] In order to stress the fraudulent dimension, legislation put an emphasis on the victim that these actions deprived of revenue. The royal treasury, or in other words, the king, occupied the dominant position as the injured party. As a victim of this criminal act, the king had the prerogative to pardon, thereby displaying the royal magnanimity, or to punish the perpetrator, thereby showing himself as the unwavering upholder of the law. Embezzlement from the king was an act not only against a person, but against Portugal and society. If the fraud victimized the king as a sovereign as well as the nation and the people he personified, the contrabandist was also a victim, because he was contravening rulings that were in everybody's, including his own, best interest. Illegal trade not only affected the king, his subjects and the contrabandists, but it also had drastic consequences for commerce in general. Illegal commerce gave the dishonest merchant a material advantage, as allowing both the contrabandist and the purchaser of smuggled goods to undercut current market prices. This pressured upright colleagues to do the same in order to compete with the contrabandists' low prices.[10] Because it was disruptive to commerce legislation condemned illegal trade as *um crime pernicioso*, (a pernicious crime.)[11]

The legislation, based on the principle that it was advantageous to society that only those persons of sufficiently high social status should engage in commerce, had an impact on everybody engaged in commercial activities. The best known example of persons prohibited from trading were the *commissários volantes*, or itinerant traders, who traveled on board the fleets to Brazil trading in the name of Portuguese and foreign merchants. Pombaline legislation tried to outlaw these peddlers, since their activities threatened conventional commerce. According to the law prohibiting these peddlers from trading between Portugal and Brazil, itinerant traders had insufficient credit and little experience in commerce and often went bankrupt or vanished.[12] Commercial activities, it was argued, should remain in the hands of honorable merchants who would support the king and his treasury. The call to restrict commercial activities to suitable and qualified persons was expressed not only in legislation, but also in official correspondence. Contrabandists were invariably described as individuals of lower social status or, to use Laura de Mello e Souza's terminology, "declassified."[13] For instance, viceroy Luís de Vasconcellos e Souza, described contrabandists in the Rio de la Plata area as "a large number of whites, Indians, and mixed bloods, who run around in those districts without any means of subsistence."[14] Such negative descriptions were repeated by merchants in Rio de Janeiro itself. Invoking legislation against itinerant traders, merchants and shopkeepers, these established merchants petitioned in 1815 for legal support against competing peddlers. They called for a new law against "These itinerant peddlers who sell their products, without having any fixed home, without profession, neither established occupation, nor assets from which they live."[15] According to these descriptions, contrabandists were invariably regarded as being of low social status.[16]

Royal legislation protected powerful and more established merchants from colleagues of inferior social status. Protagonism, support of the well-being of the Royal Exchequer, and the principle of "utility" received equal attention in such legislation in that a merchant's social status was measured by his contributions to the royal treasury. The principle of utility opened the possibility for merchants who were in good standing by means of their legal trade to engage in illegal activities as well. Since contraband trade was not immoral itself, but was condemned insofar as it produced negative consequences for the conduct of commercial activities, a merchant already contributing heavily to the royal coffers would have enough social credit to be allowed to trade illegally. His public utility made him less vulnerable to prosecution.[17] Legislation against contraband trade thus supported powerful merchants. The opprobrium associated with illegal commerce was defined not by the act itself, but by its consequences, namely the degree to which it affected the royal treasury. This allowed for elasticity between condoned and proscribed illegal trade. If a merchant had enough standing, his illegal activities would be condoned. If a merchant did not have enough social status, then his illegal activities were prosecuted.

There are many parallels between discourse on illegal trade at the local and at the international level. Like other European colonial powers, the Portuguese state was protectionist in regards to trade with its own overseas territories. In return for resources expended in colonizing the New World, the Portuguese king had reserved for himself a monopoly on the profits of commerce between Brazil and Europe.

Therefore, all trade to and from Brazil had to be conducted through the intermediary of Portugal. Legislation strictly prohibited direct commerce between Brazil and Britain, France, the Netherlands, and Spain.[18] Legislation prohibiting foreign commercial activities in Brazil was founded on the utility principle. The Marquis of Pombal formulated it thus "the whole World knows, Overseas Colonies are always established with the objective of their utility for the Metropolis to which they belong."[19] The effort expended by a European country in settling overseas colonies earned it the right to impose a monopoly on trade between colony and metropolis. Moreover, commercial activities in the colonies were expected to benefit the mother country. The circle was complete, what was beneficial to the metropolis would also be good for the colony.

The picture changed in the context of Luso-Brazilian trade with Spanish colonies. Portuguese authorities condoned illegal trade between Brazil and Spanish America.[20] This breach of the law was legitimized by invoking the same utility principle. By trading between Brazil, Rio da Plata and Peru, Portuguese merchants obtained silver from Spanish America. Moreover, illegal trade allowed the Portuguese state to make territorial claims on the regions of La Plata and the Amazon.[21] Legal discourse socially marginalized foreign contrabandists as useless persons. According to a 1757 law, individuals who engaged in illegal trade were "rejected and despised by all civilized nations."[22] Such discourse was used to discourage diplomats of other nations from defending their compatriots who were dealing illegally with Brazil.[23] Yet this rejection of foreigners' engagement in contraband was inherently at odds with Portuguese commercial policies towards Spanish America. Thus the morality of the act of contraband became linked to the degree of utility of the illegal trade to the royal treasury.

The utilitarian relationship between Portugal and Brazil was subject to challenge in contemporary discourse. Portugal, as the mother country, claimed the right of monopoly over all Brazilian commerce on the grounds of mutual utility. Such a monopoly was impossible and uneconomical, and Brazilians contested Portuguese legislation proclaiming it. One notable example of this challenge on economic grounds was the slave trade. Brazil and Portuguese India produced the major products needed in the Atlantic slave trade: tobacco from Bahia; *cachaça*, a distilled spirit made out of Brazilian sugar cane; and Indian textiles. Therefore, it was impractical to conduct the slave trade in the triangle or Europe, Africa, and Brazil. Instead, it was a trade conducted between two points of trade, namely Brazil and Africa, with the inclusion of other commodities, in this case Indian textiles, obtainable not from the mother country, but in Africa or in Brazil.[24] Invoking another principle, that of "primacy," the Portuguese crown passed legislation against the exclusion of the mother country. When, in 1772, it was reported that vessels had sailed from Portuguese India to Angola and vice versa, the Portuguese sovereign decreed

> "That it is an accorded maxim and always executed by all Nations, that it is the Capital, or Dominant Metropolis which takes the lead in commerce and navigation with the Colonies, and not the Colonies between themselves. But the officials in charge, moved by self interest have by using Angola as a point of articulation, established with general trade and navigation between Asia, Africa and America to such exclusion of Portugal."[25]

The "utility" aspect, absent from this legislation, was here replaced by the principle of primacy. The mother country, and not the colonies, claimed exclusive primacy in the pursuit of commercial activities.

A similar law in 1803 confirmed this Portuguese principle of primacy as it related to the negative impact of this trade upon the mother country.[26] In the preamble to this law, Dom Rodrigo de Souza Coutinho, the Portuguese Secretary of State, pointed out three detrimental consequences of this direct trade between India and Brazil. First, it allowed unwelcome persons to enter the market, since crews of East Indiamen engaged in this trade; secondly, it diminished the market for Portuguese goods, as gold and silver spent on directly traded products were not used for agricultural commodities of the mother country; thirdly, it decreased revenue for the royal treasury, since the king could not levy taxes over these products if they were traded in Brazil. All three arguments shared a common premise.

Portuguese-based merchants, farmers, and even the sovereign would be harmed by these commercial activities.

As prices for colonial goods rose during the wars of the French revolution, Brazilians started to contest the principle that what was advantageous for the mother country was automatically good for the colony. In fact, Brazilian merchants blamed the Portuguese administration for their underdeveloped economy, as became especially clear from an anonymous memorandum reacting to the 1803 legislation prohibiting direct commerce between Brazil and India.[27] The author of the memorandium argued that Brazil needed to increase its labor force in order to cultivate the lands. Cultivation in Brazil depended on the import of African slaves. Inclusion of Portugal in the triangular commerce between India, Brazil, and Angola would increase the costs of labor in Brazil. The author went a step further, proposing to exclude not only Portugal from this lucrative commerce, but also Indian cities under Portuguese administration. The author argued for legalization of commerce with Bengal as this trade was more profitable than that with Goa and the Malabar coast. By putting Brazilian utility above Portuguese primacy, the anonymous author undermined the basic tenets of royal policy. They based their argument on the principle of free trade to India, arguing that this would contribute most to prosperity.[28] Consequently, the author blamed Portuguese colonists' laziness for the need to import African slaves. Brazil had a labor problem, since, as the author stated, "even the most humble European emigrant, once he has left the shores of Portugal, is never again to use the plough or hoe."[29] Consequently, prevailing Portuguese attitudes towards labor were the basic problem of the Brazilian economy, whereas support for Portugal itself impeded Brazilian development.

The prohibition of manufacturing in Brazil in 1785 is another example of legislation that put the premise of "primacy" above "utility."[30] This legislation was an immediate consequence of diplomatic reports of extensive direct trade between Britain and Brazil, and complaints from Portuguese manufacturers that the Brazilian market for Portuguese textiles was declining. The Portuguese secretary of state perceived this trend as a direct threat to Portuguese primacy over Brazilian commerce, and the Portuguese administration reacted by decreeing Brazil dependent on Portuguese textiles.[31] In his memorandum, the Portuguese Secretary of State recognized as inevitable that Brazil would eventually become economically independent from Portugal because the land was more fertile, and Portugal delivered manufactured and luxury agricultural products in order to balance its imports from Brazil.[32]

Brazilians questioned both the premise that Portuguese economic "utility" took precedence over what was most advantageous to Brazil, and the formal legitimation of these policies. By the end of the eighteenth century, Brazilians started to distinguish between their interests and those of Portugal. They viewed Portuguese economic policies with suspicion, and they ignored orders to implement them. One example was Amador Patrício da Maia, a Brazilian petitioner who separated Portuguese from Brazilian interests. In a long letter to the Portuguese secretary of state, Maia granted that contraband trade was unpatriotic and harmful to Portuguese and royal interests.[33] However, he continued to explain, metropolitan economic policies had adverse effects on Brazil. Fixed prices for products such as gold and high taxes led to increased contraband trade. Moreover, the endemic involvement of administrators in illegal trade made all prohibitive measures futile. Thus, Maia declared, the secretary of state's patriotism for Portugal made him jealous, since there was no indication that this patriotism also embraced Brazil.

Conflicting economic interests between Portugal and Brazil existed before the French revolution, but it was at times of crisis that such conflicts were most in evidence. During the so-called War of the Peddlers in Pernambuco (1711), for instance, the insurrectionists demanded that two foreign vessels be freely admitted.[34] There were similar impulses to throw off the yoke of royal taxation and gain independent rule in Minas Gerais during the first three decades of the eighteenth century.[35] In 1715, the Marquis of Angeja, viceroy in Salvador, petitioned for the admission of foreign ships to the harbor of Brazil's capital, a demand repeated by rebellious shoemakers in 1798.[36] Before the 1790s, tensions between Portuguese and Brazilian interests were resolved by mutual agreement. In the 1720s, Carioca merchants sought changes in commercial practices in the name of "common well-being."[37] This consensus disappeared during the wars following the French revolution. Clashing ideas on the economic organization of the Luso-Brazilian Empire widened the division between Portuguese and Brazilian interests.

Brazilian and Portuguese pamphleteers challenged the economic organization of the Portuguese colonial empire on two fronts. The relationship between the colony and mother country and the organization of commerce changed. Although the two issues were interrelated, the first changed after 1808, the year of the opening of Brazilian ports to foreign vessels, while the other persisted. Monopolistic practices and social stratification of the Luso-Brazilian economy did not end with the opening of the ports to foreign vessels. This rethinking of the relationship between Brazil and Portugal was a long process, which began as soon as Portuguese colonists settled in the New World.

Since the 1750s, policies of active reform under Pombal sought to improve the Portuguese and Brazilian economies and to increase the mutual benefits derived from commerce by augmenting agricultural, mining and manufacturing outputs through new techniques and products.[38] Pombal increasingly monopolized and centralized the economy so as to concentrate power in the hands of entrepreneurs and administrators who were metropolitan, loyal, innovative and able to compete with foreign traders. In return for privileges, these "captains of trade" guaranteed a steady income for the royal treasury. Pombal's policies stimulated ideas about reform, but angered those excluded from privileges. After Pombal's dismissal, officials started to rethink the principle of utility through monopoly of long-distance trade, but not the colony itself. Privileged persons continued to monopolize and regulate the marketplace by means of their local connections and their jurisdictions at the same time as ideas on economic reform entered Brazil through foreign publications and Luso-Brazilian organizations such as the Academy of Sciences in Lisbon and Brazilian literary societies.[39] These ideas promoted innovations in the Luso-Brazilian economy. In contrast to the Pombaline period, late eighteenth century thinkers believed that reform could be achieved by sharing responsibility between colony and mother country, and by opening the economy to any interested person without restrictions.[40] Luso-Brazilian thinkers, profoundly influenced by the theories of free trade and by the physiocrats, contested the principle of utility through monopolization. Old mercantilist norms, dictating the submission of the colony to the mother country in tandem with the mother country's privileged access to the local economy, became outdated. Portuguese and Brazilian intellectuals alike debated these issues.[41]

Two outspoken Brazilian supporters of free trade were João Rodrigues de Brito and José da Silva Lisboa. Both were members of the colonial elite and also senior representatives of the crown government in late eighteenth-century Salvador.[42] Not only did both authors feel that free trade between Europe and Brazil was necessary, as they could see contraband trade happening every day under their very noses, but they also pleaded for a deregulated economy. João Rodrigues de Brito, a strong supporter of freedom for all commercial activities, adhered to the principle of free trade in Salvador and continued to do so after the opening of the ports in 1808. Brito was convinced that the economy in the state of Bahia would improve substantially once all monopolies were eliminated. He proposed the free sale of brazilwood and tobacco without any governmental intervention.[43] Administrative reform occupied a central place in Brito's calls for free trade. Citing Jean-Baptiste Say and Adam Smith, Brito demanded the dissolution of the Board of Inspection (*Mesa da Inspeção*) in a letter of 1807 to the Municipal Council of Salvador in which he charged that the administrators' sole contribution was to pursue their private interests, and that their interference only increased prices and stimulated illegal trade.[44] The colonial administration had become dysfunctional and was a burden to the Brazilian economy, and the same could be said of the relationship between Portugal and Brazil.

José da Silva Lisboa also voiced discontent with the organization of the economy. Like Brito, Lisboa saw illegal trade as an indicator of the decline of the Luso-Brazilian economy.[45] Lisboa also pointed to colonial administrators impeded the economic prosperity of Brazil by pursuing their own selfish interests.[46] His writings went a step further than Brito, by indirectly claiming that Portuguese policies had created problems for the Brazilian economy.[47] He asserted that it was misguided on the part of Portugal and other colonizing European states to adopt policies that stimulated monopolies and imposed regulations on their colonies. Such policies left colonies at a disadvantage because privileged persons and administrators exploited the regulations for their private gain. However, Lisboa did not exclude the possibility that a policy of mutual respect could preserve the empire. If the king based these policies on "reason and justice," then the empire could function well as an internally regulated economy.[48]

Illegal trade was a consequence of disrespect for governmental authority. Lisboa listed five points a government should respect in order to eliminate contraband trade, thereby justifying the utility principle.[49] First, a government should have a judicial system that guaranteed civil liberty and the rightful ownership of private property; secondly, the market should not be restricted; thirdly, the policies of the government should be enlightened; fourthly, there should be moderation and consistency in taxation; and, fifthly, to issue greater public confidence a government should promote policies that favored the economy and benefitted society. Lisboa emphasized that these policies were not present at the moment; on the contrary, he pointed out that self-serving Portuguese policies created an abuse of power that monopolized the Brazilian economy.[50] Lisboa did not advocate a break from Portugal, and continued to view the Luso-Brazilian Empire as a vantage point. He did see reform as a *sine qua non* to preserve the empire and its internal dynamic. His objectives were achieved when the Portuguese court arrived in Salvador in 1808 and the newly arrived prince regent "liberated" Brazilian commerce.[51] These "preservation-through-reform" notions were also present in writings of Portuguese administrators. Portuguese authorities had to cope with other realities. Portugal, and not Brazil, was their immediate object of interest, although Portuguese statesmen had since long realized that Brazil was more important than the metropolis.[52] Their policies were directed towards the preservation of Portugal, and Portugal needed financial support from Brazil in order to preserve its independence.

In the 1790s and 1800s, Portuguese administrators realized the severity of foreign threats to Portuguese territorial integrity and continuation of the monarchy, and therefore placed the principle of "primacy" far above that of "utility." Dom Rodrigo de Souza Coutinho and José Joaquim de Azeredo Coutinho well understood the importance of Brazil if a solution was going to be found to the tense economic and political situation in Portugal at the end of the eighteenth century. During the 1790s, Portugal became vulnerable to foreign invasions. Portuguese authorities had to buy off revolutionary French governments and their Spanish allies to maintain an uneasy peace.[53] In the process, the royal treasury was severely drained and the Portuguese sovereign needed to increase taxes in Portugal and its colonies. The problem demanded strong actions and forced the Secretary of State to resort to reactionary fiscal policies.

Dom Rodrigo and Azeredo Coutinho authored their memoranda on how to improve the financial situation of the royal treasury. Dom Rodrigo, the secretary of the marine, was responsible for royal finances and colonial administration. His prime concerns were to find enough money to finance the Napoleonic armistice and to make these new taxes acceptable in Portugal and its colonies. Dom Rodrigo linked Brazilian loyalty to a reconsideration of Brazil's place in the Portuguese empire.[54] He used the argument of reciprocal utility that benefitted both Portugal and Brazil by virtue of their partnership in the empire. Portugal depended for its very survival on the existence of its colonies, while Brazil and the other colonies would find the mother country a useful distribution point for the Northern European market. This mutual economic advantage united the territories of the empire as much as did their common culture, language, and monarchy. Dom Rodrigo wanted to reinforce its grip on the colony through administrative reforms. The Portuguese secretary of state's policies took two approaches, the dictum of "divide and rule" and administrative improvements. In order to weaken what was a united and coherent colonial interest group, Dom Rodrigo strongly argued that Brazil was not a single entity.[55] Therefore, he proposed that Brazil should have two viceroyalties, one in Rio de Janeiro and the other in Pará.[56] These areas bordering foreign territories would be forced to increase their defense on land and sea with two positive results, first the division of Brazil into two separate territories; second, the successful elimination of foreign contrabandists through an effective maritime force.[57]

Like Lisboa, Dom Rodrigo understood that Brazilian loyalty could not be obtained without changes in the colonial administration. The frequency of Brazilian complaints about the venality of local administrators did not go unnoticed by Dom Rodrigo. Like Lisboa, he was convinced that royal policies could be fully executed only after a profound reform of local administration.[58] Dom Rodrigo's proposals for improvements focused on the creation of an impartial judiciary. He wanted to reach this goal through the selection of administrators based on merit, the expulsion from royal service of officials involved in illegal activities, an increase in administrators' salaries, and a ban on high court judges exercising dual and concurrent functions in the commercial administration. Dom Rodrigo linked the high level of taxes to the incidence of illegal trade, but he thought that the problem could be overcome by tax reforms without decreasing income to the royal exchequer.[59] For Dom Rodrigo, Brazilian involvement in contraband trade was a question of loyalty that would eventually be solved through administrative and fiscal improvements. Rather than proposing to reconsider relations between colony and mother country and reorganize the Brazilian economy, moves that would cost the royal treasury dearly in the short term, Dom Rodrigo limited himself to suggesting administrative adjustments to the governance of Dom Rodrigo's policies, directed towards the achievement of short-term goals and solutions to pressing problems, may seem conservative and short-sighted. Still, these policies were directed to the preservation of Portugal. When the French and British military exerted pressure on Portuguese and Brazilian territorial integrity, Dom Rodrigo and other Portuguese officials were not afraid to contemplate the far-reaching consequences of the transfer of the court to Brazil, but only after this event had actually taken place in 1807-1808 were Dom Rodrigo's long-term plans given serious consideration.

That not all Brazilians were anti-Portuguese becomes clear from the case of the prelate José Joaquim de Azeredo Coutinho. The Portuguese government found in him the strongest defender of their concept of mutual utility under Portuguese primacy. Azeredo Coutinho was born the son of a powerful landowning family in Campos das Goitacazes, the rich sugar area in the captaincy of Rio de Janeiro. With this background, Azeredo Coutinho was bound to be a conservative and a staunch defender of ties between Portugal and Brazil, as the sugar farmers fared well during the price boom after the revolution in Saint Domingue.[60] He rose in both the Brazilian and Portuguese ecclesiastical bureaucracies to become the bishop and governor of Pernambuco in Brazil, as well as bishop of Elvas and chief inquisitor in Portugal. Azeredo Coutinho's loyalty to the Portuguese monarchy remained unquestioned and he defended the prime role of Portugal in the empire even after the transfer of the court to Brazil.[61] As a loyal royalist, Azeredo Coutinho reacted against the ideas of the French revolution and refused to point out that the Portuguese administration in Brazil played a key role in the problem of contraband trade. Nor did the bishop question Portugal's superiority over Brazil, agreeing that a colonizer had this right over its colonies and that it was in the common interests of both territories. For Azeredo Coutinho to question Brazil's role in the empire would have been no less than *lèse-majesté* and adherence to the Jacobin terror.

Azeredo Coutinho's conservatism was notable, but he adhered to some principles of free commerce that favored the economic interests of big landowners. Most of his economic treatises supported the social group of which he was a product. For instance, he wrote in strong defense of the slave trade, and for abolition of fixed sugar prices.[62] Only in his writings in favor of the abolition of salt and whale fishery contracts did Azeredo Coutinho contribute to a change in economic policies that did not have directly positive consequences for sugar planters in Rio de Janeiro.[63]

Contemporary economic works debated two main issues in contraband trade: Brazil's place in the Portuguese empire and the regulation of the local economy. Influenced by free traders and physiocrats, Brazilian and Portuguese authors offered different solutions. Yet, it was obvious that the external and internal reorganizations of the economy were questioned, especially during the wars following the French revolution. Still, economists did not pose the question of morality, leaving this issue to satirists and religious writers. The issue of immorality associated with illegal trade was not completely ignored by contemporaries. In the case of an acute national crisis, sermons, prose dialogues and poems condemning contraband trade found their way to the public. These works were reflective, they were meant to show contemporaries that what had brought them to this state of affairs was what was wrong in society. Decline was thus viewed as a divine punishment wrought upon Portuguese society by the Almighty as punishment for immoral behavior.

Interestingly enough, most of these critiques had been published during the seventeenth century. During the reign of king John V and his successors, censorship increased and criticism was not allowed. An attentive reading between the lines reveals critical observations.[64] A case in point are the poems in an eulogy to Gomes Freire de Andrade, published in 1753 by a literary society, the *Académia dos Selectos*.[65] The contributors described the well-regarded governor in extremely positive terms, thereby distinguishing Gomes Freire de Andrade's noble conduct from his predecessors and other members of the bureaucracy. Such hidden criticisms were rare in eighteenth century Brazil and Portugal. Only in the economic treatises discussed above at the end of the century did criticism return.

Diogo do Couto's *O Soldado Prático* stands as another landmark among writings on Portuguese corruption.[66] Couto, author of the official history of Portuguese India, completed his manuscript in 1612. He wrote his book at a time of crisis during the period of the so-called Babylonian Captivity when Portugal was part of the Spanish empire and the Dutch were defeating the Portuguese in the East and West Indies.[67] Couto's experienced and sarcastic soldier holds a staged conversation with the main character, a former governor in the East Indies, and a bureaucrat in Lisbon. The soldier explained how corruption, venality, and contraband trade were inalienable parts of the Portuguese experience in the East, and how they had contributed to the political, economic, and military defeat of the empire.

The problems in the Portuguese possessions were a consequence of greed and bad administration. Couto asserted that as soon as a Portuguese soldier set foot in India, he became bedeviled by his quest for self-enrichment.[68] No regulatory mechanisms existed to control such aspirations and, even if they had been in place, the quality of administrative personnel, themselves obsessed with self-enrichment, was such as to undermine any effective measures.[69] The most outspoken critic of the functioning of Portuguese society and economy came from the author of the book *Arte de Furtar*, or the art of thievery.[70] *Arte de Furtar* was a satire printed for moralistic purposes. With other sixteenth and seventeenth-century works such as the *O Soldado Prático* of Diogo do Couto, the satirical poetry of Gregório de Matos and the Chilean letters from Tomás António Gonzaga, they ridiculed the behavior of officials and others engaged in illegal practices. Whereas Couto had more worldly views on the Portuguese decline in the East, the author of *Arte de Furtar* explained decline in terms of divine punishment.

A consideration of time and authorship of those publications is essential to our understanding of their content. There were some reasonable doubts concerning *Arte de Furtar*. The front page of *Arte de Furtar* bears the name of the famous António Vieira S.J., and 1652 as the date of publication. The French historian Rogier Bismut has convincingly demonstrated that both the author and the date of publication were falsified.[71] Even though some of the central passages in *Arte de Furtar* were copied from Vieira's sermons, Rogier Bismut has made a case that the actual author was Padre Manuel da Costa, a contemporary of Vieira and a fellow Jesuit priest. Moreover, he proves that *Arte de Furtar* was published in 1744, but written in the 1650s.[72] The publisher used António Vieira's name to make *Arte de Furtar* respectable to a bigger readership. Contemporaries already doubted its origins, since they thought that Vieira would never have written such a satire of the monarchy, the nobility and the clergy.[73]

Arte de Furtar was written and published in restless times. Both the 1650s and the 1740s were periods of transition. In the 1650s, Brazil had just been freed of the Dutch presence in Pernambuco, but still greatly feared of foreign invasions. Portugal's political, economic and military situation left much to be desired. In the 1740s, Brazil supplied Portugal with rich cargoes of gold, but, King John V after suffering several strokes, was losing control over the empire and its administration. Both Portugal and his body remained paralyzed for almost a decade, and the king seemed to be resolved to change that situation by conspicuous consumption. In such circumstances, it was not difficult to see how a satirical book on the Portuguese administration could find an eager readership. In the eighteenth century, at least 13 works by Vieira were re-published between 1740 and 1754.[74] Only three of his works were printed before that time, and none after the Lisbon earthquake. This time frame suggests that Vieira's works were regarded as highly political and that they served as a vehicle for criticizing the regime.

In *Arte de Furtar* the world is taken over by thieves. Stealing is general and thieves are widely applauded. Thieves come in many varieties. The Spanish king who steals Portugal, a tax farmer who is able to procure a contract at a low price through his connections, and civil servants who embezzle from the state.[75] Contraband trade also figures as a form of thievery.[76] Everybody is involved in the art of thievery and the higher a person's status, the more he is allowed to steal.[77] The biggest thieves are the administrators who are charged with preventing this crime.[78] The author uses his book as a mirror in which the reader may see him or herself. *Arte de Furtar* is one of the few sources that does condemn illegal trade on moral grounds. Illegal trade and other forms of stealing from the king are deemed. Divine punishment is inevitable; even if thieves were able to get away with it in this life, they would be punished in the afterlife.[79]

Moralistic writings about illegal trade were rare. These works were mostly written during times of crisis and served as an explanation for disaster. This was especially the case after the Lisbon earthquake of 1755, whose aftermath saw an outpouring of works on individual and collective sins.[80] The successes of the Dutch in North East Brazil in 1640 had prompted António Vieira to write a sermon castigating the venality of Portuguese officials.[81] Decline was the main theme in the works of both Diogo do Couto and the author of *Arte de Furtar*. For both authors the remedy lay in curbing vices such as greed and thievery. Both opted for administrative reforms as a solution. Diogo do Couto had a more secular approach and did not shy him from bold proposals: patronage was wrong.[82] The author of *Arte de Furtar* took a more religious approach. Fear of the afterlife would be a deterrent to immoral behavior by the Portuguese population. Both writers saw defective administration embedded in a sinful society as the root of the problem.

The most colorful descriptions of a sin-saturated Portuguese society came from Gregório de Matos, a celebrated late seventeenth-century Brazilian poet who satirically chronicled his contemporaries' vices. Matos satirized the personal lives of governors, clergymen, judges, and other inhabitants of Salvador.[83] In this period of economic depression stemming from a crisis in the sugar sector, Matos's quick pen was his sharpest weapon in describing promiscuity, high-handed behavior and self-enrichment of Salvador's ruling class. His poems were personal and devastating, and earned him the nickname of "Hell's Mouth," and many highly placed enemies. One judge whose vices Matos excoriated in verse condemned him to exile in Angola. Matos' poems were very popular in Salvador, even though they were not published during the colonial period. His work was popular and contageous, as much of the poetry ascribed to him may have been written by others.[84] The usage of satirical poetry placed Matos in a special position. His poems were part of an underground culture, which challenged colonial rule directly and indirectly. Gregório de Matos went beyond personal attacks on the behavior of Salvador's elite. His poetry was a harsh indictment of colonial government, be it on the municipal, colonial, or imperial level. Matos described the city of Salvador with all its vices. In his poetry, he concentrates on three negative aspects of Bahian society that echo the work of Diogo do Couto, poor government, stealing, and unsuitable appointments to public office.[85] Matos singled out in his satire bureaucrats whose corrupt behavior and incompetence were notorious. Theft was a common theme in Matos's poetry, not only by officials and members of the clergy, but also through usury and commercial transactions. Matos also wrote about the role of mulattos in clerical and bureaucratic positions. One of his strongest poems satirizing the Portuguese government was recited after his death in 1713, shortly after the War of the Peddlers in Recife. One stanza criticizes the Overseas Council,

> "The Overseas Council is headed by a Devil to resolve all his problems he will sell and he will embezzle, and this predator of persons thinks to earn his credit, by making of insolence and arrogance a merit,
> So in Rio de Janeiro now there is not anybody who does not know

how to purchase privilege for money, and even if these covenants are thoroughly irrational, such is our good government of Portugal."[86]

In this Sebastianistic poem, the author sums up all the injustices of administrators and merchants from king to peddler, and the Almighty for a miracle to change, but not overthrow the Portuguese government. Matos used his satirical poetry as a vehicle to blame Portuguese colonization and governmental policies for Brazil's decadence.

The literary genres of satirical prose and poetry continued well into the eighteenth century. One of the most acclaimed users was the *inconfidente* Tomás António Gonzaga. The former crown judge of Minas Gerais and participant in the Inconfidência Mineira is best known for his *Cartas Chilenas*, although they were never published during his lifetime.[87] As a stratagem to criticize governors in Minas Gerais, Gonzaga used the fictitious example of a Chilean governor who abused his power through craft, corruption, illegal trade, and promiscuity. Unlike Matos, Gonzaga directly challenged the competency of such governors and their administration in Minas Gerais.[88]

Like Couto and the anonymous author of *Arte de Furtar*, Matos's poems were didactic with strong moral overtones. They were meant to change the mentality of Luso-Brazilian society and administration. The authors unanimously maintained that Portuguese decline was attributable to injustice, corruption and venality, vices not limited to the administration and economy, but pervading Luso-Brazilian society as a whole. Gonzaga went one step further, arguing that the Portuguese administration was abusive and questioning its ability to govern justly.

To conclude, illegal trade was condemned on three grounds: utility, primacy, and morality. Official discourse, i.e. legislation and administrative correspondence, condemned illegal trade mainly on grounds of utility. If the effects of illegal trade were positive, then contraband trade was to be condoned, but if the consequences were negative, then it must be condemned. On the scale between condonation and condemnation, utility was one factor, and another was the social standing of the perpetrator. Portuguese authorities employed the same principle when combating cases of illegal trade by foreigners to Brazil.

If a country or region was more committed to the preservation and economy of Portugal, then the level of condonation of such foreigners' illegal trade to Brazil was higher because of their countries' support of Portugal. Foreigners considered themselves above the law and argued that Portuguese administrators should allow their illegal activities to take place. Thus, at issue was not the morality of the act, but its utility.

Contraband trade was a barometer for the degree of primacy exercised by the mother country over the colony. Proscribed illegal trade defied the official discourse of political economy, according to which the colony should be exclusively dependent on the mother country and therefore receive no direct imports from Europe, or commercial relationships with other colonies. There were exceptions to this stance, for instance the slave trade and commerce to Rio de la Plata. As long as there was flexibility on both Portuguese and Brazilian sides, there was no problem. But in the 1710's and 1720's, the years following the first gold rushes, as well as during the wars following the French revolution, this relationship came into question.

Portuguese administrators reacted by starting to apply the principle of primacy in the service of metropolitan economic policy. They took the position that Portugal as the mother country had a right to Brazilian revenues, even if this policy was disadvantageous to the Brazilian economy. This discourse came under fire in economic treatises. The Brazilian intelligentsia followed the lead of Adam Smith on free trade, reasoning that a monopolized economy was advantageous to neither Portugal nor Brazil.

If official discourse only tangentially condemned illegal trade on moral grounds, morality was the main theme of unofficial discourse. The poems of Gregório de Matos, dialogues of Diogo do Couto, and letters of Tomás António de Gonzaga, and the social mirror held up by *Arte de Furtar* and a range of other literary genres, expressed the views, often in immoderate language, that illegal trade was but one part of the all-pervasive corruption of the Portuguese empire. The organization of administration and society was fundamentally wrong. To these writers, the Spanish occupation of Portugal, the fall of sugar prices in Bahia, the Lisbon earthquake, and the Dutch occupation of Pernambuco were all attributable to a single cause, gross immorality in government and in society. By such a measure, Portuguese decline was a well deserved and collective punishment for venality and immorality.

Both official and unofficial discourse rarely distinguished between corruption, venality, and illegal trade. Contraband trade was an integral part of a more general problem in Portuguese society: abuse of office by administrators and self-interested merchants. Official discourse marginalized the contrabandist, but condoned illegal trade by persons of a higher social status. Unofficial discourse ridiculed this double standard as destructive to the mother country and her overseas possessions. Critics of crown policies blamed the mother country alone for Brazil's failure to develop to its full economic potential.

CHAPTER 7
CONCLUSION

"This kingdom [Portugal] exist as a colony of the Court of Brazil."
Petition of Salvador Correa e Saa, in the name of Brazilian merchants settled in Lisbon. [After November 29, 1807]¹

Illegal trade in eighteenth-century Brazil should not be seen as a commercial activity that transgresses the law and runs contrary to accepted mores and values. Illegal trade, when condoned, was an integral part of colonial society. The prosecution of illegal traders was an indicator that they had crossed an unwritten boundary between what was proscribed and what was condoned.

The boundary between condonation and prosecution of illegal was fluid and subject to change. International, metropolitan, and local interests determined these limits, and how they shifted over time. Contributory factors included intra-European rivalries, diplomatic relations, and national self-interest; Portuguese crown policy, metropolitan commercial interests, and the standing of the royal treasury; and in Brazil, venality and honesty of crown officials, their relations with local officialdom, and the petty antagonisms and jealousies of appointed and elected holders of public office and their relations with the business community.

This confusion as to what comprised condoned and proscribed illegal trade was also apparent in the judicial system. Knowledge of the law was not widespread, and legislation had not been properly codified since the mid-seventeenth century. A stream of contradictory laws, decrees, dispatches, and memoranda from various Portuguese administrative entities reached Rio de Janeiro on a regular basis; to these should be added edicts of the governor or viceroy, the Municipal Council, the ecclesiastical authorities, the ranking military commander and the admiral of the fleet. At first sight, the governance of Rio de Janeiro's commerce appeared vacillating at best, and chaotic at worst.

However, close analysis has revealed that the absence of a coherent and sustained crown policy and variations in enforcement of what were perceived to be guidelines did not mean that governance was absent. On the contrary, this fluidity provided the opportunity for considerable latitude as to what was deemed legal or illegal. Local administrators could interpret policies and guidelines according to their own standards, thereby enjoying flexibility of enforcement and implementation, which revealed the degree to which effective enforcement of the law was the product of an accommodation between regal, viceregal, and gubernatorial rulings as well as local attitudes, ideologies, mores and practices. Therefore ambiguities and imprecisions become a strength, rather than a weakness, of colonial Brazilian administration. The handling of foreign vessels in Brazilian harbors and the punishment of Brazilian contrabandists are but two examples of how this legal chiaroscuro functioned to establish effective royal and local authority. If captains of foreign vessels refused to allow local officials to mediate in their legal and illegal commercial activities, their ships were liable to be confiscated. Punishment of contrabandists took the form of arrests followed by protracted imprisonment attributable to institutionalized and systematic bureaucratic procrastination. In the case of foreign vessels, the Portuguese king had the absolute authority to pardon the transgressors and restore the vessel. In the case of the Brazilian contrabandists, their appeals to higher courts often times resulted in freedom, albeit after many years. Judicial procedures leading to the punishment of foreign and Brazilian contrabandists guaranteed the upholding of local and metropolitan authority. That foreigners complained about these bureaucratic procedures is an indicator of effectiveness with which the law was implemented.

The role of the law, royal degrees, conciliar rulings, and viceregal or gubernatorial, orders as well as codified laws, in this process was arbitrary. Latitude in interpretation of regulatory laws notwithstanding, the existence of a corpus of legislation served to legitimize an official's power as an intermediary in illegal trade and was the basis of his control over illegal commercial activities. Moreover, any decision to execute the letter of the law to the full extent could be challenged. An aggressive party could bring a complaint against him or lodge a formal denunciation. Portuguese authorities took these complaints seriously, because they revealed the degree to which local officials had violated standards as to what was an acceptable degree of regulatory authority. Threats to the regularity of commerce or social stability were viewed with great concern by the sovereign's representatives. As a measure of last resort the Crown invoked the royal prerogative to intervene as an arbiter on illegal commerce even if this meant revising decisions taken by royal appointees and members of the magistracy.

Many European courts viewed Brazil as backwards. The system of monopolies deterred free trade and a policy of exclusion limited the introduction of new scientific knowledge and technology. The occurrence of contraband trade was a sign of Portuguese weakness, insofar as it underlined Portugal's inability to establish authority over its colonies. To be a proponent of or even a participant in illegal trade might have a positive dimension, but to permit unregulated contraband to occur was a sign of weakness. This phenomenon was all the more surprising, because illegal trade was not only common in Portugal, Brazil, and Latin America, but was a worldwide occurrence. Even in Britain, smuggling of tea was rampant during the eighteenth century. Illegal trade was condemned not for the deed itself, but for its consequences and ramifications.

Contraband trade was an organic and integral part of eighteenth century life: at court, on the high seas, in the marketplace. Princes of church and state, merchants and mariners, landowners and businessmen, professionals and artisans found that exposure to the realities or ramifications of contraband was unavoidable. Even the voiceless in colonial Brazil, women and slaves of African birth and descent, and those who were potential victims of persecutions, New Christians, were drawn into the web of illegal trade. Contraband was an inalienable part of colonial life. Contraband was not viewed as an aberration, nor was it seen as morally repugnant or worthy of unconditional condemnation. This flexibility cannot simply be explained in Weberian terms such as "rational" or "paternalistic". The latitude in perception and the conditional nature of the response to illegal trading served the interests of the Portuguese crown and state very well. For the metropolis and colony, the flexibility in regulation and response was an institutionalized mechanism that could benefit Portuguese relations with foreigners by easing frictions, contribute to the well-being of the royal coffers, guarantee local control over legal and illegal trade and reinforce the authority of the king as final arbiter.

The opening of the Brazilian ports to friendly foreign nations in 1808 was a *de facto* declaration of independence. As the Brazilian merchant Salvador Correa e Saa so perceptively recognized, Rio de Janeiro had become the center of the empire, and Portugal was relegated to the periphery.[2] The free acceptance of foreign merchants on Brazilian soil dramatically changed commercial practices: what had been illegal was now legal. Metropolitan and colonial interests were the beneficiaries of this foreign presence. The victims, if there were such, were local officials who suddenly found themselves stripped of the power and authority they had previously enjoyed as regulators of legal and illegal trade.

The year 1808 did not mark the end of all illegal trade, but with the influx of foreigners and changes in legislation, the conditions changed. Contraband, in its practices, participants and regulators, is a prime example of continuities and discontinuities in the history of colonial Brazil.

No less than other institutions of the colony, including the institution of slavery, it touched the lives of everybody in the colony and pervaded the political, economic, social, spiritual and moral well-being of Brazil. It helped to solidify the status of some sectors of society while depriving others. As was the case with so many other aspects of colonial society, contraband was both inclusive and exclusive.

In a society where people were neither black nor white, where slavery and freedom could be conditional, and where there was a reluctance to polarize and a willingness to accept accommodation as a sign of strength rather than weakness, Brazil stood out among its Latin American neighbors as a country that made the transition from colony to empire to republic with relative ease.

POSTSCRIPT

Any discussion of contraband leads inevitably to questions about the goods involved in illegal trade and the extent of such activity. Since these are only lightly touched on in this work, brief remarks here will provide this context. Illegal trade was conducted with any product subject to payment of duties on entering or leaving the port of Rio de Janeiro: diamonds, gold, silver, tobacco, sugar, "slaves," textiles, salt and liquor. Some of these exports and imports were illegal only nominally. For instance, gold exports between Lisbon and Falmouth were prohibited, but the crown issued licenses so that they could officially occur. Commerce between Brazil and Rio de la Plata also fell into this category of illegal but licensed trade.

Any estimate of the magnitude of contraband trade is highly speculative. The absence of official statistics makes estimates of even legal trade problematic, and for illegal trade the difficulties are naturally greater. Contemporary fiscal records and opinions by officials throw some light on estimates of, and attitudes toward, illegal trade.

The most telling reports we have about the amount of illegal trade are those by contemporaries. Still, their ideas about the extent of contraband were little better than impressions, based on personal experience. Antonil wrote about tax evasion on bullion shipments of gold.[1] He claimed in 1711 that the total amount of gold annually excavated in Brazil was three hundred arrobas [1 arroba is about 14.5 kilos], but that dues to the crown were paid on only one hundred arrobas. Some historians have taken this estimate at face value.[2] Antonil's numbers are not credible but do represent a contemporary perception of the extent of illegal trade.

Another contemporary estimate came in 1733 from Dom Pedro de Almeida, former governor of São Paulo and Minas Gerais (1717-1721).[3] He estimated illegal gold shipments by the number of vessels leaving Brazilian ports annually, namely: two arrobas of gold on each of the twenty-five vessels bound from Salvador to Lisbon; twenty-four arrobas going from Salvador to the Mina coast; four arrobas from Salvador to Angola; nine arrobas from Salvador to the Azores; two arrobas from Salvador to Colônia do Sacramento; one arroba from Salvador to either Mozambique or Madagascar; two arrobas from São Luís de Maranhão and Belém do Pará to Guiana; fifty arrobas from Rio de Janeiro; twenty arrobas from Recife; and another four arrobas from Grão Pará and Maranhão. This makes the total illegal gold trade 166 arrobas. In the manifests for the legal trade, the amount of gold transported was 990 arrobas; adding illegal gold transports to this would make a total of 1156 arrobas. The collected fifth (20% tax) on gold amounted to only 100 arrobas annually, which should have been 231 arrobas. Thus the total amount of taxes not received by the crown was 131 arrobas. This guess while more sophisticated than Antonil's, still cannot be taken at face value. Nevertheless, it is notable that Dom Pedro de Almeida's estimate of illegal trade was remarkably lower than Antonil's - an indication that contemporary perceptions of contraband trade did not consider it to be a far-reaching phenomenon.

A third estimate of the illegal gold trade came from Martinho de Mendonça de Pina de Proença, acting governor of Minas Gerais (1736-1737).[4] His estimates are based on production figures. Proença estimated that annual gold production in Brazil was around 800 arrobas, on which the fifth due to the crown should have been 160 arrobas. In fact, only 100 arrobas was collected, suggesting that contraband made up about 40 per cent of the total amount of trade in gold. As with the earlier estimates by Antonil and Dom Pedro de Almeida, Proença could not have known the actual amount of gold production in Brazil. Moreover, the *quinto* was not always levied on gold production, but alternately on slaves employed in the mining districts, as a capitation tax, and on shops and taverns. Moreover, deficient sources make it difficult to calculate gold production for Brazil, let alone for the 18th century.[5]

There are few sources available to serve as a basis for an estimation on the extent of illegal trade. One obviously insufficient source is the value of confiscations in the port of Rio de Janeiro (table 0.1).

TABLE 0.1. Confiscations by the Rio de Janeiro Customs.

Year	Amount (in reis)	Year	Amount
1753	2:324$496	1788	1:302$985
1781	479$526	1789	5:068$774
1786	3:957$481	1790	1:447$260
1787	1:520$610	1798-1802	31:571$543

Sources: Arquivo Nacional do Rio de Janeiro [A.N.R.J.], Colonial, cód.87, vol.9, fl.149r-150r; Biblioteca Nacional do Rio de Janeiro, ms. 4,3,3, fl.75v-81r; A.N.R.J., Colonial, caixa 495, pac.2; Arquivo Histórico Ultramarino, Rio de Janeiro, papeis avulsos não catalogados, caixa 207, doc.70.

These numbers say little about the total amount of illegal trade, but they are interesting as an indicator of the degree of effectiveness of measures to curb contraband. These seizures equaled the yearly income of a senior administrator — a handsome bonus supplementing the customs officers' regular salaries. Given that the tax of one tenth of the customs (*dizima da alfândega*) amounted to one hundred times the amount of seized goods, these confiscations appear to have been of questionable effectiveness.

The balance of trade has also been a matter for speculation. Between 1796 and 1808 there were official figures on trade between Portugal, its colonies and the rest of Europe. As I pointed out in chapter two, authors such as Fernando Novais, José Jobson de Arruda Andrade, Valentim Alexandre and Jorge Pedreira have based estimates on these balances.⁶ The main problem is that illegal trade is not included in these balances of trade, thereby invalidating their databases.

Trade balances were used to calculate bullion flow between Portugal and Great Britain. Virgílio Noya Pinto argued that the differences in these balances could be overcome only by the transport of noble metals, which was in itself an illegal act.⁷ However, as Noya Pinto himself pointed out, there were different levels of illegality.⁸ Gold transports from Portugal to Britain were inevitable, and to some extent, condoned. However, there was a difference between exports of coin and the illegal transport of untaxed gold dust. Such calculations do not take these differences into account.

The number of foreign vessels in Brazilian harbors is another source of speculation. Reports of "many" foreign ships in Brazilian harbors did not lead to speculation as to a quantifiable estimate of the extent of illegal trade, but only to the suggestion that it was "considerable". Although we know the numbers of foreign vessels arriving in Rio de Janeiro in the last decades before the opening of the ports in 1808, their relevance to estimates of illegal trade is limited. There is no basis for the assumption that all ships were engaged in contraband trade. Moreover, it is impossible to estimate the tonnage of these vessels or the value of the contraband. The case of Buenos Aires was different. Moutoukias has shown that only one or two vessels arrived yearly from Spain, whereas some twenty vessels entered the port from the Netherlands.⁹ But, in contrast to the lack of continuous legal commerce between Rio de la Plata and Spain, there was regular and consistent trade throughout the eighteenth century between Rio de Janeiro and Portugal.

One other potential source for contraband trade is documentation from "the other": namely foreigners who traded illegally with Brazil and left documentation on the extent of their activities. Klooster used data from the Dutch West India Company to calculate the volume of illegal cocoa trade between New Granada and Curacao.¹⁰ Unfortunately, figures on Brazilian bullion flow attributable to foreigners are scarce and, at best, sporadic.

Thus, it is difficult to give any hard figures or even estimates for illegal trade. The only extant sources are circumstantial at best, based on contemporary guesses or hearsay. At most, such sources can provide insights into how contemporaries perceived the extent of illegal trade. Fortunately, we are blessed with rich documentation on the repercussions of contraband on attitudes, the economy and society of Rio de Janeiro in the eighteenth century and, more broadly in metropolitan Portugal and her richest colony.

PORTUGAL AND BRAZIL CONFRONT THE CONTEMPORARY WORLD SERIES

The Second Line of Defense series on Portugal and Brazil provides an extraordinary journey through history, democracy, and transformation

The series reveals how catastrophe becomes catalyst, how nations reinvent themselves through crisis, and how the Portuguese-speaking world has shaped global history in ways few realize. These works connect the dots between seemingly disparate events across centuries and continents —from the Lisbon Earthquake to Brazil's contemporary political landscape.

WHAT MAKES THIS SERIES UNIQUE

Global Perspective, Local Insight: The series doesn't just tell Portuguese and Brazilian stories — it focuses on how these nations' experiences illuminate universal patterns of transformation, democracy, and renewal that resonate worldwide.

Real-Time Analysis: Written as events unfolded, these works capture the immediacy of historical moments, offering readers a "you are there" experience of witnessing history in the making.

Interdisciplinary Approach: Blending urban planning, political science, architecture, and social history, the series demonstrates how cities, nations, and civilizations evolve through the interplay of crisis and vision.

THE FIRST THREE BOOKS

1. The Tale of Three Cities: The Rebuilding of London, Paris, and Lisbon

The masterclass in urban transformation

When disaster strikes, visionaries emerge. Kenneth Maxwell reveals how three catastrophic events, London's Great Fire (1666), Lisbon's devastating earthquake (1755), and Napoleon III's radical reimagining of Paris, became the crucibles that forged modern urban civilization.

Why It Matters: This isn't just about old cities and dead architects. It's about how societies transform crisis into opportunity, how the spaces we build reflect our deepest aspirations, and how visionary leadership can literally reshape the world.

The Lisbon Revolution: Discover how the most powerful earthquake in European history launched the Enlightenment's first experiment in rational city design, creating Europe's most modern urban grid centuries before its time.

2. Perspectives on Portuguese History: The 2024 Lectures

Democracy's hidden revolution revealed

The story they don't teach in school: How Portugal's 1974 revolution was actually the "first democratic revolution of the 20th century" and why that distinction matters for understanding democracy everywhere.

Why was Portugal's decolonization a pivotal moment in global politics?

What can the Portuguese experience teach us about democracy emerging from dictatorship?

3. Brazil in a Changing World Order: Essays

A nation's journey through the contemporary landscape

Brazil in real-time: Written as events unfolded over the past decade, these essays capture Brazil's evolving role in a dramatically changing world from domestic politics to military influence to shifting foreign policy.

Historical Detective Work: Including Kenneth Maxwell's fascinating discovery of the Recueil, the U.S. constitutional documents that influenced Brazil's 1788-89 Minas conspirators, revealing hidden trans-Atlantic revolutionary connections.

FOR READERS WHO WANT TO UNDERSTAND

- ✓ How democracy emerges from dictatorship
    - ✓ How nations rebuild from catastrophe
    - ✓ How Portugal's story connects to global history
    - ✓ Why urban planning matters for civilization
    - ✓ How Brazil's evolution affects world order
    - ✓ What the Portuguese-speaking world teaches us about transformation

THE BOTTOM LINE

This series does what the best history should do: it makes the past illuminate the present while revealing patterns that help us understand where we're headed.

The series shows us that the Portuguese-speaking world isn't peripheral to global history but that it's central to understanding how societies transform, how democracy spreads, and how the future takes shape.

Available in multiple languages (English, French, Portuguese) because some stories demand to be told in the languages of the civilizations they describe.

All available on Amazon or Barnes and Noble booksellers worldwide.

NOTES

INTRODUCTION

1. Contraband" in J.A. Simpson and E.S.C. Weiner eds., *The Oxford English Dictionary* 2nd ed., (Oxford: Clarendon Press, 1989) 3: 833-834.
2. Paulo Cavalcante, *Negócios de Trapaça. Caminhos e Descaminhos na América Portuguesa (1700-1750)* (São Paulo: Editora Hucitec, 2006). His work is mostly about in-land contraband trade. There is a rising interest in illegal trade in Latin America in general, see for instance "Dossier Temático: contrabando" *América Latina en la História Económica. Revista de Fuentes e Investigación 24* (July-December 2005) 61-177.
3. John W. Tyler, *Smugglers and Patriots. Boston Merchants and the Advent of the American Revolution* (Boston; Northeastern University Press, 1986).
4. David J. Weber, *The Spanish Frontier in North America* (New Haven NC: Yale University Press, 1992) 174-175. Weber is just one supporter of these ideas arguing that Spanish economic weakness cause the lack of provisions to the desolated borderlands, and paraphrasing an author who charged the Spanish as being "indolent." For more on this idea, see Richard Kagan's "Prescott's Paradigm: American Historical Scholarship and the Decline of Spain," *American Historical Review* 101 (1996) 423-446.
5. For a good bibliography on publications of the colonial era see, Rubens Borba de Moraes, *Bibliographia Brasileira: Rare Books about Brazil published from 1504 to 1900 and Works by Brazilian Authors of the Colonial Period* 2 vols. (Los Angeles and Rio de Janeiro: Livraria Kosmos Editada, 1983).
6. Diogo do Couto, *O Soldado Prático* M. Rodrigues Lapa ed., (3rd ed. Lisbon: Sá da Costa, 1980) 9-13, and George D. Winius, *The Black Legend of Portuguese India*. Diogo do Couto, his *Contemporaries and the Soldado Prático* (New Delhi: Concept Publishing Company, 1985) 9-10.
7. Winius, *Black Legend 33*, based on Pyrard de Laval's travel account.
8. Winius 23.
9. Roger Bisnut ed., *Arte de Furtar* (Lisbon: Imprensa Nacional Casa da Moeda, 1991).
10. Pero de Magalhães de Cândavo, *História da Província Santa Cruz a que vulgaramente chamamos Brasil* (reprint from 1576; Lisbon: Biblioteca Nacional, 1984); Ronaldo Vaifas ed., *Dicionário di Brasil Colonial* (1500-1808) (Rio de Janeiro: Objetiva, 2000) 482.
11. Ambrósio Fernandes Brandão, *Dialogues of the Great Things in Brazil*, Frederick Holden Hall ed. and transl., (Albuquerque: University of New Mexico Press, 1987) 148.
12. The best edition is André João Antonil (pseud.), *Cultura e Opulência das Drogas do Brasil*, Andrée Mansuy ed. and transl. (Paris; Institut des Hautes Études de l'Amérique Latine, 1965).
13. Antonil, *Cultura e Opulência* 336-338; 416.
14. E. Bradford Burns, "The Intellectuals as Agents of Change and the Independence of Brazil, 1724-1822," in: A.J.R. Russell-Wood ed., *From Colony to Nation. Essays on the Independence of Brazil* (Baltimore: Johns Hopkins University Press, 1975) 211-246.

15. The earliest volumes have been republished recently as *Memórias Económicas da Academia Real das Ciências dee Lisboa, para o Adiamento da Agricultura, das Artes, e da Indústria em Portugal, e suas Conquistas* vols. 1-5, (Lisbon: Banco de Portugal, 1990-1991).
16. On Balthazar da Silva Lisboa's activities in Southern Bahia see Shawn W. Miller, *Fruitless Trees. Portuguese Conservation and Brazil's Colonial Timber* (Stanford: Stanford University Press, 2000) esp. 54-57
17. Many have been republished in: José da Silva Lisboa, *Escritos Económicos Escolhidos, 1804-1820* 2 vols. (Lisbon: Banco de Portugal, 1993), others can be found in the inventories of the Arquivo Histórico Ultramarino.
18. José Joaquim de Azeredo Coutinho, *Ensaio Económico sobre o Comércio de Portugal e suas Colónias 1794* (Lisbon: Banco de Portugal, 1992) and D. Rodrigo de Souza Coutinho, *Texto Políticos, Económicos e Financeiros, 1783-1811* 2 vols. (Lisbon: Banco de Portugal, 1993).
19. On Gregório de Matos see João Adolfo Hansen, *A Sátira e o Engenho. Gregório de Matos e a Bahia do Século XVII* (São Paulo: Editora Schwarcz, 1989); on Tomás Antônio Gonzaga see: Adelto Gonçalves, *Gonzaga, um Poeta do Illunismo* (Rio de Janeiro: Nova Fronteira, 1999).
20. John Hawkesworth ed., *An Account of the Voyages undertaken by the order of his present Majesty for making discoveries in the Southern Hemisphere, and successively performed by Commodore Byron, Captain Wallis, Captain Cartenet and Captain Cook, in the Dolphin, the Swallow, and the Endeavour: Drawn up from the journals which were kept by the several commanders, and from the papers of Joseph Banks esq* (London: printed for W. Stranhan and T. Cadell, 1773) 2:28-32.
21. [Abbé Raynal], *Histoire Philosophique et Politique Des Établissemens & du Commerce des Européens das les Deux Indes* (Amsterdam, 1770) 3: 397-416.
22. On this treaty itself see, A.D. Francis, *The Methuens and Portugal, 1691-1708* (Cambridge: Cambridge University Press, 1966).
23. Adam Smith, *The Wealth of Nations*, Edwin Cannan ed., (New York: the Modern Library, 2000) 586-590.
24. W.L von Eschwege, Pluto Brasiliensis. *Eine Reihe von Abhandlungen über Brasiliens Gold-Diamanten und anderen mineralischen Reichtum* (Berlin: G. Reimer, 1833), John Mawe, *Travels in the Interior of Brazil* (London: Longman, Hurst, Rees, Orme and Brown, 1822). Both have been translated into Portuguese and are published by Livraria Itatiaia Editora ltda.
25. Robert Southey, *History of Brazil* (Reprint; New York: Lenox Hill Publishers, 1970; 1st ed 1822) 1: xxiv.
26. Southey, *History of Brazil* 1:x.
27. Southey, *History of Brazil* 3:594.
28. Southey, *History of Brazil* 3:594.
29. See the index of the journal of *Revista do Instituto Histórico e Geográfico Brasileiro* year 159, vol. 400 (Jul/Sept 1998). Unfortunately, it only covers the institute in Rio de Janeiro.
30. Another such historian was José Higino Duarte Pereira a historians from Pernambuco who ordered the transcription of many Dutch documents for the historical and archeological institute in Recife. José Antônio Gonsalves de Mello, *Tempo de Journal* (Recife: Fundação Joaquim Nabuco and Editora Massangana, 1998) 182-184; Gonsalves de Mello supplemented this research and at this moment Brazilians are expanding the project through *"Operação Resgate."* For more information on this project see http://www.resgate.unb.br/rhistorico.html

31. Some of these publications are Revista do Instituto Histórico e Geographico Brasileiro, *Revista do Arquivo Publico Mineiro, Anais da Biblioteca Nacional, Documentos Históricos,* and the *Documentos Interessantes para a História de São Paulo.*
32. The inventories are published in vols. 31 (1908), 32 (1909), 34 (1911), 36 (1913), 37 (1914), 39 (1916), 46 (1924), 50 (1928), and 71 (1951). These are the reference years, which does not always coincide with the year of publication. See vol. 100 (1980) for an index.
33. Pedro Calmon, *História do Brasil* 6 vols. (Rio de Janeiro: Livraria José Olympio, 1959).
34. Calmon, *História do Brasil* 4: 1211
35. Calmon, *História do Brasil* 4: 1211.
36. Joaquim Felício dos Santos, *Memórias do Distrito Diamantino da Comarca do Sêrro Frio* (3rd ed.; Belo Horizonte: Edições o Cruzeiro, 1956, 1st ed. 1868), 166 n. 28. "Nós os sabemos da tradição e testemunho de pessoas respeitáveis e fidedignas, que tivemos o trabalho a consultar, que os ouviram dos contemporâneos de João Fernandes, que os conheceram e foram testimunhas oculares."; in the same tradition see the works of Agripa Vasconcelos especially *A Vida em Flor de Dona Beia. Romance do Ciclo do Povoamendo nas Gerais* (6th ed.; Belo Horizonte, Editor Itatiaia, 1988).
37. Dos Santos, *Memórias* 160, 164.
38. Júnia Ferreira Furtado corrected these myths using both official correspondence and notarial archives in her *Chica da Silva e o Contratador dos Diamantes. O Outro Lado do Mito* (Rio de Janeiro: Companhia das Letras, 2003).
39. The classical work on economic cycles is J. Lúcio de Azevedo, *Épocas de Portugal Económico* (1st ed. 1928; 4th ed., Lisbon: Clássica Editora, 1988).
40. Caio Prado jr., *História Econômica do Brasil* (1st ed. 1945; 35th ed., São Paulo: Editora Brasiliense, 1987) 79.
41. Caio Prado jr. *História Econômica* 92.
42. José Jobson de Andrade Arruda, *O Brasil no Comércio Colonial* (São Paulo: Editora Ática, 1980).
43. Corcino Medeiros dos Santos, *O Rio de Janeiro e a Conjuntura Atlântica* (Rio de Janeiro: Expressão e Cultura, 1993).
44. Virgílio Noya Pinto, *O Ouro Brasileiro e o Comércio Anglo-Português* (São Paulo: Ed. Nacional, 1979); Michiel Morineau, *Incroyables Gazettes et fabuleaux Méteaux. les Retours des Trésoirs Americains d'après les Gazettes Hollandeses (XVIe-XVIIIe siècles)* (London: Cambridge University Press; Paris: Maison des Sciences de l'Homme, 1985).
45. For earlier usage of statistics see the (highly unreliable) Roberto C. Simonsen, *História Econômica do Brasil (1500/1820)* (8th ed.; São Paulo, Companhia Editora Nacional, 1978
46. Jorge M. Pedreira, *Estructura Industrial e Mercado Colonial. Portugal e Brasil (1780-1830)* (Lisbon: Difel, 1994).
47. Fernando A. Novais, *Portugal e Brasil na Crise do Antigo Sistema Colonial (1777-1808)* (1st ed. 1979; 4th ed., São Paulo: Editora Hucitec, 1986).
48. Novais, *Portugal e Brasil* 175
49. See for instance, Júnia Ferreira Furtado, *Homens de Negócio. A Interiorização da Metrópole e do Comércio nas Minas Setecentistas* (São Paulo: Hucitec, 1999) (but not her book on Chica da Silva cited above), as well as Marco Antônio Silveira, *O Universo do Indistincto. Estado e Sociedade nas Minas Setecentistas (1735-1808)* (São Paulo: Hucitec, 1997).

NOTES

50. These sources have been used by American and British historians of Brazil. See for instance A.J.R. Russell-Wood, *Fidalgos and Philantropists. The Santa Casa da Misericóridai of Bahia, 1550-1755* (Berkeley: University of California press, 1968) and Rae Flory and David Grant Smith, "Bahia Merchants and Planters in the Seventeenth and Eighteenth Centuries," *Hispanic American Historical Review* 58:4 (1978) 571-594.
51. *Guia Brasileiro de Fontes para a História da África, da Escravidão Negra e do Negro na Sociedade Actual: Fontes Arquivistas* 2 vols. (Rio de Janeiro: Arquivo Nacional, 1988).
52. For two overviews of Brazilian historiography see A.J.R. Russell-Wood, *Slavery and Freedom in Colonial Brazil* (2nd ed.; Oxford: Oneworld, 2002), xiii-liii; Stuart B. Schwartz, "Somebodies and Nobodies in the Body Politic: Mentalities and Social Structures in Colonial Brazil," *Latin American Research Review* 31 (1996) 113-134.
53. João Luís Ribeiro Fragoso, *Homens de Grossa Aventura: Accumulação e Hierarquia na Praça Mercantil do Rio de Janeiro (1790-1830)* (Rio de Janeiro: Arquivo Nacional, 1992).
54. Manolo Garcia Florentino, *Em Costas Negras. Uma História do Tráfico de Escravos entre a África e o Rio de Janeiro* (Séculos XVIII e XIX) (Rio de Janeiro: Arquivo Nacional, 1995); Luiz Felipe de Alencastro, *O Trato dos Viventes. Formação do Brasil no Atlântico Sul* (São Paulo: Companhia das Letras, 2000).
55. See the debate between Pedreira and Arruda, *Hispanic American Historical Review* 80:4 (November 2000) 839-878 and between Pedreira and Pijning, *Hispanic American Historical Review* (August-November 2001) 733-744.
56. Just one example of an excellent thesis based on local archival sources is Maurídes Batista de Macêdo Filha, "A Trajetóra do Diamante em Goiás," (Masters Thesis, Universidade Federal de Goiás, 1990).
57. Maria Fernanda Bicalho, *A Cidade e o Império. O Rio de Janeiro no Século XVIII* (Rio de Janeiro: Civilização Brasileira, 2003), Hal Langfur, "Uncertain Refuge: Frontier Formation and the Origins of the Botocudo War in Late Colonial Brazil," *Hispanic American Historical Review* 82:2 (May 2002), 215-256. Newest works are by Victor Hugo Abril, *Governança no Ultramar. Conflicos e Descaminhos no Rio de Janeiro (c.1700-c.1750)*, Jundiaí: Paco Editorial, 2018), Adriana Romeiro, *Corrupção e Poder no Brasil. Uma história, séculos XVI a XVIII*, Belo Horizonte: Autêntica, 2018) and *Ladroes da República. Corrupção, moral, e cobiça no Brasil, séculos XVI a XVIII*, (Belo Horizonte: Fino Traco, 2023), Valter Lenine Fernandes, "Império e Colonização: Alfândegas e Tributação em Portugal e no Rio de Janeiro (1700-1750)," doctoral dissertation, (São Paulo: Universidade de São Paulo, 2019).

1. THE DIPLOMACY OF CONTRABAND TRADE: BETWEEN PASSIVE RESISTANCE AND PROACTIVE REFORM.

1. L.M.E. Shaw, *Anglo-Portuguese Alliance and the English Merchants in Portugal, 1654-1810* (Aldershot: Ashgate, 1998) 3.
2. Shaw, *Anglo-Portuguese Alliance* 4
3. See for instance Dom Luís da Cunha, *Instrucções Inéditas de Dom Luís da Cunha a Marco António de Azevedo Coutinho* Pedro de Azevedo ed., (Coimbra, Imprensa da Universidade, 1929); critical on these views are Abbé Raynal, *Histoire Philosphique et Politique des Établissements & du Commerce des Européens dans les Deux Indes* (Amsterdam, 1770); Adam Smith, *An Inquiry into the Nature and Causes of the Wealth of Nations* [1775], New York, The Modern Library, 1965). The best book on mercantilism is still, Eli Heckscher, *Mercantilism*, Mendel Shapiro transl. and E.F. Söderlund ed.,

(2nd ed.; New York: MacMillan Cie and London: George Allen & Unwin Ltd., 1955) 2 vols.
4. Charles R. Boxer, "Brazilian Gold and British Trader in the First Half of the Eighteenth Century," *Hispanic American Historical Review* [HAHR] 49:3 (1969) 454-472; Allan Christolow, "Great Britain and the Trades from Cadiz and Lisbon to Spanish America and Brazil, 1759-1783" *HAHR* 27:1 (1947) 2-29; A.D. Francis, *The Methuens and Portugal 1691-1708* (Cambridge: Cambridge University Press, 1966), and his *Portugal 1715-1808: Joanine, Pombaline, and Rococo Portugal as seen by British Diplomats and Traders* (London: Tamesis Books, 1985); H.E.S. Fisher, *The Portugal Trade. A Study of Anglo-Portuguese Commerce, 1700-1770* (London: Methuen & Co., 1971); Alan K. Manchester, *British Preeminence in Brazil, its Rise and Decline. A Study in European Expansion* (2nd ed.; New York: Octagon Books, 1970); V.M. Shillington and A.B. Wallis Chapman, *The Commercial Relations of England and Portugal* (1st ed.; London, 1907; Reprint: New York: Burt Franklin, 1970); L.M.E. Shaw, *The Anglo-Portuguese Alliance and the English merchants in Portugal, 1654-1810* (Brookfield VT. Ashgate, 1998); S. Sideri, *Trade and Power. Informal Colonialism in Anglo-Portuguese Relations* (Rotterdam: Rotterdam University Press, 1970); Jean-François Labourdette, *La Nation Française a Lisbonne de 1669 à 1790 entre Colbertisme et Liberalisme* (Paris: Fondation Calouste Gulbenkian, 1988), and also his "L'Ambassade de Monsieur de Chavigny a Lisbonne (1740-1743)," *Bulletin du Centre d'Histoire des Espaces Atlantiques 1* (1983) 27-80; Vitorino Magalhães Godinho, "Le Portugal, les Flottes du Sucre et les Flottes de l'Or (1670-1770)," *Annales, Économies, Sociétés, Civilisations* 5:2 (1950) 184- 197; Jorge Borges de Macedo, *A Situação Económica no Tempo de Pombal. Alguns Aspectos* (3rd ed.; Lisbon: Moraes Editores, 1989) and *Problemas de História da Indústria Portuguesa no Século XVIII* (Lisbon: Associação Industrial Portuguesa, 1963); Kenneth R. Maxwell, *Pombal: Paradox of the Enlightenment* (Cambridge: Cambridge University Press, 1995) and his seminal article: "Pombal and the Nationalization of the Luso-Brazilian Economy," *HAHR* 48:4 (1968) 608-631; Virgílio Noya Pinto, *O Ouro Brasileiro e o Comércio Anglo-Português* (2nd ed., São Paulo: Companhia Editora Nacional, 1979).
5. See for this aspect A.J.R. Russell-Wood, "Colonial Brazil: the Gold Cycle c. 1690-1750," in Leslie Bethell ed., *The Cambridge History of Latin America* (Cambridge: Cambridge University Press, 1984) 2:547-600.
6. Dom Luís da Cunha, *Instruções Inéditas de D. Luís da Cunha a Marco António de Azevedo Coutinho*, Pedro de Azevedo ed., (Coimbra: Imprensa da Universidade, 1929); Sebastião José Carvalho e Mello (1741-1742), José Barreto ed., (Lisbon: Biblioteca National, 1986).
7. Consultation of Overseas Council by António Rodrigues da Costa in 1732, *Revista do Institúto Histórico e Geográfico Brasileiro*, [RIHGB] 7 (1866) 498-507; "Parecer de António Rodrigues da Costa sobre se deveriam ou não ir os estrangeiros às conquistas," July 27, 1718, in Virginia Rau and Maria Fernanda Costa Gomes da Silva eds., *Os Manuscritos do Arquivo da Casa de Cadaval Respeitantes ao Brasil* (Coimbra: University of Coimbra, 1958) 2:200-204. Consultation of Treasury Council by José da Cunha Brochado, without date [± 1724], Quay d'Orsay [QdO] (Paris) Mémoires et Documents, Portugal, vol.21, fl.20r-21r and Biblioteca Pública de Évora, Códice CIV/1-33, fl.85r-91r.
8. For political-economic thought in the Joanine epoch see Francisco José Calazans Falcon, *A Época Pombalina (Politica Econômica e Monarquia I"ustrada)* (São Paulo: Editora Ática, 1982) 201-210.

9. On this topic see Evaldo Cabral de Mello, *O Negócio do Brasil. Portugal, os Países Baixos e o Nordeste, 1641-1669* (2nd ed.; Rio de Janeiro, Topbooks, 1998).
10. Francis, *The Methuens and Portugal* 211.
11. Labourdette, "L'Ambassade de M.r de Chavigny," 41; Dispatch of the French consul in Lisbon, Du Vernay, to Secretary of State, July 12, 1740, Archives Nationales, Paris [ANP], Affaires Étrangers [AE], B/I/671, fl.254r-256r.
12. Dispatch French ambassador to Lisbon, Abbé de Mornay, to French secretary of state, October 23, 1714, ANP, AE, B/I/653, fl.182r-185r.
13. Dispatch Du Verger to French secretary of state, July 17, 1713, ANP, AE, B/I/652, fl.405r-408r; Dispatch idem. to idem., September 25, 1713, ANP, AE, B/I/652, fl.442r-445v; Dispatch idem. to idem., November 27, 1713, ANP, A.E., B/I/652, fl.452r-459v.
14. Dispatch Du Verger to French secretary of state, December 4, 1713, ANP, AE, B/I/652, fl.46r-463r. {partly in ciphers} "quand {les flottes partent d'icy} et que l'on change {quelques Gouverneurs} on pourroit sollicíter ceux qui seroient {nommés} et par l'esperance de quelques {retribution les engager a donner parolle de recevoir tel vaisseau} qu'on leur diroit et enfin {traiter} par avance {avec eux} cette affaire."
15. Dispatch Du Verger to French secretary of state, September 25, 1713, ANP, AE, B/I/652, fl.442r-445v.
16. Dispatch Abbé de Mornay to French secretary of state, June 11, 1715, ANP, AE, B/I/653, fl.364r-365v.
17. Dispatch Abbé de Mornay to French secretary of state, July 9, 1715, ANP, AE, B/I/653, fl.387r-388r "qu'il n'est pas aisé de détruire les impressions qu'elles ont faites sur l'esprit des Portugais déja prevenues que les François estat [sic] establis dans ces conquêtes toute la nation y fera commerce en droiture."
18. [Le Gentil de la Barbinais], *Nouveau Voyage au Tour du Monde par M. le Gentil* (Amsterdam: Pierre Mortier, 1728).
19. See for instance Consultation of Overseas Council, April 16, 1709, Arquivo Histórico Ultramarino (Lisbon) [AHU], Rio de Janeiro, papeis avulsos [p.a.], caixa 8, doc. 38.
20. Dispatch Dom Rodrigo da Costa to king, September 23, 1702, Documentos Históricos 34:215.
21. Consultation of Overseas Council, January 21, 1705, AHU, Códice 232, fl.219v.
22. Andrée Mansuy, "Mémoire Inédit d'Ambroise Jauffret sur le Brésil à l'Époque de la Découverte des Mines d'Or [1704]," *Actas do V Colóquio Internacional de Estudos Luso-Brasileiros*, (Nashville: Vanderbilt University Press, 1965) 2:407-434.
23. Manoel S. Cardozo, "The Brazilian Gold Rush," *The Americas* 3 [TAm] (1946) 155-157.
24. For questions on the nomination of clergy and the employment of foreign ministers in the Portuguese empire in other contexts see Dauril Alden, *The Making of an Enterprise. The Society of Jesus in Portugal, Its Empire and Beyond 1540-1750* (Stanford: Stanford University Press, 1996) 267-272; Charles R. Boxer, *The Church Militant and Iberian Expansion, 1440-1770* (Baltimore and London: Johns Hopkins University Press, 1978) 77-84.
25. Dispatch French consul in Lisbon, Mr. Rouille, to French secretary of state, October 21, 1700, ANP, AE, B/I/651, fl.115r-117v. "On traite icy cette affaire comme affaire d'etat, l'aprehension que les etrangers ne connoissent trop ce qui se passe au Bresil est le fondement des resolutions prises"
26. Dispatch Mr. Rouille to French secretary of state, November 15, 1701, ANP, AE, B/I/651, fl.245r-248r.

27. Royal dispatch to governor of Rio de Janeiro, April 7, 1713, Biblioteca National, Rio de Janeiro [BNRJ], II-34,23,1 N.°19, and Arquivo National, Rio de Janeiro [ANRJ], Colonial, códice 60, vol.12, fl.158r.
28. Request João Adolpho Scharan to king, without date [±1730], AHU, Rio de Janeiro, papeis avulsos catalogados [p.a.c.], 6589.
29. Dispatch viceroy, Luís de Vasconsellos e Sousa, to Secretary of State, Martinho de Mello e Castro, January 22, 1789, AHU, Rio de Janeiro, p.a., caixa 143, doc.11.
30. Petition Pedro Folgman to governor, Luís Vahia Monteiro, July 4, 1726, ANRJ, Col., cód.87, vol.2, fl.134r-v.
31. Dispatch British secretary of state, Earl of Weymouth, to British plenipotentiary in Lisbon, Robert Walpole, August 13, 1776, National Archives, London [NAL], (State Papers Portugal [SP] 89, vol.82, fl.231r-232r; Dispatch James Murrier to Anthony Charier Dunkeld, August 1, 1776, NAL, SP 89, vol.82, fl.233r-v; Dispatch secretary of state, Marquis of Pombal, to Robert Walpole, September 3, 1776, NAL, SP 89, vol.83, fl.77r.
32. Charles R. Boxer, "English Shipping in the Brazil Trade, 1640-1665," *The Mariner's Mirror* 27 (1951) 197-230.
33. Dispatch British consul in Lisbon, Mr. Milner, to British secretary of state, the Earl of Sutherland, June 20, 1710, NAL, SP 89, vol.20, fl.77r-78r; Memorial British Factory at Porto, August 30, 1711, NAL, SP 89, vol.89, fl.37r-44v. Francis, Portugal 1715-1808 43-44.
34. Memorandum from the Merchants in Portugal to the British secretary of state, Earl of Galway, November 23, 1709, NAL, SP 89, vol.89, fl.3r-24v; "Representation of the Commission for Trade and Planters relating to the Grievances of the British merchant labour under in Portugal," November 23, 1709, NAL, SP 89, vol.89, fl.25r-29v
35. Da Cunha, *Instruções inéditas* 184-185; Boxer, "Brazilian Gold," 462-263; Dispatch William Poyntz to Paul Methuen, October 23, 1716, NAL, SP 89, vol.24, fl.124r-130v.
36. Report British factory at Lisbon, October 20, 1716, NAL, SP 89, vol.24, fl.124r-130v.
37. Dispatch British consul in Lisbon, William Poyntz, to British secretary of state, Paul Methuen, December 4, 1716, NAL, SP 89, vol.24, fl.139r-140v
38. Dispatch British plenipotentiary in Lisbon, Henry Worseley, to Paul Methuen, December 12, 1716, NAL, SP 89, vol.24, fl.141r-142v.
39. Dispatch Diogo Mendonça Corte Real to Henry Worseley, January 7, 1717, NAL, SP 89, vol.25, fl.3r-v.
40. Dispatch Henry Worseley to Paul Methuen, April 2, 1717, NAL, SP 89, vol.25, fl.58r-59v; Dispatch Diogo Mendonça de Corte Real to Henry Worseley, April 1, 1717, NAL, SP 89, vol.25, fl.62r-v.
41. Dispatch William Poyntz to British secretary of state, Joseph Addison, November 26, 1717, NAL, SP 89, vol.25, fl.205r-207r.
42. Dispatch Henry Worseley to Joseph Addison, December 18, 1717, NAL, SP 89, vol.25, fl.213r-215v.
43. Dispatch Diogo Mendonça de Corte Real to Thomas Lumbey, British envoy in Lisbon, February 1, 1723, NAL, SP 89, vol.30, fl.143r; Dispatch British consul in Faro, William Cayley, to British secretary of state, Lord Viscount Townshend, July 7, 1730, NAL, SP 89, vol.31, fl.232r-233r; Dispatch French consul in Lisbon, De Montagnac, to the Council of Marine, March 23, 1723, ANP, AE, B/I/661, fl.25r-v.
44. Report British factory at Lisbon, October 23, 1716, NAL, SP 89, vol.24, fl.124r-130v.

NOTES

45. Royal dispatch of March 23, 1711, AHU, Rio de Janeiro, pa., caixa 9, doc.11.
46. Secret dispatch Dutch resident in Lisbon, Houwens, to Secretary of the States General, Fagel, July 12, 1729, NADH [Nationaal Archief, Den Haag] (National Archives, The Hague, Netherlands), Staten Generaal [SG], Liassen Portugal, 7022/1; Dispatch Resident Houwens to Fagel, October 18, 1729, NADH, SG, Liassen Portugal, 7022/1.
47. Secret dispatch Dutch resident in Lisbon, F. Schonenberg to Fagel, January 18, 1712, NADH, SG, Liassen Portugal, Secreet, 7039/1. "Bij dese occasie occureerd mij aan de Hoogwijse diliberatien van Hoogh Mogenden voor te stellen, oft nu niet eenigsints te passe soude comen, dat aan den Grave Tarocca [sic] in serieuse termen bij dese gelegendheijd te verstaan gegeven wierd, hoe qualijk desselfs communiseerende onderdaanen alhier gehandeld werden, soo in de saake vande prijs van 't sout, als den graanhandel, en met ingesondenheÿd in niet te willen gedoogen, dat de Hollandsche sig in Brasil estabileeren, niettegenstaande sulx tegens de tractaaten."
48. Dispatch Robert Walpole to Earl of Rockford, October 19, 1774, NAL, SP 89, vol.78, fl.39r-44v.
49. Dispatch Henry Worseley to Lord Stanhope, November 9, 1714, NAL, SP 89, vol.23, fl.97r-98v; Dispatch idem. to idem., December 7, 1714, NAL, SP 89, vol.23, fl.104r-108r; Dispatch idem. to idem., May 10, 1715, NAL, SP 89, vol.23, fl.208r-v.v.
50. Dispatch Abbé de Mornay to Diogo Mendonça de Corte Real, September 28, 1714, ANP, AE, B/I/653, fl.153r-v.
51. Dispatch Abbé de Mornay to French secretary of state, October 2, 1714, ANP, AE, B/I/653, fl.167r-169v.
52. Dispatch Abbé de Mornay to French secretary of state, October 23, 1714, ANP, AE, B/I/653, fl.182r-185r.
53. Dispatch Abbé de Mornay to French secretary of state, February 2, 1715, ANP, AE, B/I/653, fl.238r-239v; Dispatch Du Verger to French secretary of state, April 1, 1715, ANP, AE, B/I/653, fl.238r-239v; Dispatch Abbé du Mornay to French secretary of state, March 16, 1717, ANP, AE, B/I/655, fl.18r-19v.
54. Dispatch De Montagnac to Council of Marine, August 27, 1720, ANP, AE, B/I/658, fl.169r-v; Dispatch idem. to idem., November 4, 1721, ANP, AE, B/I/659, fl.200r-201r; Dispatch vice consul of Salvador, Du Vienne to French Secretary of State, November 18, 1721, QdO, Consulaire et Commercial, Bahia, vol.1, fl.52r-53r.
55. Dispatch French consul in Fayal, Mr. de Harrangue, to French secretary of state, March 29, 1724, ANP, AE, B/I/487, fl.41r-44v. Dispatch Du Verger to French secretary of state, May 23, 1724, ANP, AE, B/I/662, fl.83r-86v.
56. Dispatch Du Vernay to French secretary of state, July 7, 1742, ANP, AE, B/I/673, fl.129r-131v, and idem. to idem., October 15, 1743, ANP, AE, B/I/674, fl.146r-147r.
57. Anonymous paper to Robert Walpole, September 22, 1792, NAL, Foreign Office [FO] 63, vol.15.
58. Fisher, *The Portugal Trade* 92.
59. See also Borges de Macedo, *A Situação Económica* 98.
60. Opinion José da Cunha Brochado, counsellor Treasury Council, without date [± 1724], QdO, Mémoires et Documents, Portugal, vol.21, fl.20r-21r and Biblioteca Pública de Évora, Cód. CIV/1-33, fl.85r-91r.
61. Boxer, "Brazilian Gold," 460; Fisher, *The Portugal Trade* 99-100.
62. Dispatch De Montagnac to French secretary of state, February 13, 1725, ANP, AE, B/I/662, fl.239r-240r. "Qu'un vaisseau de guerre Anglois sortit de ce Port 12 jours

avant rentra et mouilla aussy au milieu de cette flotte de laquelle l'on est persuadé qu'il aura chargé quantité d'or qui pouvoit y etre embarqué sans etre enregistré."
63. Boxer, "Brazilian Gold," 465.
64. On Tyrawly's stay in Lisbon see Charles R. Boxer, "Lord Tyrawly in Lisbon. An Anglo-Irish Protestant at the Portuguese Court, 1728-41," *History Today* 20 (1970) 791-798.
65. Boxer, "Brazilian Gold," 467-468; Dispatch British Secretary of State, Newcastle, to British plenipotentiary in Lisbon, Lord Tyrawly, February 2, 1734 [Old Style], British Library [BL], Additional Manuscripts [Add.Ms.]23627, fl.51r.
66. Charles R. Boxer ed., *Descriptive List of the State Papers Portugal 1661-1780* in the Public Record Office London (Lisbon: Academia das Ciências, 1979) 1:441-447; Dispatch De Montagnac to Council of Marine, January 13, 1722, ANP, AE, B/I/660, fl.2r-6r; Dispatch idem. to idem., February 2, 1722, ANP, AE, B/I/660, fl.44r-45r.
67. Copies of orders by secretary of state, Marco António de Azeredo Coutinho to *juiz da saca de moeda*, António Freire de Andrade Encerrabodes, for the export of gold from Portugal to other countries in the 1740s can be found in: Arquivo National da Torre do Tombo (Lisbon), Ministério do Reino, N.° 300. I would like to thank Tiago Costa Pinto dos Reis Miranda for this reference.
68. Fisher, *The Portugal Trade* 96-97.
69. Dispatch Du Vernay to French secretary of state, October 31, 1741, ANP, AE, B/I/672, fl.209r-211v; H.E.S. Fisher, *The Portugal Trade* 100.
70. Labourdette, *La Nation Française* 447-452; Dispatch Du Montagnac to secretary of state, September 7, 1734, ANP, AE, B/I/668, fl.158r-160r; Dispatch Du Vernay to secretary of state, August 15, 1741, ANP, AE, B/I/672, fl.162r-163v.
71. Dispatch De Montagnac to French secretary of state, January 11, 1724, ANP, AE, B/I/662, fl.6r-7r, on this case see Ernst Pijning, "Le Commerce Négrier Brésilien et la Transnationalité. Le Cas de la Compagnie Corisco (1715-1730)," *Dix-Huitième Siècle* (2001) 33:63-79.
72. Dispatch Thomas Lumley to British secretary of state, Lord Carteret, May 31, 1723, NAL, SP 89, vol.30, fl.215r-218r; Dispatch De Montagnac to French secretary of state, August 15, 1724, ANP, AE, B/I/662, fl.134r-135r.
73. Dispatch De Montagnac to French secretary of state, December 25, 1725, ANP, AE, B/I/662, fl.331r-333v.
74. Pierre Verger, *Flux et Reflux de la Traite des Nègres entre le Golfe de Bénin et Bahia de Todos os Santos* (Paris and The Hague: Mouton, 1968) 42.
75. Da Cunha, *Instruções inéditas* 137-138; 150-151.
76. See for instance Luís Ferrand Almeida, "A Fábrica das Sedas de Lisboa no Tempo de D. João V," *Revista Portuguesa de História* 25 (1989-1990) 1-48.
77. Maxwell, *Pombal: Paradox of the Enlightenment* chapter 4.
78. Jorge Borges de Macedo, "Dialéctica da Sociedade Portuguesa no Tempo de Pombal," in Manuel Antunes ed., *Como Interpretar Pombal? No Bicentário da sua Morte* (Lisbon: Edições Brotéria, Porto: Livraria A.I., w.d. [1982]) 15-16. An example of the negative explanation is António Leite, "A Ideologia Pombalina, Despotismo Esclarecido e Regalismo," in ibidem 27-54; of the positive explanation Agustina Bessa Luís, *Sebastião José* (Lisbon: Imprensa Nacional, Casa da Moeda, 1982).
79. Jorge Borges de Macedo, *A Situação Económica no Tempo de Pombal. Alguns Aspectos* (3rd ed.; Lisbon: Gradiva Publicações ltd.ᵃ, 1989) 46.
80. Maxwell, "Pombal and the Nationalization of the Luso-Brazilian Economy," *HAHR* 48:4 (1968) 608-631.
81. Maxwell, *Pombal: Paradox of the Enlightenment* 2.

NOTES

82. See for this José Luís Cardoso, *O Pensamento Económico em Portugal nos finais do Século XVIII, 1780-1808* (Lisbon, Editora Estampa, 1989).
83. See Carl A. Hanson, *Economy and Society in Baroque Portugal, 1668-1703* (Minneapolis: University of Minneapolis Press, 1981) 131.
84. Dispatch Du Vernay to secretary of state, June 3, 1749, ANP, AE, B/I/679, fl.232r-233r.
85. Opinion Alexandre de Gusmão, 1750, as reproduced in Jaime Cortesão, *Alexandre de Gusmão e o Tratado de Madrid* (Rio de Janeiro: Ministério das Relações Exteriores, Instituto Rio Branco, 1953) 5:484-493.
86. Labourdette, *La Nation Française* 338-339, 352-353, 174-178.
87. Labourdette, *La Nation Française* 358-359; Dispatch consul St. Marc to secretary of state, March 7, 1786, ANP, AE, B/I/693.
88. Dispatch consul St. Marc to secretary of state, March 14, 1786, ANP, AE, B/I/693.
89. Jorge Miguel Viana Pedreira, *Estructura Industrial e Mercado Colonial Portugal e Brasil (1780-1830)*, (Lisbon: Difel, 1994) 47-51.
90. Dispatch British plenipotentiary to Lisbon John Hort to the Earl of Egremont, March 10, 1782, NAL, FO 63, vol.3.
91. See Manuel Nunes Dias, *Fomento e Mercantilismo: A Companhia do Grão Pará e Maranhão (1755-1778)* 2 vols. (w.p. [Belém]: Universidade Federal do Pará, 1970), and José Ribeiro Júnior, *Colonização e Monopólio no Nordeste Brasileiro. A Companhia Geral de Pernambuco e Paraíba (1759-1780)* (São Paulo: Hucitec, 1976).
92. Susan Schneider, *O Marquês de Pombal e o Vinho do Porto. Dependência e Subdesenvolvi- mento em Portugal no Século XVIII*, (Lisbon: A Regra do Jogo, 1980) 18-19.
93. Schneider, *O Marquês de Pombal e o Vinho do Porto* 42.
94. Schneider, *O Marquês de Pombal* 74-75.
95. Schneider, *O Marquês de Pombal* chapter 5.
96. Schneider, *O Marquês de Pombal* 80-82.
97. Count of Kinnock, "A Remonstrance Relating to the Prejudice arising from the Establishment of Companies, for Carrying on the Brazil Trade," in *Memorials of the British Consul and Factory at Lisbon to His Majesty's Ambassador at that Court and the Secretaries of State of this Kingdom* (London: for J. Wilkie, 1766) 13.
98. Count of Kinnock, "Remonstrance Relating to the Prejudices," 42.
99. Dispatch Lord Rockford to Robert Walpole, June 28, 1774, NAL, SP 89, vol.77, fl.33r-39r.
100. [Robert Walpole], "Observations on the Answer," May 26, 1769, BL, Add.ms.9252, fl.57v-58v.
101. H.E.S. Fisher, *The Portugal Trade* 46; Borges de Macedo, *Problemas de História da Indústria Portuguesa no Século XVIII* 188; Noya Pinto, *Ouro Brasileiro* 322.
102. Fisher, *The Portugal Trade* 41-49.
103. Borges de Macedo, *A Situação Económica* chapter IV
104. Labourdette, *La Nation Française* 390-394.
105. Dispatch James Rockford to Walpole, July 19, 1774, NAL, SP 89, vol.76, fl.173r-175r; Dispatch idem. to idem., September 27, 1774, NAL, SP 89, vol.77, fl.217r-219r.
106. Dispatch Robert Walpole to Earl of Rockford, October 19, 1774, NAL, SP 89, vol.78, fl.39r-44v.
107. D. Rodrigo de Souza Coutinho, *Textos Políticos, Económicos e Financeiros*, Andrée Mansuy Diniz Silva ed., 2 vols. (Lisbon: Banco de Portugal, 1993); José da Silva Lisboa, *Escritos Económicos Escolhidos*, António Almodovar ed., 2 vols. (Lisbon: Banco de Portugal, 1993); José Joaquim da Cunha de Azeredo Coutinho, *Ensaio Económico Sobre o Comércio de Portugal e suas Colónias*, Jorge Miguel Pedreira ed.,

(Lisbon: Banco de Portugal, 1992); Domingos Vandelli, *Aritmética Política, Economia e Finanças,* José Vicente Serrão ed., (Lisbon: Banco de Portugal, 1994).
108. J.R. Amaral Lapa, "Um Agricultor Illustrado do Século XVIII," in *Economia Colonial* (São Paulo: Editora Perspectiva, 1973) 141-213.
109. Francis, *The Methuens and Portugal,* chapter 8.
110. Dispatch consul Du Vernay to secretary of state, April 23, 1737, ANP, AE, B/I/670, fl.128r-129v; Dispatch ambassador De Chavigny to secretary of state, March 26, 1743, ANP, AE, B/I/674, fl.35r-36v.
111. Jean-François Labourdette, "L'Ambassade de Monsieur de Chavigny à Lisbonne (1740-1743)," *Bulletin du Centre d'Histoire des Espaces Atlantiques* 1(1983) 27-80.
112. Dispatch consul St. Marc to secretary of state, January 1, 1785, ANP, AE, B/I/691.
113. Report Board of Trade to secretary of state, August 13, 1737, BL, Add. Mss. 23639, fl.30r-31r.
114. See also Shaw, *The Anglo-Portuguese Alliance* 109-110.
115. Memorial John Hort to Martinho de Mello e Castro, October 1, 1784, NAL, FO 63, vol.5, and its abstract in: AHU, Rio de Janeiro, p.a., caixa 134, doc.27. The abstract is published in RIHGB 10(1848) 228.
116. Secret and confidential dispatch secretary of state to Robert Walpole, October 2, 1786, NAL, FO63, vol.8.
117. "Fifteen questions put to the British Factory at Lisbon," May, 4, 1786, NAL, FO 63, vol.7.
118. Memorial Diogo de Pina Manique to Martinho de Mello e Castro, October 6, 1784, AHU, Rio de Janeiro, p.a., caixa 134, doc. 32A. Published in: RIGHB 10 (1848) 213-225.
119. Dispatch Martinho de Mello e Castro to Luís de Vasconsellos e Souza, January 5, 1785, AHU, Rio de Janeiro, p.a., caixa 135, doc. 3; Fernando A. Novais, "A Proibição das Manufacturas no Brasil e a Política Económica Portuguêsa do Fim do Século XVIII," *Revista de História. Universidade de São Paulo* 67 (1967) 145-166.
120. Pedreira, *Estructura Industrial* 295-306.
121. Fernando A. Novais, *Portugal e Brasil na Crise do Antigo Sistema Colonial* (1777-1808) (4th ed.; São Paulo: Editora Hucitec, 1986) 11.
122. Valentim Alexandre, *Os Sentidos do Império. Questão Nacional e Questão Colonial na Crise do Antigo Regime Português* (Porto: Edições Afrontamento, 1993) part 2.
123. Novais, *Portugal e Brasil* 186-188; José Jobson de Arruda Andrade, *O Brasil no Comérico Colonial* (São Paulo: Ática, 1980), 323-330.
124. Alexandre, *Os Sentidos do Império* part 1; Pedreira, *Estructura Industrial* chapter 5.
125. Pedreira, *Estructura Industrial* 280-295.
126. For instance *New Lloyds List* N.°1711 of September 27, 1785, mentioned the Stormont, captain Bennet to have sailed for the "S. Fishery," in the *New Lloyds List* N.°1793 of July 11, 1786, the same vessel and captain had returned from the "Brazils" with "50 tons of oil".
127. Dispatch Marquis de Lavradio to Martinho de Mello e Castro, June 6, 1778, AHU, Rio de Janeiro, p.a., caixa 116, doc. 53; Dispatch Martinho de Mello e Castro to Luís de Vasconsellos e Souza, August 24, 1782, AHU, Rio de Janeiro, p.a., caixa 130, doc.21; Dispatch Count de Rezende to the viceroy of La Plata, April 6, 1800, BL, Add.Ms.32606, fl.45r-v.
128. Corcino Medeiros dos Santos, *O Rio de Janeiro e a Conjuntura Atlântica* (Rio de Janeiro: Expressão e Cultura, 1993) 169-193.
129. Dispatch Martinho de Mello e Castro to Luís de Vasconsellos e Souza, August 24, 1782, AHU, Rio de Janeiro, p.a., caixa 130, doc.77.

130. On this discussion see Pedreira, "From Growth to Collapse: Portugal, Brazil and the Breakdown of the Old Colonial System (1760-1830)," *HAHR* (2000) 80, 839-864; Arruda, "Decadence or Crisis in the Luso-Brazilian Empire: a New Model for Colonization in the Eighteenth Century," HAHR (2000) 80, 865-878; Pijning, "A New Interpretation of Contraband Trade," *HAHR* (2001) 81, 733-738; Pedreira, "Contraband, Crisis, and the Collapse of the Colonial System," *HAHR* (2001) 81, 739-744
131. For instance Report Donald Campbell to secretary of state, January 1, 1801, AHU, Rio de Janeiro, p.a., caixa 196, doc. 56.
132. Dispatch Count dos Arcos to Viscount of Anadia, September 2, 1807, AHU, Rio de Janeiro, pa, caixa 241, doc.56, Ernst Pijning, "Contrabando na Legislação Portuguesa durante o Período Colonial," *Anais da Sociedade Brasileira de Pesquisa Histórica* 14 (1994) 85.
133. Dispatch Balthazar da Silva Lisboa to Martinho de Mello e Castro, April 10, 1793, AHU, Rio de Janeiro, p.a., caixa 153, doc.35.
134. Autos de Exame, February 2, 1802, AHU, Rio de Janeiro, p.a., caixa 197, doc.48.
135. Dispatch Donald Campbell to D. Rodrigo de Souza Coutinho, April 7, 1801, AHU, Rio de Janeiro, p.a., caixa 191, doc. 84.
136. Thomas Lindley, *Narrative of a Voyage to Brazil: Terminating in the Seizure of a British Vessel, and the Imprisonment of the Author and the Ship's Crew*, by the Portuguese (London: J. Johnson, 1805); Letter Brown & Ives to Ephraim Talbot, April 22, 1800, John Carter Brown Library, Providence, R.I., Brown papers, C52/1800-1801, see further on this case Berenice A. Jacobs, "The *Mary Ann*, an Illicit Adventure," *HAHR* 37 (1957) 200-212.
137. Alexandre, *Os Sentidos* 64, quadro VI.
138. Pedreira, *Estructura Industrial* 301-306; Alexandre, *Os Sentidos* 51.
139. Pedreira, *Estructura Industrial* 278-295.
140. Alexandre, *Os Sentidos* 94-162.
141. Mémoire sur le Portugal, May 26, 1797, QdO, Mémoires et Documents, Portugal, tome 1.
142. "Pneus des motifs que le directoire peut avoir pour ne pas accepter la ratification tardive de la Reine de Portugal et pour qu'il fasse la conquête de ce royaume," without date [1797], QdO, Mémoires et documents, France, tome 1967, fl.344r-345r. "L'intéret de la France exige que son gouvernement n'omette aucun moyen pour indemniser le peuple français des sacrefices qu'ils a faits, les riches magazins que les augmentont en Portugal fourniront une somme de près de cent vingt millions de livres, les riches mines du Brezil et la somme de dix millions, produits des diamants que l'on en tire, outre les autres colonies du Portugal en Asie et Afrique et surtout dixhuit vaisseaux de ligne et plus de vingt frégates que trouvent dans ces ports, voilà les dédomagemens que la répus doit exiger de ses ennemis et qui trouveroit tous au plus grand détriment de l'Angleterre qui jouit presque seule de telles avantages."
143. Luís Beltrão de Almeida, "Memória sobre a influencia da Conquista de Buenosaires pelos Inglezes em toda a America; e meios de prevenir seus effeitos," December 15, 1806, AHU, Rio de Janeiro, p.a., caixa 236, doc. 16.
144. Alexandre, *Os Sentidos* 162-163.
145. Secret instructions to Earl St. Vincent and Lieutenant General Simcoe, August 9, 1806, NAL, FO 63, vol. 51.
146. Secret and confidential dispatch Lord Strangford to George Canning, September 8, 1807, NAL, FO 63, vol.55, fl.143r-150r.

147. Dispatch Fitzgerald to Viscount of Balsemão, December 20, 1803, NAL, FO 63, vol.43.
148. See for instance Domingos Vandelli, "Modo de evitar a ruína do reino ameaçado pelos ingleses com os contrabandos, e pelos franceses com as suas excessivas pretensões," in *Aritmetica Política* 293-296.

2. REGULATING ILLEGAL TRADE: FOREIGN VESSELS IN BRAZILIAN HARBORS

1. Dauril Alden, *Royal Government in Colonial Brazil. With a Special Reference to the Administration of the Marquis of Lavradio, Viceroy, 1769-1779* (Berkeley and Los Angeles: University of California Press, 1968) 403.
2. For a full overview of the legislation see Arquivo Histórico Ultramarino [AHU] (Lisbon), códice 1193. The legislation started in 1591, during the eighty years war (the War of Dutch independence). Yet the laws of 1711 and 1715 enforced the regulations during the eighteenth century.
3. Charles R. Boxer, *The Golden Age of Brazil, 1695-1750* (Berkeley and Los Angeles: University of California Press, 1962) 30-60; A.J.R. Russell-Wood, "Colonial Brazil: the Gold Cycle c. 1690-1750," in Leslie Bethell ed., *The Cambridge History of Latin America* (Cambridge: Cambridge University Press, 1984) 2:547-600; Manoel S. Cardozo, "The Brazilian Gold Rush," *The Americas* 3 (1946) 137-160.
4. Alvará February 8, 1711 and alvará October 5, 1715, AHU, códice 1193.
5. For more detailed information on this issue see Ernst Pijning, "Contrabando na Legislação Portuguesa durante o Período Colonial," *Anais da Sociedade Brasileira de Pesquisa Histórica* 14 (1994) 85-88.
6. *La Reine de Nantes*: Dispatch French consul in Lisbon, Du Verger, to French secretary of state, April 9, 1715, Archives Nationalles, Paris [ANP], Affaires Etrangères [AE], B/I/653, fl.306r-306v; *Le Succès*: Dispatch Luís António de Sá Queiroga to king, August 8. 1718, AHU., papeis avulsos [pa], caixa 12, doc.76; *La Subtile*: Dispatch French consul to Lisbon, Du Montagnac, to Council of Marine, September 28, 1720, ANP, AE, B/I/658, fl.238r-239r; *L'Aspirant*: Declaration Captain George Bourdain, December 30, 1721, ANP, AE, B/I/660, fl.39r-41v; *Saint Jean Baptiste*: Dispatch De Montagnac to Council of the Marine, September 9, 1721, ANP, AE, B/I/659, fl.166r-169r; *Le Comte de Toulouse*: Dispatch De Montagnac to French secretary of state, May 15, 1725, ANP, AE, B/I/662, fl.270r-272r; *Saint Joseph*: Royal dispatch to viceroy, Marquis de Angeja, April 8, 1718, AHU, cód. 1193, #14; *Don Carlos*: Sentence Governor of Rio de Janeiro, Luís Vahia Monteiro, October 4, 1725, AHU, Rio de Janeiro, papeis avulsos [p.a.], caixa 16, doc. 96.
7. Dispatch Du Verger to French secretary of state, July 17, 1713, ANP, AE, B/I/652, fl.405r-408r; Dispatch idem. to idem., September 25, 1713, ANP, AE, B/I/652, fl.442r-445v; Dispatch idem. to idem., November 27, 1713, ANP, AE, B/I/652, fl.452r-459v; Dispatch idem. to idem., December 4, 1713, ANP, AE, B/I/652, fl.46r-463r; Dispatch French ambassador in Lisbon, Abbé de Mornay, to French secretary of state, October 23, 1714, ANP, AE, B/I/653, fl.182r-185r.
8. Dispatch British plenipotentiary in Lisbon, Henry Worseley, to British secretary of state, Viscount Bolingbroke, September 8, 1714, National Archives, London [NAL], State Papers [SP] 89, vol.23, fl 82r-84v; Dispatch idem. to idem., September 29, 1714, NAL, SP 89, vol.23, fl.91r-92r; Dispatch idem. to idem., October 16, 1714, NAL, SP 89, vol.23, fl.93r-94r; Dispatch Worseley to British secretary of state,

NOTES

Lord Stanhope, January 21, 1715, NAL, SP 89, vol.23, fl.153r-155v; Dispatch idem. to idem., February 8, 1715, NAL, SP 89, vol.23, fl.163r-165r.
9. Dispatch Worseley to James Stanhope, October 18, 1715, NAL, SP 89, vol.23, fl.304r-v.
10. Dispatch French consul in Salvador, De Pantigny, to French Secretary of State, March 22, 1715, Quay d'Orsay [QdO] (Paris), Bahia, Consulaire et Commercial, vol.1, fl.42r-v.
11. Dispatch Du Verger to French secretary of state, June 10, 1715, ANP, AE, B/I/653, fl.362r-363r.
12. Dispatch De Montagnac to French secretary of state, May 22, 1715, ANP, AE, B/I/662, fl.274r-275r.
13. Dispatch governor Rio de Janeiro, António de Brito de Menezes, to captain of Ilha Grande, Thomas Gomes da Silva, February 15, 1718, Arquivo Nacional, Rio de Janeiro [ANRJ], Colonial [Col.], cód.84, vol.1, fl.33r-35r, Dispatch António de Brito e Menezes to Thomas Gomes da Silva, February 17, 1718, ANRJ, Col., cód.84, vol.1, fl.35r-36v.
14. Consultation Overseas Council, August 11, 1718, and Dispatch António de Brito e Menezes to king, March 10, 1718, AHU, Rio de Janeiro, papeis avulsos catalogados [p.a.c.], 3573-3574.
15. Declaration Geslain, January 27, 1720, ANP, AE, B/I/658, fl.13r-17r, ANP, AE, B/I/658, fl.13r-17r.
16. Dispatch De Montagnac to Council of Marine, December 16, 1721, ANP, AE, B/I/659, fl.267r-269r
17. Dispatch De Montagnac to Council of Marine, September 28, 1720, ANP, AE, B/I/658, fl.238r-239r.
18. Declaration George Boudain, December 30, 1721, ANP, AE, B/I/660, fl.39r-41v.
19. Dispatch Luís Vahia Monteiro to king, September 11, 1725, AHU, Rio de Janeiro, p.a., caixa 16, doc.96.
20. [Le Gentil de la Barbinais], Nouveau Voyage au Tour du Monde par M. le Gentil 2 vols. (Amsterdam: Pierre Mortier, 1728) 2: 112-176.
21. Barbinais, *Nouveau Voyage* 2:168,169.
22. Dispatch De Montagnac to Council of Marine, November 4, 1721, ANP, AE, B/I/659, fl.196r-198v; Dispatch De Montagnac to French Secretary of State, May 1, 1725, ANP, AE, B/I/662, fl.266r-267r; Dispatch idem. to idem., September 13, 1734, ANP, AE, B/I/668, fl.164r-165v.
23. Dispatch French consul in Lisbon, St. Colombe, to Council of Marine, February 2, 1717, ANP, AE, B/I/655, fl.12r-13v; Dispatch Du Vernay to French secretary of state, ANP, AE, B/I/670, fl.228r-230r.
24. Consultation Overseas Council, January 18, 1726, *Documentos Históricos* (Rio de Janeiro: Biblioteca Nacional, 1928-1955) 96:94-97.
25. Dispatch De Montagnac to French secretary of state, May 22, 1725, ANP, AE, B/I/662, fl.274r-275r; Dispatch De Beauvegan to French secretary of state, QdO., Memoires et Documents, Amérique, vol.6, fl.523r-526r.
26. Royal Dispatch to Marquis da Angeja, April 8, 1718, AHU, cód.1193, #14; Dispatch Diogo de Mendonça Corte Real to Worsley, April 9, 1718, NAL, SP 89, vol.26, fl.36r-v.
27. Consultation of Overseas Council, May 28, 1725, *Documentos Históricos* 96:158-162; Dispatch De Montagnac to Marine Council, March 18, 1723, ANP, AE, B/I/660, fl.73r-74r; Dispatch De Montagnac to secretary of state, ANP, AE, B/I/663, fl.130r-132v.

NOTES

28. Pedro de Azevedo, "A Companhia da Ilha do Corisco," *Arquivo Histórico Português* (Lisbon, 1903) 1:422-424. For further information on this case see Ernst Pijning, "Le Commerce Négrier Brésilien et la Transnationalité. Le Cas de la Compagnie Corisco (1715-1730)," *Dix-Huitième Siècle* 33 (2001) 63-79.
29. Autos de Exame, September 12, 1725, AHU, Rio de Janeiro, pa, caixa 16, doc.96.
30. Dom Luís da Cunha, Instrucções *Inéditas de Dom Luís da Cunha a Marco António de Azevedo Coutinho*, Pedro de Azevedo ed., (Coimbra: Imprensa da Universidade de Coimbra, 1929) 152.
31. Dispatch Dutch resident in Lisbon, Houwens, to States General, July 15, 1727, Nationaal Archief, Den Haag [NADH], Staten Generaal [SG], Liassen Portugal, 7022/1. For further information on this case see Ernst Pijning, "Betwist gezag: de verhoudingen tussen de Republiek en Portugal en de confiscatie van het MCC-schip *Don Carlos* in Rio de Janeiro (1725)," *Archief. Mededelingen van het Koninklijk Genootschap der Wetenschappen* (2003) 63-78.
32. Representation Dutch resident in Lisbon, Smissaert, to King, March 25, 1782, Arquivo Nacional da Torre do Tombo [ANTT] (Lisbon), Ministério dos Negócios Estrangeiros [MNE], Arquivo Central [AC], caixa 507.
33. Alden, *Royal Government* 110-111.
34. Pepin de Bellisle, "Extrait d'un Journal de la Campagne des Vaisseaux du Roi aux Indes Orientalles en l'Année 1748," ANP, Marine, B4, N.°62, fl.281r-302v; another shorter version exists in the Biblioteca do Palácio de Ajuda, 54-XIII-4 (19). For further information about this case see Maria Fernanda Baptista Bicalho, *A Cidade e o Império. Rio de Janeiro no século XVIII* (Rio de Janeiro: Civilização Brasileira, 2003) 112-116.
35. "Extrait Journal Arc-en-Ciel," ANP, Marine, B4, N.°62, fl.284r.
36. Alden, *Royal Government* 409-410; James Cook, "An Account of a Voyage round the World in the Years MDCCLXVIII, MDCCLXIX, MDCCLXX, and MDCCLXXI", in John Hawkesworth ed., *An Account of the Voyages undertaken by the order of his present Majesty for making the discoveries in the Southern Hemisphere, and successively performed by Commodore Byron, Captain Wallis, Captain Carteret and Captain Cook* 3 vols. (London: Printed for W. Strahan; and T. Cadell 1773); and J.C. Beaglehole ed., *The Voyages of Captain James Cook on his Voyages of Discovery* vol. 1. (Cambridge: Cambridge University Press, 1955).
37. *An Account of the Voyages undertaken by the order of his present Majesty for making the discoveries in the Southern Hemisphere and successively performed by Commodore Byron* 3 vols. (London: for W. Strahan; and T. Cadell, 1773) 1:1-134; *The Voyage of Governor Philip to Botany Bay with an Account of the Establishment of the Colonies of Port Jackson & Norfolk Island*, (London: for John Stockdale, 1789); L'Abbé Courte de la Blanchediere, *Nouveau Voyage fait au Pérou* (Paris: Imprimerie de Delaguette, 1751); Louis de Bougainville, *Voyage Autour du Monde par la Frégate du Roi la Boudeuse, et la Flûte l'Étoile; en 1766, 1767, 1768 & 1769* (Paris: Chez Saillant & Nyon, 1771); Abbé de la Caille, *Journal Historique du Voyage fait au Cap de Bonne Espérance* (Paris: Chez Guillyn, 1763).
38. Dispatch of the viceroy, Count de Azambuja, to James Cook, November 18, 1768, Beaglehole ed., *The Voyages of Captain James Cook on his Voyages of Discovery* 1:488-489.
39. Dispatch Count de Azambuja to secretary of state, Francisco Xavier de Mendonça Furtado, November 28, 1768, AHU, Rio de Janeiro, p.a., caixa 93, doc. 46. For more on the transit of Venus, Cook's observations, and its importance to contemporary

NOTES

science see Peter Aughton, *The Transit of Venus. The brief, brilliant life of Jeremiah Horrocks, father of British astronomy* (London: Weidenfeld & Nicolson, 2004) 180.
40. Dispatch of Count de Azambuja to Cook, November 22, 1768, Beaglehole ed., *Voyage of the Endeavour* 1:493.
41. Joseph Banks, *The Endeavour Journal of Joseph Banks 1768-1771*, J.C. Beaglehole ed., (Sydney: Halstead Press, 1962) 1:190. See Bicalho, *A Cidade e o Império* 122-123.
42. Dispatch of Cook to Azambuja, December 1, 1768, *The Endeavour Journal of Joseph Banks* 1:497.
43. Letter of Thomas Forster to Joseph Banks, November 5, 1771, in Beaglehole ed., *The Endeavour Journal* 2:321-323.
44. Dispatch Interim Governor Patrício Manoel de Figueiredo to secretary of state, Thomé Joaquim da Costa Corte Real, August 19, 1757, AHU, Rio de Janeiro, p.a.c., 20316. I thank Maria Fernanda Baptista Bicalho for this information. For more on this case see Bicalho, *A Cidade e o Império* 60-69.
45. Instructions to Count d'Aché, January 23, 1757, ANP, Marine, B4, N.°77, fl.167r-175v.
46. Instructions to Count d'Aché, January 1757, ANP, Marine, B4, N.°77, fl.136r-150v.
47. Dispatch Count d'Aché to governor Rio de Janeiro, July 19, 1757, ANP, Marine, B4, N.°77, fl.297r-v.
48. Dispatch Patrício Manoel de Figueiredo to Count d'Aché, August 4, 1757, AHU, Rio de Janeiro, p.a.c., 20324; Dispatch British plenipotentiary in Lisbon, Edward Hay, to British secretary of state, Pitt, December 9, 1757, NAL, SP 89, vol.51, fl.63r-64r; Dispatch Dutch resident in Lisbon, C.F. Bosch de la Calmette, to States General, December 6, 1757, NADH, SG, Liassen Portugal, N.° 7028/1.
49. Dispatch Patrício Manoel de Figueiredo to king, August 4, 1757, AHU, Rio de Janeiro, pac, 20326.
50. Journal Count d'Aché, August 19, 1757, ANP, Marine, B4, N.°77, fl.305r-306v.
51. Information *provedor da fazenda*, Francisco Cordovil Sequeira e Mello, to Thomé Joaquim da Costa Corte Real, July 6, 1759, AHU, Rio de Janeiro, pac, 20771.
52. Minute of dispatch secretary of state, Sebastião José Carvalho e Mello, to governor Rio de Janeiro, Gomes Freire de Andrade, April 8. 1759, AHU, Rio de Janeiro, p.a., caixa 65, doc. 25.
53. Alden, *Royal Government* 413-415
54. Consultation Overseas Council, January 1, 1781, AHU, Rio de Janeiro, p.a., caixa 126, doc. 7; Report Robert Sherson to British secretary of state, September 17, 1781, NAL, Foreign Office [FO] 63, vol.2, Royal dispatch to viceroy, Luís de Vasconcellos e Souza, October 30, 1781, Biblioteca Nacional, Rio de Janeiro [BNRJ], ms.4,4,3, fl.14r.
55. Sentence High Court Rio de Janeiro, January 16, 1781, AHU, Rio de Janeiro, p.a., caixa 127, doc. 7.
56. Dispatch British secretary of state, James Rockford to British plenipotentiary in Lisbon, Robert Walpole, August 3, 1773, NAL, SP 89, vol.75, fl.65r-66v.
57. Dispatch Robert Walpole to Earl of Rockford, October 19, 1774, NAL, SP 89, vol.78, fl.46r-v.
58. Dispatch Robert Walpole to Earl of Rockford, March 29, 1775, NAL, SP 89, vol.79, fl.83r-84v.
59. Dispatch Martinho de Mello e Castro to Robert Walpole, October 1, 1781, NAL, FO 63, vol.2, and BNRJ, ms.4,4,3, fl.14r-v; Dispatch Luís de Vasconcellos e Souza to Martinho de Mello e Castro, May 18, 1782, AHU, Rio de Janeiro, p.a., caixa 129, doc.72, and BNRJ, ms.4,4,4, fl.99v-101v.

60. Dispatch Robert Walpole to Lord Grantham, March 23, 1783, NAL, FO 63, vol.4.
61. Dauril Alden, "Yankee Sperm Whalers in Brazilian Waters, and the Decline of the Portuguese Whale Fishery (1773-1801)," *The Americas* 20 (1964) 276-282; Myriam Ellis, *A Baleia no Brasil Colonial* (São Paulo: Edições Melhoramentos, 1969) 169-171.
62. Dispatch Robert Walpole to Martinho de Mello e Castro, April 29, 1776, NAL, SP 89, vol 82, fl.67r-v.
63. Dispatch Robert Walpole to Martinho de Mello e Castro, April 29, 1776, NAL, SP 89, vol.82, fl.67r-v; Dispatch John Hort to Viscount Weymouth, September 19, 1779, NAL, SP 89, vol.86, fl.305r-307r.
64. Meeting Privy Council on Trade, July 13, 1790, NAL, Board of Trade [BT] 5, vol.6, fl.131r.
65. Meeting Privy Council on Trade, March, 17, 1806, NAL, BT 3, vol.3, fl.132r-133v.
66. Meeting Privy Council on Trade, July, 3, 1790, NAL, BT 5, vol.6, fl.257r-v.
67. Meeting Privy Council on Trade, February 14, 1791, NAL, BT 5, vol.7, fl.26v-28r.
68. Meeting Privy Council on Trade, January 21, 1791, NAL, BT 5, vol. 7, fl.11r-12r.
69. Meeting Privy Council on Trade, January 20, 1791, NAL, BT 5, vol. 7, fl.8v-10v.
70. Report Samuel Enderby and Champion to the Privy Council on Trade, March 19, 1792, NAL, BT 5, vol.7, fl.203r-v.
71. Dispatch viceroy, Count de Rezende, to secretary of state, Luís Pinto de Souza, November 5, 1795, AHU, Rio de Janeiro, p.a., caixa 161, doc. 28. "Os debates ... são immensos, e sempre indecorosos, e ofensivos a imunidade das Reaes Ordens, ao carater do Ministro, e ao respeito que merece a signatura do Vice Rey."
72. Act of Sequestration, Relação Rio de Janeiro, March 11, 1803, NAL, FO 63, vol.43.
73. "Sentença da arribada do bergantim Inglês denominado *São Pedro*," March 10, 1803, ANRJ, Colonial, cód.157, vol.11, fl.35r-36r.
74. Dispatch Robert Stephen Fitzgerald to Lord Hawkesbury, December 17, 1803, NAL, FO 63, vol.42.
75. Dispatch Lord Strangford to George Canning, July 16, 1807, NAL, FO 63, vol.55, fl.15r-18r.
76. Sentença da arribada," April 27, 1802, ANRJ, Col., cód.157, vol.11, fl.16r-v
77. Dispatch viceroy, Dom Fernando José de Portugal, to secretary of state, Viscount de Anadia, March 18, 1802, AHU, Rio de Janeiro, p.a., caixa 200, doc. 22.
78. "Minutes taken from Daniel Morse's protest," July 31, 1798, ANTT, MNE, AC, caixa 459.
79. Representation Robert Walpole to Luís Pinto de Souza, January 28, 1800, and annexes, AHU, Rio de Janeiro, p.a., caixa 181, doc. 56.
80. Dispatch José Feliciano da Rocha Gameiro to Count de Rezende, September 11, 1801, AHU, Rio de Janeiro, p.a., caixa 194, doc. 25.
81. Dispatch Dom Fernando José de Portugal to Viscount de Anadia, November 30, 1803, AHU, Rio de Janeiro, p.a., caixa 210, doc. 38.
82. Thomas Lindley, *Narrative of a Voyage to Brazil: Terminating in the Seizure of a British Vessel, and the Imprisonment of the Author and the Ship's Crew, by the Portuguese* (London: J. Johnson, 1805).
83. Dispatch Gambier to British Secretary of State, Lord Hawkesbury, December 2, 1803, NAL, FO 63, vol.42; Dispatch D. Ships Bouns to Hammond, April 10, 1805, NAL, FO 63, vol. 47.
84. Dispatch British plenipotentiary, Fitzgerald, to Viscount de Balsemão (Luís Pinto e Souza), December 14, 1803, NAL, FO 63, vol.43, ANTT, MNE, AC, caixa 460.
85. Dispatch Viscount de Balsemão to Fitzgerald, March 13, 1804, NAL, FO 63, vol. 43.

NOTES

86. Letter Francisco José de Lima to Dom Rodrigo de Souza Coutinho, September 19, 1799, AHU, Rio de Janeiro, p.a., caixa 177, doc. 5.
87. Dispatch Fernando Joseph Correa to king, January 1, 1800, AHU, Reino, maço 267.
88. Dispatch Commander of the Brazil fleet, Donald Campbell, to Count de Rezende, May, 4, 1801, AHU, Rio de Janeiro, p.a., caixa 191, doc. 84. "Toda a nação tem direito de defender as suas rendas pelas leis que julga proprio impôr. Não posso imaginar por hum momento que Portugal esteja em estado de ceder os seus direitos em favor dos Inglezes, ou de qualquer outra nação, porem nos não tratamos de nações, tratamos de contrabandistas, que em toda a parte devem encontrar a forca da lei do pais aonde estiverem sem nunca jamais darem justos motivos de ofensa a sua mesma nação."
89. Autos de Exame, February 13, 1802, AHU, Rio de Janeiro, p.a., caixa 197, doc. 38.
90. Representation John Watson, without date, ANTT, MNE, AC, caixa 461.
91. Dispatch Viscount de Anadia to secretary of state, António de Araujo de Azevedo, February 11, 1805, ANTT, MNE, AC, caixa 461.
92. For Joanna d'Entremeusse see Dispatch French ambassador to Lisbon, General Lannes, to prince regent, April 7, 1802, ANTT, M.N.E., A.C., caixa 476; For Sauvaget see Dispatch Rayneval to António de Azevedo de Araujo, May 24, 1807, ANTT, MNE, AC, caixa 477. On this case see Maria Fernanda Baptista Bicalho, "Joana d'Entremeuse: uma contrabandista entre a insuação e circunspeção," in: Ronaldo Vainfas, Georgina Silva dos Santos and Guilherme Pereira das Neves eds., *Retratos do Império. Trajetórias individuais no mundo portugues nos séculos XVI a XIX* (Niterói, RJ: EdUFF, 2006) 99-115.
93. Dispatch Intendente Geral da Polícia, Ignacio de Pina Manique, to secretary of state, João de Almeida de Mello e Castro, May 13, 1802, Arquivo Histórico do Itamaraty (Rio de Janeiro), III-30, lata 185, maço 3.
94. Dispatch Fitzgerald to Lord Hawkesbury, August 19, 1803, NAL, FO 63, vol. 41.
95. Viscount de Anadia to António de Araujo de Azevedo, February 11, 1805, ANTT, MNE, AC, caixa 461. "Os contrabandos que os navios estrangeiros vão fazer aos portos do Brasil são tão manifestos, e escandalosos, e a astucia com que a maior parte das vezes a illudem as leis com o pretexto de arribadas forçadas, requer que essas poucas occasioens em que se prova evidentemente ... se proceda contra os culpados com as penas estabelecidas nas mesmas leis."
96. Dauril Alden, "Late Colonial Brazil," in Leslie Bethell ed., Cambridge History of Latin America (Cambridge: Cambridge University Press, 1984) 2:622.
97. For a most recent work on Colônia do Sacramento see Fabrício Prado, *Colônia do Sacramento. O extremo sul da America Portuguesa* (Porto Alegre, RS: Fabrício Prado, 2002).
98. See for instance Dispatch Marquis de la Ancennada to Don José de Andonaegue, Madrid, April 10, 1748, Biblioteca Pública do Porto, códice 903, 52.
99. Advice Alexandre de Gusmão, secretary of the Overseas Council, January 15, 1750, in Jaime Cortesão, *Alexandre de Gusmão e o Tratado de Madrid* (Rio de Janeiro, Ministério das Relações Exteriores, Instituto Rio Branco, 1953) 5:494-499.
100. Dauril Alden, *Royal Government in Colonial Brazil. With a Special Reference to the Administration of the Marquis of Lavradio, Viceroy, 1769-1779* (Berkeley and Los Angeles: University of California Press, 1968) 93-275.
101. Dispatch Don Domingo Caperetatro, December 9, 1702, ANP, AE., B/I/651, fl.367r-v; Dispatch French consul in Lisbon, Du Vernay, to French secretary of state, October 28, 1748, ANP, AE, B/I/679, fl.161r-162r; Dispatch secretary of state, Martinho de Mello e Castro to viceroy, Marquis de Lavradio, AHU, Rio de Janeiro,

pa, caixa 115, doc.45; Royal dispatch to viceroy, Luís de Vasconcellos e Souza, March 14, 1780, BNRJ, 4,4,2, fl.5r-v; Dispatch Count de Rezende to viceroy Río de la Plata, July 28, 1799, British Library, Add.ms. 32606, fl.38r-v; Representation Spanish ambassador to Lisbon, Count del Campo, to secretary of state, António de Araujo de Azevedo, May 5, 1807, ANTT, MNE, AC, caixa 434.

102. Zacharias Moutoukias, "Una Forma de Oposición" 334-335, 340.
103. Dispatch Martinho de Mello e Castro to Luís de Vasconcellos e Souza, August 24, 1782, AHU, Rio de Janeiro, pa, caixa 130, doc. 77, and BNRJ, ms.4,4,4, fl.38v-39r.
104. Dispatch British plenipotentiary in Lisbon, Robert Walpole to British secretary of state, Lord Grantham, November 23, 1782, NAL, FO 63, vol.3.
105. Dispatch Marquis de Lavradio to Martinho de Mello e Castro, June 6, 1778, AHU, Rio de Janeiro, p.a., caixa 116, doc. 53.
106. Corcino Medeiros dos Santos, *O Rio de Janeiro e a Conjuntura Atlântica* (Rio de Janeiro: Expressão e Cultura, 1993) 175-176.
107. Dispatch Luís de Vasconcellos e Souza to Martinho de Melo e Castro, February 29, 1780, AHU, Rio de Janeiro, pa, caixa 122, doc.40, and BNRJ, ms.4,1,2, fl.19r-v.
108. Dispatch Luís de Vasconcellos e Souza to Coronel Vicente Joze de Velasco Molina, March 5, 1780, Arquivo Histórico do Itamaratí, III-30, lata 188, maço 1.
109. Dispatch Luís de Vasconcellos e Souza to Martinho de Mello e Castro, March 30, 1780, AHU, Rio de Janeiro, p.a., caixa 122, doc.54., and BNRJ, ms.4,4,2, fl.22v-23v.
110. Dispatch Luís de Vasconcellos e Souza to king, March 30, 1780, AHU, Rio de Janeiro, pa, caixa 122, doc.54 and BNRJ, ms.4,4,2, fl.22r-23r. "Que embaraçase aquela transgressão tão frequente do sobredito alvará, que á vista de tudo me lembra seria publicado com o único fim de satisfazer aos estrangeiros talvez queixosos do muito contrabando, que com a introdução dos mesmos negros."
111. Dispatch Luís de Vasconcellos e Souza to Martinho de Mello e Castro, AHU, Rio de Janeiro, pa, caixa 123, doc.40, and BNRJ, ms.4,4,2, fl.47v-48r.
112. Dispatch Luís de Vasconcellos e Souza to Martinho de Mello e Castro June 22, 1780, AHU, Rio de Janeiro, p.a., caixa 123, doc. 40, and BNRJ, ms.4,4,2, fl.47r-48r.
113. Dispatch Luís de Vasconcellos e Souza to Martinho de Mello e Castro, September 22, 1780, AHU, Rio de Janeiro, p.a., caixa 124, doc. 39, and BNRJ, ms.4,4,2, fl.63v-64r.
114. Royal dispatch to Luís de Vasconcellos e Souza, AHU, Rio de Janeiro, p.a., caixa 126, doc.29, and BNRJ, ms.4,4,3, fl.9v
115. Auto de Devassa, April 20, 1780, AHU, Rio de Janeiro, p.a., caixa 123, doc. 40.
116. Medeiros dos Santos, *O Rio de Janeiro e a Conjuntura Atlântica* 184-185; Elena F. Scheuss de Studer, *La Trata de Negros en el Río de la Plata* (2.ed; Buenos Aires: Universidad de Buenos Aires, 1958).
117. Dispatch Luís de Vasconcellos e Souza to Martinho de Mello e Castro, December 7, 1781, AHU, Rio de Janeiro, p.a., caixa 128, doc. 6.
118. Dispatch Martinho de Mello e Castro to Luís de Vasconcellos e Souza, August 24, 1782, AHU, Rio de Janeiro, p.a., caixa 130, doc. 21, and BNRJ, ms.4,4,4, fl.38r.
119. Appendix of dispatch Luís de Vasconcellos e Souza to Martinho de Mello e Castro, December 16, 1781, BNRJ, ms.4,4,3, fl.58r-v.
120. "Papel que acompanhou a Carta de 4 de Agosto de 1782," AHU, Rio de Janeiro, p.a., caixa 130, doc. 77, and BNRJ, ms.4,4,4, fl.38v-39r.
121. Dispatch Luís de Vasconcellos e Souza to Martinho de Mello e Castro, September 12, 1780, AHU, Rio de Janeiro, p.a., caixa 124, doc. 22.
122. Dispatch Luís de Vasconcellos e Souza to Martinho de Mello e Castro, December 13, 1781, AHU, Rio de Janeiro, p.a., caixa 128, doc. 13; Dispatch Luís de Vasconcellos

NOTES

  e Souza to Martinho de Mello e Castro, January 1, 1782, AHU, Rio de Janeiro, p.a., caixa 129, doc. 1, and BNRJ, ms.4,4,4, fl.57r-58v.
123. Petition by 110 merchants of Rio Grande de São Pedro to Prince Regent, November 24, 1800, AHU, Rio Grande do Sul, p.a., caixa 7, doc. 47. I would like to thank Helen Osório for this and the following reference.
124. Dispatch Paulo José da Silva Gama to secretary of state, Visconde de Anadia, April 12, 1803, AHU, Rio Grande do Sul, p.a., caixa 10, doc.40.
125. Medeiros dos Santos, *O Rio de Janeiro e a Conjuntura Atlântica* 176-177; Donald Campbell, "Reflexoens imparciais sobre o trafico de escravatura entre as colonias de Portugal e Hespanha," April 30, 1802, AHU, Rio de Janeiro, p.a., caixa 199, doc. 6.
126. Joseph C. Miller, *Way of Death, Merchant Capitalism and the Angolan Slave Trade, 1730-1830* (Madison: University of Wisconsin Press, 1988) 73-78.
127. Dispatch Viscount of Anadia to Commander of the Fleet, Donald Campbell, October 12, 1801, AHU, Rio de Janeiro, p.a., caixa 195, doc.19.
128. Petition by 110 merchants of Rio Grande de São Pedro to Prince Regent, November 24, 1800, AHU, Rio Grande do Sul, p.a., caixa 7, doc.47.
129. Medeiros dos Santos, *O Rio de Janeiro e a Conjuntura Atlântica* 84-85.
130. Autos da devassa by *dezembargador ouvidor do crime*, Francisco Alvares de Andrade, July 20, 1794, AHU, Rio de Janeiro, p.a., caixa 156, doc. 66.
131. Letter Jacinto Jorge dos Anjos to João Marcos Vieira, March 8, 1794, in: correspondence found in the house of João Marcos Vieira, Autos de Devassa, June 16, 1794, AHU, Rio de Janeiro, p.a., caixa 156, doc. 66, fl.13r-56v. "O meu sentimento excede as minhas expreçoens, e não há pessoa alguma nesta Ilha que o não tenha sentido, vendo maculado o Pay destes Povos, e seu favorecido."
132. Letter Jacinto Jorge dos Anjos to João Marcos Vieira, March 8, 1794, in correspondence found in João Marcos Vieira's house, Autos de Devassa, June 16, 1794, AHU, Rio de Janeiro, p.a., caixa 156, doc.66, fl.13r-56v. "Todo o bom exito deste intrincado objecto depende do nosso amablissimo Ill.mo e Ex.mo Senhor Vice Rey, que possuhido de piedade, e compaixão que tanto resplandecem em todas as suas acçoens, e farão memoravel o seu illuminadissimo Governo, não deixará dé as praticar com Vossa Merce, em tão critica conjunctura."
133. "Carta escripta do Rio de Janeiro ao Ill.mo e Ex.mo Conde de Rezende, Vice Rei que foi do Rio de Janeiro, em que hum seu amigo lhe descreve o carater; e acções mais notaveis do seu sempre detestavel Governo," without date [± 1801], BNRJ ms.11,2,2.
134. Perguntas a Matheus Califate" (slave of João Marcos Vieira), August 1, 1794, AHU, Rio de Janeiro, p.a., caixa 157, doc. 1; Perguntas a Joaquim da Mina (slave), July 31, 1794, AHU, Rio de Janeiro, pa, caixa 156, doc. 75; "Perguntas a João Baptista" (sailor of *Santa Rita*), August 4, 1794, AHU, Rio de Janeiro, p.a., caixa 157, doc. 5.
135. "Auto de exame e revisão dos papeis que se achão no escritório de João Marcos Vieira," July 16, 1794, AHU, Rio de Janeiro, p.a., caixa 156, doc.66, fl.9r-12r; Contents of 6 letters of the former governor of Santa Catarina, José Pereira Pinto, August 16, 1794, Interrogation of the master of the *Santa Rita*, José de Aruda, August 12, 1794, and Royal order to Ouvidor Santa Catarina, August 26, 1794, AHU, Rio de Janeiro, p.a., caixa 157, doc. 4.
136. Letters found in João Marcos Vieira's office, AHU, Rio de Janeiro, p.a., caixa 156, doc. 66, fl.64r-75r; Accounts of João Marcos Vieira, correspondence Luís de Escovar, July 25, 1794, and Dispatch Dezembargador Procurador da Fazenda, José

NOTES

Soares de Barbosa to Provedor da Fazenda, João de Figueiredo, August 7, 1794, AHU, Rio de Janeiro, p.a., caixa 156, doc. 69.
137. Auto de perguntas of João Marcos Vieira, July 12, 1794, AHU, Rio de Janeiro, p.a., caixa 156, doc. 63.
138. Letter Frei António de Santa Anna Palha to João Marcos Vieira, September 3, 1791, in papers from office João Marcos Vieira, appendix T, AHU, Rio de Janeiro, p.a., caixa 156, doc. 66, fl.60r-63v.
139. Interrogation João Marcos Vieira, August 14, 1794, AHU, Rio de Janeiro, p.a., caixa 157, doc. 4. "Que este Frade por ser muyto galante chamava as molheres fazenda de contrabando."
140. Royal order to *juiz ordinário* of Villa do Rio Pardo, November 8, 1794, AHU, Rio de Janeiro, p.a., caixa 157, doc.4. Autos de Prisão of António Fernandes, *contramestre Santa Rita*, and 6 seamen from the *Santa Rita*, November 3, 1794, AHU, Rio de Janeiro, p.a., caixa 157, doc. 4.
141. Dispatch Count de Rezende to Luís José de Carvalho e Mello, ouvidor geral do crime, May 4, 1797, ANRJ, Col., caixa 492, pac.2.; Request Dona Bernadina de Azevedo Lima, wife of João Marcos Vieira, handled June 27, 1799, AHU, Rio de Janeiro, p.a., caixa 174, doc. 67.
142. See Ernst Pijning, "Conflicts in the Portuguese Colonial Administration," 403-423.
143. Dispatch João de Figueiredo to viceroy, Count de Rezende, October 31, 1796; and Dispatch idem. to idem., November 10, 1796, ANRJ, Col., caixa 485, pac.1.
144. Dispatch *juiz da alfândega*, José António Ribeiro Freire, to Count de Rezende, October 25, 1796, ANRJ, Col., caixa 495, pac.1.
145. Dispatch João de Figueiredo to Count de Rezende, December 13, 1796, ANRJ, Col., caixa 485, pac.1.
146. "Perguntas feitas a Francisco Lopes de Soiza," December 23, 1796, ANRJ, Col., caixa 490, pac.1
147. Dispatch João de Figueiredo to Count de Rezende, October 24, 1796, and Instruction João de Figueiredo to José António de Castilhos, ANRJ, Col., caixa 485, pac.1.
148. Consultation Overseas Council, March 20, 1800, AHU, Rio de Janeiro, p.a., caixa 182, doc.54.
149. Dispatch Spanish Ambassador, Marquis de Villena, to Secretary of State, Luís Pinto e Souza, March 5, 1800, ANTT, MNE, AC, caixa 431.
150. Request Gaspar Soliveres (in name of Don Pedro Dubal) to Spanish Secretary of State, Madrid, January 7, 1800, ANTT, MNE, AC, caixa 431.
151. Request Evaristo Perez de Castro to João de Almeida de Mello e Castro, February 3, 1802, AHU, Rio de Janeiro, p.a., caixa 197, doc.37
152. Dispatch viceroy, Dom Fernando José de Portugal, to Prince Regent, April 29, 1803, AHU, Rio de Janeiro, p.a., caixa 206, doc.74.
153. Dispatch Viscount de Anadia to Francisco de Borja Garção Stockler, January 12, 1805, AHU, Rio de Janeiro, p.a., caixa 218, doc.15.
154. *Belisario*: Request Ignácio Joaquim Pereira de Souza to Prince Regent, handled December 9, 1806, AHU, Rio de Janeiro, p.a., caixa 236, doc. 10; *Espada de Hierro*: Dispatch José António Ribeiro Freire, to viceroy, April 20, 1806; *Monte Toro*: Dispatch viceroy, Count dos Arcos, to Viscount de Anadia, March 27, 1807, AHU, Rio de Janeiro, p.a., caixa 237, doc. 92.
155. Dispatch Count de Rezende, to Secretary of State, Dom Rodrigo de Souza Coutinho, November 22, 1798, AHU, Rio de Janeiro, p.a., caixa 171, doc. 5; Dispatch idem. to idem., December 12, 1798, AHU, Rio de Janeiro, p.a., caixa 171, doc. 45; Dispatch Dom Fernando José de Portugal to Viscount de Anadia, October

21, 1801, AHU, Rio de Janeiro, p.a., caixa 195, doc.39; Dispatch João de Figueiredo to Count de Rezende, January 23, 1797; Dispatch José António Ribeiro Freire to Conde de Rezende, March 1, 1799, Dispatch idem. to idem. April 17, 1799, Dispatch idem. to idem., June 14, 1799, Dispatch idem. to idem. November 17, 1799, Dispatch idem. to idem. March 23, 1800, ANRJ, Col., caixa 495, pac.1; Dispatch José Caetano de Lima to Dom Rodrigo de Souza Coutinho, December 6, 1800, AHU, Rio de Janeiro, p.a., caixa 189, doc.64; Dispatch José António Ribeiro Freire to Dom Fernando José de Portugal, November 9, 1804, and Dispatch idem. to idem., September 12, 1807, ANRJ, Col., caixa 495, pac.1; Request Miguel Costa to Dom Fernando José de Portugal, April 18, 1805, ANRJ, Col., caixa 495, pac.2, Dispatch Dom Fernando José de Portugal to Viscount de Anadia, August 6, 1807, AHU, Rio de Janeiro, p.a., caixa 241, doc. 11; Count de Rezende, "Memoria do que se deve praticar a fim de se evite o extravio dos escravos," to Dom Rodrigo de Souza Coutinho, December 12, 1798, AHU, Rio de Janeiro, p.a., caixa 175, doc. 87; Memorandum chancellor High Court, Luís Beltrão de Almeida, to Viscount de Anadia, April 16, 1802, AHU, Rio de Janeiro, p.a., caixa 196, doc. 40; Campbell, "Reflexoens imparciais sobre o trafico de escravatura entre as colonias de Portugal e Hespanha," April 30, 1802, AHU, Rio de Janeiro, p.a., caixa 199, doc. 6.
156. Request Francisco Lima to Prince Regent, handled February 20, 1805, ANRJ, Col., caixa 490, pac.1.

3. MONOPOLIZING THE MARKETPLACE: REGULATING URBAN SPACE

1. See for this especially Maria Fernanda Baptista Bicalho, *A Cidade e o Império. O Rio de Janeiro no Século XVIII* (Rio de Janeiro: Civilização Brasileira, 2003) 202.
2. Harold B. Johnson, "A Preliminary Inquiry into Money, Prices and Wages in Rio de Janeiro, 1763-1823," in Dauril Alden ed., *Colonial Roots of Modern Brazil: Papers of the Newberry Library Conference* (Berkeley and Los Angeles: University of California Press, 1973) 230-283. Dauril Alden, "Price Movements in Brazil, Before, During and After the Gold Boom, with Special Reference to the Salvador Market," in Lyman L. Johnson and Enrique Tandeter eds., *Essays on the Price History of Eighteenth Century Latin America* (Albuquerque: University of New Mexico Press, 1990) 335-371.
3. On the problem of manioc in Bahia see: Caio Prado júnior, *Formação do Brasil Contemporâneo. Colônia* (7th ed.; São Paulo: Editôria Brasiliense, 1963) 157-159.
4. Alden, "Price Movements in Brazil" 360, appendix.
5. Brown, "Internal Commerce" chapters 4 and 6.
6. Johnson, "Money, Prices, Wages inn Rio de Janeiro" 268-283.
7. For a good discussion on this issue see: Eric A. Schultz, *Markets and Power. The 21st Century Command Economy* (Armonk NY: M.E. Sharpe, 2001) 3-10.
8. Luiz Mott, "Subsídios à História do Pequeno Comércio no Brasil," *Revista de História. Universidade de São Paulo* 53 (1976) 86-106.
9. Mary C. Karasch, *Slave Life in Rio de Janeiro, 1808-1850* (Princeton: Princeton University Press, 1987).
10. Luciano Figueiredo, *O Avesso da Memória. Cotidiano e Trabalho da Mulher em Minas Gerais no Século XVIII* (Rio de Janeiro: José Olympio, 1993).
11. A.J.R. Russell-Wood, "Ports of Colonial Brazil," in Franklin W. Knight and Peggy K. Liss eds., *Atlantic Port Cities. Economy, Culture and Society in the Atlantic World, 1650-1850* (Knoxville: The University of Tennessee Press, 1991) 196-239.

NOTES

12. See for instance Brooke Larson, Olivia Harris and Enrique Tandeter eds., *Ethnicity, Markets, and Migration in the Andes. At the Crossroads of History and Anthropology* (Durham and London: Duke University Press, 1995). Yet Fernanda Bicalho's *A Cidade e o Império* starts to address this issue, in the context of military threat and fear.
13. Dispatch Luís de Vasconcellos e Souza to Martinho de Mello e Souza, secretary of state, May, 25, 1789, BNRJ, ms.I-31,20,15.
14. Request by Manoel Dias Lopes and Thomas Marques, contract farmers of fish taxes, to Luís Vahia Monteiro, governor of Rio de Janeiro, and dispatch of Luís Vahia Monteiro, August 23, 1728, ANRJ, Col., cód. 7, vol.4, fl.149r-150r.
15. Order Luís Vahia Monteiro to Commander of the Fortresses at the bar, September 15, 1728, ANRJ, Col., cód.87, vol.4, fl.144r; idem. to idem., ANRJ, Col., cód.87, vol.4, fl.150v-151r.
16. Dispatch Luís Vahia Monteiro, February 19, 1732, ANRJ, Col., cód.87, vol.7, fl.211v; Petition by fishermen to interim governor, January 31, 1733, ANRJ, Col., cód.87, vol.8, fl.86r-v; Dispatch Gomes Freire de Andrade to Manoel de Campos, sargento mor of fortress São João da Barra, August 28, 1733, ANRJ, Col., cód.87, vol.10, fl.16r; Dispatch idem. to sargento mor Santa Cruz, December 12, 1733, ANRJ, Col., cód.87, vol.10, fl.75r.
17. Dispatch Luís Vahia Monteiro, February 19, 1732, ANRJ, Col., cód.87, vol.7, fl.211v; Petition by fishermen to interim governor, January 31, 1733, ANRJ, Col., cód.87, vol.8, fl.86r-v; Dispatch Gomes Freire de Andrade to Manoel de Campos, sargento mor of fortress São João da Barra, August 28, 1733, ANRJ, Col., cód.87, vol.10, fl.16r; Dispatch idem. to sargento mor Santa Cruz, December 12, 1733, ANRJ, Col., cód.87, vol.10, fl.75r.
18. Request Pedro de Souza Moreira, contract farmer of the tenths, to the governor, March 16, 1735, and dispatch of the governor, March 16, 1735, ANRJ, Col., cód.87, vol.11, fl.137v-138r.
19. "ha muito soldados atravessadores do peixe fresco que se venda na praya," (...)" o que fazem para melhor se sostentarem por não terem outro officio." Gomes Freire de Andrade to king, April 3, 1734, AHU, Rio de Janeiro, p.a., caixa 29, doc. 31.
20. Representation *juiz ouvidor da alfândega*, March 18, 1748, ANRJ, Col., cód.87, vol.17, fl.56r-v; Dispatch José António Freire de Andrade, interim governor of Rio de Janeiro to Domingos Vas de Carvalho, commander of fortress Santa Cruz, March 27, 1756, ANRJ, Col., cód.87, vol.9, fl.214r-v; Petitions Mariana Vieira Mascarenhas to Municipal Council, and idem. to governor April 11, 1760, AHU, Rio de Janeiro, p.a.., caixa 69, doc.30.
21. Dispatch Municipal Council to king, August 25, 1731, AHU, Rio de Janeiro, p.a., caixa 25, doc.25; Dispatch *juiz ouvidor de alfândega* José António Ribeiro Freire to Count de Rezende, ANRJ, Col., caixa 495, pacote 1.
22. Request José da Silva to Gomes Freire de Andrade, governor Rio de Janeiro, April 20, 1734, ANRJ, Col., cód.87, vol.10, fl.184v-185r, Dispatch Gomes Freire de Andrade to *provedor da fazenda*, March 30, 1734, ANRJ, Col., cód.87, vol.10, fl.133r; Request José da Silva Maya to José da Silva Paes, interim governor of Rio de Janeiro, ANRJ, Col., cód.87, vol.15, fl.130v-131r.
23. Information Manoel Correia Vasques, *juiz ouvidor da alfândega*, March 3, 1734, ANRJ, Col., cód.87, vol.10, fl.127v-128r.
24. Order António José Cabral de Almeida, *juiz ouvidor da alfândega* to Joaquim de Macedo Vasconcellos, *guarda mor*, May 20, 1785, ANRJ, Col., caixa 495, pac.3.

NOTES

25. For prohibition to search a Jesuit vessel see Royal order to governor of Rio de Janeiro, June 25, 1748, ANRJ, Col., caixa 495, pac.3. For an extensive discussion on the relationship between Luís Vahia Monteiro and the Religious orders see, Paulo Cavalcante, *Negócios de Trapaça. Caminhos e Descaminhos na América Portuguesa* (1700-1750) (São Paulo: Editora Hucitec, 2006) 171-194.
26. Representation José Rodrigues, contract farmer of the customs, handled February 27, 1725, AHU, Rio de Janeiro, p.a., caixa 16, doc.8; Order Luís Vahia Monteiro to ouvidor geral, April 16, 1726, ANRJ, Col., cód.87, vol.2, fl.102r; Dispatch Francisco da Silva Castro, juiz de fora, to king, December 22, 1732, AHU, Rio de Janeiro, p.a., caixa 28, doc.22.
27. Consultation Overseas Council, January 2, 1728, AHU, Rio de Janeiro, p.a., caixa 19, doc.40.
28. Consultation Overseas Council, January 30, 1696, AHU, Rio de Janeiro, p.a.c., 2019; Consultation Overseas Council, Rio de Janeiro, p.a.c., 2585; Royal dispatch to governor of Rio de Janeiro, May 2, 1733, AHU, Rio de Janeiro, p.a., caixa 28, doc.54; Royal dispatch to governor of Rio de Janeiro and Minas Gerais, September 17, 1748, ANRJ, Col., caixa 495, pac.3; Dispatch Count de Rezende to Luís Pinto de Souza, secretary of state, September 3, 1795, AHU, Rio de Janeiro, p.a., caixa 160, doc.37.
29. Request José Ferreira da Veiga, contract farmer of the customs, to king, handled January 10, 1747, AHU, Rio de Janeiro, p.a., caixa 47, doc.3.
30. Dispatch Luís Vahia Monteiro to D. Manoel Henriques de Noronha, commander of the fleet, July 2, 1929, ANRJ, Col., cód.87, vol.5, fl.128v-129r; Royal dispatch to governor of Rio de Janeiro, May 2, 1733, AHU, Rio de Janeiro, p.a., caixa 28, doc.54; for similar disputes in Salvador see: José Roberto do Amaral Lapa, *A Bahia e a Carreira da Índia* (São Paulo: Companhia Editora Nacional, 1968) 219-225.
31. Dispatch Count de Rezende to Luís Pinto da Souza, September 3, 1795, AHU, Rio de Janeiro, p.a., caixa 160, doc.37.
32. Dispatch Manoel da Cunha Sottomayor to Luís Pinto de Souza, July 26, 1796, AHU, Rio de Janeiro, p.a., caixa 163, doc.22.
33. Dispatch José António Freire de Andrade, interim governor Rio de Janeiro, to Domingos Vas de Caminho, commander fortress Santa Cruz, June 1, 1756, ANRJ, Col., cód.87., vol.9, fl.220v-221r.
34. Royal dispatch to Francisco de Tavora, governor of Rio de Janeiro, April 31 [sic], 1715, ANRJ, Col., cód.60, vol.12, fl.243v-244r.
35. Dispatch José António Freire de Andrade to Domingos Vas de Caminho, ANRJ, Col., cód.87, vol.9, fl.220v-221r.
36. Dispatch José António Freire de Andrade to Domingos Vas de Carvalho, March 27, 1756, ANRJ, Col., cód.87, vol.9, fl.214r-v.
37. Royal dispatch to Luís Vahia Monteiro, August 22, 1730 and his reply, July 9, 1731, AHU, Rio de Janeiro, p.a., caixa 23, doc.39.
38. Royal dispatch to Gomes Freire de Andrade, May 7, 1733 and answer Gomes Freire de Andrade, April 3, 1734, AHU, Rio de Janeiro, p.a., caixa 29, doc.31.
39. Consultation Overseas Council, July 23, 1738, AHU, Rio de Janeiro, p.a.c. 11844.
40. Dispatch José Soares de Barbosa to Count de Rezende, November 29, 1798, ANRJ, Col., cód.807, vol.23, fl.221v-222r, "Ellas não deixarão vir, hum piqueno espasso de praya livre, e as ruas que dessem da cidade, apareceriaõ embarracadas com ranchos, e estadas. Huma grande parte destas tem cazinhas com chave, chegando não só tomar toda a Praya, mas ainda do Mar, com estacadas, em que se achão portinhas,

e lancelas particulares, outros tantos vieiros, para a introdução dos contrabandos, e asilo dos contrabandistas."
41. This is well demonstrated for women in colonial Minas Gerais in Luciano Figueiredo, *O Avesso da Memória* 38-50.
42. Petition Municipal Council to Prince Regent, July 21, 1792, AHU, Rio de Janeiro, p.a., caixa 151, doc.87.
43. Representation Municipal Council of Rio de Janeiro to king, August 21, 1728, AHU, Rio de Janeiro, p.a., caixa 20, doc.72.
44. Royal dispatch to Luís Vahia Monteiro, December 10, 1726, BNRJ, ms.II-34,15,49.
45. See for instance Dispatch Count de Rezende to Martinho de Mello e Castro, February 3, 1791, AHU, Rio de Janeiro, p.a., caixa 148, doc.44.
46. Letter Clemente Pereira de Azevedo Coutinho and António Mendeira da Cruz to king, August 2, 1731, AHU, Rio de Janeiro, p.a., caixa 25, doc.53.
47. Advice Luís Vahia Monteiro to king, October 11, 1732, AHU, Rio de Janeiro, p.a., caixa 26, doc.4.
48. Representation of Municipal Council to king, June 12, 1739, AHU, Rio de Janeiro, p.a., caixa 38, doc.53; Advice Count da Cunha to king, January 23, 1767, AHU, Rio de Janeiro, p.a., caixa 87, doc.17.
49. Dispatch João Soares de Barboza, *procurador da coroa e fazenda real*, to Count de Rezende, November 29, 1798, ANRJ, Col., cód.807, vol.23, fl.221v-222v; Representation António José da Silva Lourenço to prince regent, handled January 10, 1807, AHU, Rio de Janeiro, p.a., caixa 237, doc.11. Arno and Maria José Wehling also noted similar disputes between the governor and the *desembargador provedor da fazenda* in 1798. They argued that these disputes *might* be related to contraband trade give the connections of the high court judges and merchants as well as the prevalent smuggling in these areas. *Direito e Justiça no Brasil Colonial. O Tribunal da Relação do Rio de Janeiro (1751-1808)* (Rio de Janeiro, São Paulo, and Recife: Renovar, 2004) 312-313.
50. Sérgio Tadeu de Niemeyer Lamarão, *Dos Trapiches ao Porto, um Estudo sobre a Área Portuária do Rio de Janeiro* (Rio de Janeiro: Secretaria Municipal de Cultura, 1991) 27-31.
51. See for instance Opinion Municipal Council to viceroy, May 30, 1804, AHU, Rio de Janeiro, p.a., caixa 213, doc.35; Representation André Martins Brito, *escrivão câmara municipal* of Rio de Janeiro, handled March 12, 1760, AHU, Rio de Janeiro, p.a., caixa 66, doc.48.
52. Anonymous, "Carta ao Conde de Rezende", w.d. [± 1801], BNRJ, ms.11,2,2; Afonso Carlos Marques dos Santos, *No Rascunho da Nação: Inconfidência no Rio de Janeiro* (Rio de Janeiro: Prefeitura da Cidade do Rio de Janeiro, 1992) 31-51.
53. Advice Count de Rezende, March 5, 1796, AHU, Contrato do Sal, p.a., caixa 2, doc.37.
54. Representation of Municipal Council to prince regent, July 21, 1792, AHU, Rio de Janeiro, p.a., caixa 151, doc.87.
55. Dispatch Count de Rezende to Martinho de Mello e Castro, Secretary of State, November 29, 1792, AHU, Rio de Janeiro, p.a., caixa 152, doc.62.
56. "Autos de Summário em publica forma," drawn by juiz de fora, Balthazar da Silva Lisboa, November 19, 1792, AHU, Rio de Janeiro, p.a., caixa 152, doc.59.
57. The prices of wheat flour and manioc were indeed higher as compared to the previous decade, during the regency of Rezende, see: Johnson, "Money, Prices, Wages in Rio de Janeiro" 272, 276.

NOTES

58. Devassa Balthazar da Silva Lisboa, November 16, 1792, AHU, Rio de Janeiro, p.a., caixa 152, doc.40.
59. "Discurso sobre o Celleiro da Bahia," w.d. [±1807], ANRJ, Col., cód.807, vol.17, fl.20r-27v.
60. Catharine Lugar, "The Merchant Community of Salvador, Bahia, 1780-1830," Ph.D. dissertation, State University at Stony Brook, New York, 1980, chapter 2.
61. Caio Prado júnior, *Formação do Brasil* 157-159.
62. "Discurso sobre o Celleiro da Bahia," ANRJ, Col., cód.807, vol.13, fl.20r.
63. "Discurso sobre o Celleiro," ANRJ, Col., cód.807, vol.13, fl.20r-v.
64. "Discurso sobre o Celleiro," ANRJ, Col., cód.807, vol.13, fl.21r.
65. "Discurso sobre o Celleiro," ANRJ, Col., cód.807, vol.13, fl.21r-v.
66. "Discurso sobre o Celleiro," ANRJ, Col., cód.807, vol.13, fl.22r.
67. "Discurso sobre o Celleiro," ANRJ, Col., cód.807, vol.13, fl.22v-23r.
68. "Discurso sobre o Celleiro," ANRJ, Col., cód.807, vol.13, fl.23v-24r.
69. Livro das Condemnações do Senado da Câmara de Salvador 1703-1805, Arquivo Municipal de Salvador, livro 36.1, *passim*.
70. Myriam Ellis, "O Monopólio do Sal no Estado do Brasil. (1631-1801). (Contribuição ao Estudo do Monopólio Comercial Português no Brasil, durante o Período Colonial)," Bolletim da Universidade de São Paulo, Faculdade de Filosofia, Ciências e Letras 14 (1955) 1-265.
71. Royal dispatch to Governor of Rio de Janeiro, June 2, 1734, AHU, Rio de Janeiro, p.a., caixa 30, doc.22; Miriam Ellis, "O Monopólio do Sal" 183-184.
72. D.Rodrigo de Souza Coutinho, "Memória sobre o Melhoramento dos Domínios de Sua Majestade na América," (1797-1798), in D. Rodrigo de Souza Coutinho, *Textos Políticos, Económicos e Financeiros*, Andrée Mansuy Diniz Silva ed., (Lisbon: Banco de Portugal, 1993) 2:56; Dispatch Diogo Ignacio de Pina Manique to secretary of state, July 18, 1797, AHU, p.a., Contrato do Sal, caixa 2, doc.44; Domingos Vandelli, "Memoria relativa à extinção do contrato do sal," w.d., ANRJ, Col., cód.807, vol.24, N.°61.
73. "Alvará de abolição do contrato do estanque do sal e da pescaria das baleias no Brasil, 24 de Abril de 1801," in Souza Coutinho, *Textos Políticos* 2:247-256.
74. Ellis, "O Monopólio do Sal" 82, 111-113.
75. Representation Municipal Council of Paratí, December 3, 1735, AHU, Rio de Janeiro, p.a., caixa 31, doc.30.
76. Representation Municipal Council of Paratí, March 14, 1739, ANRJ, Col., cód.87, vol.16, fl.31v-33v.
77. Representation Municipal Council of Paratí, July 15, 1757, AHU, Rio de Janeiro, p.a., caixa 62, doc.9.
78. Representation Municipal Council of Angra dos Reis, July 14, 1727, AHU, Rio de Janeiro, p.a., caixa 19, doc.55; Representation Municipal Council of Cabo Frio, September 29, 1747, AHU, Rio de Janeiro, p.a., caixa 48, doc.30.
79. John Hunter, *An Historical Journal of the Transaction at Port Jackson and Norfolk Island* (London: Printed for John Stockdale, 1793) 23.
80. Russell-Wood, "Ports of Colonial Brazil," 225.
81. John Luccock, *Notes on Rio de Janeiro, and the Southern Parts of Brazil; taken during a Residence of ten Years in that Country, from 1808 to 1818* (London: Printed for Samuel Leigh, 1820) 102.
82. Jean-Baptiste Debret, *Voyage Pittoresque au Brésil, Sejour d'un Artiste Français au Brésil, depuis 1816 jusqu'en 1831 inclusif* 3 vols. (Paris: Institut de France, 1835) 2:45.
83. Karasch, *Slave Life* 207.

NOTES

84. Mary C. Karasch, "Suppliers, Sellers, Servants, and Slaves," in Louisa S. Hoberman and Susan M. Socolow eds., *Cities and Society in Colonial Latin America*, (Albuquerque: University of New Mexico Press, 1986) 269.
85. Karasch, *Slave Life* 89, 207
86. Note of "Principal Sousa", w.d., BNRJ, ms.I-29,14,50, N°5.
87. Karasch, *Slave Life* 196.
88. See for instance A.J.R. Russell-Wood, "Colonial Brazil," in David W. Cohen and Jack P. Greene ed., *Neither Slave Nor Free* (Baltimore: The Johns Hopkins University Press, 1972) 89-90.
89. See for instance Petition *provedor and irmãos Santa Casa da Misericórdia* to king, handled September 29, 1755, AHU, Rio de Janeiro, p.a., caixa 50, doc.31; A.J.R. Russell-Wood, *Fidalgos and Philanthropists. The Santa Casa da Misericórida of Bahia, 1550-1755* (Berkeley and Los Angeles: University of California Press, 1968) 234-259.
90. See for instance Alvará de Fiança João Velho e Marcella, slaves of Bento da Costa, AEB, Provincial e Colonial, livro 500, Relação, registros 1704-1707, fl.121v.
91. Dispatch Manoel da Costa Mimiz, *ouvidor geral*, to king, July 7, 1730, AHU, Rio de Janeiro, p.a., caixa 23, doc.22.
92. Dispatch Luís Vahia Monteiro to king, July 9, 1728, AHU, Rio de Janeiro, p.a., caixa 20a, doc.73.
93. Dispatch João Pachedo Pereira, *chancellor da relação*, to king, October 6, 1753, AHU, Rio de Janeiro, p.a., caixa 54, doc.9.
94. Petition *Quitandeiras* to Municipal Council, handled May 29, 1775, ANRJ, Col., cód.807, vol.19, fl.63r-v.
95. Advice João Antunes de Araujo Lima, procurator of the Municipal Council to the Senate, July 3, 1776, ANRJ, Col., cód.807, vol.19, fl.68r-v.
96. Dispatch Francisco Cordovil Sequeira e Melo to king, March 17, 1753, AHU, Rio de Janeiro, p.a., caixa 53, doc.44. "Este produto não tem natureza de monopolio ... alem de que este licor hé no Brazil remedio approvado para qualquer ferida, ou contuzão, e seria grande incommodo prohibir-se o uzo fora da Cidade"
97. Petition of 108 Carioca merchants to Prince Regent, handled April 25, 1815, BNRJ, ms.II-34,27,24.
98. See Kenneth R. Maxwell, *Pombal: Paradox of the Enlightenment* (Cambridge: Cambridge University Press, 1995) 59-60; Jorge Borges de Macedo, *A Situação Económica no Tempo de Pombal. Alguns Aspectos* (3nd ed.; Lisbon: Morães Editores, 1989) 66-67.
99. [Robert Walpole] "Observations on the answer," May 26, 1769, BL, Add. Mss. 9252, fl.57v-58v.
100. I found the following six references: an itinerant trader who requested to stay in Rio de Janeiro for a year: Request Manoel Pereira de Carvalho to Luís Vahia Monteiro, ANRJ, Col., cód.87, vol.5, fl.212v; a "homem volante" on Ilha Grande: Dispatch Luís Vahia Monteiro to Manoel da Costa, *juíz ordinário Ilha Grande*, May 22, 1731; a transfer of money to a comissário volante: Order José António Freire de Andrade to juiz ouvidor da alfândega, November 15, 1754, ANRJ, Col., cód.87, vol.18, fl.85r; two arrests: Dispatch João Tavares de Abreu to Francisco Xavier Mendonça Furtado, April 3, 1763, AHU, Rio de Janeiro, p.a., caixa 75, doc.86, and Petition José Mendes Guimaraes to viceroy, June 17, 1771, ANRJ, Col., caixa 485, pac.1; and one license to sale: Francisco de Sousa Pinto e Masuelos, "Compilação," November 16, 1775, BNRJ, ms.8,1,9, fl.28v, note (a).
101. Dispatch Count da Cunha to Francisco Xavier de Mendonça Furtado, April 18,

NOTES

1766, printed in RIGHB 254 (1962) 345-346. "nesta perjudicialima Rua se metem a titolo de Ourives, quantos ladroens, e quantos vagabundos que vem ao Brasil."
102. Dispatch José Mauricio da Gama e Freitas to Count da Cunha, August 9, 1767; and Dispatch Conde da Cunha to Francisco Xavier Mendoça Furtado, August 14, 1767, in RIGHB 262 (1962) 401-404.
103. Yet Antonio Carlos Jucá de Sampaio argues that one can never speak about a complete monopoly. His point is about Carioca merchants and Lisbon based long distance traders. Neither of them did monopolize the long-distance trade, and he pleads for autonomy of the Carioca merchants vis-à-vis their Lisbon counterparts. Moreover, long-distance traders in Rio de Janeiro, did not shy away to diversify and compete with small local merchants in the local market. *Na Encruzilhada do Império: hierarquias sociais e conjunturas econômicas no Rio de Janeiro (c.1650-c.1750)* (Rio de Janeiro: Arquivo Nacional, 2003) 254.
104. João L.R. Fragoso, Homens da Grossa Ventura: Acumulação e Hierarchia na Praça Mercantil do Rio de Janeiro (1790-1830) (Rio de Janeiro: Arquivo Nacional, 1992) 171-172.
105. Luccock, *Notes on Rio de Janeiro* 104.

4. THE POLITICS OF PUNISHMENT: DEFINING THE BOUNDARY BETWEEN CONDONED AND PROSCRIBED ILLEGAL TRADE

1. Request Captain António José Ribeiro de Faria to Prince Regent, handled October 30, 1805, Arquivo Histórico Ultramarino [AHU], Rio de Janeiro, papeis avulsos [p.a]., caixa 221, doc.51. "A Soberana Magestade he superior a todas as leijs, e protege os vassalos oprimidos por virtude das mesmas leijs infringidas, e com ellas capeadas as paixões particulares e caprixos dos seus executores."
2. António Manuel Hespanha, *As Vésperas de Leviathan. Instituições e Poder Político Portugal- séc. XVII* (Coimbra: Livraria Almedian, 1994), for a good overview of Hespanha's argument see: Maria Fernanda Baptista Bicalho, "O que significa ser citadão nos tempos coloniais," in: Martha Abreu and Rachel Soilhet eds. *Ensino de História. Conceitos, Temáticas e Metodologia* (Rio de Janeiro: Casa da Palavra, 2003) 140.
3. Lauren Benton, Law and Colonial Cultures. *Legal Regimes in World History, 1400-1900* (Cambridge: Cambridge University Press, 2002) 61-64.
4. Arno and Maria José Wehling, *Direito e Justiça Colonial. O Tribunal da Relação do Rio de Janeiro (1751-1808)* (Rio de Janeiro: Renovar, 2004) 347-348.
5. António Manuel Hespanha, "A Punição e a Graça," in José Matoso ed., *História de Portugal, o Antigo Regime (1620-1807)*, António Manuel Hespanha ed., (Lisbon: Editorial Estampa, 1993) 239-266, and "Da 'Iustitia' a 'Disciplina,' Textos, Poder e Política no Antigo Regime," *Boletim da Faculdade de Direito de Coimbra* (1989) 3-98; Timoty J. Coates, *Degraods e Órfãs: Colonização dirigida pela Coroa no Império Português, 1550-1755*, José Vieira Lima transl., (Lisbon, Comissão Nacional para as Comemorações dos Descobrimentos Portugueses, 1998), Patricia A. Aufderheide, "Order and Violence: Social Deviance and Social Control in Brazil, 1780-1840," Ph.D. dissertation University of Minnesota, 1976.
6. See for instance David Higgs, "Unbelief and Politics in Rio de Janeiro during the 1790s," *Luso-Brazilian Review* 21 (1984) 41-61, Adriana Romeiro, *Um Visionário na Corte de D. João V. Revolta e Milenarísmo nas Minas Gerais* (Belo Horizonte: Editora UFMG, 2001).

NOTES

7. Aufderheide, ""Order and Violence" 228.
8. Stuart B. Schwartz, *Sovereignty and Society in Colonial Brazil: the Judges of the High Court of Bahia, 1586-1750* (Berkeley: Los Angeles and London: University of California Press, 1973) 151.
9. Stuart B. Schwartz, *Sovereignty and Society in Colonial Brazil: the Judges of the High Court of Bahia, 1586-1750* (Berkeley: University of California Press, 1974). Arno Wehling is now writing a book on the High Court of Rio de Janeiro in which he will include a study on the handling of civil court cases.
10. Silvia Hunold Lara, *Campos da Violência, Escravos e Senhores na Capitania do Rio de Janeiro 1750-1808* (Rio de Janeiro: Paz e Terra, 1988); Patricia A. Aufderheide, "Order and Violence: Social Deviance and Social Control in Brazil, 1780-1840" Ph.D. dissertation, University of Minnesota, 1976, Patricia A. Aufderheide, "Upright Citizens in Criminal Records Investigations in Cachoeira and Geremoabo, Brazil, 1780-1836," *TAm* 38 (1981) 173-184; Leila Mezan Algranti, "Slave Crimes: The Use of Police Power to Control the Slave Population of Rio de Janeiro," *Luso-Brazilian Review* 25 (1988) 27-48.
11. A.J.R. Russell-Wood, *Fidalgos and Philanthropists. The Santa Casa da Misericórdia of Bahia, 1550-1755* (Berkeley and Los Angeles: University of California Press, 1968) 234-259. A.J.R. Russell-Wood, "A Cause Célèbre of Colonial Brazil: António Fernandes' Personal Struggle for Justice," *Revista da Sociedade Brasileira de Pesquisa Histórica* 4 (1987-1988) 1-8.
12. Zacarias Moutoukias, *Contrabando y Control Colonial en el Siglo XVII, Buenos Aires, el Atlantico y el Espacio Peruano* (Buenos Aires: Bibliotecas Universitarias, 1988) 84-92.
13. See Paulo Cavalcante, *Negócios de Trapaça. Caminhos e Descaminhos na América Portuguesa (1700-1750)* (São Paulo: Editora HUCITEC, 2006) chapter 4, for an excellent discussion about contraband trade under Luís Vahia Monteiro, as well as the governor's disputes with the Municipal Council and the Ecclesiastical authorities.
14. Dispatch Louis Houwens, Dutch resident in Lisbon, to States General, January 11, 1724, Nationaal Archief, Den Haag [NADH], Staten Generaal [SG], Liassen Portugal, N.° 7021/1.
15. Dauril Alden, *Royal Government in Colonial Brazil. With a Special Reference to the Administration of the Marquis of Lavradio, Viceroy, 1769-1779* (Berkeley and Los Angeles: University of California Press, 1968) 426, note 18.
16. Petition 88 merchants to the king, handled July 1, 1727, AHU, Rio de Janeiro, p.a., caixa 19, doc.46.
17. Charles R. Boxer, *The Golden Age of Brazil 1695-1750, Growing Pains of a Colonial Society* (Berkeley, Los Angeles and London: University of California Press, 1962) 201-202.
18. Dispatch Luís Vahia Monteiro to viceroy in Salvador, October 18, 1725, Arquivo Nacional, Rio de Janeiro [ANRJ], Colonial [Col.], cód. 84, vol.3, fl.96r-99v.
19. See 3 dispatches of French Consul, De Montagnac to French Secretary of State, October 23, 1732; December 12, 1731, Archives Nationalles, Paris [ANP], Affaires Étrangères [AE], B/I/666, fl.134r-137r, fl.292r-293v, and fl.337r-339v; Dispatch British Consul, Charles Compton to the Duke of Newcastle, National Archives, London [NAL], State Papers, Portugal [SP] 89, vol.37, fl.141r-145v.
20. Boxer, *Golden Age of Brazil* 201-202.
21. A.J.R. Russell-Wood, "Colonial Brazil: The Gold Cycle, c. 1690-1750," in Leslie Bethell ed., *The Cambridge History of Latin America* (Cambridge: Cambridge Univer-

sity Press, 1984) 2:590; Edict Luís Vahia Monteiro, March 21, 1730, ANRJ, Col., cód.87, vol.5, fl.206r-v.
22. Directive Luís Vahia Monteiro to Manoel Salgado da Crus, May 23, 1730, ANRJ, Col., cód.87, vol.5, fl.226v.
23. Guilt of Manoel de Araujo Lima, Joaquim Ferreira Varella, Agapitto Miz' Figueira and João Francisco Muzzi in: Dispatch Bernardo Leyte Lebo, ouvidor geral of Rio de Janeiro to king, August 23, 1731, AHU, Rio de Janeiro, p.a., caixa 25, doc.61; Guilt of Manoel Rodrigues Chaves in: Request Manoel Rodrigues Chaves to Luís Vahia Monteiro, handled August 14, 1730, ANRJ, Col., cód.87, vol.7, fl.59v.
24. Directive Luís Vahia Monteiro to Provedor of Casa de Moeda, July 9, 1730, ANRJ, Col., cód.87, vol.7, fl.7r.
25. Directive Luís Vahia Monteiro to provedor da fazenda, June 16, 1730, ANRJ, Col., cód.87, vol.7, fl.39r.
26. Copy of the letter exchange between Luís Vahia Monteiro and the governor of São Paulo, May and July 1730, AHU, Rio de Janeiro, p.a.c., 6813-6815.
27. Royal letter to Luís Vahia Monteiro, September 13, 1730 and Reply Luís Vahia Monteiro to king, July 12, 1731, AHU, Rio de Janeiro, p.a., caixa 26, doc.9.
28. Luís Lisanti, *Negócios Coloniais (uma Correspondência Comercial do Século XVIII)* (Brasília: Ministério da Fazenda, 1973) volume III. On this correspondence see: Dauril Alden, "Vicissitudes of Trade in the Portuguese Atlantic Empire during the First Half of the Eighteenth Century: A Review Article," *TAm* 32 (1975) 282-291, William M. Donovan, "Commercial Enterprise and Luso-Brazilian Society during the Brazilian Gold Rush: the Mercantile House of Francisco Pinheiro and the Lisbon to Brazil Trade" Ph.D. dissertation, Johns Hopkins University, 1990, and Júnia Ferreira Furtado, *Homens de Negócio. A Interiorização da Metrópole e do Comércio nas Minas Setecentistas* (São Paulo, Hucitec, 1999).
29. Luís Lisanti, *Negócios Coloniais (uma Correspondência Comercial do Século XVIII)* (Brasília: Ministério da Fazenda, 1973) volume III. On this correspondence see: Dauril Alden, "Vicissitudes of Trade in the Portuguese Atlantic Empire during the First Half of the Eighteenth Century: A Review Article," *TAm* 32 (1975) 282-291, William M. Donovan, "Commercial Enterprise and Luso-Brazilian Society during the Brazilian Gold Rush: the Mercantile House of Francisco Pinheiro and the Lisbon to Brazil Trade" Ph.D. dissertation, Johns Hopkins University, 1990, and Júnia Ferreira Furtado, *Homens de Negócio. A Interiorização da Metrópole e do Comércio nas Minas Setecentistas* (São Paulo, Hucitec, 1999).
30. For a short account of Muzzi's arrest see also William M. Donovan, "Commercial Enterprise" 277-278.
31. Letter João Francisco Muzzi to Francisco Pinheiro, July 1, 1730, Negócios Coloniais 3:377-386.
32. For the case of the expulsion of the Dutchman Pedro Folgman Petition Pedro Folgman to governor, Luís Vahia Monteiro, July 4, 1726, ANRJ, Col., Cód.87, vol.2, fl.134r-v.
33. Petition Municipal Council to king, March 30, 1731, AHU, Rio de Janeiro, papeis avulsos catalogados [p.a.c.], 7111; Petition Municipal Council to king, April 24, 1731, AHU, Rio de Janeiro, p.a., caixa 24, doc.62 .
34. Consultations Overseas Council, January 23, 1731 and January 31, 1731, AHU, Rio de Janeiro, p.a.c., 6766 and 6786.
35. Royal Letter to Luís Vahia Monteiro, February 16, 1731, AHU, Rio de Janeiro, p.a., caixa 24, doc.22.

NOTES

36. Petition João Francisco Muzzi to the governor, June 19, 1730, ANRJ, Col., cód.87, vol.7, fl.120r-v.
37. Letter João Francisco Muzzi to Francisco Pinheiro, February 2 and August 20, 1731, in *Negócios Coloniais*, 3:411-416.
38. Letter João Rodrigues Silva, Faustinho de Lima and António de Araujo Pereira to Francisco Pinheiro, July 29, 1732, in *Negócios Coloniais*, 3:495-496.
39. Letter João Francisco Muzzi to Francisco Pinheiro, December 2, 1732, in *Negócios Coloniais*, 3:485-488.
40. Royal letter to Luís Vahia Monteiro, February 22, 1731, AHU, Rio de Janeiro, p.a., caixa 24, doc.24.
41. Request João Francisco Muzzi, handled July 17, 1732, AHU, Rio de Janeiro, p.a., caixa 26, doc.47.
42. Letter Eugenio Martini to Francisco Pinheiro, July 2, 1734, in *Negócios Coloniais* 3:535-536.
43. Letter João Francisco Muzzi to Francisco Pinheiro, June 6, 1735, in *Negócios Coloniais* 3:558-564.
44. Letter João Francisco Muzzi to Francisco Pinheiro, August 15, 1736, in: *Negócios Coloniais* 3:589-593.
45. See for this phenomenon Patricia Aufderheide, "Order and Violence" chapter 7.
46. For instance: António Gomes Souto, suspect of gold smuggling received such a license, but had to pay a 100$000 reis bail, Request handled July 9, 1736 by Overseas Council, AHU, Rio de Janeiro, p.a., caixa 32, doc.52.
47. For instance, the case of Francisco José de Andrade, arrested for diamond smuggling, Dispatch Manoel Francisco da Sylva e Freire to Secretary of State, September 28, 1772, AHU, Rio de Janeiro, p.a., caixa 103, doc.38.
48. For instance, the case of Bento Coelho Ramos, accused of diamond smuggle, Consultation Overseas Council, September 23, 1778, AHU, Rio de Janeiro, p.a., caixa 117, doc.76.
49. See on this theme Patricia Aufderheide, "Order and Violence" chapter 7.
50. Opinion Luís de Vasconcellos e Souza, viceroy in Rio de Janeiro, to Martinho de Mello e Castro, Secretary of State, September 23, 1779, AHU, Rio de Janeiro, p.a., caixa 120, doc.69.
51. Royal letter to Provedor da Fazenda, April 25, 1745, ANRJ, Col., cód.60, vol.25, fl.113r-v.
52. Between 1727 and 1733 at least 35 gold smuggling suspects were imprisoned by Luís Vahia Monteiro.
53. Dispatch British plenipotentiary, Abraham Castres to Mr. Amyand, February 23, 1754, NAL, SP 89, vol.48, fl.250r-251r; Dispatch French Chancellor, Mr. Ferrand, to French Secretary of State, February 19, 1754, ANP, AE, B/I/681, fl.20r-21r; Secret dispatch Dutch resident, C.T. Bosch de la Calmette to Fagel, February 26, 1754, NADH, SG, Liassen Portugal, N.° 7040/1.
54. See chapter 2 for the issue of the implementation of the sumptuary laws in Portugal.
55. Minute of a royal letter to Chancellor of Rio de Janeiro, June 1, 1753, AHU, Rio de Janeiro, p.a., caixa 53, doc.134.
56. Dispatch Diogo de Mendonça Corte Real, secretary of state, to Mathias Coelho de Souza, governor a.i. of Rio de Janeiro, June 1, 1753, AHU, Rio de Janeiro, p.a., caixa 88, doc.57.
57. "Relação das fazendas que se confiscarão na alfândega desta Cidade," July 1, 1753, AHU, Rio de Janeiro, p.a., caixa 54, doc.45.

NOTES

58. Petition of 88 merchants to the king against the *casa de moeda*, handled July, 1, 1729, AHU, Rio de Janeiro, p.a., caixa 19, doc.46.
59. "Auto de justificação testimunhal," September 6, 1753, AHU, Rio de Janeiro, p.a.c., 16208.
60. Information José António Freire de Andrade, November 2, 1753, AHU, Rio de Janeiro, p.a.c., 16946
61. Edict José Freire de Andrade, October 11, 1753, AHU, Rio de Janeiro, p.a.c., 16196.
62. Request Capitães de Mar e Guerra, October 10, 1753, AHU, Rio de Janeiro, p.a.c., 16198
63. Petition homens de negócio, October 10, 1753, AHU, Rio de Janeiro, p.a.c., 16201.
64. 3 Requests 128 homens de negócio, dispatches governor, juiz da corroa e fazenda and juiz ouvidor da alfândega, October 17, 19 (twice), 1753, AHU, Rio de Janeiro, p.a.c., 16204, 16205, and 16206.
65. "Copia do asento dos dezembargadores sobre as fazendas prohibidas que vieram na prezente frota," October 7, 1753, AHU, Rio de Janeiro, p.a.c., 16207.
66. Dispatch José António Freire de Andrade to Mathias Coelho de Souza, May 18, 1754, AHU, Rio de Janeiro, p.a., caixa 88, doc.57.
67. Royal Dispatches to governor of Rio de Janeiro and Chancellor of the High Court, February 23, 1754, AHU, Rio de Janeiro, p.a.c., 16967-16968.
68. Compromiso Mesa do Bem Comum, December 15, 1753, AHU, Rio de Janeiro, p.a.c., 17065.
69. Petition merchants of Rio de Janeiro, December 15, 1753, AHU, Rio de Janeiro, p.a.c., 17065.
70. 2 Petitions Mesa do Bem Comum to king and governor, w.d. [1755], AHU, Rio de Janeiro, p.a.c., 18329 and 18330; Request Mesa do Bem Comum to king, handled November 8, 1756, AHU, Rio de Janeiro, p.a.c., 19724.
71. Opinion João Soares Tavares, May 20, 1755, AHU, Rio de Janeiro, p.a.c., 18327.
72. Thomas da Costa Pereira, *Sermão do Espirito Santo, Prégado na Igreja do Bom Jesus do Rio de Janeiro à Meza do Negocio no Anno de 1754, em que a mesma Meza o Elegeo por seu Protector* (Lisbon: Officina de Miguel Manescal da Costa, 1755).
73. Susan Schneider, *O Marquês de Pombal e o Vinho do Porto. Dependência e Subdesenvolvimento em Portugal no Século XVIII* (Lisbon: A Regra do Jogo, 1980) 136-137; João Lúcio d'Azevedo, "Política de Pombal Relativo ao Brasil," in *Novas Epanáforas. Estudos de História e Literatura* (Lisbon: Livraria Clássica Editora, 1932) 42.
74. Dispatch viceroy, Count Sabugoza to Gomes Freire de Andrade, December 29, 1734, ANRJ, Col., cód.87, vol.11, fl.108v-109v.
75. Dispatches Gomes Freire de Andrade to viceroy, January 27, 1735, and idem. to Duarte Sodre Pereira, governor of Pernambuco, March 6, 1735, ANRJ, Col., cód.84, vol.5, fl.125r-126r and fl.166r-169r, Consultation Overseas Council, May 4, 1735, AHU, Rio de Janeiro, p.a.c., 8564.
76. For a description of Gomes Freire's Government of Rio de Janeiro see Robert A. White, "Gomes Freire de Andrada: Life and Times of a Brazilian Colonial Governor," Ph.D. dissertation, University of Texas at Austin, 1972, 18-97.
77. Gomes Freire de Andrade to Duarte Sodre Pereira, March 6, 1735, ANRJ, Col., cód.84, vol.5, fl.166r-169v, "que em breves annos estarião poderosos".
78. Gomes Freire de Andrade to Duarte Sodre Pereira, March 6, 1735, ANRJ, Col., cód.84, vol.5, fl.166r-169v.
79. This case was referred to in a petition of the merchants of Rio de Janeiro to the Governor of Rio de Janeiro, October 10, 1755, AHU, Rio de Janeiro, p.a.c., 16197.
80. See the cases cited in Dauril Alden, *Royal Government in Colonial Brazil* 399-403.

NOTES

81. Royal letter to Count da Cunha, December 16, 1762, AHU, Rio de Janeiro, p.a., caixa 76, doc.38.
82. Dispatch Count da Cunha to Luís Diogo Lobo da Silva, governor of Minas Gerais, January 6, 1764, AHU, Rio de Janeiro, p.a., caixa 77, doc.73, The two suspects in Minas Gerais were Sebastião Lucena e Silva "homem de naçao" and José Gomes da Sª.
83. "Interrogation of António de Souza, September 14, 1765 in: "Traslado de Devassa," N.° 65, June 7, 1767, AHU, Rio de Janeiro, p.a., caixa 90, doc.73.
84. Royal Letter to Conde da Cunha, December 16, 1762, AHU, Rio de Janeiro, p.a., caixa 76, doc.38.
85. Interrogation of Francisco Xavier Telles, May 17, 1764, Arquivo Nacional da Torre do Tombo, Lisbon [ANTT], Intendência Géral da Polícia [IGP], maço 601, appenso 4, fl.3v. "Se elle respondente merece hir para caconda, ou galés o mandem."
86. Extensive records on these interrogations can be found in "Autos de Sequestros e Perguntas sobre o ouro e brilhantes pertencentes a individuos do Rio de Janeiro," ANTT, IGP, maço 601.
87. "Auto de perguntas feitas ao Francisco Xavier Telles," May 17, 1764, ANTT, IGP, maço 601, appenso 4, fl.2r-v.
88. "Autos de perguntas," August 4, 1764 and September 3, 1764, ANTT, IGP, maço 601, appenso 4, fl.28r and fl.30r.
89. "Perguntas feitas a Domingos Lourenço," February 6, 1764, ANTT, IGP, maço 601, N.°21, fl.4r.
90. "Perguntas feitas ao Francisco Xavier Telles," July 8, 1764, ANTT, IGP, maço 601, appenso 4, fl.19r-20r.
91. "Perguntas feitas a Domingos Lourenço," February 6, 1764, ANTT, IGP, maço 601, N.°21, fl.4r.
92. "Perguntas feitos a Francisco Xavier Telles prezo na cadeia desta Corte," March 18, 1765, ANTT, IGP, maço 601, appenso 4.
93. Request Francisco Xavier Telles to king, handled February 15, 1777, AHU, Rio de Janeiro, p.a., caixa 111, doc.25.
94. Dispatch José Mauricio da Gama e Freytas to Count da Cunha, August 5, 1767, AHU, Rio de Janeiro, p.a., caixa 89, doc.3; Dispatch idem to idem, October 26, 1767, AHU, Rio de Janeiro, p.a., caixa 90, doc.10.
95. Dispatch Count de Azambuja, viceroy, to Francisco Xavier de Mendonça Furtado, secretary of state, August 26, 1768, AHU, Rio de Janeiro, p.a., caixa 92, doc.52.
96. This case was considered a murder. Dispatch Manoel Luís Condeiros, juiz de fora, to king, March 5, 1718, AHU, Rio de Janeiro, p.a., caixa 11, doc.22.
97. On the theme of bails and pardons see Patricia Aufderheide, "Order and Violence" chapter 7.
98. Hespanha, "Da 'Iustitia'" 3-98.
99. Hespanha, "Da 'Iustica'" 22, 31.
100. Consultation Overseas Council after request of Manoel Rodrigues Veiga, April 1, 1754, AHU, Rio de Janeiro, p.a., caixa 55, doc.27.
101. "La prison est moins récente qu'on ne le dit lorsqu'on la fait naître avec les nouveaux Codes. La forme-prison préexiste à son utilisation systématique dans les lois pénales. Elle s'est constituée à l'extérieur de l'appareil judiciaire, quand se sont élaborées, à travers tout le corps social, les procédures pour répartir les individus, les fixes et les distribues spatialement, les classer, tirer d'eux le maximum de temps,

NOTES

et le maximum de forces" (...) Michel Foucault, *Surveiller et Punir. Naissance de la Prison* (reprint; Saint-Amand, Bussière Camedan Imprimeries, 2000) 267.

102. Dispatch Count da Cunha to Francisco Xavier de Mendonça Furtado, April 18, 1766, with annex of the number of people employed in the Rua dos Ourives, AHU, Rio de Janeiro, p.a., caixa 85, doc.60, Dispatch idem. to idem., August 14, 1767, AHU, Rio de Janeiro, p.a., caixa 89, doc.2. The dispatches are published in RIGHB 254 (1962) 344-345; 401-403.

103. Request Captain António José Ribeiro de Faria to Prince Regent, handled October 30, 1805, AHU, Rio de Janeiro, p.a., caixa 221, doc.51.

5. INSTITUTIONALIZED ILLEGALITY: COLONEL ADMINISTRATION AND CONTRABAND TRADE

1. See for instance Padre António Vieira, "Sermão da Visitação de Nossa Senhora," in Hernani Cidade ed., *Padre António Vieira no Brasil* (Lisbon: Agência Geral das Colônias, 1940) 2:189-218; Gregório de Matos, Obra Poética, James Amado and Emanuel Araújo eds., (3rd ed; Rio de Janeiro: Editora Record, 1992) 1:135-191, 311-329; Thomas Lindley, *Narrative of a Voyage to Brazil: Terminating in the Seizure of a British Vessel, and the Imprisonment of the Author and the Ship's Crew, by the Portuguese* (London: J. Johnson, 1805); Dispatch Count dos Arcos to Viscount of Anadia, September 2, 1807, Arquivo Histórico Ultramarino [AHU], Rio de Janeiro, papeis avulsos [p.a.], caixa 241, doc. 56.

2. Clarence Haring, *The Spanish Empire in America* (1st ed. 1947; reprint: San Diego, New York and London: Harcourt Brace Jovanovich, 1975); Graça Salgado *et al*, *Fiscais e Meirinhos. Administração no Brasil Colonial* (Rio de Janeiro: Editora Nova Fronteira, 1985) 17.

3. On the role of the chief treasurer see Ernst Pijning, "Conflicts in the Portuguese Colonial Administration. Trials and Errors of Luís Lopes Pegado e Serpa, Provedor-Mor da Fazenda Real in Salvador, Brazil 1718-1721," *Colonial Latin American Historical Review* 2:4 (1993) 403-423.

4. *Privilégios dos Cidadãos da Cidade do Porto, Armando de Castro intro.*, (Lisbon: Imprensa Nacional-Casa da Moeda, 1987), Maria Fernanda Baptista Bicalho, "O que significava ser cidadão nos tempos coloniais," in: Martha Abreu and Rachel Soihet eds., *Ensino de História. Conceitos, temáticas e metodologia* (Rio de Janeiro: Casa da Palavra, 2003) 149-155.

5. I have found only a few *residências* in the Portuguese archives. None of them were of governors or viceroys, but of senior magistrates, namely: *Residência* of *ouvidor* and *juiz de fora*, Caetano Furtado de Mendonça and Mateus Franco Ferreira, April 23, 1740 and April 25, 1740, AHU, Rio de Janeiro, p.a., caixa 37, doc. 19 and 20; *Residência* of *ouvidor* Luís António da Cunha, September 4, 1750, AHU, Rio de Janeiro, p.a., caixa 50, doc. 98; *Residência* of *juiz de fora* Lourenço José Vieira Souto, October 22, 1787, AHU, Rio de Janeiro, p.a., caixa 140, doc. 73; *Residência* of *juiz de fora*, Bacharel José Bernardes de Castro, April 13, 1804, AHU, Rio de Janeiro, p.a., caixa 212, doc. 22; *Residência Capitão-Mor* of Cabo Frio, Manoel Alvares de Afonseca April 15, 1729, AHU, Rio de Janeiro, p.a., caixa 21, doc.33. For a reference to a *residência* of governor of Rio de Janeiro, Aires de Saldanha e Albuquerque, see Dispatch *ouvidor geral*, Manoel da Costa Mimoza to king, July 2, 1728, AHU, Rio de Janeiro, p.a., caixa 20, doc. 37.

NOTES

6. Request *ouvidor geral*, Roberto Car Ribeiro to king, handled in 1723, AHU, Rio de Janeiro, papeis avulsos catalogados [p.a.c.], 4429; Royal message to Overseas Council, September 9, 1774, AHU, Rio de Janeiro, p.a., caixa 106, doc. 12.
7. Royal order to viceroy, April 10, 1779, AHU, Rio de Janeiro, p.a., caixa 94, doc. 37.
8. Royal dispatch to Gomes Freire de Andrade, June 26, 1748, AHU, Rio de Janeiro, p.a., caixa 48, doc. 4; Request Gonsalo Teixeira de Carvalho, handled September 15, 1783, AHU, Rio de Janeiro, p.a., caixa 132, doc. 29.
9. Dauril Alden, "Late Colonial Brazil, 1750-1808," in Leslie Bethell ed., *The Cambridge History of Latin America*, (Cambridge: Cambridge University Press, 1984), 2:605. The most reliable estimate of the Brazilian population remains still Dauril Alden, "The Population of Brazil in the Late Eighteenth Century: A Preliminary Study," HAHR 43 (1963) 173-205.
10. See for instance Royal provision, February 27, 1671, Arquivo Nacional da Torre do Tombo [ANTT] (Lisbon), Papeis do Brasil, vol.9, fl.100r, Arquivo Nacional do Rio de Janeiro [ANRJ], Colonial, cód.807, vol.19, fl.4v-5r. For an imperial vision of governors and their rotation through the empire see Maria de Fátima Gouvêa, "Poder político e administração na formação do complexo atlântico português (1645-1808)," in João Fragoso *et al* eds.,*O Antigo Regime nos Trópicos: a dinâmica imperial portuguesa (séculos XVI-XVIII)*, (Rio de Janeiro: Civilização Brasileira, 2001) 299-309.
11. Alvará August 29, 1720, AHU, Rio de Janeiro, p.a., caixa 13, doc.28.
12. Consultation Overseas Council, December 24, 1692, AHU, Códice 232, fl.79r-82v.
13. Consultation Overseas Council, December 24, 1692, AHU, Códice 232, fl.79r-82v.
14. Consultation Overseas Council, December 24, 1692, AHU, cód.232, fl.80r-81r.
15. Consultation Overseas Council, December 24, 1692, AHU, cód.232, fl.81r-v.
16. Alvará August 29, 1720, AHU, Rio de Janeiro, p.a., caixa 13, doc.28.
17. Opinions Francisco Barreto and Ruy de Moura Telles, August 12, 1711, Biblioteca do Palácio de Ajuda (Lisbon), 51-IX-32, p.419-428; for another occasion where this became questioned see: Consultation Overseas Council, July 24, 1715, *Documentos Históricos* (Rio de Janeiro: Biblioteca Nacional, 1928-1953), 96:175-187.
18. Law (*alvará*), March 27, 1721, AHU, Rio de Janeiro, p.a., caixa 13, doc. 28.
19. See for instance: Dispatch Luís Beltrão de Gouvea d'Almeida, Chancellor of the High Court, to Viscount of Anadia, April 16, 1802, AHU, Rio de Janeiro, p.a., caixa 196, doc. 40.
20. See for instance Luiz dos Santos Vilhena, *Recopilação de Noticias Soteropolitanas e Brasilicas*, Braz do Amaral ed., 2 vols., (Salvador: Imprensa Official do Estado, 1921-1922) 1:49. "Basta pois, que saibas que alguns [negociantes] poderá haver mais do que deixo dito e que alguns destes commerceão so com o seu nome, e com cabedaes de personagens a quem seia menos decente o saber-se commerceão."
21. Ayres de Saldanha e Albuquerque: AHU, cód.1177, Biblioteca Pública de Évora, cód. CXX/2-3, fl.58r-60v; Dom Fernando José de Portugal, Coleção Aguiar, Biblioteca Nacional do Rio de Janeiro [BNRJ], I-4,17. For two other cases see Maria Júlia de Oliveira e Silva, *Fidalgos-Mercadores no Século XVIII. Duarte Sodré Pereira* (Lisbon: Imprensa Nacional-Casa de Moeda, 1992) and Virginia Rau, "Fortunas Ultramarinas e a Nobreza Portuguesa no Século XVII," in *Estudos sobre a História Económica e Social do Antigo Regime*, José Manuel Garcia ed., (Lisbon: Editorial Presença, 1984) 29-46.
22. *Procuração Bastante*, May 13, 1765, BNRJ, 15-2-24, Livro de Notas Brandão, fl.67v-68v.

23. Dispatch De Montagnac, French consul in Lisbon, to French secretary of state, September 23, 1732, and idem. to idem. April 14, 1733, Archives Nationalles, Paris [ANP], Affaires Étrangeres [AE], B/I/666, fl.113r-118v and fl.224r-249r; Adriana Romeiro, "Confissões de um Falsário: as Relações Perigosas de um Governador em Minas," in: Eunici Nodari *et al* eds., *História: Fronteiras XX Simpósio Nacional da ANPUH* (São Paulo: Humanitas/FFLCH/USP, ANPUH, 1999) 321-337, Carlos Leonardo Kelmer Mathias, "No exercício de atividades comerciais, na busca da governabilidade: D. Pedro de Almeida e sua rede de potentados nas minas do ouro durante as duas primeiras décadas do século XVIII," in João Luis Ribeiro Fragoso *et al* eds., *Conquistadores e Negociantes. Histórias de elites no Antigo Regime nos trópicos. America lusa, séculos xvi a xviii* (Rio de Janeiro: Civilização Brasileira, 2007) 196-222.

24. Visconde de Santarém, *Quadro Elementar das Relaçoes Politicas e Diplomáticas de Portugal com as diversas Potencias do Mundo desde o Princípio da Monarchia Portuguesa até aos nossos Dias* (Lisbon: Académia Geral das Sciencias, Paris: J.P. Aillard, 1842-1860) 5:cclxvii, note 1.

25. Letter "Friends of the British Nation" to Viscount Strangford, November 10, 1805, National Archives, London [NAL], Foreign Office [FO] 63, vol. 48.

26. *Inventário Post Mortum*, Luís de Vasconcellos e Souza, Count of Figueiró, April 29, 1812, ANTT, Casa de Supplicação, Inventários, Letra L, maço 12, caixa 2467. I would like to thank Nuno Gonçalves Monteiro for this reference. Nuno Gonçalves Monteiro is somewhat ambivalent about the fortunes acquired by viceroys, "Trajetórias socias e governo das conquistas: Notas preliminares sobre os vice-reis e governadores-gerais do Brasil e da Índia nos séculos XVII e XVIII," in Fragoso *et al* eds, O Antigo Régime nos Trópicos 275-279.

27. *Notícias Históricas de Portugal e Brasil (1751-1800)* (Coimbra: Coimbra Editorial Ltd.ª, 1964) 2:187, 213, and 219.

28. *Noticias Históricas* 2:222-223

29. *Noticias Históricas* 2:217-218.

30. Anonymous letter to Count of Rezende, w.d., BNRJ, ms.11,2,2.

31. Dispatch Pedro de Sante da Silva to secretary of state, July 7, 1802, AHU,Rio de Janeiro, p.a., caixa 201, doc. 55. For an exposé on the procedures of such gold inspections see: A.J.R. Russell-Wood, "As Frotas de Ouro do Brasil, 1710-1750," *Estudos Econômicos* 13 (1983) 701-717.

32. Benguella: Royal Dispatch to Alexandre José Botelho de Vasconcellos, September 7, 1795, ANTT, Ministério do Reino, maço 604, caixa 707; Santa Catharina: Petition Manoel Soares Coimbra to Luís Pinto e Souza, February 2, 1796, AHU, Rio de Janeiro, p.a., caixa 162, doc. 7; Colônia de Sacramento: Dispatch João Ricardo Pereira, Chancellor High Court Rio de Janeiro, to king, October 15, 1753, AHU, Rio de Janeiro, p.a., caixa 54, doc. 10.

33. Consultation Overseas Council, February 4, 1714, AHU, Rio de Janeiro, p.a.c., 3315. I would like to thank Maria Fernanda Baptista Bicalho for this reference

34. Request Dona Maria de Tavora Leito, handled in 1731, AHU, Rio de Janeiro, p.a.c., 7058-71.

35. Letter of Marquis do Lavradio to his brother, Dom Martinho Lourenço de Almeida, May 1, 1769, in: Marquês do Lavradio, *Cartas da Bahia, 1768-1769* (Rio de Janeiro: Arquivo Nacional, 1972) 153-155. "Estimo que ainda me não tenham por lá na opinião de ladrão, régulo, ou voluntário, que são os honrados títulos a que estão expostos os mizeráveis Governadores da América; creio que o não se terem ainda lembrado de me chamar estes infames nomes, nasce do favor que eu devo ao nosso ministério."

NOTES

36. Letter Marquis do Lavradio to Joaquim Ignacio da Cruz, Salvador, July 20, 1769, in Marquês do Lavradio, *Cartas da Bahia* 244-246; Letter Marquis do Lavradio to Principal de Almeida, September 11, 1770, in Marquês do Lavradio, *Cartas do Rio de Janeiro* (Rio de Janeiro: Arquivo Nacional, 1978) 44-45; Letter Marquis do Lavradio to José de Seabra e Silva, February 1772, in Marquês do Lavradio, *Cartas do Rio de Janeiro* 94-95.
37. Letter Marquis do Lavradio to Count of Rezende, November 18, 1770, in Marquês do Lavradio, *Cartas do Rio de Janeiro* 57-58.
38. See on the subject of debts see Nuno Gonçalves Monteiro, "O Endividamento Aristocrático (1750-1830): Alguns Aspectos," *Análise Social* 116/117 (1992) 263-283, and his excellent book on the Portuguese nobility, *O Crepúsculo dos Grandes (1750-1832)* (Lisbon: Imprensa Nacional-Casa da Moeda, 1998).
39. For royal subsidies to Marquis do Lavradio and his father see two *Cartas de Padrão* September 8, 1767, ANTT, Chancellaria Dona Maria I, Livro 75, fl.388v-393r, fl.393r-395r; for Gomes Freire de Andrade: Alvará para se lhe fazer pagamento de 25:597$320 reis rendimento Caza de Moeda, April 25, 1752, ANTT, Chancellaria Dom José I, livro 64, fl.374r.
40. Dispatch French consul Du Vernay to French secretary of state, July 23, 1748, ANP, AE,B/I/670, fl.113r-114r.
41. Charles R. Boxer, *Portuguese Society in the Tropics. The Municipal Councils of Goa. Macao, Bahia, and Luanda, 1510-1800* (Madison and Milwaukee: The University of Wisconsin Press, 1965) 5-7.
42. Maria Fernanda Baptista Bicalho, "As Representações da Câmara do Rio de Janeiro ao Monarca e as Demonstrações da Lealdade dos Súditos Coloniais Séculos XVII e XVIII," in: Alberto Vieira ed., *O Município no Mundo Português. Seminario Internacional* (Funchal: Centro de Estudos de História do Atlântico, 1998) 523-543. João Fragoso elaborated on this by demonstrating the netwokrs of families related to the Municipal Councillors "Fidalgos e parentes de pretos: notas sobre a nobreza principal da terra do Rio de Janeiro (1600-1750), in Fragoso *et al* eds., *Conquistadores e negociantes* 35-120.
43. Representation Municipal Council to king, June 20, 1685, AHU, Rio de Janeiro, p.a., caixa 5, doc. 75; Representation Municipal Council to king, August 6, 1678, AHU, Rio de Janeiro, p.a., caixa 4, doc. 105.
44. Representation Municipal Council to king, July 23, 1757, AHU, Rio de Janeiro, p.a., caixa 62, doc. 27.
45. Representation Municipal Council to king, June 26, 1709, AHU, Rio de Janeiro, p.a., caixa 8, doc. 39.
46. Royal Dispatch to Municipal Council, May 6, 1747, AHU, Rio de Janeiro, p.a., caixa 47, doc. 39; Representation merchants to king, handled August 3, 1746, AHU, Rio de Janeiro, p.a., caixa 46, doc. 51.
47. See for instance against the clergy, Consultation Overseas Council, November 28, 1697, AHU, Rio de Janeiro, p.a.c., 2082-2083; against the governor: Consultation Overseas Council, December 15 & 16, 1704, AHU, Rio de Janeiro, p.a.c., 2815; 2818-32; in favor of the governor: Royal dispatch to Dom Alvaro da Silveira de Albuquerque, March 26, 1709, Virginia Rau and Maria Fernanda Costa Gomes da Silva eds., *Os Manuscritos do Arquivo da Casa de Cadaval Respeitantes ao Brasil* (Coimbra: University of Coimbra, 1958) 2:61-62; against *ouvidor*: Request Municipal Council, February 18, 1709, AHU, Rio de Janeiro, p.a.c., 3155; in favor of *ouvidor*: Request Municipal Council to king, December 6, 1722, AHU, Rio de Janeiro, p.a., caixa 13,

NOTES

doc. 159; commercial affairs: Request Municipal Council to king, August 3, 1720, AHU, Rio de Janeiro, p.a., caixa 12, doc. 72.

48. This happened three times under Luís Vahia Monteiro's government in 1727, 1730 and 1732, Request Municipal Council to king, August 13, 1727, AHU, Rio de Janeiro, p.a., caixa 19, doc. 77; Dispatch *juiz de fora* to Luís Vahia Monteiro, June 30, 1730, ANRJ, Col., cód.87, vol.7., fl.34v-35r; Petition Municipal Council, handled July 24, 1732, AHU, Rio de Janeiro, p.a.c., 7545.

49. See for instance Request *ouvidor geral*, Manoel da Costa Mimosa to king, August 5, 1728, AHU, Rio de Janeiro, p.a., caixa 20, doc. 40.

50. See for instance Request Municipal Council to king, February 15, 1730, AHU, Rio de Janeiro, p.a., caixa 25, doc.51.

51. Paulo Cavalcante de Oliveira Junior, *Negócios de Trapaça: Caminhos e Descaminhos na América Portuguesa (1700-1750)* (São Paulo: Editora HUCITEC, 2006), 195-210.

52. Dispatch Luís Vahia Monteiro to king, July 28, 1731, AHU, Rio de Janeiro, p.a., caixa 25, doc. 29.

53. Request Municipal Council to king, April 24, 1731, AHU, Rio de Janeiro, p.a., caixa 24, doc. 62; see chapter 6.

54. Consultation Overseas Council, September 2, 1700, AHU, Rio de Janeiro, p.a., caixa 7, doc. 27; "Regimento que deo o Sr. Governador Luís Vahia Monteiro para se administrarem pela Alfandega os impostos," May 18, 1729, ANRJ, Col., cód.87, vol.5, fl.120r-122r; Consultation Overseas Council, November 12, 1729, AHU, Rio de Janeiro, p.a.c., 6078, Alden, *Royal Government in Colonial Brazil* 309-310.

55. Request procurator Municipal Council, October 10, 1747, AHU, Rio de Janeiro, p.a., caixa 47, doc. 107; Request Municipal Council to king, A.H.U., Rio de Janeiro, p.a., caixa 52, doc. 17; Request Municipal Council to king, May 17, 1753, AHU, Rio de Janeiro, p.a., caixa 53, doc. 83; Petition Francisco de Almeida to king, handled August 2, 1760, AHU, Rio de Janeiro, p.a., caixa 67, doc. 26.

56. Dispatch Count da Cunha to Francisco Xavier de Mendonça Furtado, March 24, 1767, in: "Para a História do Rio de Janeiro (Vice-Reinato) - Século XVIII - Correspondência do Conde da Cunha," *Revista do Instituto Histórico e Geográfico Brasileiro*, (1962) 254:389-391; 2 dispatches João Carlos Lemos to Marquis do Lavradio, January 22, 1769 and June 22, 1769, ANRJ, Col., caixa 481, pacote 1, fl.23r-v; 23v-25r.

57. Ronald Raminelli, "Baltazar da Silva Lisboa: a honra e os apuris do juiz naturalista," in Ronaldo Vainfas *et al* eds., *Retratos do Império. Trajetórias individuais no mundo português nos séculos XVI a XIX* (Niteroí, RJ: Editora da Universidade Federal Fluminense, 2006) 279-295 discusses the Balthazar's career as a *juiz de fora* in Rio de Janeiro.

58. Request Municipal Council Paratí to king, July 6, 1719, AHU, Rio de Janeiro, p.a., caixa 11, doc. 58; Dispatch Municipal Council Angra dos Reis to king, July 15, 1719, AHU, Rio de Janeiro, p.a., caixa 11, doc. 80; Request Municipal Council Cabo Frio to king, July 1, 1726, AHU, Rio de Janeiro, p.a., caixa 19, doc. 46.

59. The sale of offices was common in most European empires. For this issue see: Mark A. Burkholder ed., *Administrators of Empire* (Aldershot UK and Brookfield VT: Ashgate Publishing Company, 1998) xviii.

60. Consultation Overseas Council, November 24, 1696, AHU, Rio de Janeiro, p.a.c., 2043.

61. Message Governor Rio de Janeiro to Manoel Correa Vasques, November 4, 1705, ANRJ, Col., cód.61, vol.14, fl.330r-331r; Consultation Overseas Council, July 1, 1706, AHU, Rio de Janeiro, p.a.c., 2906.

62. See Pijning, "Conflicts in the Portuguese Colonial Administration," 403-423; Alden, *Royal Government* 22-25.
63. Consultations Overseas Council, March 30, 1709, AHU, Rio de Janeiro, p.a.c., 3206, and AHU, cód.232, fl.254v.
64. Consultation Overseas Council, April 11, 1714, AHU,cód.233, fl.64v-66v.
65. Request Coronel Francisco de Amaral Gurgel, 1716, AHU, Rio de Janeiro, p.a.c., 3520.
66. Dispatch Aires de Saldanha e Albuquerque to king, June 28, 1719, AHU, Rio de Janeiro, p.a., caixa 11, doc. 53.
67. Sentence Casa da Supplicação, November 5, 1720, AHU, Rio de Janeiro, p.a., caixa 12, doc. 98.
68. Consultation Overseas Council, November 29, 1720, AHU, Rio de Janeiro, p.a.c., 3820. See also Eduardo Castro e Almeida, "Inventário dos Documentos Relativos ao Brasil Existentes no Archivo de Marinha e Ultramar de Lisboa - Rio de Janeiro," *Annaes da Bibliotheca Nacional* 39 (1917) 376.
69. Request Francisco Cordovil de Sequeira e Mello to king, June 26, 1736, AHU, Rio de Janeiro, p.a., caixa 32, doc. 46. "Com aquella mesmo amor, zelo, e desinteresse."
70. Dispatch Mathias Coelho e Souza to Gomes Freire de Andrade, January 4, 1738, ANRJ, Col., cód.84, vol.6, fl.171r-172v; Request Francisco Cordovil Sequeira e Mello to Mathias Coelho de Souza, January 4, 1738, ANRJ, Col., cód.87, vol.15, fl.29r.
71. Petition Francisco Cordovil de Sequeira e Mello to king, handled July 28, 1739, AHU, Rio de Janeiro, p.a., caixa 36, doc. 67.
72. Dispatch Gomes Freire de Andrade to João Alvarez Simões, *ouvidor geral*, June 10, 1743, ANRJ, Col., cód.87, vol.9, fl.28v.
73. Message Governor, July 28, 1748, ANRJ, Col., cód.87, vol.17, fl.63r-v.
74. Dispatch Count of Bobadella to Francisco Xavier de Mendonça Furtado, July 7, 1761, AHU, Rio de Janeiro, p.a.c., 21622; Consultation Overseas Council, August 14, 1764, AHU, cód.920, fl.78v-79r.
75. Petition Francisco Cordovil de Sequeira e Mello to king, handled June 16, 1764, AHU, Rio de Janeiro, p.a., caixa 77, doc. 76.
76. *Auto de Devassa* by José Mauricio da Gama e Freitas, September 24, 1770, AHU, Rio de Janeiro, p.a., caixa 98, doc. 48.
77. Private letter Marquis do Lavradio, viceroy, to Count da Cunha, president of the Overseas Council, February 20, 1770, in Marquês de Lavradio, *Cartas do Rio de Janeiro* 21-22; Opinion Francisco José Brandão to Marquis of Angeja, January 26, 1769, AHU, Rio de Janeiro, p.a., caixa 94, doc. 11.
78. Alden, *Royal Government* 24, note 87.
79. Alvará, March 3, 1770, Opinion Luís José de Pinto to secretary of state, July 31, 1777, Opinion Count da Azambuja to Marquis de Angeja, October 8, 1777, Petition Felipe Cordovil de Sequeira e Mello to Queen, w.d., all in AHU, Rio de Janeiro, p.a., caixa 94, doc. 11; Wehling, *História Administrativa do Brasil* 116; see also Alden, *Royal Government* 285 note 20.
80. Opinion Luís José de Britto to queen, June 19, 1781, AHU, Rio de Janeiro, p.a., caixa 94, doc. 11.
81. Opinion Count da Azambuja to Marquis de Angeja, October 8, 1777, AHU, Rio de Janeiro, p.a., caixa 94, doc. 11.
82. Petition Felipe Cordovil e Sequeira to queen, handled June 15, 1781, AHU, Rio de Janeiro, p.a., caixa 94, doc. 11.

NOTES

83. Petition Felipe Cordovil e Sequeira to queen, w.d., AHU, Rio de Janeiro, p.a., caixa 94, doc. 11.
84. Representation Municipal Council, May 24, 1788, A.H.U., Rio de Janeiro, p.a., caixa 141, doc. 44.
85. Favor princes regent, Dona Catherina da Bragança to Manoel Correa Vasques, March 6, 1705, ANRJ, Col., cód.61, vol.14, fl.276r-280r.
86. Opinion António Menezes de Souza to secretary of state, May 8, 1758, AHU, Rio de Janeiro, p.a., caixa 63, doc. 62; Message Luís de Vasconcellos e Souza, February 17, 1786, ANRJ, Col., caixa 495, pac.3; Dispatch António Martins Britto to queen, March 24, 1786, AHU, Rio de Janeiro, p.a., caixa 137, doc. 25; Request António Martins Britto to queen, February 28, 1787, AHU, Rio de Janeiro, p.a., caixa 139, doc. 22.
87. *Fiscais e Meirinhos* 254-259, 261-262, 268-269.
88. *Fiscais e Meirinhos* 347-349.
89. Alden, *Royal Government* 12, note 33; *Fiscais e Meirinhos* 371.
90. See for instance about the interference with the elections of the Municipal Council Dispatch Luís de Vasconcellos e Souza to Martinho de Mello e Castro, March 14, 1783, AHU, Rio de Janeiro, p.a., caixa 131, doc. 25.
91. *Fiscais e Meirinhos* 349-350.
92. Francisco de Souza Massuelos, "Compilação," October 15, 1760, BNRJ, ms.8,1,9, fl.54r-v.
93. See for this Alden, *Royal Government* 282-286.
94. Kenneth R. Maxwell, "The Generation of the 1790s and the Idea of Luso-Brazilian Empire," in Dauril Alden and Warren Dean eds., *Colonial Roots of Modern Brazil: Papers of the Newberry Library Conference* (Los Angeles: University of California Press, 1973), 107-146; A.J.R. Russell-Wood, "António Alvares Pereira: a Brazilian Student at the University of Coimbra in the Seventeenth Century," in F.W. Hodcroft ed., *Medieval and Renaissance Studies on Spain and Portugal in Honour of P.E. Russell* (Oxford: Society for the Studies of Medieval Languages and Literature, 1981) 192-209; Stuart B. Schwartz, *Sovereignty and Society in Colonial Brazil: the Judges of the High Court of Bahia, 1586-1750* (Berkeley: Los Angeles and London: University of California Press, 1973) 320-323.
95. The *provedores da fazenda*, Francisco de Cordovil e Sequeira e Mello and their son, Filipe de Cordovil e Sequeira had all received a degree in Coimbra. This was not the case with their predecessor Bertholomeu de Cordovil e Sequeira. The old judge of the customs, Manoel Correa Vasques was also Coimbra-trained, but his two successors not: João Martins Britto and António Martins Britto. "Estudantes da Universidade de Coimbra Nascidos no Brasil," *Brasília* supplement 4 (1949) 647, 1565, 318.
96. Stuart B. Schwartz, *Sovereignty and Society* chapter 13
97. High Court Judges could not marry locally, this was extended to all *ministros de letras* in 1734. Wehling and Wehling, *Direito e Justiça* 308. Royal Dispatch to Gomes Freire de Andrade, March 27, 1734, AHU, Rio de Janeiro, p.a., caixa 29, doc. 24 and BNRJ, ms.3,4,3, N.°31; for the same issue in Salvador see Schwartz, *Sovereignty and Society* 340-341
98. Petition Mathias Pinheiro da Silveira Bothelho to king, handled January 7, 1754, AHU, Rio de Janeiro, p.a., caixa 55, doc. 7.
99. Two letters of Bishop Rio de Janeiro to king, January 13, 1755, and January 19, 1756, AHU, Rio de Janeiro, p.a.c., 18183 and 19342; Opinion Gregorio Dias da Silva, chancellor High Court, January 12, 1754, AHU, Rio de Janeiro, p.a., caixa 55, doc. 7.

NOTES

According to Arno and Maria José Wehling the judge was allowed to marry. *Direito e Justiça no Brasil Colonial. O tribunal da relação do Rio de Janeiro (1751-1808)* (Rio de Janeiro: Renovar, 2004) 309.

100. Petition Mathias Pinheiro da Silveira Bothelho to king, AHU, Rio de Janeiro, p.a., caixa 55, doc. 7, commentary in marge: "Por repetidos decretos se tem ordenado que os Dezembargadores do Ultramar não cazem sem expressa licença de Sua Magestade pelas consequencais que destes cazamentos tem rezultado; este Dezembargador está no principio do seu lugar, e poderá ter muitas dependencias na caza da sua futura exposa que dependão dos pleitos, e assim me parece que por hora he intempestido este requerimento; porem como he matrimonia de graça Sua Magestade poderá fazer, sendo servido." For a treatment of this issue in Salvador: see Schwartz, *Sovereignty and Society* 314-356, Wehling and Wehling *Direito e Justiça* 308-309.
101. Petition *juiz de fora*, José de Lourenço Borges da Camara to Prince Regent, handled June 27, 1805, AHU, Rio de Janeiro, p.a., caixa 221, doc. 89A; and Petition idem. to idem, handled May 21, 1806, AHU, Rio de Janeiro, p.a., caixa 229, doc. 32; Representation Joaquim de Amorim Castro to Prince Regent, handled July 16, 1805, AHU, Rio de Janeiro, p.a., caixa 222, doc. 42. Arno and Maria José Wehling found four more cases of marriages, namely of Francisco Lopes de Sousa Faria Lemos in 1799, who obtained authorization tp marry his niece and of José Fortunato de Brito Abreu Sousa e Menezes in 1806. They also found references to two other locally married high courts judges (installed in 1794 and 1798) of whom they did not find records of official authorization.
102. Wehling and Wehling, *Direito e Justiça* 290-309, 619-620.
103. See listing by João Carlos Correa Lemos, September 2, 1786, BNRJ, 3,3,4, fl.269r-311v.
104. Royal Dispatch to Gomes Freire de Andrade, December 23, 1740, AHU, Rio de Janeiro, p.a., caixa 38, doc.6.
105. See for instance Dispatch António Martins Britto, *juiz ouvidor da alfândega*, to king, March 24, 1755; Consultation Overseas Council, January 8, 1756, AHU, Rio de Janeiro, p.a.c. 19237.
106. Royal dispatch to governor Rio de Janeiro, AHU, Rio de Janeiro, p.a., caixa 50, doc.26, November 12, 1749, "nunca foi da minha Real intenção, que se admeticem nas serventias dos officios pessoas inhabeis"; Dispatch Count da Azambuja to Francisco Xavier de Mendonça Furtado, May 16, 1768, AHU, Rio de Janeiro, p.a., caixa 91, doc. 65.
107. Consultation Overseas Council, March 6, 1760, AHU, Rio de Janeiro, p.a., caixa 66, doc. 45.
108. List of officials by João Marcos Correa Lemos, September 22, 1786, BNRJ, 3,3,4, fl.269r-311v.
109. Zacharias Moutoukias, "Réseaux Personnels et Autorité Coloniale: les Négociants de Buenos Aires au XVIIIe Siècle," *Annales E.S.C.* 4 (1992) 889-914.
110. Dispatch José António Ribeiro Freire to Conde dos Arcos, September 19, 1806, ANRJ, Col., caixa 495, pac.1. "A falta de execução da sobredita lei, tem dada cauza, a que não trabalharem os Officiaes e Guardas d'Alfândega com zelo nestas arrecadaçoens dos Reaes Direitos; por que como vão para os Armazens Reaes as fazendas fruto do seo trabalho feito com o nome injurozo de Denunciantes, Malsins, e Beleguins, com que são odiados, não só pelos Contrabandistas, e seos Socios, mas tambem pelo mesmo Povo, que os olha com horror, ameaçados a cada passo, com evidente perigo a sua vida, não querem ser efficazes nestas deligencias;

NOTES

mas antes se podem fazer contravençoens, ajustes, e compoziçoens, deixarão passar, debaixo dos seus olhos, qualquer genero de contrabando; o que hé de pessimas consequencias."
111. "Termo de Determinação" António José Cabral de Almeida, March 4, 1786, ANRJ, Col., caixa 495, pac.3; Dispatch José António Ribeiro Veiga to viceroy, March 12, 1787, ANRJ, Col., caixa 495, pac.3.
112. Dispatch António Martins do Britto to queen, March 24, 1786, AHU, Rio de Janeiro, p.a., caixa 137, doc. 25.
113. Dispatch António José Cabral de Almeida to Council of the Treasury (in Rio de Janeiro), June 8, 1786, ANRJ, Col., caixa 495, pac.3; Dispatch António Martins Britto to queen, February 28, 1787, AHU, Rio de Janeiro, p.a., caixa 139, doc. 22.
114. Dispatch António José Ribeiro Veiga to Council of the Treasury, June 27, 1789, ANRJ, Col., caixa 495, pac.3, Dispatch Louis da Souza Gurgel de Amaral to queen, April 30, 1791, AHU, Rio de Janeiro, p.a., caixa 149, doc. 35.
115. Alden, *Royal Government* 281; Kenneth R. Maxwell, *Conflicts and Conspiracies: Brazil and Portugal 1750-1808* (Cambridge: Cambridge University Press, 1973) 65-66.
116. D. Rodrigo de Souza Coutinho, "Memória sobre o Melhoramento dos Dominios de Sua Majestade na America (1797-1798)," in Andrée Mansuy Diniz Silva ed., *D. Rodrigo de Souza Coutinho, Textos Políticos, Económicos e Financeiros (1783-1811)* (Lisbon: Banco de Portugal, 1993) 2:51-52.
117. Request Luís de Noronha Sorrizão to prince regent, April 23, 1800, AHU, Rio de Janeiro, p.a., caixa 183, doc. 69.
118. Auto de Devassa, October 13, 1800, AHU, Rio de Janeiro, p.a., caixa 188, doc. 40.
119. Dispatch José António Ribeiro Freire to Dom Rodrigo de Souza Coutinho, secretary of state, November 11, 1800, AHU, Rio de Janeiro, p.a., caixa 189, doc. 45
120. Dispatch Dom Fernando José de Portugal to Viscount of Anadia, secretary of state, December 22, 1802, AHU, Rio de Janeiro, p.a., caixa 196, doc. 26.
121. For the same phenomenon in Minas Gerais see Maxwell, *Conflicts and Conspiracies* 67-69.
122. "Estatutos Junta do Comércio, Cap.17, §7," September 30, 1755, Arquivo Histórico do Itamaraty, (Rio de Janeiro) Lata 197, maço 6.
123. Request Don Juan Perales to viceroy, July 7, 1789, with information José António Ribeiro Veiga, July 1, 1789, ANRJ, Col., caixa 495, pacote 3; 2 Dispatches *provedor da fazenda*, João de Figueiredo to viceroy, November 5, 1796, and October 15, 1796, ANRJ, Col., caixa 485, pac.1.
124. Dispatch José António Ribeiro Freire to viceroy, January 15, 1799; Petition officials of the Customs, handled October 5, 1798, and 3 Petitions guards and officials of the customs, w.d. [1804], ANRJ, Col., caixa 495, pac.1.
125. Message judge of the customs to Count dos Arcos, viceroy, July 27, 1807, ANRJ, Col., caixa 495, pac.1.

6. DISCOURSE ON ILLEGALITY

1. Laura de Mello e Souza, *Desclassificados do Ouro. A Pobreza Mineira no Século XVIII* (3rd ed.; Rio de Janeiro: Edições Graal, 1990) 11-18.
2. For a similar notion about Spain see: Richard L. Kagan, "Prescott's Paradigm: American Historical Scholarship and the Decline of Spain," *American Historical Review* 101 (1996) 423-446.
3. José Luís Cardoso, *O Pensamento Económico em Portugal nos Finais do Século XVIII 1780-1808* (Lisbon: Editorial Estampa, 1989)

NOTES

4. Joel Serrão, "Decadência," in Joel Serrão ed., *Dicionário de História de Portugal* (Porto: Livraria Figueirinhas, w.d.) 2:270-274.
5. Fernando A. Novais, *Portugal e Brasil na Crise do Antigo Sistema Colonial (1777-1808)* (4th ed.; São Paulo: Editora Hucitec, 1986).
6. Anonymous comment [±1802] on: Autos de Examem, American vessel *Palmeira*, Arquivo Nacional, Rio de Janeiro [ANRJ], Colonial, Códice 76, volume 9, fl.41r.
7. For the debate on the "Sistema Colonial": José Roberto do Amaral Lapa, *O Sistema Colonial* (São Paulo: Editorial Estampa, 1991) Lapa supports Novais' views.
8. João L.R. Fragoso, *Homens da Grossa Ventura: Acumulação e Hierarchia na Praça Mercantil do Rio de Janeiro (1790-1830)* (Rio de Janeiro: Arquivo Nacional, 1992); Larissa V. Brown, "Internal Commerce in a Colonial Economy: Rio de Janeiro and its Hinterland, 1790-1822" Ph.D. dissertation, University of Virginia, 1986.
9. "Contrabando," in: António de Morais Silva ed., *Grande Dicionario da Lingua Portuguesa* (10th ed.; Lisbon: Editorial Confluência, 1949) 3:479.
10. Alvará com força de Lei, November 14, 1757, *Colleção de Leis, Decretos e Alvarás*, vol.1.
11. See for instance alvará de declaração, forbidding trade between Brazil and Mozambique, December 12, 1772, *Collecção das Leis, Decretos, e Alvarás* (Lisbon: Officina de Antonio Rodrigues Galhardo, 1797) 3:252-254.
12. Alvará com força de Lei, November 14, 1757, *Colleção de Leis, Decretos e Alvarás* vol.1.
13. . Mello e Souza, *Desclassificados do Ouro passim*
14. Dispatch Luís de Vasconcellos e Souza to Martinho de Mello e Castro, October 2, 1784, Biblioteca Nacional, Rio de Janeiro [BNRJ], ms.4,4,6, fl.213r. "Falo de grande numero de Individuos brancos, Indios, e Mestiços, que andão vagando por aqueles Districtos sem meios de subsistencia."
15. Petition merchants of Rio de Janeiro, handled April 25, 1815, BNRJ, ms.II-34,27,24."Estes homens errantes aqui, e ali, que não tem morada fixa, que não tem profissão, nem officio certo, nem bens, dos quaes subsistão."
16. Antonil was another example. He described the miserable conditions of contrabandists and their families once they were caught after being tempted to engage in this lucrative illegal trade. André João Antonil, *Cultura e Opulência do Brasil por suas Drogas e Minas*, Andrée Mansuy ed., (1st ed. 1711; Paris: Institute des Hautes Études de l'Amérique Latine, 1965) 334-340.
17. See for example request Captain António José Ribeiro de Fariato to prince regent, handled October 30, 1805, Arquivo Histórico Ultramarino (Lisbon) [AHU], Rio de Janeiro, papeis avulsos [p.a.], caixa 224, doc.51.
18. For this legislation see Ernst Pijning, "Contrabando na Legislação Portuguesa Durante o Período Colonial," *Anais da Sociedade Brasileira de Pesquisa Histórica* 14 (1994) 85-88.
19. "Das Leys Geraes de toda a Europa, e das Fundamentaes da Monarquia Portugueza, que prohibem a entrada dos Navios Estrangeiros nos Portos dos Dominios Ultramarinos de Portugal," w.d., Arquivo Nacional da Torre do Tombo (Lisbon) [ANTT], Ministério dos Negócios Estrangeiros, caixa 927, "Todo o Mundo sabe, que as Colonias Ultramarinas sendo sempre estabelecidas com o precizo objecto da utilidade da Metropolo, a que são pertencentes."
20. "Papel que acompanhou a Carta de 4 de Agosto de 1782," AHU, Rio de Janeiro, p.a., caixa 130, doc.77, and BNRJ, ms.4,4,4, fl.38v-39r.
21. Dauril Alden, "Late Colonial Brazil" in Leslie Bethell ed., *Cambridge History of Latin America* (Cambridge: Cambridge University Press, 1984) 2:622.
22. Alvará com força de Lei, November 14, 1757, *Colleção de Leis, Alvarás e Decretos* vol.1.

NOTES

"são os mesmos Contrabandistas a abjecção e o desprezo de todas as Nações Civilizadas."

23. See for instance dispatch Lord Strangford to George Canning, July 16, 1807, National Archives London, Foreign Office 63, vol.55, fl.15r-18r; Dispatch Commander of the Brazil fleet, Donald Campbell, to Count de Rezende, May, 4, 1801, A.H.U., Rio de Janeiro, p.a.n.c., caixa 191, doc. 84; "Pneus des motifs que le directoire peut avoir pour ne pas accepter la ratification tardive de la Reine de Portugal et pour qu'il fasse la conquête de ce royaume," without date [1797], Quay d'Orsay (Paris), Mémoires et documents, France, tome 1967, fl.344r-345r.

24. Pierre Verger, *Flux et Reflux de la Traite des Nègres entre le Golfe de Bénin et Bahia de Todos os Santos* (Paris and The Hague: Mouton, 1968) 27-53; José Roberto do Amaral Lapa, *A Bahia e a Carreira da Índia* (São Paulo: Companhia Editora Nacional, 1968) 253-299.

25. Alvará June 19, 1772, ANRJ, Col., caixa 495, pacote 3. "Que sendo hua maxima geralmente recebida, e constantamente praticada entre todas as Nasçoens, que da Capital, ou Metropoli-Dominante; hé que se deve fazer o Comercio, e Navegação pra as Colonias, e não as Colonias entre si, tenhão os ditos Officiaes enteresados e [en]carregados estabelecido por meyo do Intreposto de Angola hum Comercio Geral, e Navegação entre a Azia, Africa, e America com tal excluzão destes Reinos."

26. Alvará com força de Lei, January 11, 1803, AHU, Rio de Janeiro, p.a., caixa 204, doc. 9.

27. Memorandum, 1803, AHU, Rio de Janeiro, p.a., caixa 204, doc. 9.

28. Memorandum, 1803, AHU, Rio de Janeiro, p.a., caixa 204, doc. 9.

29. Memorandum, 1803, A.H.U., Rio de Janeiro, p.a., caixa 204, doc. 9. "Que o Emigrado Europeo da mais humilde classe, depois que sahe do Reino, nunca mais pega no Arado, nem na Enchada."

30. Memorandum Martinho de Mello e Castro to Luís de Vasconcellos e Souza, January 5, 1785, AHU, Rio de Janeiro, p.a., caixa 134, doc.32A.

31. For the impact of the legislation on Brazilian manufactures see Fernando A. Novais, "A Proibição das Manufacturas no Brasil e a Política Econômica Portuguêsa do Fim do Século XVIII," *Revista de História. Universidade de São Paulo* 67 (1967) 145-166.

32. Memorandum § 17, Martinho de Mello e Castro to Luís de Vasconcellos e Souza, January 5, 1785, AHU, Rio de Janeiro, p.a., caixa 134, doc. 32A.

33. Dispatch Amador Patrício da Maia to Martinho de Mello e Castro, February 15, 1794, AHU, Rio de Janeiro, p.a., caixa 156, doc.21.

34. "Capitulação que fizerão os levantados," [1711], in Virginia Rau and Maria Fernanda Costa Gomes da Silva eds., *Os Manuscritos do Arquivo da Casa de Cadaval Respeitantes ao Brasil* (Coimbra: University of Coimbra, 1958) 2:352-354.

35. Charles R. Boxer, *The Golden Age of Brazil 1695-1750, Growing Pains of a Colonial Society* (Berkeley, Los Angeles and London: University of California Press, 1962) 30-83; 162-203; A.J.R. Russell-Wood, "Manuel Nunes Viana: Paragon or Parasite of Empire?" *The Americas* 87 (1981) 479-498. For the theme of revolts in colonial Brazil see: Luciano Raposo de Almeida Figueiredo, "Protestos, Revoltas e Fiscalidade no Brasil Colonial," *LPH: Revista de História* 5 (1995) 56-87 and his *Rebeliões no Brasil Colônia,* (Rio de Janeiro: Jorge Zahar Editor, 2005).

36. Consultation Overseas Council, July 17, 1715, in: *Documentos Históricos* (Rio de Janeiro: Biblioteca Nacional, 1952) 96:165-175; Denunciation Joaquim José de Santa Ana, August 27, 1798, in *Anais do Arquivo Público da Bahia* 8 (1921) 46.

37. Petition merchants of Rio de Janeiro to king, handled July 1, 1727, AHU, Rio de Janeiro, p.a., caixa 19, doc. 46.
38. Kenneth R. Maxwell, "Pombal and the Nationalization of the Luso-Brazilian Economy," *Hispanic American Historical Review* 48:4 (1968) 608-631.
39. E. Bradford Burns, "The Intellectuals as Agents of Change and the Independence of Brazil, 1724-1822," in A.J.R. Russell-Wood ed., *From Colony to Nation. Essays on the Independence of Brazil* (Baltimore: The Johns Hopkins University Press, 1975) 211-246.
40. Kenneth R. Maxwell, "The Generation of the 1790s and the Idea of Luso-Brazilian Empire," in Dauril Alden and Warren Dean eds., *Colonial Roots of Modern Brazil: Papers of the Newberry Library Conference* (Los Angeles: University of California Press, 1973) 107-146.
41. José Luís Cardoso, *O Pensamento Económico em Portugal nos Finais do Século XVIII, 1780-1808* (Lisbon: Editórial Estampa, 1989) 289-300.
42. João Rodrigues de Brito, *Cartas Economico-Politicas Sobre a Agricultura e Commercio da Bahia* (Lisbon: Imprensa Nacional, 1821), José da Silva Lisboa, *Escritos Económicos Escolhidos,* António Almodovar ed., 2 vols., (Lisbon: Banco de Portugal, 1993).
43. Rodrigues de Brito, *Cartas Economico-Politicas* 18, 24.
44. Letter João Rodrigues de Brito to Câmara Municipal, May 28, 1807, in: Rodrigues de Brito, *Cartas Economico-Politicas* 89.
45. José da Silva Lisboa, "Princípios de Economia Política, para Servir de Introducção á Tentativa Economica," in José da Silva Lisboa, *Escritos Económicos Escolhidos (1804-1820),* António Almodovar ed., (Lisbon: Banco de Portugal, 1993) 1:12
46. Silva Lisboa, "Princípios da Economia Política" 1:19.
47. . Silva Lisboa, "Princípios" 1:14-16.
48. Silva Lisboa, "Princípios" 1:28.
49. Silva Lisboa, "Princípios" 1:35.
50. Silva Lisboa, "Princípios" 1:36-43.
51. Silva Lisboa, "Observações Sobre o Commercio Franco no Brasil," in Silva Lisboa, *Escritos Económicos Escolhidos* 1:187.
52. See for example Dom Luís da Cunha, *Instrucções Inéditas de Dom Luís da Cunha a Marco António de Azevedo Coutinho,* Pedro de Azevedo ed., (Coimbra: Imprensa da Universidade de Coimbra, 1929) 211
53. Valentim Alexandre, *Os Sentidos do Império. Questão Nacional e Questão Colonial na Crise do Antigo Regime Português* (Porto: Edições Afrontamento, 1993) 97-164.
54. Dom Rodrigo de Souza Coutinho, "Memória Sobre o Melhoramento dos Domínios de Sua Majestade na América," in Dom Rodrigo de Souza Coutinho, *Textos Políticos, Económicos e Financeiros (1783-1811),* Andrée Mansuy Diniz Silva ed., (Lisbon: Banco de Portugal, 1993) 2:48-53.
55. Dom Rodrigo de Souza Coutinho, "Memória Sobre o Melhoramento" 2:49-50.
56. Souza Coutinho, "Memória sobre o Melhoramento" 50.
57. Souza Coutinho, "Memória sobre o Melhoramento" 51.
58. Souza Coutinho, "Memória sobre o Melhoramento" 51-52.
59. Souza Coutinho, "Memória sobre o Melhoramento" 56.
60. José Joaquim da Cunha de Azeredo Coutinho, *Ensaio Económico Sobre o Comércio de Portugal e as suas Colónias,* Jorge Miguel Pedreira ed., (1st ed. 1794; reprint: Lisbon: Banco de Portugal, 1992) xiv-xvi.
61. Azeredo Coutinho, *Ensaio Económico* 99-102.
62. Azeredo Coutinho. Ensaio Económico xii, xvi.
63. Azeredo Coutinho, *Ensaio Económico* xvi.

NOTES

64. See for instance the analysis of Gregório de Matos by Hansen João Adolfo Hansen, *A Sátira e o Engenho. Gregório de Matos e a Bahia do Século XVII* (São Paulo: Companhia das Letras, 1989) esp. chapter 2.
65. Manoel Tavares de Sequira e Sá ed., *Júbilos da América, na Gloriosa Exaltação, e Promoção do Illustrissimo e Excellentissimo Senhor Gomes Freire de Andrada*, (Lisbon: Na Officina do Dor. Manoel Alvares Sollano, 1754).
66. Diogo do Couto, *O Soldado Prático*, M. Rodrigues Lapa ed., (3rd ed.; Lisbon: Livraria Sá da Costa, 1980).
67. For revisionist historiography on this issue see Sanjay Subrahmanyam, *The Portuguese Empire in Asia, 1500-1700: A Political and Economic History* (London and New York: Longman Group, 1993) 107-143.
68. Couto, *O Soldado Prático* 155.
69. See for instance Couto, *O Soldado Prático* 128-130.
70. *Arte de Furtar*, Rogier Bismut ed., (Lisbon: Imprensa Nacional Casa de Moeda, 1991).
71. *Arte de Furtar* 13-24.
72. *Arte de Furtar* 31.
73. *Carta Apologetica, em que se mostra que não he Author do Libro, intitulado Arte de Furtar o insigne P. Antonio Vieira, da Companhia de Jesus; escrita por hum Zeloso da Illustre Memoria deste grande Escritor* (Lisbon: Na Regia Officina Sylviana, e da Academia Real, 1744) 4-5, 43.
74. Gordon R. Williams et al ed., *The National Union Catalogue. Pre-1956 Imprints* (London: Mansell Publishing, 1979) 636:456-466
75. *Arte de Furtar* 117-160, 97-100, 287-291
76. *Arte de Furtar* 77-79.
77. *Arte de Furtar* 64-66.
78. *Arte de Furtar* 71-76.
79. *Arte de Furtar* 371-374
80. T.D. Kendrick, *The Lisbon Earthquake* (London: Methuen & Co., 1956) 72-92.
81. Padre António Vieira, "Sermão da Visitação de Nossa Senhora," in Hernani Cidade ed., *Padre António Vieira no Brasil,* (Lisbon: Agência Geral das Colônias, 1940) 2:189-218.
82. Couto, *O Soldado Prático* 156, 157.
83. Gregório de Matos, *Obra Poética*, James Amado and Emanuel Araújo eds., 2 vols., (3rd ed; Rio de Janeiro: Editora Record, 1992).
84. Emanuel Araújo, "716 Poemas à Procura de um Autor," in Gregório de Matos, *Obra Poética* 2:1285-1289.
85. Matos, *Obra Poética* 1:33-58.
86. Matos, "Este é o bom governo de Portugal," *Obra Poética* 2:1232-1245. "O Conselho de Ultramar / donde preside um Diabo / que assim vai dado o cabo / vendendo o que se há de dar: / e espera de se salvar / este assolador de gente / tão soberbo e insolente / que o Rio de Janeiro / todos dizem que por dinheiro / vendera este irracional / Este é o bom governo de Portugal"
87. Tomás Antônio Gonzaga, *Cartas Chilenas,* Joaci Pereira Furtado ed., (São Paulo: Companhia das Letras, 1995).
88. Gonzaga, *Cartas Chilenas* 251-253

7. CONCLUSION

1. Petition Salvador Correa e Sa to king, w.d. [after November 20, 1807], Arquivo Histórico Ultramarino, Rio de Janeiro, papeis avulsos, caixa 243, doc. 23. "em quanto este reyno existir, em qualidade de huma Collonia da Corte do Brasil."
2. For this concept see Maria Odila Silva Dias, "A Interiorização do Metropole," in Carlos Guilherme Mota ed., *1822: Dimenções* (2nd ed.; São Paulo: Edições Perspectiva, 1986) 160-184. The significance of 1808 will always remain controversial. For the latest discussions see José Jobson de Andrade Arruda, *Uma Colônia entree dois Impérios. A abertura dos portos brasileiros* (Bairú, SP: EDUSC, 2008) and Luís Valente de Oliveira and Rubens Ricupero eds., A Abertura dos Portos (São Paulo, Editora SENAC, 2007).

POSTSCRIPT

1. André João Antonil, *Cultura e Opulência do Brasil por suas Drogas e Minas*, Andrée Mansuy ed., (1st ed. 1711; Paris: Institute des Hautes Études de l'Amérique Latine, 1965) 388-389.
2. For a discussion of this see: Jaime Cortesão, *Alexandre de Gusmão e o Tratado de Madrid* (Rio de Janeiro: Ministério das Relações Exteriores, Instituto Rio Branco, 1953) 1:1, 53-63.
3. Cortesão, *Alexandre de Gusmão* 1:1, 53-63.
4. Cortesão, *Alexandre de Gusmão* 1:1, 53-63.
5. The most widely used calculation comes from: Virgílio Noya Pinto, *Ouro Brasileiro e o Comércio Anglo-Português* (2.ed.; São Paulo: Companhia Editora National, 1979) 39-117.
6. Novais, *Portugal e Brasil na Crise do Antigo Sistema Colonial*; José Jobson de Andrade Arruda, *O Brasil no Comércio Colonial* (São Paulo: Ática, 1980); Valentim Alexandre, *Os Sentidos do Império. Questão Nacional e Questão Colonial na Crise do Antigo Regime Português* (Porto: Edições Afrontamento, 1993); Jorge Miguel Viana Pedreira, *Estructura Industrial e Mercado Colonial. Portugal e Brasil (1780-1830)* (Lisbon: Difel, 1994).
7. Noya Pinto, *Ouro Brasileiro* 285-315.
8. Noya Pinto, *Ouro Brasileiro* 299-300.
9. Moutoukias, *Contrabando y Control Colonial* chapter 4.
10. Klooster, Illicit Riches, chapter 9.

BIBLIOGRAPHY

I. Archival materials.
Brazil, Rio de Janeiro
(1) Arquivo Nacional, Rio de Janeiro
Capitania e Vicereinato
Caixas:
Caixa 485: Correspondência diversas autoridades.
Caixa 486: Correspondência Fazenda Real.
Caixa 490, 491: Correspondência diversa.
Caixa 492, 493: Autos de Exames Embarcações estrangeiras.
Caixa 495: Correspondência Alfandega de Rio de Janeiro.
Caixa 502: Correspondência Governador de Angola.
Caixa 715: Ministério da Marinha e Ultramar.
Caixa 716: Idem.
Caixa 717: Idem.
Caixa 746: Correspondência Capitania do Rio de Janeiro.
Caixa 747: Correspondência Colonia Sacramento.
Caixa 750: Correspondência Provedor da Fazenda.
Caixa 751: Correspondência diversas autoridades.
Códices:
Códice 60, vols. 12, 25, 27: Registro Original da Provedoria da Fazenda.
Códice 61, vols. 14, 15: copiados e restaurados de códice 60.
Códice 76: Autos de Embarcações.
Códice 87, vols. 2-18: registro original da correspondência dos governadores do Rio de Janeiro. Portárias, Ordens, Bandas etc. 1725-1763.
Códice 104, vol. 108: Correspondência com o governador e mais pessoas do Rio Grande do Sul sobre demarcações de limites etc. 1779-1807.
Códice 157: Fianças embarcações.
Códice 807, vols. 3-14, 16, 19-25: Coleção memórias.
(2) Arquivo Histórico do Itamaraty.
Documentos anterior à 1822
Lata 169, Maço 4; Lata 181, Maço 4; Lata 182, Maço 3;
Lata 183, Maço 1; Lata 185, Maços 1-5; Lata 186, Maços 1-3; Lata 188, Maços 1-3; Lata 197, Maço 6.
(3) Biblioteca Nacional, Rio de Janeiro.
1,4,1/#25; 3,1,30; 3,4,3/#13,26,31,33; 4,4,3-13; 6,3,9; 7,1,32; 7,3,1/#5,10; 7,3,44; 8,1,9; 11,2,2; 12,2,2; 15,2,24; 22,1,26.
I-4,17,1-101 (Coleção Aguiar).
I-12,1,9/#14; I-17,12,1/#7,9,10-1,14,19; I-17,12,4/#4;
I-28,25,11.

BIBLIOGRAPHY

I-29,13-16, 20 (Coleção Linhares).
I-31,4,1/#10; I-31,20,15; I-32,14,5/#3; I-34,15,19.
II-34,3,1/#10; II-34,15,49; II-34,18,9;
II-34,23,1/#19,43-45,53; II-34,24,15; II-34,27,24;
II-34,30,45; II-35,5,32/#5,7.
(4) Instituto Histórico e Geográfico Brasileiro.
Arquivo 1.1.22; 1.1.25; 1.1.26; 1.2.12; 1.4.31.
Lata 4, Pasta 23; Lata 16, Pasta 6; Lata 48, Pasta 19; Lata 188, Maço 3; Lata 581, Pasta 1.
Salvador:
(1) Arquivo Público do Estado da Bahia.
Seção Colonial e Provincial.
Livro 158: Cartas do Governo a várias autoridades 1798-1800.
Livro 202: Cartas ao Governo 1800-1801.
Livro 449: Registo de Alvarás, Relação da Bahia 1700-1702.
Livro 500: Relação da Bahia: Alvarás, provisões, registros 1704-06.
Livro 501: Idem. 1707-11.
Livro 502: Idem. 1712-15.
Livro 503: Idem. 1715-18.
Livro 512: Idem. 1734-35.
(2) Arquivo Municipal da Bahia:
Livro 5.3: Condemnações 1769-99.
Livro 36.1: Condemnações do Senado, vereações 1703-1805.
Livro 92: Posturas 1696.
Livro 238: Posturas 1716-42.
Livro 364: Condemnações que fizeram os Almocreves 1777-85.
Livro 929: Actas da Camara 1718-31.
France
Paris.
(1) Archives Nationales.
Affaires Étrangeres B/I 647-86 (Inventoried by Cícero Dias).
B/III 385.
(2) Quay d'Orsey.
Memoires et Documents.
Ameriques, vol. 6.
France, vol. 1967, 1996, 2115.
Portugal, vol. 1, 2, 11, 21, 28.
Correspondance Consulaire et Commercial.
Bahia, vol. 1.
Lisbonne, vol. 53.
(3) Biblioteque Nationale.
Clairembaut, cod. 1005.
Great Britain
London
(1) British Library.
Additional Mss. 9252, 23627, 38395 and 43441.

Egerton 528.
(2) National Archives
SP 89 State Papers Portugal, vols. 15-34.
FO 63 Correspondence Portugal, vols. 1-10.
FO 179, vol. 1.
Netherlands.
The Hague
Nationaal Archief.
Staten Generaal/Liassen Portugal:
7016, 7021/1-2, 7022/1-2, 7027/1-2, 7028/1-2, 7037/1-2, 7039/1-2, 7040/1.
Portugal.
Lisbon
(1) Arquivo Histórico Ultramarino.
Rio de Janeiro, papeis avulsos catalogados by Eduardo Castro e Almeida.
Rio de Janeiro, papeis avulsos caixas 1-244; 295-301.
Códices 232,233,234,912,920,1177,1193.
(2) Arquivo Nacional da Torre de Tombo.
Casa da Suplicação:
Juizos Diversos, Inventios, Letra L, Maço 12, Caixa 2467: Inventário dos bens de Luís de Vasconcellos e Souza.
Chancelarias:
Dom José I: Livro 64, fl.347r-v.
    Livro 70, fl.276r-277r.
Dona Maria I: Livro 22, fl.334v.
    Livro 75, fl.388v, 393r-395r.
    Livro 181.
Intendência Geral da Polícia:
Maço 601.
Ministério dos Negócios Estrangeiros:
Caixas 93,147,414,416,417,427,429-34,454,456,457,459-61, 507,561,865,918-22,927,952; Livro 120.
(3) Arquivo do Tribunal de Contas:
Erário Regio:
Códices 3976, 4042, 4044, 4047, 4057.
(4) Biblioteca Nacional, Lisboa.
Coleção Pombalina:
41, 42, 49, 107, 613, 614, 616, 637, 638.
(5) Biblioteca do Palácio de Ajuda:
Documents inventoried by Ferreira:
49-I-58, 51-IV-36, 51-VI-02, 51-IX-32, 51-IX-33, 53-XIII-16/#136, 51-IX-31, 54-2-14, 54-V-12/#5, 54-XIII-4/#74, 54-VII-27, 54-XIII-4/#9,72.
Porto
Biblioteca Municipal do Porto.

BIBLIOGRAPHY

Códices 235 and 903.
Évora
Biblioteca Pública de Évora:
Códices CIV/1-33; CV/2-17; CXVI/2-12,#1,18,20; CXVI/2-13,#25,27; CXVI/1-39,#24; CXVI/2-13,#25,27; CXX/2-3.

II. Contemporary Accounts and Printed Primary Sources.

Account of the Voyages undertaken by the order of his present Majesty for making the discoveries in the Southern Hemisphere, and successively performed by Commodore Byron, Captain Wallis, Captain Carteret and Captain Cook, An, John Hawkesworth ed., 3 vols. (London: for W. Strahan and T. Cadell 1773).

Antonil, André João, *Cultura e Opulência do Brasil por suas Drogas e Minas*, Andrée Mansuy ed., (1st ed. 1711; Paris: Institute des Hautes Études de l'Amérique Latine, 1965).

Arte de Furtar, Rogier Bismut ed., (Lisbon: Imprensa Nacional Casa de Moeda, 1991).

Banks, Joseph, *The Endeavour Journal of Joseph Banks 1768-1771*, J.C. Beaglehole ed., (Sydney: Halstead Press, 1962).

[Barbinais, le Gentil de la], *Nouveau Voyage au Tour du Monde par M. le Gentil* 2 vols. (Amsterdam: Pierre Mortier, 1728).

Brito, João Rodrigues de, *Cartas Economico-Politicas Sobre a Agricultura e Commercio da Bahia* (Lisbon: Imprensa Nacional, 1821).

Bougainville, Louis de, *Voyage autour du Monde par la Frégate du Roi la Boudeuse, et la Flûte l'Étoile; en 1766, 1767, 1768 &1769* (Paris: Chez Saillant & Nyon, 1771).

Burke, Edmund, *An Account of the European Settlements in the Americas* 2 vols. (London: Printed for R. and J. Dodsey in Pall-Mall, 1757).

Caille, Abbé de la, *Journal Historique du Voyage fait au Cap de Bonne Espérance* (Paris: Chez Guillyn, 1763).

Carta Apologetica, em que se Mostra que não he Author do Libro, Intitulado Arte de Furtar o Insigne P. Antonio Vieira, da Companhia de Jesus; Escrita por hum Zeloso da Illustre Memoria deste Grande Escritor (Lisbon: Na Regia Officina Sylviana, e da Academia Real, 1744).

Collecção das Leis, Decretos, e Alvarás, 8 vols. (Lisbon: Officina de Antonio Rodrigues Galhardo, 1797).

Cook, James, *The Voyages of Captain James Cook on his Voyages of Discovery*, J.C. Beaglehole ed., vol.1 (Cambridge: Cambridge University Press, 1955).

Coutinho, José Joaquim da Cunha de Azeredo, *Ensaio Económico Sobre o Comércio de Portugal e suas Colónias*, Jorge Miguel Pedreira ed., (Lisbon: Banco de Portugal, 1992).

Couto, Diogo do, *O Soldado Prático*, M. Rodrigues Lapa ed., (3rd ed.; Lisbon: Livraria Sá da Costa, 1980).

Courte de la Blanchediere, Abbé, *Nouveau Voyage fait au Pérou d'Alonso-Carillo-Lazo*,(Paris: Imprimerie de Delaguette, 1751).

Coutinho, Dom Rodrigo de Souza, *Textos Políticos, Económicos e Financeiros*, Andrée Mansuy Diniz Silva ed., 2 vols., (Lisbon: Banco de Portugal, 1993).

Cunha, Dom Luís da, *Instrucções Inéditas de Dom Luís da Cunha a Marco António de Azevedo Coutinho*, Pedro de Azevedo ed., (Coimbra: Imprensa da Universidade de Coimbra, 1929).

Débret, J.R., *Voyage Pittoresque au Brésil, Sejour d'un Artiste Français au Brésil, depuis 1816 jusqu'en 1831 inclusif*, 3 vols. (Paris: Institut de France, 1835).

Documentos Históricos 110 vols. (Rio de Janeiro: Biblioteca Nacional, 1928-1955).

BIBLIOGRAPHY

"Estudantes da Universidade de Coimbra Nascidos no Brasil," *Brasília* supplement (1949) vol.4.

Gonzaga, Tomás Antônio, *Cartas Chilenas*, Joaci Pereira Furtado ed., (São Paulo: Companhia das Letras, 1995).

Hunter, John, *An Historical Journal of the Transaction at Port Jackson and Norfolk Island* (London: for John Stockdale, 1793).

Júbilos da América, na Gloriosa Exaltação, e Promoção do Illustrissimo e Excellentissimo Senhor Gomes Freire de Andrada, Manoel Tavares de Sequira e Sá ed., (Lisbon: Na Officina do Dor. Manoel Alvares Sollano, 1754).

Koster, Henry, *Travels in Brazil in the years 1809 to 1815*, 2 vols, (Philadelphia: M. Carey & Son, 1817).

Lavradio, Marquês do, *Cartas da Bahia, 1768-1769* (Rio de Janeiro: Arquivo Nacional, 1972).

Lavradio, Marquês do, *Cartas do Rio de Janeiro* (Rio de Janeiro: Arquivo Nacional, 1978).

Lindley, Thomas, *Narrative of a Voyage to Brazil: Terminating in the Seizure of a British Vessel, and the Imprisonment of the Author and the Ship's Crew, by the Portuguese* (London: J. Johnson, 1805).

Lisanti, Luís, ed., *Negócios Coloniais (Uma Correspondência Comercial do Século XVIII)* (Brasília: Ministério da Fazenda, 1973) volume III.

Lisboa, José da Silva, *Escritos Económicos Escolhidos*, António Almodovar ed., 2 vols. (Lisbon: Banco de Portugal, 1993).

Luccock, John, *Notes on Rio de Janeiro, and the Southern Parts of Brazil; taken during a Residence of ten Years in that Country, from 1808 to 1818* (London: Printed for Samuel Leigh, 1820).

Manuscritos do Arquivo da Casa de Cadaval Respeitantes ao Brasil, Os, Virginia Rau and Maria Fernanda Costa Gomes da Silva eds., 2 vols. (Coimbra: Imprensa da Universidade de Coimbra, 1958).

Matos, Gregório de, *Obra Poética*, James Amado and Emanuel Araújo eds., 2 vols. (3rd ed; Rio de Janeiro: Editora Record, 1992).

Mello, Sebastião José de Carvalho e, *Escritos Económicos de Londres (1741-1742)*, José Barreto ed. (Lisbon: Biblioteca Nacional, 1986).

"Mémoire Inédit d'Ambroise Jauffret sur le Brésil à l'Époque de la Découverte des Mines d'Or [1704]," *Actas do V Colóquio Internacional de Estudos Luso-Brasileiros* Andrée Mansuy ed. (Nashville: Vanderbilt University Press, 1965) 2:407-434.

Memorials of the British Consul and Factory at Lisbon to His Majesty's Ambassador at that Court and the Secretaries of State of this Kingdom (London: for J. Wilkie, 1766).

Notícias Históricas de Portugal e Brasil (1751-1800) vol. 2 (Coimbra: Coimbra Editora, 1964).

Ordinações Filipinas, Mário Júlio de Almeida Costa ed. (Lisbon: Fundação Gulbenkian, w.d.; reprint of 1870 Edition) 5 vols. in 3.

"Para a História do Rio de Janeiro (Vice-Reinato) - Século VIII - Correspondência do Conde da Cunha," *Revista do Instituto Histórico e Geográfico Brasileiro* 254 (1962) 241-410.

Pereira, Thomas da Costa, *Sermão do Espirito Santo, Prégado na Igreja do Bom Jesus do Rio de Janeiro à Meza do Negócio no Anno de 1754, em que a mesma Meza o elegeo por seu Protector* (Lisbon: Officina de Miguel Manescal da Costa, 1755).

Raynal, Abbé, *Histoire Philosophique et Politique, des Établissemens & du Commerce des Européens dans les Deux Indes* (Amsterdam: w.p., 1770).
Turnbull, John, *A Voyage Round the World, in the Years 1800, 1801, 1802, 1803 and 1804* (2nd ed.; London: printed for C. Chapple, 1813).
Vandelli, Domingos, *Aritmética Política, Economia e Financas 1770-1804*, José Vicente Serrão ed. (Lisbon: Banco de Portugal, 1994).
Vilhena, Luiz dos Santos, *Recopilação de Noticias Soteropolitanas e Brasilicas*, Braz do Amaral ed., 2 vols. (Salvador: Imprensa Official do Estado, 1921- 1922).
2^0 Visconde de Santarém, *Quadro Elementar das Relaçoes Políticas e Diplomáticas de Portugal com as Diversas Potencias do Mundo desde o Princípio da Monarchia Portuguesa até aos nossos Dias* (Lisbon: Académia Geral das Sciencias, (Paris: J.P. Aillard, 1842-1860) 19volumes.
Voyage of Governor Philip to Botany Bay with an Account of the Establishment of the Colonies of Port Jackson & Norfolk Island, The, (London: for John Stockdale, 1789).
III. Books and Articles.
Abreu, Martha and Rachel Soilhet eds. *Ensino de História. Conceitos, Temáticas e Metodologia* (Rio de Janeiro: Casa da Palavra, 2003).
Abril, Victor Hugo, *Governança no Ultramar. Conflictos e Descaminhos no Rio de Janeiro c 1700-c.1750)* (Jundiaí, SP: Paco Editorial, 2018).
Alden, Dauril and Warren Dean eds., *Colonial Roots of Modern Brazil: Papers of the Newberry Library Conference* (Los Angeles: University of California Press, 1973).
Alden, Dauril, "Late Colonial Brazil, 1750-1808," in Leslie Bethell ed., *The Cambridge History of Latin America* (Cambridge: Cambridge University Press, 1984) 2:601-660.
Alden, Dauril, *The Making of an Enterprise. The Society of Jesus in Portugal, Its Empire and Beyond, 1540-1750* (Stanford: Stanford University Press, 1996).
Alden, Dauril, "The Population of Brazil in the Late Eighteenth Century: A Preliminary Study," *HAHR* 43 (1963) 173-205.
Alden, Dauril, "Price Movements in Brazil, Before, During and After the Gold Boom, with Special Reference to the Salvador Market," in: Lyman L. Johnson and Enrique Tandeter eds., *Essays on the Price History of Eighteenth Century Latin America* (Albuquerque: University of New Mexico Press, 1990) 335-371.
Alden, Dauril, *Royal Government in Colonial Brazil. With a Special Reference to the Administration of the Marquis of Lavradio, Viceroy, 1769-1779* (Berkeley and Los Angeles: University of California Press, 1968).
Alden, Dauril, "Vicitudes of Trade in the Portuguese Atlantic Empire during the First Half of the Eighteenth Century: A Review Article," *The Americas* 32 (1975) 282-291.
Alden, Dauril, "Yankee Sperm Whalers in Brazilian Waters, and the Decline of the Portuguese Whale Fishery (1773-1801)," *The Americas* 20 (1964) 267-288.
Alencastro, Luiz Felipe de, "The apprenticeship of colonization," in: Barbara Solow ed., *Slavery and the rise of the Atlantic System* (Cambridge: Cambridge University Press, 1991),
Alencastro, Luiz Felipe de, *O Trato dos Viventes. Formação do Brasil no Atlântico Sul Séculos XVI e XVII* (São Paulo: Companhia das Letras, 2000).
Alexandre, Valentim, *Os Sentidos do Império. Questão Nacional e Questão Colonial na Crise do Antigo Regime Português* (Porto: Edições Afrontamento, 1993).
Algranti, Leila Mezan, "Slave Crimes: The Use of Police Power to Control the Slave Population of Rio de Janeiro," *Luso-Brazilian Review* 25 (1988) 27-48.

BIBLIOGRAPHY

Almeida, Eduardo Castro e, "Inventário dos Documentos Relativos ao Brasil Existentes no Arquivo de Marinha e Ultramar, organizado para a Biblioteca Nacional do Rio de Janeiro," *Anais da Biblioteca Nacional do Rio de Janeiro*, vols. 39 (1917), 46 (1934), 50 (1936), and 71 (1951).

Almeida, Luís Ferrand, "A Fábrica das Sedas de Lisboa no Tempo de D. João V," *Revista Portuguesa de História* 25 (1989-1990) 1-48.

Arruda, José Jobson de Andrade, "Decadence or Crisis in the Luso-Brazilian Empire: a New Model for Colonization in the Eighteenth Century," *HAHR* (2001) 865-878.

Arruda, José Jobson de Andrade, *Uma Colônia entre dois Impérios. A abertura dos portos brasileiros* (Bairú, SP: EDUSC, 2008).

Arruda, José Jobson de Andrade, *O Brasil no Comércio Colonial* (São Paulo: Ática, 1980).

Arruda, José Jobson de Andrade, *Planos para o Brasil Projetos para o Mundo. O novo imperialismo britânico e o processo de Independência (1800-1831)*, São Paulo: Almedina, 2022).

Araújo, Emanuel, "716 Poemas à Procura de um Autor," in Gregório de Matos, *Obra Poética*, James Amado and Emanuel Araújo eds., (3rd ed; Rio de Janeiro: Editora Record, 1992) 2:1285-1289.

Aufderheide, Patricia A., "Order and Violence: Social Deviance and Social Control in Brazil, 1780-1840," Ph.D. dissertation University of Minnesota, 1976.

Aufderheide, Patricia A., "Upright Citizens in Criminal Records Investigations in Cachoeira and Geremoabo, Brazil, 1780-1836," *The Americas* 38 (1981) 173-184.

Aughton, Peter, *The Transit of Venus. The brief, brilliant life of Jeremiah Horrocks, father of British astronomy* (London: Weidenfeld & Nicolson, 2004).

Azevedo, João Lúcio d', "Política de Pombal Relativa ao Brasil," in: *Novas Epanáforas. Estudos de História e Literatura* (Lisbon: Livraria Clássica Editora, 1932) 8-62.

Azevedo, Pedro de, "A Companhia da Ilha do Corisco," *Arquivo Histórico Português* (Lisbon, 1903) 1:422-424.

Benton, Lauren, *Law and Colonial Cultures. Legal Regimes in World History, 1400-1900* (Cambridge: Cambridge University Press, 2002).

Bernstein, Harry, *The Brazilian Diamond in Contracts, Contraband and Capital* (Lanham, NY: University Press of America, 1986).

Betancour, Arturo Ariel, *Contrabando y Contrabandistas: Historias Coloniales* (Montevideo: Aria Editorial, 1982).

Bicalho, Maria Fernanda Baptista, *A Cidade e o Império. O Rio de Janeiro no Século XVIII* (Rio de Janeiro: Civilização Brasileira, 2003).

Bicalho, Maria Fernanda Baptista, "Joana d'Entremeuse: uma contrabandista entre a insuação e circunspeção," in: Ronaldo Vainfas, Georgina Silva dos Santos and Guilherme Pereira das Neves eds., *Retratos do Império. Trajetórias individuais no mundo portugues nos séculos XVI a XIX* (Niterói, RJ: EdUFF, 2006) 99-115.

Bicalho, Maria Fernanda Baptista, "O que significa ser citadão nos tempos coloniais," in: Martha Abreu and Rachel Soilhet eds. *Ensino de História. Conceitos, Temáticas e Metodologia* (Rio de Janeiro: Casa da Palavra, 2003) 139-151.

Boschi, Caio Cesar, *Roteiro Sumário dos Arquivos Portuguezes de Interesse para o Pesquisador da História do Brasil* (São Paulo: Edições Arquivo do Estado, 1986).

Boxer, Charles R., "Brazilian Gold and British Traders in the First Half of the Eighteenth Century," *HAHR* 49 (1969) 454-472.

BIBLIOGRAPHY

Boxer, Charles R., *The Church Militant and Iberian Expansion, 1440-1770* (Baltimore and London: Johns Hopkins University Press, 1978).

Boxer, Charles R., ed. *Descriptive List of the State Papers Portugal, 1661-1780, in the Public Record Office, London* 3 vols. (Lisbon: Académia das Ciências, 1979-1980).

Boxer, Charles R., "English Shipping in the Brazil Trade, 1640-1665," *The Marinier's Mirror* 27 (1951) 197-230.

Boxer, Charles R., *The Golden Age of Brazil 1695-1750, Growing Pains of a Colonial Society* (Berkeley, Los Angeles and London: University of California Press, 1962).

Boxer, Charles R., "Lord Tyrawly in Lisbon. An Anglo-Irish Protestant at the Portuguese Court, 1728-41," *History Today* 20 (1970) 791-798.

Boxer, Charles R., *Portuguese Society in the Tropics. The Municipal Councils of Goa, Macao, Bahia, and Luanda, 1510-1800* (Madison and Milwaukee: The University of Wisconsin Press, 1965).

Boxer, Charles R., *Salvador de Sá and the Struggle for Brazil and Angola, 1602-1686* (London: The Athlone Press, 1952).

Brown, Larissa V., "Internal Commerce in a Colonial Economy: Rio de Janeiro and its Hinterland, 1790-1822," Ph.D. dissertation, University of Virginia, 1986.

Burkholder, Mark A. ed., *Administrators of Empire* (Aldeshot UK and Brookfield VT: Ashgate Publishing Company, 1998).

Burkholder, Mark A., and D.S. Chandler, *From Impotence to Authority, the Spanish Crown and the American Audiencias, 1687-1808* (Columbia and London: University of Missouri Press, 1977).

Burns, E. Bradford, "The Intelectuals as Agents of Change and the Independence of Brazil, 1724-1822," in: A.J.R. Russell-Wood ed., *From Colony to Nation. Essays on the Independence of Brazil* (Baltimore: The Johns Hopkins University Press, 1975) 211-246.

Calmon, Pedro, *História do Brasil* 6 vols. (Rio de Janeiro: Livraria José Olympio, 1959).

Canabrava, Alice P., *O Comércio Portugues no Rio de la Plata (1580-1640)* (1st ed. 1944; Belo Horizonte and São Paulo: Editora Itatiaia Ltda. and Editora da Universidade de São Paulo, 1984).

Canny, Nicolas, and Anthony Pagden eds., *Colonial Identity in the Atlantic World, 1500-1800* (Princeton: Princeton University Press, 1987).

Cardoso, José Luís, *O Pensamento Económico em Portugal nos Finais do Século XVIII, 1780-1808* (Lisbon: Editorial Estampa, 1989).

Cardozo, Manoel S., "The Brazilian Gold Rush," *The Americas* 3 (1946) 137-160.

Cardozo, Manoel S., "The Collection of the Royal Fifths in Brazil, 1695-1709," *HAHR* 20:3 (1940) 359-379.

Cavalcante, Paulo, *Negócios de Trapaça. Caminhos e Descaminhos na América Portuguesa (1700-1750)* (São Paulo: Editora Hucitec, 2006).

Christelow, Allan, "Great Britain and the Trades from Cadiz and Lisbon to Spanish America and Brazil, 1759-1783," *HAHR* 27 (1947) 2-29.

Cohen, David W., and Jack P. Greene eds., *Neither Slave Nor Free* (Baltimore: The Johns Hopkins University Press, 1972).

Como Interpretar Pombal? No Bicentenário da sua Morte (Lisbon: Edições Brotéria, Porto: Livraria A.I., w.d. [1982]).

Cooney, Jerry W., "Neutral Vessels and Platine Slavers: Building a Viceregal Merchant Marine," *Journal of Latin American Studies* 18 (1986) 25-39.

BIBLIOGRAPHY

Cortesão, Jaime, *Alexandre de Gusmão e o Tratado de Madrid*, 10 vols. (Rio de Janeiro: Ministério das Relações Exteriores, Instituto Rio Branco, 1953).

Dias, Cícero, ed. *Archives Nationales. Catálogo de Documentos Relativos ao Brasil* ([Brasília]: Ministério das Relações Exteriores, 1975).

Dias, Manuel Nunes, *Fomento e Mercantilismo. A Companhia de Grão Pará e Maranhão (1755-1778)* 2 vols. (w.p. [Belém]: Universidade Federal de Pará, 1970).

Dias, Maria Odila Silva, "A Interiorização do Metropole," in: Carlos Guilherme Mota ed., *1822: Dimenções* (2nd ed.; São Paulo: Edições Perspectiva, 1986) 160-184.

Donovan, William M., "Commercial Enterprise and Luso- Brazilian Society during the Brazilian Gold Rush: the Mercantile House of Francisco Pinheiro and the Lisbon to Brazil Trade" Ph.D. dissertation, Johns Hopkins University, 1990.

Ellis, Myriam, *A Baleia no Brasil Colonial* (São Paulo: Edições Melhoramentos, 1969).

Ellis, Myriam, "O Monopólio do Sal no Estado do Brasil (1631-1801). (Contribuição ao Estudo do Monopólio Comercial Português no Brasil, durante o Período Colonial)," *Bolletim da Universidade de São Paulo, Faculdade de Filosofia, Ciências e Letras_14* (1955) 1-265.

Falcon, Francisco José Calazans, *A Época Pombalina (Politica Econômica e Monarquia Illustrada)* (São Paulo: Editora Ática, 1982).

Faoro, Raymundo, *Os Donos do Poder, Formação do Patronato Político Brasileiro*, 2 vols. (2nd. ed.; São Paulo and Porto Alegre: Editora Globo and Editora da Universidade de São Paulo, 1973).

Fernandes, Valter Lenine, "Império e Colonização: Alfândegas e Tributação em Portugal e no Rio de Janeiro (1700-1750)," Doctoral Dissertation, Universidade de São Paulo, 2019.

Ferreira, Carlos Alberto ed., *Inventário dos Manuscritos da Biblioteca da Ajuda Referentes a América do Sul* (Coimbra: Faculdade das Letras, 1946).

Figueiredo, Luciano, *O Avesso da Memória. Cotidiano e Trabalho da Mulher em Minas Gerais no Século XVIII* (Rio de Janeiro: José Olympio, 1993).

Figueiredo, Luciano Raposo de Almeida, "Protestas, Revoltas, e Fiscalidade no Brasil Colonial," *LPH: Revista de História* 5 (1995) 56-87.

Figueiredo, Luciano, *Rebeliões no Brasil Colônia*, (Rio de Janeiro: Jorge Zahar Editor, 2005).

Fisher, H.E.S., *The Portugal Trade. A Study of Anglo-Portuguese Commerce, 1700-1770* (London: Methuen & Co., 1971).

Florentino, Manolo Garcia, *Em Costas Negras: Uma História do Tráfico Atlântico dos Escravos entre a África e o Rio de Janeiro (Séculos XVIII e XIX)* (Rio de Janeiro: Arquivo Nacional, 1995).

Foucault, Michel, *Surveiller et Punir. Naissance de la Prison*, (Saint-Amand : Bussière Camedan Imprimeries, 2000).

Fragoso, João et al eds., *O Antigo Regime nos Trópicos: a dinâmica imperial portuguesa (séculos XVI-XVIII)*, (Rio de Janeiro: Civilização Brasileira, 2001).

Fragoso, João Luis Ribeiro et al eds., *Conquistadores e Negociantes. Histórias de elites no Antigo Regime nos trópicos. America lusa, séculos xvi a xviii* (Rio de Janeiro: Civilização Brasileira, 2007).

Fragoso, João Luis Ribeiro, "Fidalgos e parentes de pretos: notas sobre a nobreza principal da terra do Rio de Janeiro (1600-1750)," in Fragoso et al eds., *Conquistadores e Negociantes*, 35-120.

BIBLIOGRAPHY

Fragoso, João L.R., *Homens da Grossa Ventura: Acumulação e Hierarchia na Praça Mercantil do Rio de Janeiro (1790-1830)* (Rio de Janeiro: Arquivo Nacional, 1992).

Francis, A.D., *The Methuens and Portugal 1691-1708* (Cambridge: Cambridge University Press, 1966).

Francis, A.D., *Portugal 1715-1808: Joanine, Pombaline, and Rococo Portugal as seen by British Diplomats and Traders* (London: Tamesis Books, 1985).

Furtado, Júnia Ferreira, *Chica da Silva e o Contratador dos Diamantes. O Outro Lado do Mito* (Rio de Janeiro: Companhia das Letras, 2003).

Furtado, Júnia Ferreira, *Homens de Negócio. A Interiorização da Metrópole e do Comércio nas Minas Setecentistas* (São Paulo: Hucitec, 1999).

Godinho, Vitorino Magalhães, "Le Portugal, les Flottes du Sucre et les Flottes de l'Or (1670-1770)," *Annales, Économies, Sociétés, Civilisations* 5 (1950) 184-197.

Gonçalves, Adelto, *Gonzaga, um Poeta do Illuminismo* (Rio de Janeiro: Nova Fronteira, 1999).

Gouvêa, Maria de Fátima, "Poder político e administração na formação do complexo atlântico português (1645-1808)," in: João Fragoso *et al* eds.,*O Antigo Regime nos Trópicos: a dinâmica imperial portuguesa (séculos XVI-XVIII)*, (Rio de Janeiro: Civilização Brasileira, 2001) 287-315.

Grahn, Lance R., "Cartagena and its Hinterland in the Eighteenth Century," in: Franklin W. Knight and Peggy K. Liss eds., *Atlantic Port Cities. Economy, Culture and Society in the Atlantic World, 1650-1850* (Knoxville: The University of Tennessee Press, 1991) 168-195.

Grahn, Lance R., "Contraband (Colonial Spanish America)," in: Barbara A. Tenenbaum ed., *Encyclopedia of Latin American History and Culture* (New York: Charles Scribner's Sons, 1996) 2:257-259.

Grahn, Lance R., *The Political Economy of Smuggling. Regional Informal Economies in Early Bourbon New Granada* (Boulder CO: Westview Press, 1997).

Guia Brasileiro de Fontes para a História da África, da Escravidão Negra e do Negro na Sociedade Actual: Fontes Arquivistas 2 vols. (Rio de Janeiro: Arquivo Nacional, 1988).

Hansen, João Adolfo, *A Sátira e o Engenho. Gregório de Matos e a Bahia do Século XVII* (São Paulo: Companhia das Letras, 1989).

Hanson, Carl A., *Economy and Society in Baroque Portugal,1668-1703* (Minneapolis: University of Minneapolis Press, 1981).

Haring, Clarence, *The Spanish Empire in America* (1st ed. 1947; reprint: San Diego, New York, and London: Harcourt Brace Jovanovich, 1975).

Heckscher, Eli, *Mercantilism*, Mendel Shapiro transl. and E.F. Söderlund ed., (2nd ed.; New York: MacMillan Cie and London: George Allen & Unwin Ltd., 1955) 2 vols.

Hendrick, T.D., *The Lisbon Earthquake* (London: Methuen & Co., 1956).

Hespanha, António Manuel, *A História do Direito de Portugal* (Lisbon: Livros Horizonte, 1978).

Hespanha, António Manuel, *História das Instituições, Épocas Medieval e Moderna* (Coimbra: Livraria Almeda, 1982).

Hespanha, António Manuel, "Da 'Iustitia' a 'Disciplina,' Textos, Poder e Política no Antigo Regime," *Boletim da Faculdade de Direito de Coimbra* (1989) 3-98.

Hespanha, António Manuel, *As Vesperas do Leviathan. Instituições e poder político Portugal - Século XVII* (Coimbra: Livraria Almedina, 1994).

BIBLIOGRAPHY

Higgs, David, "Unbelief and Politics in Rio de Janeiro during the 1790s," *Luso-Brazilian Review* 21 (1984) 41-61.
Hoberman, Louisa S., and Susan M. Socolow eds., *Cities and Society in Colonial Latin America* (Albuquerque: University of New Mexico Press, 1986).
Jacobs, Berenice A., "The Mary Ann, an Illicit Adventure," *HAHR* 37 (1957) 200-212.
Johnson, Harold B., "A Preliminary Inquiry into Money, Prices and Wages in Rio de Janeiro, 1763-1823," in: Dauril Alden ed., *Colonial Roots of Modern Brazil: Papers of the Newberry Library Conference* (Berkeley and Los Angeles: University of California Press, 1973), 230-283.
Johnson, Lyman L., and Enrique Tandeter eds., *Essays on the Price History of Eighteenth-Century Latin America* (Albuquerque: University of New Mexico Press, 1990)
Kagan, Richard L., "Prescott's Paradigm: American Historical Scholarship and the Decline of Spain," *American Historical Review* 101 (1996) 423-446.
Karasch, Mary C., *Slave Life in Rio de Janeiro, 1808-1850* (Princeton: Princeton University Press, 1987).
Karasch, Mary C., "Suppliers, Sellers, Servants, and Slaves," in Louisa S. Hoberman and Susan M. Socolow eds., *Cities and Society in Colonial Latin America* (Albuquerque: University of New Mexico Press, 1986) 251-283.
Klooster, Wim, *Illicit Riches. Dutch Trade in the Caribbean, 1648-1795* (Leiden: KITLV Press, 1998).
Knight, Franklin W. and Peggy K. Liss eds., *Atlantic Port Cities. Economy, Culture and Society in the Atlantic World, 1650-1850* (Knoxville: The University of Tennessee Press, 1991).
Labourdette, Jean-François, "L'Ambassade de Monsieur de Chavigny à Lisbonne (1740-1743)," *Bulletin du Centre d'Histoire des Espaces Atlantiques* 1 (1983) 27-80.
Labourdette, Jean-François, *La Nation Française a Lisbonne de 1669 à 1790 entre Colbertisme et Liberalisme* (Paris: Fondation Calouste Gulbenkian Centre Cultural Portugais, 1988).
Lamarão, Sérgio Tadeu de Niemeyer, *Dos Trapiches ao Porto, um Estudo sobre a Área Portuária do Rio de Janeiro* (Rio de Janeiro: Secretaria Municipal de Cultura, 1991).
Langfur, Hal, *The Forbidden Lands: Colonial Identity, Frontier Violence, and the Persistence of Brazil's Eastern Indians, 1750-1830*, (Stanford: Stanford University press, 2006).
Langfur, Hal, "Uncertain Refuge: Frontier Formation and the Origins of the Botocudo War in Late Colonial Brazil," *HAHR* 82:2 (May 2002), 215-256.
Lapa, José Roberto do Amaral, "Um Agricultor Illustrado do Século XVIII" in: *Economia Colonial* (São Paulo: Editora Perspectiva, 1973) 141-213.
Lapa, José Roberto do Amaral, *A Bahia e a Carreira da Índia* (São Paulo: Companhia Editora Nacional, 1968).
Lapa, José Roberto do Amaral, O Sistema Colonial (São Paulo: Edições Ática, 1991).
Lara, Silvia Hunold, *Campos da Violência, Escravos e Senhores na Capitania do Rio de Janeiro 1750-1808* (Rio de Janeiro: Paz e Terra, 1988).
Larson, Brooke, Olivia Harris and Enrique Tandeter eds., *Ethnicity, Markets, and Migration in the Andes. At the Crossroads of History and Anthropology* (Durham and London: Duke University Press, 1995).
Leite, António, "A Ideologia Pombalina Despotismo Esclarecido e Regalismo," in: *Como Interpretar Pombal? No Bicentenário da sua Morte* (Lisbon: Edições Brotéria, Porto: Livraria A.I., w.d. [1982]) 27-54.

BIBLIOGRAPHY

Linhares, Maria Yedda and Francisco da Silva, *História da Agricultura Brasileira* (São Paulo: Brasiliense, 1980).

Lugar, Catharine, "The Merchant Community of Salvador, Bahia, 1780-1830," Ph.D. dissertation, State University at Stony Brook, New York, 1980.

Luís, Agustina Bessa, *Sebastião José* (Lisbon: Imprensa Nacional Casa da Moeda, 1982).

Macedo, Jorge Borges de, "Dialéctica da Sociedade Portuguesa no Tempo de Pombal," in: *Como Interpretar Pombal? No Bicentenário da Sua Morte* (Lisbon: Edições Brotéria, Porto: Livraria A.I., w.d. [1982]) 15-23.

Macedo, Jorge Borges de, *Problemas de História da Indústria Portuguesa no Século XVIII* (Lisbon: Associação Industrial Portuguesa, 1963).

Macedo, Jorge Borges de, *A Situação Económica no Tempo de Pombal. Alguns Aspectos* (3rd ed.; Lisbon: Morães Editores, 1989).

Macêdo Filha, Maurídes Batista de, "A Trajetóra do Diamante em Goiás," (Masters Thesis, Universidade Federal de Goiás, 1990).

Manchester, Alan K., *British Preeminence in Brazil, its Rise and Decline. A Study in European Expansion* (2nd ed.; New York: Octagon Books, 1970).

Mansuy, Andrée, "Mémorie inédit d'Ambroise Jauffret sur le Brésil à l'Époque de la Découverte des Mines d'Or [1704]," *Actas do V.Colóquio International de Estudos Luso-Brasileiros*, (Nashville : Vanderbilt University Press, 1965) 2: 407-434

Marcílio, Maria Luiza, "The Population of Colonial Brazil," in: Leslie Bethell ed., *The Cambridge History of Latin America* (Cambridge: Cambridge University Press, 1984) 2:37-63.

Mathias, Carlos Leonardo Kelmer, "No exercício de atividades comerciais, na busca da governabilidade: D. Pedro de Almeida e sua rede de potentados nas minas do ouro durante as duas primeiras décadas do século XVIII," in: João Luis Ribeiro Fragoso *et al* eds., *Conquistadores e Negociantes. Histórias de elites no Antigo Regime nos trópicos. America lusa, séculos xvi a xviii* (Rio de Janeiro: Civilização Brasileira, 2007) 196-222.

Matoso, José ed., *História de Portugal, O Antigo Regime (1620-1807)*, António Manuel Hespanha ed., (Lisbon: Editorial Estampa, 1993).

Maxwell, Kenneth R., "The Generation of the 1790s and the Idea of Luso-Brazilian Empire," in: Dauril Alden and Warren Dean eds., *Colonial Roots of Modern Brazil: Papers of the Newberry Library Conference* (Los Angeles: University of California Press, 1973) 107-146.

Maxwell, Kenneth R., *Pombal: Paradox of the Enlightenment* (Cambridge: Cambridge University Press, 1995).

Maxwell, Kenneth R., "Pombal and the Nationalization of the Luso-Brazilian Economy," *HAHR* 48 (1968) 608-631.

Meilinck-Roelofsz, M.A.P., *Asian trade and European Influence in the Indonesian Archipelago between 1500 and about 1630* (The Hague: Martinus Nijhof, 1962).

Melo, Isabele de Mattos Pereira de, *Magistrados a Serviço do Rei. Os ouvidores-gerais e a adminstração da justiça na comarca do Rio de Janeiro*, (Rio de Janeiro: Arquivo Nacional, 2015)

Miller, Joseph C., *Way of Death, Merchant Capitalism and the Angolan slave Trade, 1730-1830* (Madison: University of Wisconsin Press, 1988).

Miller, Shawn W., *Fruitless Trees. Portuguese Conservation and Brazil=s Colonial Timber* (Stanford: Stanford University Press, 2000).

Monteiro, Nuno Gonçalves Freitas, *O Crespúlo dos Grandes (1750-1832)* (Lisbon: Imprensa Nacional Casa da Moeda, 1998).

Monteiro, Nuno Gonçalves, "O Endividamento Aristocrático (1750-1830): Alguns Aspectos," *Análise Social* 116/117 (1992), 263-283.

Monteiro, Nuno Gonçalves, "Trajetórias socias e governo das conquistas: Notas preliminares sobre os vice-reis e governadores-gerais do Brasil e da Índia nos séculos XVII e XVIII," in: Fragoso *et al* eds, *O Antigo Régime nos Trópicos* 251-283.

Moraes, Rubens Borba de, *Bibliographia Brasileira: Rare Books about Brazil Published from 1504 to 1900 and Works by Brazilian Authors of the Colonial Period* 2 vols. (Los Angeles and Rio de Janeiro: Livraria Kosmos Editada, 1983).

Morineau, Michel, *Incroyables Gazettes et Fabuleux Métaux.Les Retours des Trésoirs Americains d'après les Gazettes Hollandeses (XVIe-XVIIIe siècles)* (London: Cambridge University Press; Paris: Maison des Sciences de l'Homme, 1985).

Mott, Luiz, "Subsídios à História do Pequeno Comércio no Brasil," *Revista de História. Universidade de São Paulo* 53 (1976) 86-106.

Moutoukias, Zacarias, *Contrabando y Control Colonial, Buenos Aires y el Espacio Peruano en el Siglo XVII* (Buenos Aires: Bibliotecas Universitarias, 1988).

Moutoukias, Zacarias, "Una Forma de Oposición: el Contrabando," in: Massimo Ganci and Ruggiero Romano, eds., *Governare il Mondo l'Imperio Spagnolo dal XV al XIX Secolo* (Palermo: Società Siciliana per la Storia Patria, Instituto di Storia Moderna, Facultà di Lettere, 1991) 333-368.

Moutoukias, Zacharias, "Power, Corruption, and Commerce: The Making of the Local Administrative Structure in Seventeenth Century Buenos Aires," *HAHR* 68 (1988) 771-801.

Moutoukias, Zacharias, "Réseaux Personnels et Autorité Coloniale: les Négociants de Buenos Aires au XVIIIe Siècle," *Annales E.S.C.* 47 (1992) 889-914.

Novais, Fernando A., *Portugal e Brasil na Crise do Antigo Sistema Colonial (1777-1808)* (4th ed.; São Paulo: Editora Hucitec, 1986).

Novais, Fernando A., "A Proibição das Manufacturas no Brasil e a Política Económica Portuguêsa do Fim do Século XVIII," *Revista de História. Universidade de São Paulo* 67 (1967) 145-166.

Oliveira, Luís Valente de, and Rubens Ricupero eds., *A Abertura dos Portos* (São Paulo, Editora SENAC, 2007).

Parrela, Ivana, *O Teatro das Desordens. Garimpo, contrabando e violência no sertão diamantina, 1768-1800*, (São Paulo: Annablume, 2009).

Pearson, Michael N., "Corruption and Corsairs in Sixteenth Century Western India: a Functional Analysis," in: *Coastal Western India. Studies from the Portuguese Records* (New Delhi: Concept Publishing Company, 1981) 18-40.

Pedreira, Jorge Miguel Viana, ""Contraband, Crisis, and the Collapse of the Colonial System," *HAHR* (2001) 81:739-744.

Pedreira, Jorge Miguel Viana, *Estructura Industrial e Mercado Colonial. Portugal e Brasil (1780-1830)* (Lisbon: Difel, 1994).

Pijning, Ernst, "Betwist gezag: de verhoudingen tussen de Republiek en Portugal en de confiscatie van het MCC-schip *Don Carlos* in Rio de Janeiro (1725)," *Archief. Mededelingen van het Koninklijk Genootschp der Wetenschappen* (2003) 63-78.

Pijning, Ernst, "Contrabando, ilegalidade e medidas políticas no Rio de Janeiro do século XVIII," *Revista Brasileira de História* (2001) 21:42, 397-414.

Pijning, Ernst, "Le Commerce Négrier Brésilien et la Transnationalité. Le Cas de la Compagnie Corisco (1715-1730)," *Dix-Huitième Siècle* 33 (2001) 63-79.

Pijning, Ernst, "Conflicts in the Portuguese Colonial Administration. Trials and Errors of Luís Lopes Pegado e Serpa, Provedor-Mor da Fazenda Real in Salvador, Brazil 1718-1721," *Colonial Latin American Historical Review* 2:4 (1993) 403-423.

Pijning, Ernst, "Contraband as a way of government, Rio de Janeiro in the 18th century," in: Michelle Sauer ed., *Proceedings 11th Annual Meeting of the Northern Great Plains Conference in Early British Literature*, (Minot: Minot State University, 2003) 115-123.

Pijning, Ernst, "Contrabando na Legislação Portuguesa durante o Período Colonial," *Anais da Sociedade Brasileira de Pesquisa Histórica* 14 (1994) 85-88.

Pijning, Ernst, "Guidelines for Research in the Arquivo Histórico Ultramarino: the Most Important Archive for Research on the Former Portuguese Colonies," *Portuguese Studies Review* 3:2 (1994-1995) 9-42.

Pijning, Ernst, "A New Interpretation of Contraband Trade," *HAHR* (2001) 81: 3-4, 733-738.

Piñero, Eugenio, *The Town of San Felipe and Colonial Cacao Economies*, (Philadelphia: American Philosophical Society, 1994).

Pinto, Virgílio Noya, *Ouro Brasileiro e o Comércio Anglo- Português* (2.ed.; São Paulo: Companhia Editora National, 1979).

Posthumus, N. W., *Inquiry into the History of Prices in Holland* vol. 1 (Leiden: E.J. Brill, 1946).

Prado, Fabrício, *Colônia do Sacramento. O extremo sul da America Portuguesa* (Porto Alegre, RS: Fabrício Prado, 2002).

Prado júnior, Caio, *Formação do Brasil Contemporâneo. Colônia*, (7th ed.; São Paulo: Editôra Brasiliense, 1963).

Raminelli, Ronald, "Baltazar da Silva Lisboa: a honra e os apuris do juiz naturalista," in: Ronaldo Vainfas *et al* eds., *Retratos do Império. Trajetórias individuais no mundo português nos séculos XVI a XIX* (Niteroí, RJ: Editora da Universidade Federal Fluminense, 2006) 279-295.

Rau, Virginia, *Estudos sobre a História Económica e Social do Antigo Regime*, José Manuel Garcia ed., (Lisbon: Editorial Presença, 1984).

Ribeiro Júnior, José, Colonização e Monopólio no Norteste Brasileiro. A Comapnhia Geral de Pernambuco e Paraíba (1759-1780) (São Paulo: HUCITEC, 1976).

Romeiro, Adriana, *Corrupção e Poder no Brasil. Uma história, séculos XVI a XVIII*, (Belo Horizonte: Autêntica Editora, 2017).

Romeiro, Adriana, *Ladroes da República. Corrupção, moral, e cobiça no Brasil, séculos XVI a XVIII*, (Belo Horizonte: Fino Traco, 2023).

Romeiro, Adriana, *Um Visionário na Corte de D. João V. Revolta e Milenarísmo nas Minas Gerais* (Belo Horizonte: Editora UFMG, 2001).

Rosenn, Keith S., "*The Jeito*, Brazil's Institutional Bypass of the Formal Legal System and its Developmental Implications," *The American Journal of Comparative Law* 19 (1971) 514-549.

Russell-Wood, A.J.R., "António Alvares Pereira: a Brazilian Student at the University of Coimbra in the Seventeenth Century," in: F.W. Hodcroft ed., *Medieval and Renaissance*

BIBLIOGRAPHY

Studies on Spain and Portugal in Honour of P.E. Russell (Oxford: Society for the Studies of Medieval Languages and Literature, 1981) 192-209.

Russell-Wood, A.J.R., *The Black Man in Slavery and Freedom in Colonial Brazil* (New York: St. Martin's Press, 1982).

Russell-Wood, A.J.R., "A Cause Célèbre of Colonial Brazil: António Fernandes' Personal Struggle for Justice," *Revista da Sociedade Brasileira de Pesquisa Histórica* 4 (1987-1988) 1-8.

Russell-Wood, A.J.R., "Colonial Brazil," in: David W. Cohen and Jack P. Greene ed., *Neither Slave Nor Free* (Baltimore: The Johns Hopkins University Press, 1972) 84-133.

Russell-Wood, A.J.R., "Colonial Brazil: the Gold Cycle c. 1690-1750," in: Leslie Bethell ed., *The Cambridge History of Latin America* (Cambridge: Cambridge University Press, 1984) 2:547-600.

Russell-Wood, A.J.R., *Fidalgos and Philanthropists. The Santa Casa da Misericórdia of Bahia, 1550-1755* (London: MacMillan, 1968).

Russell-Wood, A.J.R., ed., *From Colony to Nation. Essays on the Independence of Brazil* (Baltimore: The Johns Hopkins University Press, 1975).

Russell-Wood, A.J.R., "As Frotas de Ouro do Brasil, 1710- 1750," *Estudos Econômicos* 13 (1983) 701-717.

Russell-Wood, A.J.R., "Local Government in Portuguese America: A Study in Cultural Divergence," *Comparative Studies in Society and History* 16 (1974) 187-231.

Russell-Wood, A.J.R., "Manuel Nunes Viana: Paragon or Parasite of Empire?" *The Americas* 87 (1981) 479-498.

Russell-Wood, A.J.R., "Ports of Colonial Brazil," in: Franklin W. Knight and Peggy K. Liss eds., *Atlantic Port Cities. Economy, Culture and Society in the Atlantic World, 1650-1850*, (Knoxville: The University of Tennessee Press, 1991) 196-239.

Salgado, Graça et al., *Fiscais e Meirinhos. Administração no Brasil Colonial* (2nd. ed.; Rio de Janeiro: Editora Nova Fronteira, 1985).

Sampaio, António Carlos Jucá de, *Na Encruzilhada do Império: hierarquias sociais e conjunturas econômicas no Rio de Janeiro (c.1650-c.1750)* (Rio de Janeiro: Arquivo Nacional, 2003).

Santos, Afonso Carlos Marques dos, *No Rascunho da Nação: Inconfidência no Rio de Janeiro* (Rio de Janeiro: Perfeitura da Cidade do Rio de Janeiro, 1992).

Santos, Corcino Medeiros dos, *O Rio de Janeiro e a Conjuntura Atlântica* (Rio de Janeiro: Expressão e Cultura, 1993).

Santos, Joaquim Felício dos, *Memórias do Distrito Diamantino da Comarca do Sêrro Frio* (3rd ed.; Belo Horizonte: Edições o Cruzeiro, 1956, 1st ed. 1868).

Schneider, Susan, *O Marquês de Pombal e o Vinho do Porto. Dependência e Subdesenvolvimento em Portugal no Século XVIII* (Lisbon: A Regra do Jogo, 1980).

Schultz, Eric A., *Markets and Power. The 21st Century Command Economy*, (Amonk: M.E. Sharpe, 2001).

Schumpeter, Elisabeth B., *English Overseas Trade Statistics 1697-1808* (Oxford: Clarendon Press, 1960).

Schwartz, Stuart B., *Sovereignty and Society in Colonial Brazil: the Judges of the High Court of Bahia, 1586-1750* (Berkeley: Los Angeles and London: University of California Press, 1973).

BIBLIOGRAPHY

Schwartz, Stuart B., "Somebodies and Nobodies in the Body Politic: Mentalities and Social Structures in Colonial Brazil," *Latin American Research Review* 31 (1996) 113-134.

Serrão, Joaquim Veríssimo, *História de Portugal* vol. 6 (Lisbon: Editorial Verbo, 1981).

Serrão, Joel, "Decadencia," in: Joel Serrão ed., *Dicionário de História de Portugal* (Porto: Livraria Figueirinhas, w.d.) 2:270-274.

Shaw, L.M.E., *The Anglo-Portuguese Alliance and the English merchants in Portugal, 1654-1810* (Brookfield VT. Ashgate, 1998)

Shillington V.M., and A.B. Wallis Chapman, *The Commercial Relations of England and Portugal* (1st ed., London, 1907; Reprint: New York: Burt Franklin, 1970).

Sideri, S., *Trade and Power. Informal Colonialism in Anglo-Portuguese Relations* (Rotterdam: Rotterdam University Press, 1970).

Silva, António de Morais ed., *Grande Dicionário da Lingua Portuguesa* (10th ed.; Lisbon: Editorial Confluência, 1949).

Silva, Maria Beatriz Nizza da, ed., *Dicionário da História da Colonização Portuguesa no Brasil* (Lisbon and São Paulo: Editorial Verbo, 1994).

Silva, Maria Júlia de Oliveira e, Fidalgos-Mercadores no Século XVIII. Duarte Sodré Pereira (Lisbon: Imprensa Nacional-Casa de Moeda, 1992).

Silveira, Marco Antônio, *O Universo do Indistincto. Estado e Sociedade nas Minas Setecentistas (1735-1808)* (São Paulo: Hucitec, 1997).

Simonsen, Roberto C., *História Económica do Brasil (1500/1820)* (8th ed.; São Paulo, Companhia Editora Nacional, 1978).

Socolow, Susan M., *The Bureaucrats of Buenos Aires, 1769- 1810: Amor al Real Servicio* (Durham N.C.: Duke University Press, 1987).

Socolow, Susan M., "Port and Hinterland in the Río de la Plata Region at the End of the Eighteenth Century. The Activities of Gaspar de Santa Coloma," in: Jeanne Chase ed., *Géographie du Capital Marchand aux Amériques 1760-1860* (Paris: Éditions de l'École des Hautes Études en Sciences Sociales, w.d.) 109-128.

Souza, Laura de Mello e, *Desclassificados do Ouro. A Pobreza Mineira no Século XVIII* (3rd. ed.; Rio de Janeiro: Graal, 1990).

Steensgaard, Niels, *The Asian Trade Revolution of the Seventeenth Century. The East India Companies and the Decline of the Caravan Trade* (Chicago and London: University of Chicago Press, 1974).

Studer, Elena F. S. de, *La Trata de Negros en el Río de la Plata* (2 ed.; Buenos Aires: Universidad de Buenos Aires, 1958).

Subrahmanyam, Sanjay, *The Portuguese Empire in Asia, 1500- 1700: A Political and Economic History* (London and New York: Longman Group, 1993).

Tyler, John W., *Smugglers and Patriots. Boston Merchants and the Advent of the American Revolution* (Boston; Northeastern University Press, 1986).

Vainfas, Ronaldo, Georgina Silva dos Santos and Guilherme Pereira das Neves eds., *Retratos do Império. Trajetórias individuais no mundo portugues nos séculos XVI a XIX* (Niterói, RJ: EdUFF, 2006).

Vasconcelos, Agripa, *A Vida em Flor de Dona Beia. Romance do Ciclo do Povoamendo nas Gerais* (6th ed.; Belo Horizonte, Editor Itatiaia, 1988).

Verger, Pierre, *Flux et Reflux de la Traite des Nègres entre le Golfe de Bénin et Bahia de Todos os Santos* (Paris and The Hague: Mouton, 1968).

BIBLIOGRAPHY

Weber, David J., *The Spanish Frontier in North America* (New Haven NC: Yale University Press, 1992)

Wehling, Arno, *Administração Portuguesa no Brasil de Pombal a D. João (1777-1808)* (Brasília: Fundação Centro de Formação do Servidor Público, 1986).

Wehling, Arno and Maria José, *Direito e Justiça Colonial. O Tribunal da Relação do Rio de Janeiro (1751-1808)* (Rio de Janeiro, São Paulo and Recife: Renovar, 2004).

White, Robert A., "Gomes Freire de Andrada: Life and Times of a Brazilian Colonial Governor," Ph.D. dissertation, University of Texas at Austin, 1972.

Williams, Gordon R. *et al* ed., *The National Union Catalogue. Pre-1956 Imprints* (London: Mansell Publishing, 1979) vol. 636.

Winius, George D., *The Black legend of Portuguese India* (New Delhi: Concept Publishing, 1985).

www.ingramcontent.com/pod-product-compliance
Lightning Source LLC
Chambersburg PA
CBHW060459090426
42735CB00011B/2044